IRAN

Map of Iran, showing author's
route to and from Mashhad.

شیخی بزن ماحسته کفتا مستی
هر روز بدام دیگری پا بستی
کفتا شیخا هر آنچه کوئی هستم
اما تو چنانکه می نمائی هستی؟

"A Sheikh said to a drunken prostitute:
'Everyday you are caught by some person's snare,
She answered 'Sheikh, I am everything you say
But are you everything you pretend to be?'"

Omar Khyyam

مشکلی دارم ز دانشمندان مجلس بازپرس
توبه فرمایان چرا خود توبه کمتر می کنند.
حافظ شیرازی

"I have a problem; ask the learned men of the gathering,
Why do those who command repentance rarely repent themselves?"

Hafiz Shirazi

بی افکندم از نظم کاخی بلند که از باد و باران نیابد گزند
نمیرم از این پس که من زنده ام که تخم سخن را پراکنده ام.

"I made a castle with my might and main,
which will withstand the strongest wind and rain.
Since I have sown the seed of living words,
I shall not die, but henceforth must remain."

Firdawsi

بنی آدم اعضای یکدیگرند که در آفرینش ز یک گوهرند
چو عضوی بدرد آورد روزگار دگر عضوها را نماند قرار
تو کز محنت دیگران بی غمی نشاید که نامت نهند آدمی.
سعدی شیرازی

"Human beings are members of one another.
They are created from the same essence,
When a member is in pain
Other members will not rest,
If you do not care about others' pain
You ought not to be called a human-being."

Sa'di Shirazi

"When colourlessness became enslaved by colour.
A Moses became an enemy with a Moses.
When you removed this colour (materialism)
Moses and Pharoes became friends."

Rumi

چونکه بی رنگی اسیر رنگ شد موسی با موسی در جنگ شد
چونکه این رنگ از میان برخاستی موسی و فرعون کردند آشتی
مولانا جلال الدین رومی

IRAN

A Child's Story, A Man's Experience

GHOLAM-REZA
SABRI-TABRIZI

MAINSTREAM
PUBLISHING

First published in Great Britain in 1989 by
MAINSTREAM PUBLISHING COMPANY (EDINBURGH) LTD
7 Albany Street
Edinburgh EH1 3UG

ISBN 1 85158 178 2 (cloth)

British Library Cataloguing in Publication Data

Sabri-Tabrizi, Gholam-Reza
   Iran : a child's own story.
   1. Iran. Social life, 1925-1979 —
   Biographies
   I. Title
   955'.052'0924

   ISBN 1-85158-178-2

Typeset in 10 on 11½ Vladimir by
Pioneer Associates, Perthshire.
Printed in Great Britain by Butler & Tanner Ltd, Frome, Somerset

Contents

The sons of Adam are limbs of each other
Having been created of one essence.
When the calamity of time afflicts one limb [member]
The other limbs [members] cannot remain at rest.
If thou hast no sympathy for the troubles of others
Thou art unworthy to be called by the name of man [human being].

(Sa'di Shirazi)

Foreword

The birth of this book is in the combination of ecstasies and agonies, joys and sorrows, the innocence of a child and experience of a man. A number of factors, however, have given birth to this book. Leaving one's homeland and all relatives, friends and objects that one has become used to during childhood, creates a mental vacuum. This vacuum is filled partly with new impressions, experiences and the cultural wealth of other countries. To fill the other part one uses the imagination and begins to recreate, perhaps out of intellectual necessity, one's own past memories. This is a kind of rediscovery which is indeed essential for human existence and identity, especially when one is surrounded by an alien social and political atmosphere, which often ignores the identity and cultural values of other nations.

I became acutely conscious of the identity of the Iranian people, who have taken the blame for the misdeeds of ignorant and irresponsible rulers both in the past and the present who, ironically, have been discreetly supported by the West. I used my inner rediscovery of my childhood memories, or rather self-awakening, as a bridge between a child's memories and a man's experience and between Eastern and Western cultures.

In my talks and lectures I have referred, and still do, to my own past experiences and memories of Iran during 1940-1969 and in the later years of 1970-1979. A number of friends and scholars had suggested that I record on paper these memories and experiences.

I once gave a talk to the North American Studies Seminar at Edinburgh University on the modern history of Iran, in which I referred to my experience of the periods during the government of the Democratic Party of Azerbaijan (1945-1946) and Mossadeq's government (1951-1953). After the talk, my distinguished colleagues and friends Mr Owen Dudley Edwards and Professor Victor Kiernan strongly urged me to write my memories of Iran during the Revolution of 1979 which ousted the Shah. Owen Dudley Edwards kindly encouraged me to the extent that he not only introduced me to Mainstream Publishing in Edinburgh, but also helped me to actually start on the book. I perhaps owe most to him, but, indeed, without the encouragement of all my friends both in Iran and Britain the birth of this book would not have taken place. Mr Rahim Raisniya (historian) and Mr Muhammad-Ali Mahmid (poet and writer), both from Tabriz, and Dr H. Philsooph (University of Edinburgh) also gave me valuable suggestions.

When I returned from Iran in 1979 (after spending almost a year there during and after the Revolution) and expressed my observations to my friends and my wife, they suggested that I record my impressions as soon as possible.

Now the product of all those ideas is born in the form of this book. It combines my childhood experiences through society and history both in Iran and Britain. Here and there I have included some photographs to help give a visual idea of the environment in which I grew up. This book is thus a social, cultural and political history of Iran related through my own impressions and experience. Whenever I refer to the social conditions of women or criticise the unjust social relationships in Iran, I do not intend to use either the capitalist or the socialist world as criteria in my observations. I have not lived in a socialist country, but I have lived for over 20 years in Britain, and know that there are many anomalies and injustices in the position of women and the different social classes in the West as a whole; but there are many competent native writers who can tell about these and record their own stories. Whatever I tell in this book is essentially about what I have seen and experienced and I hold myself responsible for all shortcomings and errors.

Many of the names in the following pages have been transliterated by different writers in different ways. Since this book is intended for the general reader I have not wished to burden the text with a large number of diacritical marks. In addition, I have always tried to give the better known names in the forms in which they will be familiar to the Western reader. I hope therefore that specialist colleagues will not be alarmed if they find certain vulgarisms in the spelling of these names.

Finally, I wish to express again my deep gratitude to Owen Dudley Edwards and also Dr Reza Navabpour (University of Durham), Dr M. McDonald (University of Edinburgh) and my wife, who kindly read the manuscript and made valuable suggestions. I also thank Miss J. Crawford, our departmental secretary, for her kind assistance, Michelle Kendrick, my editor, Mrs Bennet for her patience in typing from my handwriting and tackling so many Persian and Azerbaijani names and the staff of Edinburgh University Library and the National Library of Scotland for their generous assistance. I must add that I am in debt, above all, to the peoples of Iran and my students and friends in Britain who have been the source of my inspiration and encouragement in writing this book.

Humai, my nurse, and my mother bore most of my childhood troubles and also suffered most during my absence from home during the past 25 years or so. Knowing that the heaviest burden of life is on the shoulders of mothers, who live on through their children, I have therefore decided to dedicate this book to the world's mothers:

O Mother, O Mother,
I wish I was an ocean, millions of fish would swim in my heart,
Or I was land, millions of flowers would blossom in my heart,
Or at least I was a clod of clay,
When the cattle returning in the evening from the mountains to our village
Pass over me — Mother.

Introduction

Iran occupies a key strategic position in the world, being bounded to the west by Turkey and Iraq, to the north by the USSR, to the east by Afghanistan and Pakistan and to the south by the waters of the Persian Gulf. When Iran has been strong, it has been the centre of a succession of mighty empires, and when it has been weak its geographical position, together with its oil and other rich resources, have ensured that outside powers have competed for influence or domination over the country.

Iran covers a very large area, six times the size of the United Kingdom, and despite the fact that much of it is desert or mountain, it has a population of over 50 million. The climate varies greatly, from the scorching heat of the Gulf to the moist and rainy shores of the Caspian Sea, where much of the country's rice crop is grown. The major part of Iran, however, consists of a vast highland plateau ringed by mountains, from which rise the rivers on which the country's irrigation depends. Much of the land is best suited to grazing and until recently a large part of the population has consisted of nomadic tribal peoples.

The central plateau contains the major cities of Tehran, Esfahan, Shiraz and, in the east, Mashhad, and is the home of the major linguistic group, the speakers of Persian, or Farsi, who have traditionally dominated the state. However, there are many other languages spoken in Iran, including Azerbaijani, with ten million speakers and the second most important language, as well as Kurdish, Arabic, Baluchi, Turkmen and many others.

The history of Iran goes far back into the past, but the country rose to prominence after the arrival of the Indo-European tribes who were to become the Persians. The first Persian Empire, founded by Cyrus the Great, lasted from 550 to 320 BC and included the Middle East, Egypt, the territory which is today Turkey, Central Asia and much of today's Pakistan. This empire was followed by the Parthians (247 BC to AD 224) and the Sasanians (AD 226 to 651). It was particularly under the rule of the latter dynasty that the Zoroastrian religion was most fully developed and became the state religion of Iran.

The Sasanian period was one of the great artistic, literary and musical achievements, but the full flowering of Iran's cultural talents was to come after the Arab conquest of the seventh century and the adoption by Iranians of the religion of Islam.

The new Islamic state absorbed influences from Arabia, Greece, Iran and India which, combined with a dynamically evolving Islam, produced the characteristic Islamic civilisation, of whose leading exponents so many were themselves Iranian or had Iranian blood.

As the Islamic state began to decline and the control of Baghdad weakened, political independence reasserted itself in Iran and there was a revival of literature in the Persian language. Poetry has always been the most important literary form in Iran, and we should mention especially the national poet of Iran, Firdausi, as well as Sa'di, Hafiz and Omar Khayyam.

Iran has suffered much from its proximity to Central Asia, and was periodically overrun by various nomadic Turkish tribes before being overwhelmed by the Mongols.

It was not until the foundation of the Safavi dynasty at the beginning of the 16th century that Iran was recreated as a nation-state. Under the Safavis also, Shia Islam was adopted as the religion of the state, thus distinguishing Iran from its neighbours in terms of religion as well as national identity. Under the Safavis Iran was strong and united, but by the beginning of the 19th century, under the Qajar dynasty, it was beginning to find that it was no match for the aggressive, newly industrialised European nations. It was forced to cede much territory to the Russians, including the northern part of Azerbaijan, while British influence in the south grew stronger and stronger.

By the beginning of the 20th century Iran was virtually partitioned between Russia and Britain, and its economy too was largely foreign-dominated. With Western political domination, however, there also came Western ideas and it was as a result of both factors that the Constitutional Revolution of 1905-1909 took place. Although the gains of the Constitutional Revolution were largely destroyed by Russian intervention, its ideals did not die and continued to inspire those struggling for Iranian freedom and independence.

After the First World War Reza Shah Pahlavi succeeded in winning a measure of political independence for Iran and laid the foundations for the modernisation and industrialisation of the country. However, his authoritarian and ruthless methods allowed no room for individual freedom or political evolution, and contributed to the social problems facing the country. Reza Shah was deposed by Britain during the Second World War because of his attempts to maintain Iranian neutrality, and the next few years saw a measure of free speech and political activity.

This period culminated in the premiership of Mossadeq, whose nationalisation of Iran's oil provoked a royalist coup and the installation of Muhammad Reza Shah as absolute ruler of Iran. During the latter part of his reign, increasing popular dissatisfaction was met with increasing repression, mostly at the hands of the dreaded secret police, SAVAK, and the destruction of all political opposition finally meant that the only force capable of confronting the regime was Islam and the ayatollahs.

The fact that the Shah had relied so heavily in the latter years upon the United States meant that the Islamic Revolution, when it came, was strongly anti-Western in character. It is too soon to pass judgement on this latest revolution, but it is clear that much still has to be achieved before the ideals of the Constitutionalists of 1905 are realised.

The events recounted in the following pages took place during the later years of Reza Shah's reign and the disturbed period of the Second World War and after. At this time the influence of the West was beginning to affect the lives of ordinary Iranians, but by and large the traditional life of the country continued undisturbed. The way of life described here has almost vanished today, but I hope that I have been able to preserve a little of it in my description of the life of one ordinary Iranian family in these years.

1

I am Born

But my actual birthday is unknown. I discovered this when I wanted to take
a secondary school examination. My teachers at my previous school told me
that I was outspoken and that I answered questions out of turn so I left
school when I was 13 (as I thought), working during the day in a chemist's
shop and attending classes in the evening. The only educational way forward
left to me was to take part in the voluntary examination, which meant that I
would have to be not less than 16 years of age. Although by the end of the
year I had managed to compress two years' education into one, when I went
to register my name for the final examination in June I was told that I was
too young to enter.

In my neighbourhood lived a lawyer called Mr Karrubi who was also
the editor of a newspaper, *Akhtar Shomal* (Northern Star). I told him my
story and asked if he could increase my age from 14 to 16. He suggested that
I should write a letter of complaint to the law court against my father, in
which I should say that my father had made a mistake in registering my
birth and that I should be two years older than the age on my certificate.
After receiving this letter, the court would make investigations, call both my
father and myself, come to a final decision and either refuse or accept it. Mr
Karrubi added, "Since I am part of the court I will make things go smoothly,
and you will be able to have your age increased." So I started to carry out all
his suggestions, writing letters and finding witnesses, going to the law court
and spending almost three months at the Department of Justice, going from
one room to another. Finally the court voted in my favour. So I was now 16
according to my birth certificate, but I still did not know my exact birthday.

The confusion arose because my father could neither read nor write. He
could not register the birth at the back of the Quran as Muslims usually do;
nor did he ask somebody else to write it down for him. I remembered,
however, that everybody told me I was born on the first day of spring, which

is also the Iranian New Year, Nawruz, celebrated in Afghanistan, Iran and Central Asia. Thus I came to the conclusion that I was born on New Year's Day 1313 according to the Iranian solar calendar, which is something quite different from the Islamic lunar calendar.

My father was born after his own father's death and had to go out to work when he was six years of age. By the time I was born he was comfortably off and could afford to keep servants in the house. Not being able to read or write did not mean that he was not educated as such. He could tell stories from the Quran, the Bible and our Persian national history. In other words he was orally literate, but could not write down the product of his imagination. He had a tremendous creative imagination and was rather poetic. This imagination had been manifested in colourful carpets which he had designed, one of which — *Mahi* (fish) — is called after him. His name was Muhammad-Ali Sabri-Tabrizi. Since he had been to Mecca he bore before his name the title Haji. In fact, visiting holy shrines in any city gave a person a title: on my return from a visit to Mashhad in north-eastern Iran, where Imam-Riza is buried, I became known as Mashhadi Gholam-Reza in my district and family circle.

My father did not say much about his background. All he talked about was working as a child labourer in different carpet factories. He used to tell me about his mother's dependence on him and her dedication to his well-being. One of his clear memories was of saving his money to buy his mother an oil lamp, which at that time was a novelty, replacing candles. When he returned home he found that the room was dark and his mother was sitting in the corner of the room. She did not know how to light the modern lamp. I could often sense two very different personalities within him: one was the suppressed child in him and the other was an enthusiasm to help others. This was reflected in his relationship with me. On the one hand he rejected modern education in favour of religious, mosque education, which was very much influenced by the religious mullahs who denounced modern education as being Western and non-Islamic in influence. Yet he encouraged me to learn my craftsmanship and trade and gave me great encouragement in dealing with daily life. For example, he would never check the amount of money I had spent, or what I did in the house. But he was always anxious that I should spend more time at the carpet factory which he managed and of which he was part-owner. He wanted me to spend more time with the workers. During the Second World War, he lost a lot of carpets in the storeroom in Baghdad which caught fire. It was then that he himself started working at the factory and from then on I helped him, preparing carpet looms and cutting and trimming the carpets after they were finished.

Then his character seemed to change from what it had been a few years previously. When I was a child of three or four, ten years earlier, I remember that he used to visit the factory like a god, pacing about and filling everyone

My father's patented carpet design.

with silent dread. I remember, too, that he hit one worker so violently with a wooden block that the man's head started bleeding. Now, however, he was to be found sitting alongside the workers, a mild person, listening to what they said, and even enjoying eating with them and chatting about their work and lives. He was quite a different person and most likeable. Those months of working with him left a deep impression of his loving personality. He cared much more about the welfare of the workers, and in a way defended their rights against others. One day I myself hit one of the workers when he was out, assuming that as his son I need not worry about the consequences; when he returned in the evening to pay the workers' wages for the day he learned that I had hit Mr Jabbar, one of the senior craftsmen in the factory. He called me and called Mr Jabbar and asked Mr Jabbar to return the slap on my face, which he refused to do. Then my father slapped me so hard that I keeled over onto the factory floor. I felt very bitter towards him at the time. Before slapping me, however, he said, "The redness on your cheek and mine is because of the work of people like Mr Jabbar."

Years later, after I had been studying at university for a few years and my father was an old, retired man, I used to see him sitting with Mr Jabbar in his little hut where he had his sock-making machine. Mr Jabbar had changed his profession, but my father's friendship followed him wherever he went.

Another event I remember clearly occurred one bright winter's morning. There was a lot of snow on the ground but the sun was shining. The weather was so cold that many schools remained closed and I had to stay at home. My father came home looking very sad and almost in tears. He told my mother of a woman in our neighbourhood who had given birth to a child the previous night. Both the mother and child had died afterwards because of the severe cold and lack of heating. He said, "We are all responsible for this tragedy — I feel really sick and sad that this has happened."

This feeling of sympathy for the common people and for the poor grew with my father so much that he turned a blind eye to my political activities in later life. Again his split personality worked against his real convictions. He warned me not to bring my friends to the house in case I should be arrested, thereby placing my family in danger. He was a dedicated Muslim, opposed to government schools and modern education, the Democratic Party of Azerbaijan and the leadership of Jafar Pishavari, who was accused by the mullahs of being Communist and anti-Islam. Yet when the Democratic Party of Azerbaijan (1945-46), among its many other social reforms, allocated one day per week for free bathing and the free use of all bath-houses in the town for all workers, as well as free health services, my father, despite his dislike of the Party, agreed to send his workers. He also encouraged them to join the trade unions being formed under the auspices of Pishavari. When I asked him why he sent the workers to trade union meetings and supported Pishavari's policy while denouncing him as a Communist, he said, "I oppose him because the mullahs think he is a Communist, but he is very helpful in a practical way to our workers." My father was very much influenced by the mullahs, and used to hold regular religious meetings in our house. For a child it is a very haunting and very confusing experience to wake up in the early morning to hear the sound of people howling in the next room with the mullah chanting verses about the death of the martyred Hussein (grandson of the prophet Muhammad, who was martyred in AD 675). Reza Shah, the ruler of Iran during my boyhood, had forbidden religious ceremonies being held in public, so they used to take place in darkness or in the early morning. This ceremony in honour of Hussein had been specifically forbidden, as it was still politically sensitive. Hussein had been killed in Karbala, in Iraq, and at the time I am writing the Iran-Iraq war has that event as one of its causes. The more fanatical Shi'ites see the death of Hussein as a source of inspiration and revenge.

While my father was anxious to help and encourage me to work in the factory, he did not want to know about my problems in establishing the date of my birth and changing its presumed time, or about my education. In fact he was against my going to university, and realised that my legal complaint against my unknown birthday was the beginning of a change in my career. "Why should you be bothered about when you were born?" he asked me when I told him of my intention. But the support of my mother and her mother, who came from an educated family — my grandmother's father had been a medical doctor — gave me the fullest encouragement and put pressure on my father to accept my needs in the matter of my birth registration. There was peace and friendship while I worked with him in the factory, but as soon as I changed my course and decided to continue my education through evening classes I was faced with an objecting and negative attitude from my father. For this reason I spent days with my grandmother, knowing that my mother, while secretly supporting my ambitions, could not openly oppose my father.

My problem about getting satisfactory evidence for my age in order to be allowed to sit the necessary state examination was solved, but I still did not know my real age. In Iran children usually go to school when they are seven years of age. I was in the second year of primary school when the Democratic Party of Azerbaijan (which had come to power in 1945), ordered a change in the language taught in schools from Persian to Azerbaijani. My father came home one evening and suddenly announced, "Tomorrow you will not go to your school, both you and your brother, because our mullah at the mosque has denounced the state school." The following day he took me and my young brother Ibrahim to a *maktab*, a traditional Islamic school where the Quran and the Arabic language were taught. This suggests that at that time I must have been nine or ten years of age and the date of the Democratic Party's coming to power puts the year of my birth at 1935 or 1936. I have to assume that my parents kept an accurate count of the years: yet by the solar date 1313 I would have been born in 1934, and later my successful court action made the year of my birth 1932.

When I registered at Edinburgh University as a postgraduate student in 1963, I had to state the year on my birth certificate, which effectively committed me to 1932, now also inscribed on my passport. When I became a lecturer in 1965 I certified the same date, although knowing I was younger.

On the other hand, if the year of my birth is unknown, the day should be clear enough: the first day of spring, the 21st of March. Before I came to Britain I did not celebrate my birthday at all because such ceremonies were not the custom in Iran at that time, but since being in Britain, first as a single and later a married person, my friends and my wife and children wanted to know my exact birthday, and I could tell them this, although I could not tell them how old I was. This became a great source of amusement. Since I was born on the first day of Nawruz, this much was clear: but the festival sometimes coincides with the 19th of March, sometimes the 20th and sometimes the 21st or 22nd. So my friends used to ask me first which date was my birthday, and then how old I was. Either I answered by joking that I was still under 20, or it took me a long time to explain the situation. The joke was also quite common in my family, especially with my daughters, who would ask whether I had yet reached 20 or 25, at each birthday, and did I want my birthday this year on the 19th, 20th, 21st or 22nd? In the official calendar the first day of Nawruz is put against the 21st of March. But the hour on which the year changes differs from year to year. For example, in this year in which I write (1988) the New Year started just before 9.39 on the 19th of March. So my family celebrated my birthday that evening instead of the 21st or even the 20th or 22nd. This confusion and amusement is a common thing in our family circle, which to my delight makes my unknown birthday and age a source of joy, causing the children to be both curious and entertained.

To be rather philosophical, Persians believe that every day can be a birthday, because a birthday is not only a natural day of birth but also the process of becoming. To rise with the sun every dawn is to achieve birth. Fitzgerald may not be an accurate translator of Omar Khayyam, but he captures his spirit very well:

> Awake! for Morning in the Bowl of Night
> Has flung the Stone that puts the Stars to Flight,
> And Lo! the Hunter of the East has caught
> The Sultan's Turret in a Noose of Light.
>
> Dreaming when Dawn's Left Hand was in the Sky,
> I heard a Voice within the Tavern cry,
> "Awake, my Little ones, and fill the Cup
> "Before Life's Liquor in its Cup be dry."
>
> And, as the Cock crew, those who stood before
> The Tavern shouted — "Open then the Door!
> "You know how little while we have to stay,
> "And, once departed, may return no more."
>
> Now the New Year reviving old Desires,
> The thoughtful Soul to Solitude retires,
> Where the White Hand of Moses on the Bough
> Puts out, and Jesus from the Ground suspires.
>
> . . .
>
> Come, fill the Cup, and in the Fire of Spring
> The Winter Garment of Repentance fling:
> The Bird of Time has but a little way
> To fly — and Lo! the Bird is on the Wing.

(From the *Rubaiyat* of Omar Khayyam.)

Fitzgerald's translation helps us to cross the divide between British and Persian cultures by showing in conventional English metaphor the likeness of a day to a lifetime; however, in Persian this is not metaphor but an article of belief. Even my mother used to say every morning, with a special charm and smile on her face, "Wake up! The sun is about to rise! Get up and offer your prayer, as all Muslims do." (Muslims offer prayer five times a day.) Being a lively, happy and charming woman, she used to make a happy start to every morning before my father would come out of his private section of the building to take us down to breakfast.

She always had a smile on her face, but my father seemed thoughtful and withdrawn. He would perhaps be worried about how many workers would show up to work at the factory, and how many would not. I gathered this because as soon as he sat down he used to say to me, "Have your breakfast quickly and go and bring the children of so-and-so. If they refuse to come and demand more wages, say that they will have them in the near future."

There was a kind of perpetual semi-strike in the factory. Some people would refuse to come to work, and I would have to go and persuade their children to get their parents to bring them to the factory. The children were the chief workers with whom I had to deal. Sometimes I had to persuade adults who were over 20 to go themselves. I was often reluctant to go, and my mother used to give me some encouragement in order to avoid my father's anger.

My reluctance was rooted in several experiences I had had in the past. One day, in the very cold midwinter, I had been sent to bring two boys and a girl from a family from the outskirts of our city, Tabriz. When I entered their house I saw that it consisted of a bedroom and a vestibule, which was used as a kitchen and for storage. To my surprise and shock I saw three young children sleeping under one cover, and two buckets of water at the corner of the room which were frozen like white fat. The parents were squatting in the corner of the room preparing tea and breakfast for them. Seeing this situation and comparing my own breakfast and lifestyle with theirs made me so ashamed that I abandoned any idea of asking them to come to the factory. While standing in the middle of the room, I noticed that the girl of about nine and the boys of about eleven and 14 had their middle fingers wrapped with cloth. Children often cut their fingers while making carpets, yet were forced to continue working even though their hands were bleeding; often the blood made a red ribbon along the white cotton strands of the carpet on the loom. This really horrified me. When I returned home I was told off but I made the excuse that they were unwell. I composed the following lines in later years:

> I am six years of age and play only in my dreams,
> I get up early morning while it is still dark
> And the streets are deserted and frightening.
> I find my way to the carpet factory.
> In summer I walk through dust;

In winter I walk through snow.
I have shoes, but without soles,
And clothes without warmth.
My face is as white as snow;
My legs are as thin as a bird's.
I work from dawn to sunset,
Make no complaints, for I have no choice.
I make colourful carpets to cover your floors
And write my history on beautiful Persian rugs.
The roses are coloured red by my finger's blood
And the twisted patterns are my life's perilous path!

The parents of most children like these came from the villages and became either very cheap labour or unemployed. They had to sell their children's labour, and indeed the children themselves, to the best bidder from any factory. This bound the children to work only in that factory. As a matter of fact I came to know and love these children and often played with them. I found them most affectionate children, who were kind to me, much kinder than the children of the rich people. When I came home on that particular day I told the story to my mother. She could sympathise but she could have no personal feelings about it, because she had not experienced that life. She said, "Don't make yourself sick about their situation. Don't worry about them. Allah will care for them." But I did not understand how Allah could care for them. When I asked her she said, "It is the secret of life that we do not know. Don't ask about that." And then I pressed her further, saying, "Compare your situation with that of their mother." She said, "Every person will meet their destiny. Perhaps you exaggerated, perhaps they should ask Allah to give them more." But still I was doubtful as to how they were to ask Allah to change their situation, because Allah, as far as I could see, was always on the side of the rich. My mother and father deeply believed that all their fortune was given by Allah and that it was the blessing of Allah which protected them against all the evils and misfortunes of life. Nevertheless, my mother was a very sincere and loving person. She used to work alongside the servants, and she often acted as a buffer against my father's anger at the servants and children.

I had two stepsisters, one of whom married a government clerk, and the other, a few years older than me, lived with us. Their real mother had died of an illness two years before my father married my mother. My father was then about 40 and my mother 15 years of age and my elder stepsister was about the same age as my mother. My mother treated them very well and my stepsisters were extremely kind to my three other sisters and five brothers. My two stepsisters were Sakineh Sultan and Khanum Sultan. My own sisters were Batul, Bozorg and Aghdas. My brothers were Ibrahim, Ismail, Yunis (universally known as Mohsen), Muhammad Reza and Akbar. Batul

Looms and workers.

was older than me; all the rest were younger. Ismail died of tuberculosis when he was about 18. He apparently caught this from a fair-haired and blue-eyed girl who worked in the factory. Ismail was in love with her. He died but she survived. He used to go from school and work alongside her, to help her. His death affected me very deeply. He was the first of our family to die. I was then about 21. We had shared the same room and exchanged our feelings, sorrows and happinesses. He was the most sensitive companion in my family circle. He was ever-happy for the happiness of others, and sad for their griefs. He could offer everything of his own to anyone who needed it. And we called him "the philosopher of the family".

Ismail was full of jokes and pranks. Once we were on holiday, camping near Lake Urmiyeh, which lies to the east of Tabriz next to Urmiyeh city and is a very salty lake, without any outlet. A villager was selling milk and he asked my father if we would have some. My father said yes, and asked Ismail to see how much it cost and how good it was. Ismail said, "I cannot see how good it is without tasting it," and asked the milk-seller if he could taste. With his consent he took a half-kilo-sized jar of milk and drank it all at one go. He then put the empty jar on the floor and said to my father, "Excellent. He should be paid twice." My father, with a grim look, took some money out of his pocket, gave it to the milkman and said "Thank you", and so we didn't have any milk. This became a family joke, so that for the rest of the week when there was any occasion to buy anything we would ask Ismail if he wanted to "try and then buy".

It might be added that Ismail was very hostile to the mullahs. Mullahs used to come to the house, and there was one who habitually arrived on a donkey to preach to the women about anything and everything from how to sleep with their husbands to problems of menstruation. I used to keep some sal-ammoniac for small batteries with which I would feed the electric light. Ismail managed to put some of the sal-ammoniac up the backside of the mullah's donkey, which was always left at the gate of the house, tied up at the electric pole. (Some rich mullahs used to have servants to run alongside and look after their donkeys, but this one didn't.) As soon as the mullah came out and mounted the donkey, the donkey went up in the air and threw the mullah off. The children were hiding behind the wall to see what would happen. There was a roar of laughter and the joke lasted the entire evening throughout the district. The mullah had to be brought back into the house, and it was Ismail who looked after him, bringing him fruit. (Mullahs are reputed to be big eaters and lovers of women, which no doubt explains their interpretation of the Quran in favour of polygamy.) Ismail then helped the mullah to remount the donkey and start safely on his journey homeward.

The following evening I asked Ismail why he did such a silly thing. Without hesitation he said, "It wasn't a silly thing at all. It was delightful. It was a good lesson for a mullah who comes and feeds his eyes on the bosoms and beautiful faces of women, and talks about nothing but the hinder parts of women. He deserves nothing but to be buried in a grave alive. I really loathe them. They have nothing to do but eat and enjoy themselves with women, and make women and the people forget about having minds for themselves. I really doubt whether there is any Allah. If there is I don't accept him because he has such stupid representatives."

But Ismail had his own convictions and his own very deeply rooted human feeling. A few months before his death he knew that his TB had developed to such an extent that it had become dangerous. In a last desperate attempt to get help, we travelled together to Tehran to see a specialist. He told me, "I wish to die sooner rather than harm anybody else." Unhappily, his wish was granted very soon afterwards.

I remember Ismail telling me, "You have finished university and I am not educated as you are. But my opposition to mullahs is against neither the Quran nor Islam. In fact I would follow the progressive Muslim writers like Omar Khayyam, Rumi and Hafiz, who, quoting the Quran, believed that there was no priestcraft in Islam, and Allah is indeed nearer to us than our arteries. I tell you in fact that mullahs play on the weaknesses of men. They accuse people of loving each other without marriage and drinking wine while they are doing thousands of things that are worse than adultery or drinking wine, things that are against ordinary decent human feeling. As Khayyam says, 'If you don't drink, don't blame those who do drink. You have placed the foundation of your life on hypocrisy and scandal. Don't be proud that you do not drink, while you eat hundreds of things to which drinking wine can be considered as auxiliary.' Or as Hafiz said, 'When I drink I drink the blood of the grapes. But you drink the blood of the people.' I tell you, my brother, frankly, mullahs have always supported the rich and the ruling class. Haven't you seen that whenever the Shah goes away from the country or returns, he is whispered to by an ayatollah (a senior priest or mullah), whose caste has been always against the people and Islam.

"Yesterday Zari asked me if I did not mind loving her without marriage, when I was the son of a higher class compared with her parentage. I answered her, 'Laws of religion destroy love and there is no class and gender in love. I can love you without religion and without class and I don't care what others think.' She said, 'Yes, but what about your mother and father, who regard me as only a little worker in their factory? And you know I often do not dare to appear in front of anyone in your company in case they think that I am interested in your position and wealth.' 'Stop talking this nonsense, Zari,' I said. 'When I embrace you secretly at night and in the moonlight in the corner of our orchard the whole world becomes like a nutshell under my feet and I feel on top of the world. I really see the meaning of creation then. Then I talk the language of nature and the stars. When the cock crows and the birds sing in the early morning they are conveying the same language of love, saying that yesterday has passed and a new day is starting again, and my love for you has nothing to do with the past — it is ever fresh and ever created every day. If I were you I wouldn't worry about these things. The most important thing is to love and to be loved, and not to let external matters stain it.'"

My mother once asked Ismail, "What will happen if you make her pregnant? For then people will talk about it and say that you have made a poor worker in your factory pregnant, and besides it doesn't seem appropriate to marry either one's own servant or one's own worker. This would not be a lasting companionship." She added, "We had a relative who made love with his servant, giving her two children, and the girl served in his house as a servant until the end of her life while the man married another woman. The thing I must do is to inform your father so that he sends her back to the village to live with her grandfather before she gets pregnant." But none of this happened. My brother died before my mother had taken any action and Zari left the factory after his death, telling me, "I cannot see the same streets, the same trees, the same flowers, even the same stains in the carpets without

Ismail." She left Tabriz. We never heard of her again.

Actually Zari's first friendship had been with my mother, before she and my brother fell in love with one another. She, her grandfather and her little brother had been given a bedroom and large vestibule in our basement and my mother had given Zari many gifts such as dresses. I never learned what had happened to her mother and father. The grandfather and little brother left Tabriz at the same time as Zari. The day before they left Zari had lunch with my mother, and the grandfather had dinner with my father separately. The girls and boys in the factory had made a very small rug and the names of Ismail and Zari were woven into it, because they all knew that they loved each other. I well remember Zari leaving our big garden in tears, looking carefully at all the corners of the high-walled orchard in which she was used to meeting Ismail.

Though Ismail and Zari left the family circle and our community, the story of their love and kindliness to others continued among both workers and our family circle. I suppose Zari would have been 15 or 16 when all this happened. I have no idea as to whether they ever had sexual relations or not: in Azerbaijani and Persian the word "love" does not carry the implication of a sexual relationship and what was important to Ismail was this love in the terms of which he spoke of it. Today in English "love" and "love affair" carry the assumption of a sexual association, but it was not always used with that exclusive meaning, or even with that assumption. Perhaps Ismail and I spoke Azerbaijani as the Victorians spoke English! Ismail died in 1956. I left Tabriz for Istanbul in 1959. His death was one of the causes of my departure.

My brother Ismail was three years younger than I, my other brother Ibrahim two. When Ibrahim was about eight or nine he was playing with me in the garden in front of our house. There was a large vineyard divided from the fruit trees in the orchard. It was early spring. The vineyard and orchard were very wet because of the previous night's continuous rain. The vineyard was farther away from the main building, but connected by a wide path which was laid next to the high walls surrounding the house. A large pool was situated next to the rose garden in front of the building. It was used for washing dishes and the laundry, for watering the garden and for rinsing newly dyed carpet wool; we also used it as a swimming pool in the summer. But it was now much fuller and deeper than normal.

An electric wire, coming from the street, was hanging over the orchard and it was joined to the house at one corner, next to the drainpipe which carried rain from the roof to the garden. This rainwater was deemed essential for the orchard and was not diverted underground into sewers as is done in the West. In fact there is not, to this day, an underground sewage system in Tabriz, or Tehran, or other big cities in Iran.

Since it was a very wet day there must have been contact between the

My father, standing by the pool in our garden, 1960.

My mother, 1965.

My brother Mohsen, 1968.

My brother Ibrahim, in our garden, 1962.

*My brother Ismail,
aged 15.*

electric wire and the drainpipe. The clothesline which was tied to the drainpipe stretched from the basement windows round the back of the house. We were playing just in front of the last window of the basement. As soon as my brother touched the clothesline he screamed. For a second I thought he was joking, and I was angry at him. Then, in front of my eyes, he was thrown to the ground of the orchard a few metres away. When my mother and our womanservant arrived in response to my shouts for help, they tried to rescue my brother but were caught and thrown back by the electric voltage.

The wire was wrapped around my brother's neck. Though my mother and the servant were not caught by the wire, they received a violent shock. My eldest sister, Sakineh, ran around the garden, shouting for help, and caught sight of my father entering the house from the vineyard end of the garden, about 400 metres away. She shouted to my father that Mother and Ibrahim and Kubra (the servant) were caught by the electric wire. My father, who was carrying dyed carpet wools in his hands, threw them to the ground, ran back into a passage between the garden and the gate, and switched off the electricity at the mains.

My mother and Kubra got up and rushed towards Ibrahim, who could not move. It looked as if he was dead. He was as white as bread-flour. My father fetched a shovel and covered my brother's body with soil from the orchard. Only Ibrahim's head remained uncovered. After a few minutes he moved and twitched, and Father exclaimed, "Thank Heaven, he is alive. Gholam-Reza, run and bring the doctor!" I ran through the garden into the street, and to the house of the doctor in our neighbourhood, a hundred metres away from our house. The doctor, knowing my father, came immediately.

When, later, I was sent to buy medicine it was a dark night, the streets were very wet and muddy, and I could hardly run because I was shaken by fear at having seen what had happened to my brother. I brought home the medicine, and only then did I realise that my brother's neck had been badly burnt. It took him months to recover. He still carries a big scar around his neck. In fact electric wires still hang over houses, alleys and streets in the cities of Iran, and people walk amidst death. And when there is a rainy day or thunder, our people fall victim to electric shock. At other times many fires are caused by these open wires.

Many years later, when my father realised that I did not want to stay in the carpet business he asked Ibrahim to join him in the factory. Ibrahim was then at secondary school — I suppose he was about 15. He was put in charge of all the financial affairs of the family and the factory. I even used to ask him to give me pocket money in the year before I entered university, when I had no job. It was, as I remember, very hard to extract money from him. He may, understandably, have resented my studying while he was working in the factory. My father was a reputable businessman and my brother helped to build the business up.

After my father's death in 1963, my wife and our nine-month-old daughter Sarah visited Iran with me for the first time in 1965. When my wife first saw the garden she said, "This is like a garden from the Arabian Nights!" We had travelled along a dusty, twisted alley, entered through a big gate and double archway, and had arrived tired from the journey to be greeted by the perfume of roses, the breeze through the huge willow trees and the fruit trees — peaches, pears, apricots, pistachio nuts — at the corner of the house. All these added to her sense of the exhuberance and the exoticism of the garden. And she added, "My God, how could you bear the mist and cloud and cold of Britain, and a dark basement flat, after spending your childhood here?" I replied that the images of these memories were exactly what kept me going. We came back on at least two other occasions with Sarah and the younger children when the garden was as I had remembered it. But when we returned in 1973 after an interval of about four years, the entire garden had been split into two, one part being the house (with pool) occupied by my mother, while the other had been taken over by a huge building housing Ibrahim and his family. The orchard and vineyard were gone. I felt sad and lost, as though I had not returned to the same house at all. I felt an exile as never before: in the end I felt myself an alien in the grounds of my own home.

Ibrahim was taken away from school, as I have said, and probably with reluctance, however much he realised that the factory would give him prospects that continuing his education might not. If he was later to become a man of property, he had paid the price for it, and while I encountered harder times I was doing what I wanted. Mohsen, my third brother, who would have been about three years younger than Ismail, and four years younger than Ibrahim, was the only one of our family who refused to go to school at all. He had three years of elementary school and then quit. He also refused to eat cheese, because he had been told that if you eat cheese you become unintelligent. So the fact that Mohsen went to such lengths to save himself from cheese makes it clear that his decision to stay away from school did not mean he despised intelligence! He was very popular with the workers in the factory because he worked with them, ate with them and spent his social life with them. He was the only one in the family in Iran who did not prohibit himself the consumption of alcohol. I found this out when I visited Iran for the first time with my wife: to my surprise he asked me if I wanted some whisky. I said, "Of course". He had never known me to drink when I was in Iran. So whenever I went to Iran I added to my gifts a bottle of whisky from Scotland, which was not something I had ever expected to do when I started out on my first return visit.

Mohsen was a man with whom two things never lasted: grief in his mind and money in his pocket. He helped the sick who needed hospitalisation, the poor to find lodgings and unmarried men to find wives — and was always popular with children and (particularly) women, who were always conspicuous at his parties and in his company. He was the one of the family who married a farmer's daughter, and throughout his life everybody mocked him and his wife because of this. Whenever sisters-in-law quarrelled, his wife Munireh (who was loved by all our children) was called "stupid peasant daughter". She complained to me several times about this. I said, "Quite frankly, I always desired and planned to marry a peasant's daughter, and I am glad Mohsen did it. I idealised the notion of it." This reply put a smile back on Munireh's face, but of course it didn't solve the problem that she lived in a two-roomed flat with two children when she had grown up in the freedom of the countryside. It was some time before Mohsen's family were able to move from their cramped quarters with my mother to share Ibrahim's big new house.

In 1977, when I was arrested by the SAVAK, the Shah's secret police, during a visit to Iran from Britain without my family, it was Mohsen and his police-officer friend who managed to save my life. This man had become close to Mohsen because of their long companionship and common enjoyment of alcohol. Mohsen and I both took part in the Revolution of 1979, the only members of our family to do so; he was wounded, and spent a whole year in hospital. I like to feel that if Ismail had survived there would have been three of us.

My last two brothers were much younger than I: there were 20 or 21 years between us. Muhammad Reza afterwards joined me in Edinburgh, while Akbar became a civil engineer, and is the one really devout religious male member of our family. Like Ibrahim and Mohsen, he is still in Tabriz.

My half-sister Sakineh (whom I called Baji-jan) married a son of my father's partner Haji Ali. Haji Ali was educated and quite well-off, and in fact before he died he managed the books of both the factory and the marketing business which depended on it.

Baji-jan had married when I was about three years of age. She went with her husband, Muhammad Kamali, to Khalkhal near the Caspian Sea, where he was in charge of a registry office dealing with birth and death certificates, properties and so forth. I had only a vague notion about my sister and her husband until they returned from Khalkhal to Tabriz when I would have been about eight years of age. They had two sons, Javad and Hussein. Javad would have been about five, and Hussein three. I could play with Javad. My first impression of my sister was the time when I noticed her sea-blue eyes with light-brown hair and attractive face. She looked, in fact, very like my brother Ismail who was then quite young. Then she told me, "You know, I always wanted to have a brother, and you are my brother." This made me very pleased, and from then on I felt attached to her.

They stayed with us for some time until my father discovered that my brother-in-law was addicted to opium. Then they had to move into two rooms in a building next to the factory. When my brother-in-law went to Khalkhal he had become acquainted with some big landowners and high-ranking officials who used to get together in the evenings, twice or three times a week, and smoke opium on charcoal through the special pipes and eat together. According to my father and my sister herself, when they went to Khalkhal they took with them very expensive rugs, and other household effects. During their time in Khalkhal Muhammad Kamali had to sell them all to keep up his supplies of opium and maintain other social habits. In fact when they came back home they had nothing but their suitcases full of old clothes. My sister was at first reluctant to tell my father the whole story, but finally my father decided, in order to protect the children and my sister's life and well-being, to put Muhammad under the supervision of a doctor to cure him of his addiction to opium.

This situation continued for a year while my brother-in-law was working in the same profession, but in an office in Tabriz. However, the reduction of his opium to a very limited amount affected him so much that he decided to stay at home and not to go to his office. One summer evening news came that Muhammad Kamali had thrown himself into a water-well in their garden. My father and others rushed for a doctor and for people to go down and bring him out. When he emerged, he was alive, but his left leg was badly broken, and it took over two years to heal. Thenceforward my brother-in-law never said much, but spent all his days in the house or outside in the blazing sunshine.

The effects of these tragedies pressed heavily on Baji-jan. Although my father gave her a lot of help and financial support with Muhammad's doctors and medicine, and despite the salary which still came to him (later cut back to a pension), she still could not manage financially, especially since two other boys, Faridun and Hassan, arrived two and three years respectively after the fall in the well.

Just before their return from Khalkhal, Haji Ali had died, of typhoid: he had been a rich man but that had not helped him, although if the disease had been diagnosed and treated in time his life could have been saved. Muhammad Kamali was one of six sons, of whom the other five were from a second marriage. They claimed that Haji Ali had already given him his share of the inheritance when he married, so that there was nothing more to come to him. In any case Haji Ali had put most of his money into property and left very little personal wealth: he had lived up to the extent of his considerable income. Naturally Muhammad's stepmother supported her five sons against him. Muhammad had always been something of an outsider, having been very outspoken and somewhat politically conscious, talking about the need for constitutional revolution. He was more educated than his half-brothers, having a natural fluency as a writer. Baji-jan, on the other hand, was illiterate. Muhammad's stepmother was in fact my own mother's sister: my father and Haji Ali, both widowers, had married sisters as their second wives. This meant that Muhammad and Baji-jan were not themselves related but had been very much thrown together. This quarrel in his family over the legacy of Haji Ali became very bitter and dragged on for many years; it was ultimately settled by giving Muhammad a share in Haji Ali's house which he then sold back to his half-brothers. But before that time came Baji-jan had to live a life of great privation and suffering, all the harder as she had started out so comfortably and with such high hopes and pride in her clever husband.

The striking thing in my memory was the change in my brother-in-law's position and my sister having to move to relatively poor lodgings, which altered people's attitudes towards her and her husband to such an extent that I could not fail to notice. She would no longer be invited to parties where once she would have naturally have been a deeply honoured guest. Even my father's attitude changed towards her. I remember she used to send the children to our house in cold winters for charcoal, tea, sugar and even bread, which were not always supplied willingly. My love and affection for my sister had not changed at all. In fact by the time I came to know her Muhammad Kamali had already lost all their money, though she had managed to keep up appearances for a time. Then when the truth became known, all was changed. The successive steps of Muhammad's ceasing to go to work, followed by his accident, deepened the extent to which Baji-jan seemed to be treated by my parents as an outcast. For me, nothing had changed. She was my sister and I continued to love her as I had learned to do.

Baji-jan lived about a hundred metres away from our house. There was a chimney which connected to her kitchen and vestibule, and was visible from the alley which led to our gate. If I could see smoke rising from there in the evening I knew that my sister had food cooking in her kitchen or some fire in her stove. Seeing the smoke used to make my heart warm and happy, but if there was no smoke I would worry about her. In fact several times I went in to find that my feeling was correct — they had no hot food and only bread and cheese.

When Javad was ten and Hussein eight years of age they were taken away from their school and sent to work in my father's factory; my sister's bedroom and sitting-room windows faced the factory window and there was a door between her yard and the factory. Baji-jan herself went to work for my father, preparing dyed wools for the looms, a task she could perform at home. Sometimes she grew very upset because my father, in moments of irritation, would accuse her of stealing some of the wool. It was never an open accusation, but he would maintain that the material she produced was less than the raw wool she had been given: the implication of theft was there. She spoke bitterly of this to me several times. Another thing which made her deeply sad and upset, later when Faridun and Hassan had joined their brothers in the factory, was hearing her children cry because of their maltreatment by the foreman. She used to rush into the factory in tears and ask him why he treated her children like this. "I do not want them to have to work. If I had had the chance and if I had money, I would never have sent them to work here. They should be at school." I remember the anger on her face. This scene occurred several times in my presence when I had gone to work in the factory myself.

I wanted to help Baji-jan by any means possible. I used to feel that if she did steal wool from my father, she was justified. One evening when she asked me for a very small sum of money I gave her what I had, and she was so tragically grateful that it shocked me. She sent one of her sons with the money to buy some tea and paraffin, which was used in their oil stove to cook food. The next day I had a talk with her when my father was out of the factory: I could not leave my work when he was there. She told me, "I don't mind being poor, I don't mind living in two rooms with four children, I don't mind bringing water from the neighbours" — she did not have piped water — "I don't even mind working day and night very hard. Working is an honour to me. But what really makes me sad is the insecurity and loneliness as a result of the situation that I am put in. When we put the bread and the meal on the tablecloth, we don't have a table, and the tablecloth has to be on the ground. I cannot swallow food properly, it chokes me, thinking of my children's labour. Their crying faces at the carpet looms appear in front of me. I am against child labour and also I see how helpless women are in this society, not being able to get either government help or secure jobs. You know, my brother, I tell you the truth. Since we have returned from Khalkhal and my husband has lost his job, people look at us as if we had been cast out. I hate this feeling. But I can put up with poverty. The disease is insecurity. The disease is insult."

Some time later, when I was attending evening classes, I was returning home one evening and saw a large crowd outside my sister's house. When I asked the reason they told me she had fainted and still lay unconscious. They said that a rich neighbour, Haji Piramoon, had made an accusation of attempted burglary against her sons. Javad and the others had been playing football, and the ball had been kicked onto the neighbour's roof. Javad and Hussein climbed up to the roof, whereupon the neighbour said that they clearly intended to break into his house to steal his goods. When I heard this, and realised that the accusation had been responsible for my sister's collapse in her weakened and undernourished condition, I flung my books on the road, rushed down to the neighbour's house, announced my name to the servant and, when the neighbour appeared, flung him down on the ground, attempting to strangle him. I had almost choked him to death when my father appeared, dragged me off the neighbour's chest and struck me, telling me to stop. He did not support me, but the people around knew what I had done and why I had done it and, I thought, had some sympathy for my anger. My fury had boiled up at the thought of all that my sister had endured over the years, and at last I was able to take revenge on those who had treated her as an outcast.

When I left Iran perhaps the saddest person who saw me off was Baji-jan. By the time my wife and Sarah visited Iran, Javad had become a coach-driver and Hussein kept a photography shop, but the younger boys were still working in the factory. My wife, Jacqueline, liked Baji-jan very much. Baji-jan and her family had now moved from what we used to call "the factory yard" to a rented flat on the other side of the town. When we visited Iran for the second time, she was complaining of high blood pressure, and she died of this in 1970. She was about the same age as my mother, but my mother survived 15 years longer. One thing which pleased me and her was that Sarah and her first grandchild Maryam were almost the same age and played together while we were there.

Muhammad survived Baji-jan and lived with Hussein. He married another woman, two years younger than himself, but after a few years he divorced her. Now as an old man he still lives with Hussein and has become very religious, constantly telling Hussein's wife what to do and what not to do. But she is very kind to him, and they get on very well. I have numerous letters from him which I regard as masterpieces of Persian writing, and beautiful calligraphy. But all these do not change my memory of my sister's life.

My other stepsister Khanum Sultan was six or seven years younger than Baji-jan, about ten years older than myself, very active, helpful and loving. As my mother was contemporary with Baji-jan and was about 17 years old when I was born, this helps to confirm the period of time separating us. Khanum Sultan did not go to school either, not because she did not want to, but because she was not sent. Both of them were sent, each in turn, to a Quran school, for rote learning and to read the Quran in Arabic without understanding it. All our prayers were in Arabic but relatively few people understood their meaning, save by their own intuition. The mullahs now and then translated some prayers into our native language, Azerbaijani.

The relationship between Khanum Sultan and my mother was very good, and was not at all that of stepdaughter and stepmother. In fact my mother was much more loving to Khanum Sultan than was my father. Whenever Khanum Sultan burned food, or broke something in the house, my mother's reaction was quite sympathetic, but my father responded harshly. I remember once that Khanum Sultan burned the bottom of the pot when she was cooking rice: my father tried to beat her, but my mother intervened.

I regarded Khanum Sultan as a sister and a very good friend, because she carried out my childish demands. For example, I used to ask her to catch me sparrows, and she used to bring a ladder and put it against the wall, reaching up to the nests and bringing me baby sparrows into the house to feed. Some of them used to die and some of them used to fly away. The birds would of course have been happier with their parents, but I liked having them around me. We also kept lambs and sheep in a separate section of the garden. Khanum Sultan knew that I liked birds and animals and used to help me play with them. She would climb up the trees to bring me fruits and once she was caught by my father and punished. But she did not mention that she had done it for my sake, and I thought it very fine of her. One day she was teasing me and my father arrived to find me chasing her. He asked me why I was so angry. I said, "Khanum Sultan is calling me mad", and she was told off. When I was really furious I had the habit of shouting as an insult "Come and eat my buttock!" (Western readers may be familiar with an equivalent phrase.) I used to annoy Khanum Sultan by shouting this until eventually my mother said to her, "Why don't you do it the next time he says it?" So the next time I shouted it Khanum Sultan bit me very hard on the buttock, and hurt me so much that I never did it again.

She was the only one of my sisters who mixed with boys when we were growing up. Whenever bigger boys attacked me or threatened me she used to defend me. I never remember her losing her temper or being depressed but I did see her cry now and then, usually when my mother was away or was unhappy. Ismail's illness affected both of them very much indeed. She was a very lively girl, all through. One very memorable event is a good example of this. Before she was married, on her engagement day, all my younger brothers, sisters and the children of other relations were kept in another house while my mother was entertaining the women. When the party finished and we returned home, and we were sure that my parents had gone to their room and were asleep, Khanum Sultan got hold of the keys and brought out all the sweetmeats and fruits from the cellar. She brought them into the garden saying, "Let us have our own celebration". We had a party which lasted all night. The following day we asked Khanum Sultan if Mother had asked what happened to the cakes and sweets. She said, "Yes, and I told her the cats got into the cellar." My mother didn't say anything, but she knew that there was something else behind the unusual rapacity of the cats.

Khanum Sultan's husband was very charming, and about seven or eight years older than her (she would have been 17 when she married — this was older than my own sisters, most of whom would have been 15 or 16 when they married). He was called Mashhadi Hassan and was in the tea business. He was a very kind and remarkable man, in the sense that he would support my sister against all criticisms and unjust accusations she used to receive from her sister-in-law and mother-in-law, both of whom were living in the same house. It was unusual for a husband to protect his wife and take her side against his own mother. I remember once that my sister came and stayed with us for some weeks without her husband, longer than usual for such a visit, and I suspected that all was not well. There had been a row which took longer than usual to resolve, and one in which for once her husband was not able to support her. In the extended family situation every woman had her own private trunk in which she kept her valuables. Khanum Sultan had been accused of opening her mother-in-law's trunk and stealing some gold and money. It took a long time to straighten out this situation. My mother tried desperately to solve the problem. She even took my sister to the fortune-teller in order to discover where the stolen gold bracelet and the money would be, and to do something to improve relations between my sister and her husband.

There were fortune-tellers, male and female, in every city. The fortune-teller would write some lines from the Quran on a piece of paper and ask the visitor to keep it with him or her in a leather or cloth bag, often hanging from the neck. Or the fortune-teller would instruct that the paper be placed in water to let the words dissolve. Then the water would have to be drunk. I do not know what mysterious hand solved this particular problem for Khanum Sultan, but the gold and money were found and my brother-in-law came and took my sister away. It had to be done fairly elaborately: my father went to Mashhadi Hassan's shop and brought him back to our house. In fact, my father had never broken contact with Mashhadi Hassan and used to call at his shop and drink tea with him all the time that Khanum Sultan was living at our house. They stayed with us for two or three days and then returned to his house.

Most of Mashhadi Hassan's customers were Kurdish, from that part of Kurdistan which is in the north-west of Iran. He used to bring the headmen of the Kurds to his house whenever they visited Tabriz, and spoke with them either in Farsi (the Persian language) or Kurdish. It was the first time I had seen and met Kurds. It was also the first time I had seen such beautiful women, who went about in tribal costume, and without the *chadors* (veils) always worn by Persian women at this time. The most striking things were their height, their blue eyes and sharp looks, embroidered skirts and colourful sari-like scarves.

The first four years of marriage for brides in the Tabriz of my youth were very difficult, especially when like Khanum Sultan they had to live with their mother-in-law and with brothers-in-law and their wives. Mashhadi Hassan was in a fairly typical situation. His father had had four sons, and during his

Children wearing Kurdish costume.

lifetime two of them had taken their inheritance and formed households elsewhere, although the younger of those first two chose to live in the house adjoining his father's. The third brother, Gholam-Ali, owned a coach which he drove between Tehran and Tabriz. He was a very different figure from Mashhadi Hassan, a forceful, sensual, hard-drinking fellow, very sure of himself and of his rights. He had two wives, one living with Khanum Sultan and the others, the other living in another part of Tabriz. She was younger and prettier. His first wife knew that he had a second wife, but resented having to see her. The whole family knew about it, and the way they talked about it made it clear they did not accept the idea. Gholam-Ali used to stay two or three days in the other wife's house, and then he was also away travelling. Sometimes he was drunk when he returned, though in fact this often made him generous. But his first wife used these occasions to attack him — in words, not with blows — and he used to sit there, playing with his moustache. She was by nature a pleasant and affectionate woman, and his good humour dried up any bad feeling when he was there.

He had two sons and two daughters. I never saw any tension in the house when he was there, and I used to play with his son Jalil and his daughter Fatimeh, whom I found very attractive. We did not play with children outside the family, but there were enough of them in it to give me plenty of friends. Although I saw nothing of the tension, I suppose the fact that the second wife was never seen meant that the first wife might work off her resentment towards her by irritation and suspicion against Khanum Sultan, who was also younger and more attractive than herself. The mother of Gholam-Ali and Mashhadi Hassan was probably also critical of my sister for the same reason. It would not have surfaced often, but it could be unpleasant when it arose. I never saw any sign of it myself, apart from the one occasion when Khanum Sultan returned to my father's house for an exceptional length of time. The mother never showed any resentment of me, and when I was a child she used to give me sweets and always displayed a warm affection. We used to roam through the rooms of the house, taking fruit when we felt like it, and Jalil and I were never told off; we could explore wherever we liked and there was a great sense of freedom and assurance.

There was a big pool, in the house, which we used for swimming in the summer. Their garden was as large as the one in my father's house. The pools in such houses were a source both of joy and tragedy, the joy for children over five years of age in hot summer, and the tragedy for younger children who while their parents were asleep at midday used to go off and play by the pool and often fall in and drown. Khanum Sultan lost her two-year-old boy who fell into the pool. When they found him it was too late: he was dead. Child mortality is high in Iran, both because of dysentery and because of this kind of accident. I remember Khanum Sultan being in mourning for her beautiful child for many months, until she had her second child, Davood. She and her husband left the house soon afterwards and went to live in a flat on the other side of town. They lived happily after that: like most young married couples they only started their true life after finding their independence.

Mashhadi Hassan left the tea trade, and bought a coach, travelling between Tabriz, Kurdistan and Tehran. When he died in 1980 he had a great long vehicle which was driven by his son Davood between Abadan and other cities, carrying goods from the Persian Gulf in connection with the oil refinery. My sister has four daughters and three sons who are literate; her second son Maghsood is a technical teacher in Zanjan, halfway between Tabriz and Tehran and famous for its steel knives and scissors. Whenever people travelled through Zanjan we small children used to expect them to bring some of the famous small handicrafts as presents.

Mashhadi Hassan was very good to his family. When his coach was not in use — they used to be taken off the regular route two or three days a month — he used to take the entire family to different cities in Azerbaijan and on the Caspian Sea. Every summer he used to take his family and my brother Muhammad Reza to Ardabil near the Caspian Sea: nearby there is what in the West would be called a spa, with various restorative hot mineral waters. Khanum Sultan's story, after the first difficult years, was a happy one; many families live together in Iran with brothers and sisters and their families all inhabiting one house. Working-class families in towns and peasant families in villages who had to work all together either in the factory or on the farm did not have much time for jealousy, backbiting and major conflicts, and often worked together in harmony more than seems to be the case with families where there is more time to breed suspicion and conflict.

As regards polygamy as a cause of conflict, even remote conflict, I had little opportunity of witnessing other cases. Yusef was born to my father's partner Haji Ali as his eldest son by his second wife, my mother's sister, so he was my cousin, and also half-brother to my half-sister's drug-addict husband Muhammad Kamali. Yusef had moved from Tabriz to Tehran, where he worked as a telecommunications engineer. He had married a first wife in Tabriz, the daughter of a button-maker, and they had two daughters and four sons. But after they had been married for 15 years he was repairing the telephone of a lady, fell in love with her and made her his second wife. He had a son and a daughter by this marriage. His first wife discovered about the second wife after two years, and she went very quiet, he told me later, and seemed very sad. This was worse than her shouting at him, which she never did, or demanding a divorce. Yusef told me that whatever I did I should keep away from polygamy: "It is all right to fall in love and forget for a time, but when you wake up and face reality it becomes unfair for the first and the second. Both suffer." He said that for some months he had felt like a yo-yo between the two of them. Finally, with the consent of the second wife, he kept their son and they divorced. She married someone else and kept their daughter. I believe that they are now on quite good terms and that his first wife is very good to her stepson, but I don't know what is going on in the mind of that lovely boy. When I look at his large bright eyes I see a story untold. Recently I heard that the boy, by consent of his father, has joined his own mother and lives with her.

In my immediate family, apart from my cousin Yusef, the only other case of polygamy — long before his experience in the early 1970s — was something of which his own mother, my aunt, was a victim. After her husband Haji Ali Kamali died, she remained a widow for a few years. Then my grandfather, her father, told her that a certain man wanted to marry her, and gave as his name Haji Seyyid Ismail Taheri. She refused, arguing that she had grown-up sons of 16 and 17, and it would not be appropriate for her to remarry. But Seyyid Taheri, a mullah, had stressed to my grandfather that because he bore the name Seyyid this testified to his direct descent from Muhammad and in his anxiety to have his family mingled with the blood of Muhammad my grandfather renewed his attempts to convince my aunt. She

ultimately agreed that it was desirable for her to have some connection with
Seyyid. She also agreed that it would be useful to have his financial support,
and she was lonely without a husband.

Because of his being a Seyyid, Yusef and her other children respected him
and did not openly resent his being their stepfather. My aunt continued to
live in her own house, and gave birth to a girl and boy by him. The girl
married my brother Ibrahim when she was about 15 and Ibrahim was about
21. But the point was that Seyyid Taheri already had another wife living in
Tabriz, and he normally spent the night-time with her although he would
remain for much of the day with my aunt: being a mullah, of course, he did
not work. I gradually discovered, however, that in addition to these two
wives, Seyyid Taheri had made a number of temporary marriages. He used
to bring girls from villages, marry them and after a few months divorce them
and marry them to other people. I guessed that his sons by his first wife used
to sleep with these girls too. He used to keep them in his first wife's house.
His first wife and my aunt used to meet and got along well with one another,
but the first wife had a nervous breakdown and I saw her in a pitiful
condition on many occasions as a result of her husband's actions.

We made something of a joke about the situation; but my detestation of
Seyyid Taheri grew fairly open when I heard, after the death of my father,
that he then approached my mother with the suggestion that he should
marry her also. She had replied, "No thank you, sir, you put Muhammad to
shame. I do not need a husband; I have five men, and whenever they enter
the house I know that each of them represents my husband. I am quite
fulfilled." From then on he was regarded as lower than a diseased dog by our
household and none of my brothers and sisters could bear to see him, but
since he was my brother Ibrahim's father-in-law and was constantly visiting
the house and enjoying his hospitality my mother had to be courteous.
Otherwise she said that we should not connect him in our minds with Islam
and Muhammad; he would, she said, have sexual cravings for a dog on the
street.

One question remained in my mind. Like many mullahs and Seyyids he
spent most of his time either at home or in the offices of big merchants in the
bazaar. I wondered how he was able to live without working, and where his
income came from. Some said he received money from merchants by virtue
of his being a Seyyid; some said he worked as an informer for the SAVAK
because of his excellent contacts with so many people. Or others believed
that like many leading mullahs he received money from the British
Government or Embassy. The British Government used to support the
mullahs as their main source of information and influence in Iran and in
Islamic communities in India. I have never been able to solve this mystery.
He ate well, and had a high standard of living which the middle classes

could not afford to enjoy. He ultimately went to Tehran with his first wife. My aunt followed him and settled there.

When the Revolution took place and the Shah was overthrown Seyyid Taheri went underground for a whole year, perhaps for one of two reasons. The first was that he was a follower of Ayatollah Shariatmadari, who had millions of followers in Azerbaijan and posed a threat to Khomeini. Or else he was afraid that the source of his income would be discovered. He is back now in ordinary life once more.

My full sister Batul was four or five years younger than Khanum Sultan, and about two years older than me. She too was not sent to the state school, but went to the Quran school. She attended dressmaking classes as well, and had many more regular Quran classes than my other sisters, which rather pleased my father. I used to play with her too, but not so much as I did with Khanum Sultan. Khanum Sultan taught me how to swim in our pool but Batul rarely joined us. She was more introverted and concerned with household matters. At the age of ten she was the best cook in the family apart from my mother, whereas Khanum Sultan was much less domesticated, for which my father criticised her. Generally, Tabriz girls were famous for their kitchens and cooking, which they regarded as very important. A special type of long-grained rice is used in Iran, with an odour peculiar to the rice which comes from near the Caspian Sea, called *dom-e siyah*. They make from this a dish called *chilo kebab* which is one of the national dishes of Iran. Batul was particularly good at cooking this dish, which everybody admired.

Along with all these qualities as an outstanding cook and housekeeper, Batul was very strict with us and refused to give us sweets, fruits or cheese. She locked them in a cupboard and told us that we should restrict ourselves to meals. In this way she became the controller of household affairs second in command to my mother, while Khanum Sultan enjoyed her time playing with us and my cousins in our basement in winter and in summer in the garden. Batul had more or less taken after my maternal grandmother who was a quiet and rather thoughtful person.

I considered Batul to be more intelligent than Khanum Sultan; she could have made a good nurse or even doctor if she had been sent to a modern school and been educated. The signs of frustration were obvious in her reactions to men who tried to touch her: once a boy approached her in the street and tried to touch her arm and she slapped his face. She was very sharp in this way, and very outspoken and independent. Although interested in the house, she was not anxious to show herself as being feminine and attractive. I never saw her laughing and chatting to men, even my father. At the same time she was very attractive, tall with large black eyes and long hair. She did not have any inferiority complex and had a strong personality.

However, this strong personality was seriously challenged when she became engaged to Guli Ahmadabadi. Guli had moved to Tabriz from Ahmadabad after his father's death with his mother, sister and two brothers, Muhammad and Ahmad, some years before the engagement. They had a large spice and tea merchants' store in the Davachi Bazaar. Since they had good social connections in Ahmadabad and surrounding villages, most of their customers were peasants and farmers who used to bring their goods from the villages — charcoal, wheat, barley, lentils, split peas, chickpeas and many other things — to be sold in the bazaar either through Guli's shop or independently. From the profits from these crops the peasants bought tea, sugar, loaf-sugar, spices and tobaccos. The prosperity of merchants like Guli depended on the villagers from the surrounding area, and he and his brothers made much money from them. When there were bad harvests the villagers were forced to sell their trees and their orchards, sometimes even their land, very cheaply to Guli simply in order to survive. Guli and other merchants prospered while the peasants became poorer.

Guli's mother visited our house with her daughter Aazam and took a liking to Batul. After a few weeks they sent the lady who usually went between families to arrange engagements, who came with a proposal for a meeting and an engagement. Batul was about 15. It was arranged that Batul would go to Guli's shop with my mother and Baji-jan pretending to be customers, to give Batul a chance to see Guli's appearance and decide whether she wanted to enter into discussions about an engagement with him. When they returned, with Batul's consent and my mother's encourage-ment, they arranged another meeting with his mother, and Guli visited our house. After Batul and Guli had expressed some interest, each family decided to send their delegation, which met in our house to negotiate the marriage in detail.

Traditionally in Iran, the bride's father gives a carpet (or, if rich, several carpets), a bed, furniture, literally everything needed for a kitchen, bedrooms and sitting-rooms. The bridegroom makes a marriage settlement of money on the wife in case it should ever be necessary for her to seek a divorce; sometimes it would be gold, sometimes in the country livestock (where the father's contribution may also be livestock). The difference is that the husband simply has to set aside the marriage settlement: he does not pay it over, and may never do so if it is not necessary. The father must pay over his share at the time of the marriage. Also, from the time a daughter is two years of age, her mother will have been setting aside for her a trousseau to be built up over the years — clothes, china, toilet articles, glasses, watches, embroidery and all sorts of other things needed for her and her husband. Nevertheless, the worry of the dowry, especially in lower-middle-class and working-class households, hangs over the parents and the girls. Even the girls themselves start working from eight years of age to build up the money for their dowry and often are worried whether their dowry will be accepted by the mother-in-law, sisters-in-law and the husband; even if they are accepted at the time of the marriage, their supposed inadequacies may be a source of dispute and recrimination for years afterwards. For this reason mothers of girls are usually very anxious to send the best presents and goods for the prospective mother-in-law and sisters-in-law in order to please them and keep them quiet. This was very true in Batul's case.

After the contract had been agreed they set the date of the marriage. Before the marriage takes place the dowry is moved from the house of the girl's parents' to her own new home in a special ceremony which varies in different parts of the country. In many places the goods are carried on special trays on the heads of big, strong men, or transported in cars or on animals. From the number of these huge trays, or the number of cars, camels or mules, people would learn or recognise how rich or poor the bride was. If the number of trays in Tabriz were over ten, it would have been regarded as a rich person's bride, or a rich person's daughter. Since bulky goods like carpets and furniture could not be carried on the human head, they would be carried on a large cart pulled by a horse at the back of the procession. We called this cart a *dashga*. People would pass the news from one to the other, remarking on the number of trays.

It is very difficult to see how a married couple can enjoy their wedding, even their wedding night, with this sort of thing hanging over the whole occasion, and wondering what sort of talk is taking place about it. It is a kind of torture. While the procession was moving from one house to the other, people would stand at their doors to see what was being carried and being given, and some would even climb up trees or on housetops for a better view. Usually the brothers and close relatives accompanied the procession. I went to Guli's house and helped deliver the things, and after having tea and cakes, returned home. While I was there I saw swarms of women entering the house from the neighbours' to find out what was being brought. One could instantly tell by the reception one got whether the bridegroom's family were pleased or not — and at least were pleased in Guli's house as Batul had quite a good dowry. The wedding took place a week later.

Marriage for all of my sisters — I am thinking chiefly of the ones whose wedding celebrations impinged most on my youth, Khanum Sultan and Batul — was the end of the sweet days of laughter, games, flirtation, childhood. The change in their way of life made for a drastic alteration in personality, appearance and behaviour. It meant a leap from childhood dependence on parents to dependence on a husband, a virtual stranger, combined with responsibility to him. When I first visited Batul after her marriage the house, with its high walls within which Batul was physically and mentally imprisoned, seemed to me like a fortress. While I was there I could hardly sit and talk to her. She was up and down the whole time bringing either tea or food to her mother-in-law, sister-in-law, brothers-in-law and husband, while all of us were sitting on the ground having our meal. When she had brought the last dish her husband quietly said, "Why don't you sit down, Batul?" She answered equally quietly, "I am not hungry." I knew what this meant in Batul's terms: "I do not like to eat this kind of food." And she was too tired to eat. She was reduced to the level of being a mere servant for two ladies and three gentlemen. Admittedly, she did not have to attend to her sister-in-law for very long, as she in her turn was married.

For the first two years that I visited my sister, she had hardly any time to talk to me. I wanted to talk to her, but had no opportunity and ultimately was forced to ask to go to the toilet. This meant that I would have to go to the other end of the garden, and she would have to go with me, carrying a lantern to light the way. Then and only then did I have any chance at all to exchange confidences with her, and what little I got out of her, in her hesitation, caution, withdrawal and short bursts of disclosure told me many stories. I was convinced that the situation had become a bad one, and so I was most anxious to have the chance of talking to her in my father's house.

Batul had two miscarriages before she had her first child, a girl called Maliheh, born prematurely. In an effort to console her for the miscarriages, my mother would say, "Perhaps Allah did not want you to have a child this time." These were Batul's only words of comfort; her husband and mother-in-law taunted her by saying that she was too puny to bear a child. This was humiliation and disgrace. Batul felt extremely bitter about marrying too young and once said to me in private: "My parents did me a great injustice in giving me over to this man who regards me as his land or cattle. They treat me like a servant in the house, at everyone's beck and call. I work all day and by the evening I am so exhausted I can't eat or enjoy my husband's company." From her conversation I also gathered that she was bitter about the miscarriages and blamed not the will of Allah, but her hard life. She thought if she had married at an older age and had been given more opportunity to rest during her pregnancy, with a balanced diet of food, then she would not have suffered unnecessary miscarriages. She always complained about constant tiredness and backache and I overheard her confiding to my mother that she had not been taken to the doctor nor had any medical help been sought.

At that time, and still today, the majority of women in Iran receive no proper ante- or post-natal medical care. Neither the government nor a family like that of Batul's husband paid any heed to this essential issue for women. It seems a common belief that women should not become sick and that if they became ill because of pregnancy or gynaecological problems, then it was not really a serious matter, merely one of the hazards of being female.

Left alone, they would recover naturally. Thus Batul's complaints were ignored or taken as signs of ill-temper.

This common concept that women should not be ill had perhaps both psychological and practical causes. Batul bore the brunt of the household chores. Her illness meant the disruption of day-to-day life. It therefore suited the interests of everyone in the house to assume that she was well. Children, especially, feel lost when their mother is ill in bed. I remember my own feelings of desolation when my mother took to her bed. At the same time, I grew to realise how my mother and sisters bore sickness and pain more stoically than the males in the family. They would suffer for months before being taken to a specialist. Illiterate and veiled, they could not make or keep appointments by themselves. My sister Bozorg suffered for weeks with post-natal bleeding until I intervened and took her to a doctor in Tehran. This was in 1970. I first took her to a state-run hospital which was dirty, run-down and chaotic. The building was full of women waiting for treatment. When one of the doctors realised my anxiety, he advised me to take my sister to a private clinic. I told him, "I am prepared to take my sister to a private clinic and I can afford it, but what about those who are suffering like my sister but cannot afford private treatment?" The doctor could not answer this because he himself was a victim of an inadequate health service. I took Bozorg to a private clinic and she was cured in a week.

Of course, not all women suffered from this lack of concern. Some wives and mothers discovered that constant ill-health was a certain way to ensure continual attention; although they waited until they were well-established in the family before making this particular claim to fame.

Most women in Iran, of my mother's and sisters' generation, gave birth at home. Their babies were delivered by traditional midwives who had learned their profession by experience, but who often knew more about reciting the Quran than anything other than the most rudimentary health care. Most educated people, who could afford it, had their children delivered by properly trained midwives either at home or in hospital. All of my sisters and brothers were born at home. I clearly remember the births of my sisters Bozorg and Aghdas, and brothers Muhammad-Reza and Akbar. We older children were ushered to a distant corner of the house or to a neighbour's house. I used to hear my mother's screams, although I do not remember being frightened. Once, being curious, I hung around. I saw my mother leaning against two walls at the corner of a room, supported by two of her sisters. Underneath, on the floor, was a large copper bowl half-full of charcoal ashes. The midwife was squatting in front of my mother, waiting for the baby's arrival. At this point I was hurriedly shooed away by one of my older sisters. After half an hour I was called in to see the baby. My mother was lying in her bed. She looked very pale but her smile and kiss on my cheek made me happy. We were lucky — my mother never lost a baby;

but sometimes children died at birth because of problems which were beyond the capabilities of traditional midwives.

Batul had her children at home. Following the usual custom, my mother went to look after her, as she did with all my sisters following a birth or miscarriage. She usually stayed for ten days, cooking, cleaning and receiving visitors. When visitors came to see the baby and mother, the grandmother would take the baby out of the room beforehand. When everyone was seated the baby would be ceremonially brought in. This custom was followed until the baby was 40 days old. The idea behind it was to prevent a visitor bringing the evil eye or bad luck to a baby. My sister Bozorg lost her first child from pneumonia when he was two weeks old. People had openly admired his beauty which, according to popular belief, had caused the "evil eye to fall on him".

New-born babies are traditionally swaddled in Iran, as in biblical times. The child is wrapped in layers of wide strips of soft white cotton, over which a colourful shawl is wound. The whole bundle is secured by a narrow strip of cotton criss-crossed round the baby. The baby stays thus cocooned between feeds and changing. Many babies remain swaddled until they are near the crawling stage when, like impatient caterpillars, they wriggle and squirm along the ground.

I remember when Batul had her first child. She lay in a basement room and my mother had to continually climb up and down the stairs, cooking for and serving Batul and her guests. She used to become tired but I never heard her complain. My mother used to help her daughters in other ways. Whenever they held a big party, she assisted with the cooking and organisation, much to the annoyance of her own children at home, who wanted her to stay with them.

Ten days after giving birth, my sisters would come to our house and stay for about a month to recover. They also learned from my mother how to feed and care for the baby. This was an excellent arrangement. Mother and baby could bond together and feeding could be established without the demands of housework or husbands.

Most women breast-fed their children. When I visited Iran in 1964 and later years, however, I noticed that bottle-feeding had become fashionable, especially among women of the younger generation. They used milk powder imported from abroad. Unfortunately, lacking proper guidance, they did not always make up the feeds or sterilise the feeding utensils correctly. I saw many children who, as a result, were malnourished or suffered from gastro-enteritis. The companies who advertised and sold baby milk made good profits but many children suffered because of this fashion. In this respect, my sisters' children were protected by the family's adherence to traditional patterns of child care.

For a traditional Iranian bride, the new mother-in-law is as important as her husband — she might spend the night with her husband but she will be every day with her mother-in-law. An unsympathetic or critical mother-in-law can cause misery to the young wife, as Batul's experience had shown.

Guli's and his brothers' trade was similar to that of my grandfather and Uncle Rahim. Guli was often very rude, in front of Batul and even my mother, towards my Uncle Rahim. This upset my mother, but she kept quiet because of her daughter's position. This tension was, perhaps, due to business competition, because I did not know of any other reason for such animosity between Guli and my mother's relatives. Our family was deeply upset by what was happening to Batul. It was constantly talked about, and Ismail and I both felt angry and frustrated, yet we could hardly have understood the full extent of Batul's misery.

Although Guli was very good to his brothers and defended them, he was badly betrayed by them and almost made bankrupt when they divided up their property about 15 years later. Guli had left the family house about seven years previously, and had established his own house where four more children were born to Batul and himself — Mahmud, Shafiqeh, Samad and Abdulrahim — in addition to the two that had already been born in his mother's house, Maliheh and Farideh. Once Guli had moved to his own house, his behaviour improved. In fact, his whole attitude changed; his relationship with my sister started to blossom and the marriage began to work. This is a pattern often repeated in many traditional families; until the couple have their independent life and privacy it is not a true marriage. Of course, children also serve to strengthen the wife's position. Guli's financial crisis and near bankruptcy further improved his behaviour and finally gave my sister the upper hand.

For the first time, I noticed that Batul was dictating to him what to do. She would say to him, in front of me, "Look at all the insults and misery and bad treatment to which you subjected me because of them and at their behest, and look at what they have finally done to you." He made no reply, but blushed shamefacedly. On other occasions, in his presence, Batul would invite me and my brothers to the house and I used to say, "If that is acceptable to Haji Guli." (His name had formally become "Haji Guli" when he had undertaken a pilgrimage to Mecca two years after his departure from his mother's house.) He would answer, "The word is Batul Khanum's. I agree with anything she says." And this was genuine. It seemed to me that he had absolutely surrendered to her after the near-bankruptcy and bitterly regretted what he had done in the past. Batul's children were her powerful supporters. Haji Guli, who used to come home as a lion, now seemed to me like a lamb. Batul had gained authority and strengthened her own personality, but she always regretted that her parents had not given her a chance to be educated, to study and to live and direct her own life. Perhaps her personality influenced her daughters in certain ways. None of them married before they were 22 years of age, and they all had very strong personalities. All six of the children were literate and educated, although Maliheh was not interested in studies. Nevertheless, her daughters Farideh and Shafiqeh were not allowed to go to university, which they resented very much. It was not the fault of Batul alone; she was helpless in the face of old ways and customs which would not let them fulfil their potential.

Haji Guli had been forced to sell his shop because of the rapacity and cheating of his brothers, but he started another one and did well. Although Batul experienced no trouble with her children — she was an iron disciplinarian and their obedience to her was well known, and most unusual, in our family — I always felt that she had pent-up energy like that of a volcano which wants to erupt. Perhaps her sons-in-law Rahim, the husband of Maliheh, and Akbar, the husband of Farideh, paid the price for it. Rahim and Akbar seldom visit Batul, and receive rather rough treatment from her: she is very insistent on her daughters' rights and not much inclined to give credit to the husbands for good intentions. The girls' marriages seem to work out well.

As for Guli's brothers, all social connection with them had ceased after the near-bankruptcy episode: the old mother had died shortly before Guli went to Mecca, and no doubt her death played its part in improving Guli's attitude to Batul. His brothers stopped living together, and Muhammad, the elder one, married. One of the conditions made by Muhammad's prospective father-in-law, who was a very rich man, was that his daughter should have an independent house. The other brother, Ahmad, lived on in his mother's house, although he had been the youngest of the three. He got most of the property at the carve-up: Muhammad had not benefited much from the near-bankruptcy of Guli. It really would seem to be the case that Ahmad, although only 20, had acquired a very powerful influence over both of his brothers, no doubt with the assistance of his mother; but what is frightening to realise is that such a person could impose his own will on his sisters-in-law and any women who were subject to the men whom he found it possible to control. It is clear that when they were all living in that terrible house and Batul was suffering so much, one reason for her humiliation was that Guli and his brothers had come from a lower stratum in society than my father, and took satisfaction in degrading the girl from that society who was now in their power. Again, it would seem that these feelings of bitter and almost psychotic resentment stemmed from Ahmad. Guli had been much more of a weakling than a brute; but his brother had made him a brute. Batul on her own won her battle within her own family — but with what pain! Guli died in December 1987.

The story of Batul is not only one of a woman oppressed ultimately fighting her adverse situation and winning, partly by her own efforts and partly by making the most of every opportunity thrown in her way: it is also the story of a highly intelligent woman thrown into frustration and disappointment by being denied an education and opportunity to make her own destiny in a healthy society. In a society which is wholly illiterate, intelligence can make its way and take its effect, and despite the world-wide exploitation of women throughout human history, many women have in fact taken the leadership in their own households and sometimes even in public affairs in non-literate societies. But Iran, when I was growing up, was partly literate, partly illiterate, and the problem for many intelligent people, especially intelligent women, was that they had been intended by nature to be literate and often intellectual, but that this had been denied them. They could see others, less intelligent than themselves, making the most of their education and becoming owners of stores of book-learned knowledge and aptitudes, and the frustration created by such a situation for the intelligent illiterate is always a very cruel one. Batul would almost certainly have been an outstanding woman in any of the professions she could have entered: yet here she was condemned to a horrible physical and sexual slavery to a man and his brothers who were far less intelligent than herself. Quite apart from Ahmad's jealousy of her family, her own intellect threatened him and angered him, and because of her remarkable qualities she had a much harder life with these men, who resented her not being on their level.

After her first terrible shock, she gradually made the most of her husband's weaknesses, and built up a family as she thought it best. I have occasionally thought that it has made her contemptuous of the low social stature of others, as though she had adopted some of the materialism of Guli and his brothers. But, in fact, she had no alternative other than to adopt it, and make much more of it than they could. The story of societies such as ours is one in which talented individuals are often dragged back and prevented from realising themselves through education; but this is far more the case with women than men, and for one intellectual who can congratulate himself on having gained professional success, there are the many who do not so much fail as are held back.

My two other sisters, Bozorg and Aghdas, are so much younger than I that they hardly come into this narrative of my family and youth. Bozorg was about 13 years younger than me, and Aghdas about three more than that. (The reader may be getting tired of these "about"s when we come to age: but it may be useful to keep reminding ourselves what a completely different frame of reference people have in societies without the organisation of literacy and numeracy that most Western cultures take for granted.)

It is striking that both girls, when they had grown up, also greatly regretted the fact that they, like all of their sisters, were denied literacy and education. Both of them in fact are much more politically conscious than the rest of their sisters, and Bozorg is a very strong advocate of the rights of the poor. Her daughter Fahimeh, who was educated until the age of 15, has benefited from being brought up in the capital city, Tehran, and she took part on the fringes of the Revolution which overthrew the Shah. She is very strongly for women's rights, is highly articulate, and sold off all her valuables to obtain money for the revolutionaries. She occasionally asks me why I did not ensure that her mother had an education; I tell her that I argued a great deal with my father about it, but that I was powerless in the matter. It was Fahimeh who visited the place where the dead and wounded were being brought in during the Revolution and saw on "Black Friday", 8 September 1978, the number "3672" on one of the dead, indicating the number of people who had been disposed of by the Shah's troops. She was particularly horrified at the fact that several pregnant women had been killed.

Aghdas, like Bozorg, is happily married, but she has been less fortunate in the fate of her most politically conscious child. Samad was a great reader, the philosopher of the family, someone in whom I saw again my brother Ismail. He had built up a fine library and seemed destined to make the most of the education denied to so many of his relatives. In 1982 he was killed in the Iran-Iraq war.

2

A Walk Through Space and Time

My mother often used to take me to her parents' house when I was a little boy. We used to walk through twisted alleys and pass by the women's bath-house and hear the roar of conversation, shouting and rushing water, and the screams of excited children. It was called Haj-Ali Baba, and was like most of the bath-houses, built underground, about ten to 15 steps below street level. When one entered, there was a vestibule opening onto the street and then the main hall which was round, with a small pool and fountain in the middle, lower still.

We did not go in during these expeditions to my grandparents', but Haj-Ali Baba was one of the women's bath-houses to which my mother took me once every two weeks in winter and once a week in summer. Of course my father took me occasionally as well, in his case to the bazaar bath-house where the men went. It was a very different experience, going with my father rather than with my mother. With my father it took much less time, an hour or at most two, but with my mother the bathing lasted several hours. My father used to buy me sherbet and milk-pudding after the bath, whereas my mother used to bring food from the house which we would have together after a bath which sometimes lasted from nine in the morning till two in the afternoon. After so many hours the soles of my feet would be all wrinkled up and I could hardly put on my shoes to walk. I always had to proceed slowly on the walk from the women's bath-house, my mother treating me to fruit from the nearby grocer's shop which helped me to endure the pain.

It was never tedious to stay so many hours in the women's bath-house. I used to play with other children; play with water and the fountain; watch the women and listen to them talk and hear my mother and sisters having long, long conversations with the other women about their dresses, weddings, marriages, husbands, mothers-in-law and new houses. This lively and leisurely exchange of gossip and information continued each time I returned, with an endless succession of women sitting around the pillars and circular steps. In the men's bath-houses the talkers used to be more business-like as a rule, and — when it was safe to do so — conversed about politics and governmental changes, and perhaps exchanged private information about particularly officious and repressive policemen or guards.

The bath-houses had been meeting-places in Tabriz for hundreds of years. For example, a story passed down, and certainly garbled down, the centuries (especially after reproduction in the somewhat condescending renditions of English orientalists — an Irish friend of mine remarks that when the English find they cannot understand something they know it is time to patronise it) tells of the great poet Sa'di of Shiraz who died a very old man, supposedly aged over 100, around AD 1292, meeting with Humam-al-Din Tabrizi, whose own poems greatly reflect Sa'di's influence. Sa'di had travelled to Tabriz and wished to meet Humam (whose dates are roughly 1236-1314). He was told that the Tabrizi poet had a very beautiful son whom he guarded carefully from meeting with strangers, so that he would always accompany the boy when going to the baths. Sa'di discovered the day on which Humam would be likely to appear, hid in a corner and waited: it would seem that Humam had chosen an hour when few people would be present, and the bath itself is termed a private one, though presumably this would merely mean fairly expensive as Sa'di experienced no noticeable difficulty in gaining entrance. Humam was disconcerted to see him, seated his son behind him and enquired what was the stranger's profession and where he came from. He evidently wanted to rebuff the unwanted foreigner for their exchanges were rude in the extreme. Sa'di told Humam he was from the holy land of Shiraz, and that he was a poet. The two cities were as far apart as London and Aberdeen — in all senses. Humam replied testily that the Shirazis were as numerous as dogs in Tabriz. Sa'di said that it was the converse in Shiraz, where the Tabrizis were less in number and in public estimation than were dogs. Humam then picked up the water-pitcher and, having emptied it, inverted it and observed that the heads of the Shirazis were bald, like the bottom of the pitcher. Sa'di, in turn, said that the heads of the Tabrizis were empty, like the inside of the pitcher. Next Humam, seeking to test whether the visitor knew anything about poetry or him, or both, asked whether the Shirazis recited any of Humam's poetry; Sa'di promptly declaimed a couplet exactly in Humam's form (which so resembled his own), presumably grinning in the direction of the beautiful youth almost hidden behind his father:

> Humam is a veil between me and my love,
> I hope that the veil will rise from betwixt us.

All was now clear. Humam knew that the stranger had recognised him and why he was so churlish, and the stranger's way of elegantly turning the tension into a charming little joke gave the father just the clue he needed. "I think," said Humam, "you are Sheikh Sa'di? There is nobody else who can have such a spirit!" He kissed Sa'di's hand, introduced his son, and brought him back to his house where he entertained him for several days. In Sa'di's very civilised culture it was as appropriate to compliment a parent on the beauty of a son as of a daughter, but he showed his appreciation of Humam's wise anxiety to protect his son from more sinister strangers. And down to my own time, children continued to be accompanied to the baths, and to meet interesting persons who wished to know their parents and do them honour.

Every district had several bath-houses, at varying cost for different social classes. Whenever my nurse took me to a bath-house it would be to one in which there were no attendants and all the women washed and dressed their own hair; but when my mother took me it would be to a bath-house in which there were three or four women looking after the customers, washing their hair and helping them by pouring water on their bodies and hair while the ladies were sitting and talking. Sometimes they would bring tea or cold drinks while their well-to-do clients conversed. Every New Year my mother would give presents to the attendants in the bath-house she particularly favoured, and she might also give gifts in other ones if she was going to them at all frequently. She would also invite one or two of the attendants to lunch at our house. This was a way of ensuring particular attention, especially when there might be many customers. Conversely, my mother might take her custom elsewhere for a time if she was not getting the service she sought, and when she did return to the slighted bath-house later she would explain politely but firmly when asked that it was because they seemed too over-crowded to be able to serve her. But my nurse's bath-house showed simplicity at every level. The big cloth in which she would place our clothes would not be white, but would be old and threadbare.

The conversations in my mother's bath-house often supplied the basis for later discussions at home with my father and might be of considerable importance. The talks among women might lead to proposals for marriage alliances between their children, and details might be worked out there, as well as the preliminaries which would set the idea in motion in the first place. But my nurse took far less time; and there were far fewer conversations, and their content was much more a matter of the conventional mechanics. For myself, I preferred to be looked after by my nurse in the bath-houses because she was so gentle, whereas the busy attendants who had reason to be so careful with my mother were quick and rough with me. They pushed me this way and that as they pummelled and rubbed me to get rid of the dirt, frequently putting soap in my eyes and taking no heed of my protests in their efforts to complete my toilet and move on to their other clients. Then, there were other rites in men's bath-houses. It was considered requisite for men who saw friends of theirs in a bath-house to pay their bill if they should leave before their friends: it would be analogous to the British custom of "standing rounds" in a pub. Women often shared the food and drink they had brought with their friends. However, even as I was growing up something of the communal spirit was disappearing with the advent of modernisation; the common hot pool began to give way to single showers.

As a child I was curious as to why the women, after entering the main bath-house, disappeared into a place that looked like a toilet in the corner of the great hall, later returning with a faint green colour on their bodies. This also happened, even more frequently, with men. When I first went to the men's bath-house with my father he disappeared saying he would soon return and when he did he, too, had this strange green colour on his body. Later on I found out that it was a caustic depilatory paste. Both men and women in hot countries considered it healthy and attractive to remove all hair from the body, and often it was taken so seriously by deeply religious people that it was regarded as obligatory to remove all hair from the body, especially for men. Ironically, to have very large, rich beards is regarded as holy by the same people: head-hair is holy; body-hair is unholy. Perhaps the long hair and beards of the ayatollahs — I have no experience of their bodies — is a sign of their holiness!

Some years later I was living in London and a Jewish friend of mine, Larry, told me he was travelling to Tabriz, so I sent him to our home where my parents, who were orthodox Muslims, welcomed him into the home and treated him as a son of the family. Larry was a charming man, and very popular with my brothers, but like many Europeans who are discovering the East he became a little too enthusiastic about some of its customs, in this instance customs common to Jews and Muslims. One day he had gone to the bath-house with one of my brothers and decided to apply the depilatory paste as my brother did, but having a fairer skin and not being used to this harsh ointment, Larry found himself burning in some parts of his body, especially those normally out of sight and polite conversation. When they had returned home Larry kept repeating that his body was burning, and it took my brother some time to realise that he was too embarrassed to indicate where he was really suffering. They managed to clean the paste off him and get the doctor, but he was in real pain for about a week. I saw him in Tehran about ten years later, and his mind still went back forcibly to this incident as his introduction — since neither of us were from Christian backgrounds I can hardly call it "baptism by fire". But he was also able to bring with him the much more delightful memories of my mother's tasty and special Tabrizi dishes which Larry had liked so much and which had comforted him in his affliction. He told me he could find no equivalent of her *chilo kebab* anywhere in Tehran. He was also very proud of the carpet he brought from my brother's factory, which he was still using in Tehran. He used to return to my family two or three times every year, but I never heard that he showed any further interest in depilation. Of course he still went on expeditions to the bath-house with my brothers, but from then on he only went for the water, despite satirical enquiries from time to time as to whether he would like to employ its other accessories!

But all this lay far in the future — Larry did not visit Tabriz until 1961 — and we must return to my walks with my mother to my grandfather's house. Naturally, when we passed the bath-house I did not stop there, apart from listening for a moment or two to make out snatches of conversation or find out what the children were shouting about as they played. But after that interruptions were frequent.

We would walk through a common burial ground, where some graves were open to the sky, and my mother would warn me to be careful in case I fell in. In fact a few times my feet did fall into the graves, but with no serious results; these would have been shallow graves, very old and whose former tenants had completely disintegrated. At the exit of this burial ground there was a huge door with a dark entrance whence descended a huge stairway of hundreds of steps leading to a spring and used by a constant traffic of men, women and children carrying their buckets and going down and up. There are striking symbols in this juxtaposition of death and life, and water or its absence was indeed the frontier of death and life in our culture — you may get some idea of the climate of Tabriz from the name of our river, Quri Chay, which means "dry river". But the steps at the graveyard did not lead down to the Quri Chay, whose water, when it had water, was polluted and undrinkable. The water-seekers and water-carriers at the graveyard were going far below the level of the Quri Chay to an underground spring, or cheshma as it is called in both Azerbaijani and Persian. I suppose there were many springs in Tabriz, though few were as deep.

The use of the springs was chiefly limited to the poorer people: richer families like my own had a private reservoir. But my father's office in the bazaar used a cheshma, unlike his factory which relied on his reservoir at home. I would often have the task of hauling the water from the bazaar cheshma. The bazaar cheshma only involved some 25 or 30 steps, but the graveyard cheshma was much deeper and to me as a child seemed to stretch for at least a hundred steps. I was fascinated by it and would annoy my mother by wanting to gaze down its depths instead of getting on my way. In the summer, too, I would beg one of the water-carriers to let me have some water, and would sink gratefully on the bucket when it was lowered to me, drinking it in greedily like a fish. My mother found that we would set out at 8.00 a.m. and would generally not reach her father's house until midday. She complained that with my delaying it was like making a journey from one city to another.

The people chattered happily as they met one another at the steps of the *cheshma*, supremely untroubled by the proximity of the graveyard, not even finding time for reflections like those of Omar Khayyam:

> Into this Universe, and *why* not knowing
> Nor *whence*, like Water willy-nilly flowing:
> And out of it, as Wind along the Waste,
> I know not *whither*, willy-nilly blowing.

The district in which the graveyard and *cheshma* were situated was Davachi Gapisi, which is Azerbaijani for "the Gate of the Camel-Drivers" and was the North Gate of the four Gates of Tabriz. My mother's father, to whose house we were making such slow progress, lived in Gajil Gapisi, "the Gate of the Builders", since most of the construction industry operated there: this was the West Gate. Davachi Gapisi, our own district, still retained its own clear identity. In addition to the poorer inhabitants of the area, the camel-drivers and mule-drivers used it extensively. Many of them had come from adjoining villages, but some had come on the silk road which led from China through Afghanistan to Turkey and ultimately connected with Europe. This was the northern silk route: there was a southern one also, which passed through Esfahan and Shiraz to the Persian Gulf and Arabia. Tabriz was hence a very important link on the old line of communications between East and West, and opposite the graveyard was a great *karvan-sarai*. The words survive in English as caravanserai: but they are pronounced like the English personal pronoun "I" in its Azerbaijani and Persian forms, although in FitzGerald's *Rubaiyat* it is given a different rhyme.

> Think, in this batter'd Caravanserai
> Whose Portals are alternate Night and Day,
> How Sultan after Sultan with his Pomp
> Abode his destin'd Hour, and went his way.

The *karvan-sarai* was a huge house — it literally means "caravan house" — with stables at the bottom and bedrooms at the top, and I loved to race across to it and goggle at the camel-drivers and dealers as they leaned back on their great loads of merchandise, swigging tea, boasting, telling each other stories, narrating their adventures on the roads, giving news of their towns, even discussing the government's attitudes to them and swapping political news as well as information about the doings of their own families. This was the one way of passing news across the country. And those who came from foreign cities or had specific regular trading with them became regularly known by the names of those cities. I would have been looking at men known as Istanbulchi, Tehranchi, Moscowchi, Baghdadchi, Kabulchi,

Bakuchi, Khorasanchi, Calcuttachi and hearing without comprehending exchanges of information on developments in Russia, India, Iraq, Turkey and Afghanistan as well as from other major cities in Iran as the great men from Istanbul, Tehran, Moscow, Baghdad, Kabul, Baku (in Soviet Azerbaijan), Khorasan (in north-eastern Iran near Afghanistan) and Calcutta smoked their hubble-bubble, or as it is often called by the British, their hookah (the pipe whose smoke is filtered through water). My mother was forever having to drag me back from my efforts to abide my undestined hour at the *karvan-sarai*. I must have been a terrible child!

If we remember that Muhammad, the founder of Islam, was a camel-driver, we can get some sense of the historic role of such men and their meetings in the development and migration of ideas in world history. History is so often written in terms of battles and famous men; in fact the changes were often the product of the journeyings of people completely unknown outside their own generation. The importance of Tabriz is primarily that it was a meeting-place for ideas and cultures over thousands of years, and the men I watched were fulfilling the roles that their predecessors had also sustained far before the dawn of recorded history.

Islam no doubt arrived by camel like everything else, but it also arrived by conquest. In fact it encountered great resistance in Tabriz — we seem to welcome the arrival of ideas there when they come from peaceful rather than warlike communication — and found it very hard to make headway against the local religion of Zoroastrianism. There were specific reasons for that. Tabriz is interested in the outside world; but it is also very conscious of its own traditions, and Zoroaster was a local hero.

As is often the case our real clues can be found in names. Tabriz is the capital of Azerbaijan, whose old name before the Islamic invasion was Atropad. It meant "land of fire". And Tabriz itself means "warm-flowing". The identification in both instances with heat would seem to be allied to the religion of Zoroaster, who believed in the worship of fire. The warm-flowing place in the land of fire would imply that the capital status of Tabriz existed in some form before the Birth of Christ, that it was the heart of the country which gave birth to Zoroaster. He could certainly have been born in Tabriz himself as Muhammad was born in Mecca; or it could have been associated with his winning success in some way, as was the case of Muhammad at Medina. But Tabriz evidently had a symbolic pre-eminent status in his identification with the country of his birth, as lava is a condition of extreme heat in the heart of fire. As for the date of all this, Zoroaster has been claimed as having been born 1500 years before the birth of Moses, but more sober historians today are inclined to settle for around 600 BC. In any case trade made the city a breeding-ground for religion, and religion was extensively exported from it along with trade; or, to put it another way, Tabriz would have owed its status both to being a critical point on the northern silk route and to being the heartland of the Zoroastrian religion. It seems reasonable to suggest that Mecca would have been as popular in Tabriz after Muhammad, as America was popular in Britain after George Washington, or Moscow was popular in America after Lenin. In religion as in politics the newer fashions are seldom in vogue with the centres which have determined the shape of the old.

The religion which sprang from the philosophy of Zoroaster (or, as Nietzsche and others call him, Zarathustra) was by no means the first Aryan religion, but it differed from its predecessors in one crucial aspect. In evaluating the popular faiths of Aryans, Zoroaster was appalled that most of them centred on Ahura, the Lord of War and Destruction whose wrath had to be constantly appeased by human sacrifice. (Similar figures are to be found in the Greeks' Ares, the Romans' Mars, the Carthaginians' Moloch and the Hindus' Shiva.) Zoroaster bitterly opposed human sacrifice and instead believed in two forces guiding Man's life, represented by Ahuramazda and Angro Maina, or Ahriman. Ahuramazda was the god of light and the creator of all that is pure and good. Opposing him was Ahriman, symbol of evil and destruction, of darkness and death. In preaching these ideals Zoroaster was the first to propose that Man was involuntarily trapped in the context between good and evil, and that Ahuramazda in his mercy gave him the freedom to choose his own destiny. The idea of worship of fire is manifested in the nature of the land of Azerbaijan, where you can find flames or boiling springs in severe winter amidst snow. I myself bathed in a pool near Ardabil (a city close to the Caspian Sea) in cold midwinter: the water seemed almost boiling and I could not endure it for more than ten minutes. The opposition of heat and cold arises also from our very cold winters and hot summers, and from our huge mountains covered with trees and greenery on the one hand, and barren desert for miles within sight of it. When one looks at nature the sunrise has a glorious feeling each morning. I find the words I want in my beloved William Blake:

> "What," it will be questioned, "when the sun rises, do you not
> see a round disc of fire somewhat like a guinea?" "O no, no,
> I see an innumerable company of the heavenly host crying
> 'Holy, Holy, Holy is the Lord God Almighty'".
>
> (*A Vision of the Last Judgment*, 1810.)

So Zoroaster's idea is not really worship of fire, so much as admiration of the sun in nature and the creative imagination of Man which both he and his followers, either poets or philosophers, stressed through their creative imaginations and their songs. Night and darkness were regarded as transitory and a result of absence of sun, and so in Man transgression and Fall are seen as the want of imagination and essentially transitory. Some travellers lose their way at night and they think that they will move always in darkness.

Zoroaster was primarily concerned with Man and the society in which he lived and he believed that Ahuramazda ought to be seen through Man and his actions only, therefore he put all his thought and philosophy into three words: Good Thoughts, Good Words, Good Deeds. (I said *three* words, but the thoughts, words and actions cannot be separated from their united spirit and goodness.) Among the lines which survive from him, he is perhaps best summed up by his prayer:

> With the help of Truth and Good Mind, give Mankind Power to
>   bring rest and happiness to the world,
> Of which Thou, my Lord, O Ahuramazda, art indeed the first
>   possessor.

The idea of Ahuramazda influenced later religious thinkers, literary figures and social revolutionaries. The idea of dualism in human nature which consists of the qualities of good and evil and their extension into principles of warring forces, is a feature of religions, Christian and non-Christian, pre-Reformation and post-Reformation. Yet in my study of Blake I found in his message a clear development of Zoroaster's dualistic theory. "There is not an Error," wrote Blake in *A Vision of the Last Judgment*, "but it has a man for its . . . Agent, that is, it is a Man. There is not a Truth but it has also a Man. Good and Evil are Qualities in Every Man . . . Man is a twofold being, one part capable of evil and the other capable of good . . . both evil and good cannot exist in a simple being, for thus two contraries would spring from one essence, which is impossible . . ."

Omar Khayyam wrote, in his *Rubaiyat*:

> I sent my Soul through the Invisible,
> Some letter of that After-life to spell:
> And by and by my Soul return'd to me,
> And answer'd "I Myself am Heav'n and Hell":
>
> Heav'n but the Vision of fulfill'd Desire,
> And Hell the Shadow from a Soul on fire,
> Cast on the Darkness into which Ourselves,
> So late emerg'd from, shall so soon expire.

In 1976 when I was attending the 41st International PEN Congress in London, I found that the opening speech by Arthur Koestler enlivened my imagination and made me go back to my origins. There must have been about 200 writers present in the Queen Elizabeth Hall, all of them Europeans or Americans: there were no African or Asian writers, a point which surprised and angered me. I talked to Koestler after the speech: he had aroused my curiosity. He was a short man, sharp in manner, quick in replies, with a bright, engaged eye. I liked him because he was concerned with the destiny of man. At some points he seemed a child lost in a crowd; he did not sit peacefully within himself. He seemed to me to be searching for something. Yet he treated me very kindly, and spent a lot of time with me: he seemed interested in my views on writers' missions. His speech, delivered on 23 August, was defending imagination against materialism and selfishness. It was entitled "The Vision that links the Poet, the Painter and the Scientist" (and was reported in *The Times*, 25 August 1976) and it began by attacking the theme of the Congress "The Truth of Imagination" and its context, Keats' letter to Benjamin Bailey of 22 November 1817 in which the poet said:

> I am certain of nothing but of the holiness of the heart's affections and the truth of Imagination. What the Imagination seizes as Beauty must be Truth, whether it existed before or not; — for I have the same idea of all our passions as of Love: they are all, in their sublime, creative of essential Beauty . . . The imagination may be compared to Adam's dream: he awoke and found it truth. I am more zealous in this affair, because I have never yet been able to perceive how anything can be known for truth by consecutive reasoning, — and yet [so] it must be.

Koestler observed dispassionately, "This, frankly, does not seem to make much sense. Nor does it help much to find an echo of that passage in the famous last lines of the *Ode on a Grecian Urn*, written two years later:

> 'Beauty is truth, truth beauty,' — that is all
> Ye know on earth, and all ye need to know.

No doubt there is beauty in the lines," continued Koestler, "but do they speak the truth?"

In some ways I had answered Koestler's question when Mother finally got me away from gazing rapturously at the *karvan-sarai* and she succeeded in dragging me as much as a hundred yards till we reached the bazaar where there was yet another delay while I drank in its wonders. As one approached the bazaar there was a large tea-house filled with peasants, workers and travellers, some sitting outside because the inside was full, putting lumps of sugar in their mouths and sipping hot tea through the sugar lump, or smoking their hookahs and looking very relaxed as if they had no worry in the world. What fascinated me was the man with the samovar, an enormous receptacle, from which he was filling several glasses with tea, first from the pot on the top and then from a tap at the side, and moving with extraordinary expedition through the great crowd. He was placing glass after glass of tea on their saucers in front of each storekeeper. At first I thought the service was free, and then I noticed that at each counter he would pick up a token, a piece of metal called *pata*, which my father later told me were bought in bulk at the beginning of the week. Once I insisted on having a cup of tea, but my mother said "The glasses are not clean, and, besides, good boys don't have tea outside." When I persisted she said, "Honestly, it doesn't taste good out of doors", and when I asked "How do you know?" she was silent. But she bought me ice-cream from the shop where they sold hot beetroot in slices out of the pot in winter, and ice-cream in the summer. Ice-cream was made in front of the customers, the eggs and milk being beaten in a huge wooden box, then poured into tins, put in crumbled ice or snow brought from the mountains and turned round until the ice-cream set. As soon as the seller finished one huge tin of the ice-cream he followed with other ones. There were several people working in the shop. This was the only shop in the bazaar where I saw the wife, daughter and husband working together.

When we passed on, my eyes would be attracted by peasant men and women, in colourful clothes and dresses. The women didn't wear veils, but had scarves, very pretty long skirts and embroidered waistcoats. Some were mounted on mules, some walking alongside the horses. The men from the villages were distinguished by their hats, some made of felt. I remember some schoolboys found it amusing to take the peasants hats and run away. When the peasants chased them they would throw away the hat and escape. This was regarded as a great source of enjoyment for the city boys. Further up the bazaar could be found shops full of material for women's dresses and men's garments. The travellers from the villages who came to do their shopping were watched constantly by the shopkeepers with very searching eyes, like those of cats studying the movements of mice: I vividly remember their expressions. Some of the villagers would have come from 150 kilometres away, as far as Ahar to the north-east, for instance, or other places to the west, on the other side of Lake Urmiyeh.

On several occasions, to my mother's annoyance, I asked the mule- and camel-drivers to let me mount their animals, which they finally helped me to do. I well remember the first time I mounted a camel. When I was allowed on the beast, while it was sitting down, the driver said a quick word and I was very frightened to see the ground falling away as my steed lurched upward from the rear and then the front, and when I was finally settled on the standing camel, holding tight to the saddle of straw and cloth, I could see over the whole bazaar and felt the proudest boy in the place, as well as the most grateful to a camel-driver.

This Davachi Bazaar, beginning with the *cheshma* and *karvan-sarai*, ended in a huge square which had great shops on two sides. These sold dried fruit in winter and fresh fruit in summer and autumn. I must admit that I used to spend a lot of time watching these shops — in winter dried figs, almonds, raisins, dried peaches and pears and dates captured my zealous eyes, and in summer green water-melon and great varieties of grapes, of all colours, piled like mountains to a child's vision. In winter the shopkeepers would sit in a small office or outside next to their goods, lazing comfortably in front of a brazier full of ash and burning charcoal. In summer, standing in front of the shop, shouting how sweet their watermelons and grapes were, they incited customers and often employed young people to attract them. Once I persuaded my mother to buy me a bunch of grapes. She agreed with the one condition that we keep it until we reached home and then wash and eat it. Although I agreed, I ate almost half the bunch on the way through a hole in the handkerchief we were carrying. When we arrived she was surprised that half the grapes were eaten, and grimly expressed the hope that I would not become ill.

Beyond the square, across the Quri Chay, lay another big bazaar, this time devoted to carpets, jewellery and kitchen utensils. Once more my little eyes lit up, and my poor mother found her journey lengthened almost beyond endurance. Yet here above all I was amid a great and long tradition going back at least 600 years. The great Muslim topographer, Ibn Battuta (1304-1368/9), records a visit to Tabriz in his *Travels in Asia and Africa* (extending from 1325 to 1354): he is not speaking of the bazaar I knew, but of one which had since perished and was located some short distance away. It may perhaps seem strange to a European that Ibn Battuta writes of Tabriz so much with the air of a man visiting a foreign country, since it is easy to assume that different parts of the Near East are very like one another. But in his time Tabriz was very much part of a foreign country — it was the Mongols' capital in Persia. He would have arrived there in about 1328, travelling north across the mountains from Baghdad.

> We reached the town after ten days' travelling, and encamped outside it in a place called ash-Sham. Here there is a fine hospice, where travellers are supplied with food, consisting of bread, meat, rice cooked in butter, and sweetmeats. The next morning I entered the town and we came to a great bazaar, called the Ghazan bazaar, one of the finest bazaars I have seen the world over. Every trade is grouped separately in it. I passed through the jewellers' bazaar, and my eyes were dazzled by the varieties of precious stones that I beheld. They were displayed by beautiful slaves wearing rich garments with a waist-sash of silk, who stood in front of the merchants, exhibiting the jewels to the wives of the Turks, while the women were buying them in large quantities and trying to outdo one another. As a result of all this I witnessed a riot — may God preserve us from such! We went on into the ambergris and musk market, and witnessed another riot like it or worse.
>
> We spent only one night at Tabriz.

Understandably, you might feel. My fellow-citizens, however exotic their goods and exciting their markets, seem to have been a little too much for the great topographer. There is a slightly absurd fashion in Britain and America today for defining anyone very reactionary as "to the Right of Genghis

One of the Tabriz bazaars and fruitmarkets through which I roamed.

Khan" (a popular English spelling for the great Mongol leader known in Persian as "Chingiz Khan"): I suppose that the rioters might have come into that category for Ibn Battuta. But in fact they were not the cause of his departure.

> Next day the amir received an order from the sultan to rejoin him, so I returned along with him, without having seen any of the learned men there.

So Tabriz for him was a centre of intellectualism as well as of commerce and riots. He also knew it as a place dear to its inhabitants, and wide-ranging in its influence and reputation. He travelled as far away as Grenada in Moorish Spain where he found a company of Persian dervishes, wandering spiritual men, some of them mystics, and among them a native of Tabriz who told him that they had made their home in Grenada because of its resemblance to their homelands. Tabriz in his time had reached its greatest importance to date, having displaced Baghdad as the chief commercial centre of western Asia and attracting large numbers of merchants from Europe. One wonders why a man such as that dervish in Grenada, with his great love for Tabriz, should have decided to make his home so far from it. The theme is one which constantly repeats itself throughout history, through to the present day. Thousands of intellectuals and patriots spread over the world because of regimes as oppressive in their own ways as was the Mongols'. The movement of dervishes, which took place between the 13th and 14th centuries and greatly influenced Persian poets like Sa'di and Hafiz Shirazi, was against social injustice and dogmatic religion. And the saddest thing is that those who criticise the shortcomings of governments in the more liberal regimes where they make their homes find themselves reproached: "If you don't like it here, why don't you go back to your own country?" So many would have been only too happy to return home, if they could have done so with any real hope of retaining their liberty or even lives.

A dervish means literally a "poor man", but metaphorically a "wandering mind", and the man from Tabriz whom Ibn Battuta met in Grenada would have been in the fullest sense a wandering mind, carrying with him his whole city, the houses, bazaars and streets, the people among whom he used to tell his stories and hold his philosophical and theological disputations — all carried within him to the other end of the Mediterranean where he tried to convince himself he found something of his lost and loved Tabriz. Something of the personality of these exiled intellectuals may be derived from the Shirazi poet Sa'di; Story 11 in the first chapter of his *Gulistan* (*Rose Garden*) tells of the confrontation between a dervish (or darwish) and a tyrant ruler. This particular dervish was famous above all for the fact that his prayers were answered: this was not true of every dervish, but those of whom it was were much respected and feared. People were particularly anxious not to provoke them, for if angered they might utter some curse which in calmer moments they would restrain: but so great was their power that their malediction would be fulfilled. In other cultures it was felt to be unlucky to meet a holy man when out walking, and above all to block his way. In any case, as Sa'di tells it:

> A darwish, to whose prayers were given answers, was
>   beheld in the land,
>
> And Hejaj Yusuf summoned him, saying: "Speak a good
>   prayer for me".
>
> The darwish prayed "O lord, upon this man may the Angel
>   of Death stretch out his hand".
>
> And Hejaj Yusuf cried out "In God's name is this the good
>   prayer I asked of thee?"
>
> And the darwish replied "It is a good prayer for thee
>   and for all the children of Islam".
>
> Tyrant, thy savage rule
>   How long must thy people thole?
> Thou usest power but as a fool,
>   Death is thy better goal.

A little later, in Story 15 of the same chapter, Sa'di tells of a vizier who had been disgraced and removed from office, and had entered a circle of dervishes where he grew to find himself content, so that when the king resolved to take him back into favour and ordered him to return to office he refused, saying: "Retirement is better than profession":

> Those who sit down, safe, poor and far from thee
> Have bound the teeth of dogs and jaws of men:
> They tore the paper up and broke the pen,
> And froze the hand and tongue of calumny.

To which the king replied:

Verily we stand in need of a man of sufficient intelligence who is able to carry on the administration of the government.

And in answer, said the dervish who had been his vizier:

It is a sign of sufficient intelligence not to engage in such matters.

About the same time as Sa'di, lived the great writer Mawlana Jalalu'ddin Rumi (1204-1271), born in Balkh (south-west of Samarkand). He travelled to Tabriz and wrote of it, including a poem about a dervish. It seems worth including, apart from its richness of imagery and quizzical humour, for it suggests that not all wandering intellectuals found themselves at odds with figures of authority in Tabriz. At least one of them seems to have found the most benevolent police inspector in literature. Here is Reynold Nicholson's translation of part of the passage from the sixth book of the *Mathnawi*:

A certain dervish, who was in debt, came from the outlying provinces to Tabriz.
His debts amounted to nine thousand pieces of gold. It happened that in Tabriz was a man named Badru'ddin 'Umar.
He was the Police Inspector, but at heart he was an ocean of bounty: every hair's tip of him was a dwelling-place worthy of Hatim.
Hatim, had he been alive, would have become a beggar to him and laid his head before him and made himself as the dust of his feet.
If he had given an ocean of limpid water to a thirsty man, such was his generosity that he would be ashamed of bestowing that gift;
And if he had made a mote as full of splendour as a place of sunrise, even that would seem to his lofty aspiration to be an unworthy action.
That poor stranger came to Tabriz in hope of him, for to poor strangers he was always a kinsman and relative.
That poor stranger was familiar with his door and had paid unnumerable debts from his bounty.
In reliance upon that generous protector he ran into debt, for the poor man was confident of receiving his donations.

He had been made reckless by the Inspector and almost eager to incur debts in hope of his enrichment by that munificent sea.

His creditors looked sour, while he was laughing happily, like the rose, on account of that garden of generous souls. . . .

The poor stranger, afflicted with fear on account of his debts, set out on the way to that Abode of Peace.

He went to Tabriz and the rose-garden district: his hope was to lie supine on roses.

From the glorious imperial city of Tabriz darted light upon light on his hope.

His spirit was laughing for that orchard of noble men and the fragrant breeze from Joseph and the Egypt of union.

He cried, "O cameleer, let my camel kneel for me to alight: my help is come and my need is flown.

Kneel down, O my camel! My affairs are flourishing: verily, Tabriz is the place where princes alight.

Graze, O my camel, round the meadows: verily Tabriz is for us the most excellent source of bountifulness.

O camel-driver, unload the camels: 'tis the city of Tabriz and the district of the rose-garden.

This garden hath the splendour of Paradise: this Tabriz hath the brilliance of Heaven.

At every moment of time joy-enkindling odours diffused by the Spirit are floating down from above the empyrean upon the inhabitants of Tabriz."

When the poor stranger sought the Inspector's house, the people told him that the loved one had passed away.

"The day before yesterday," they said, "he removed from this world: every man and woman is pale with grief for the calamity that has overtaken him.

That celestial peacock went to Heaven, when the scent of Heaven reached him from invisible messengers.

Although his shadow was the refuge of people, the Sun rolled it up very quickly.

He pushed off his boat from this beach the day before yesterday: the Khwaja had become sated with this house of sorrow."

The man shrieked and fell senseless: you would say that he too had given up the ghost on the heels of the Inspector.

Then they threw julep and water on his face: his fellow-travellers wept and bewailed his plight.

He remained unconscious till nightfall, and then his soul returned, half-dead, from the Unseen.

The rest of the poem is a prayer of the wretched survivor to Allah asking pardon for having put an earthly being on the same level as Allah as a protector and provider, and thanking Allah for giving him his existence and the means for enjoying what his friend had formerly given him. Elsewhere Rumi wrote: "When imagination becomes imprisoned in colour or materialism, Moses acts against Moses. When you free imagination from bondage, Moses and Pharaoh become friends." This was his message — that materialism is only acceptable as the means of human unity, not as an end in itself (which brings only division). But how the bereaved bankrupt escaped from his creditors, Rumi does not say.

So my city had always had its incomers and outgoers, not that all of those coming were bankrupt seekers of philanthropy, or those going limited to alienated intellectuals. And if the *karvan-sarai* confronted me with the obvious fact of the traffic in and out, the bazaar showed the results, most especially in the part where the various carpets from all over the East were bought and sold. It was a meeting across time as well as distance. Some of the carpets I would have seen being sold, while my mother still begged me to make haste, could have been as much as 500 years old; others would certainly have been of very recent manufacture. And the customers in my day, as formerly, came from West as well as East, although now there was far more traffic from the West than in the past.

The great bazaar through which we were making such slow progress was an enormous building, called the Muzaffaria, which was lit by huge skylights. It had been rebuilt in the 19th century, but it had had many ancestors. A short distance from the great bazaar many *sarais*, or houses, were situated, surrounded by offices, and in the middle of the area — which is open, unlike a bazaar — could be seen sacks of dried fruit, pistachio nuts, walnuts, almonds, raisins, dried figs and all sorts of spices, which were to be sold all over Europe and in other parts of the world. The offices surrounding the area were occupied by merchants who dealt with famous cities in other countries, and whose camel-drivers we had noticed earlier. The *sarais* were reached through huge gateways, some of them having as many as three or four, which opened onto different bazaars, streets and parts of the city. The great gates were usually closed at sunset, by *sarai-dars*, and for those who left last of all the *sarai-dars* opened a small door at the bottom of the great gate so that the final exits had to be made crouched down and almost crawling: they then locked up even the small doors for the night. These doors were intended to keep the goods safe from possible thieves and marauders at night, but during the daytime the *sarai-dars* turned a blind eye to small children who found these huge yards an excellent place for hide-and-seek and also to feed themselves on the dried fruits when they were hungry. My father's office was quite nearby, and children from different offices and I, when I was older, used to congregate to play in one of these *sarais*. Naturally there was more dried fruit to be obtained from sacks which were old and had holes, or were torn open, and from there we fed ourselves whenever we wanted to. We used to eat anything we liked, but we never took anything away, and I remember that no one ever told us off at any time for touching these things.

One of the very few early European accounts of Tabriz comes from the witness of a boy not much older than myself and my friends when we were raiding the bags of dried fruit. Marco Polo was about 17 when he first saw

Tabriz, around 1271, just before the death of Rumi, and he conveys the excitement of the place as a hub of competing civilizations. He was highly conscious of Rumi's Muslim co-religionists — most of them much more orthodox than Rumi — and he and his father and uncle were bound on their journey deeper and deeper into the Mongol Empire; and of course for all of his enforced cosmopolitanism he retained the prejudices of his native Venice:

> Since Tabriz is the most splendid city in the province, I will tell you about it.
>
> The people of Tabriz live by trade and industry; for cloth of gold and silk is woven here in great quantity and of great value. The city is so favourably situated that it is a market for merchandise from India and Baghdad, from Mosul and Hormuz, and from many other places; and many Latin merchants, especially Genoese, come here to buy the merchandise imported from foreign lands. It is also a market for precious stones, which are found here in great abundance. It is a city where good profits are made by travelling merchants. The inhabitants are a mixed lot and good for very little. There are Armenians and Nestorians, Jacobites and Georgians and Persians; and there are also worshippers of Mahomet, who are the natives of the city and are called Tabrizis. The city is entirely surrounded by attractive orchards, full of excellent fruit. The Saracens of Tabriz are wicked and treacherous. The law which their prophet Mahomet has given them lays down that any harm they may do to one who does not accept their law, and any appropriation of his goods, is no sin at all. And if they suffer death or injury at the hands of Christians, they are accounted martyrs. For this reason they would be great wrong-doers, if it were not for the government. And all the other Saracens in the world act on the same principle. When they are on the point of death, up comes their priest and asks whether they believe that Mahomet was the true messenger of God; if they answer "Yes", then he tells them that they are saved. That is why they are converting the Tartars and many other nations to their laws, because they are allowed great licence to sin and according to their law no sin is forbidden.
>
> Within the confines of Tabriz is a monastery named in honour of the Venerable St Barsamo. Here there is an abbot with many monks who wear a habit in the style of Carmelites. These monks, so as not to give themselves up to idleness, are continually weaving woollen girdles, which they afterwards lay on the altar of St Barsamo when they celebrate Mass. When they go through the province begging (like the friars of the order of the Holy Ghost), they give some of them to their friends and to noblemen, because they are efficacious in relieving the body of pain; and for this reason everyone devoutly wishes to have one.
>
> (From Marco Polo, *The Travels*.)

When I was with my mother, I never dared to enter the *sarais*. This was not because I was afraid, but because I realised that such an action would bring my mother to great trouble. She was wearing her *chador*, and it was impossible for her to see me clearly with it; she would have difficulty in following me and would be in danger of being tripped up by the huge sacks of the merchants' produce. I myself would be in serious danger of losing her because when veiled she simply looked like hundreds of other women similarly protected. Indeed, several times in the past I had lost her for this very reason. In much less populated places I had only been able to recognise her by the shape of her shoes and by a hand gesturing in my direction under her garment. But when we used to arrive at the Great Mosque — Masjed-Jami' — I used to sit on the platform next to the great gate with my mother standing next to me. I used to watch the merchants rolling open great carpets in front of the mosque and displaying them to their customers. While these beautiful carpets were lying in front of the gate of the mosque I noticed people walking over them, and I drew my mother's attention to this as it was strictly forbidden at home for us to walk on the carpets with our shoes on. She explained to me that here this did not matter, as the merchants wanted the carpets to look older than they actually were, so that they would be taken to be valuable antiques and would therefore sell for a better price.

Sometimes I would say to my mother that I wanted to go to the toilet, and she would tell me to find a wall and go behind it and relieve myself that way. But I was shy and didn't want to, and besides I liked the adventure of finding a public, official toilet and going there myself just like a man. So when we came to the mosque on this occasion I was allowed to go to the toilets situated in front of it to use the facilities. This meant that I had to go into the dark, where it was frightening, since there was only one light at the far end of the passage, but it was also most welcome in its cool, soothing air, so different from the hot day outside. When I reached the open space I found many men washing in a large pool, preparing themselves to go in and pray, for which they had to be scrupulously clean. Beside the pool were little toilets. When I went in I found a great deep hole in the ground, into which a little boy might fall, and I could hear the noise of the sewer far below. So when I returned I told my mother of my fears and she said, yes that was why she had wanted me to go behind the wall.

I wanted to know why my mother would not come into the mosque with me, especially since it was so cool and agreeable after the open air. But she would only say that it was the wrong time. It was not until much later that I realised this was the time of the month when she was having her period, and it was forbidden for women to enter the mosque and pray during the days of their menstruation. She would remain outside while I would be allowed a few minutes to savour the quiet, peace and cool temperature.

Many men and boys were sleeping in some corners of the mosque, and when there was no mass prayer in progress the porters who had been carrying heavy carpets and loads on their backs and in their arms through the bazaar would go there to rest and have their meal. In fact after a few years when I was in my father's office, I myself slept in the mosque once or twice. Often, instead of going to collect my father's debts I would retire to the mosque and read my books in a quiet, cool place. Outside the mosque there were many rooms, including classrooms, where religious students read and studied. In fact it was the place where in later years I studied the *Gulistan* of Sa'di and the Arabic languages.

Immediately after we had passed the mosque we came to a huge open area with willow trees which was surrounded by these classrooms. I really wanted to go and paddle in the great pool there, but it contained pure water, reserved for the students who were at work, so that they could wash their hands and face, according to the religious rites, before prayer, and my mother forbade me in case I should be thought to be desecrating the water. The mosque itself was no more than two centuries old, but like most mosques in Tabriz it had been rebuilt many times over the centuries. The chief cause of the destruction of the mosques was the persistent recurrence of terrible earthquakes. One of the oldest surviving poems by a Tabrizi writer, the work of Qatran Tabrizi, deals with one of these earthquakes. It was written almost two centuries before Rumi and Marco Polo visited Tabriz, and long before the Mongols made their fierce conquest which resulted in Tabriz becoming so powerful and important a city. He speaks of the earthquake as the work of Yazdan, God.

Gaze on the might of Yazdan. Gaze on the mighty work of his hand.
Such deeds seem as little or naught to the hand of Yazdan.
No man can comprehend in its fullness the power of God.
No man can comprehend in its fullness the valour of God.
He makes gardens into barren hills and plains — such is his power.
He converts barren hills and plains into rich gardens in flower.
If contemplation makes you aware of humility — that is but fitting . . .
If you are cast into confusion by his might and his mystery — that, too, is fitting.
You who would reach to the innermost sense of these things,
You who would master the innermost motive of all of these things,
Make your way to Tabriz, learn how God's mighty hand cast it down,
Make your way to Tabriz, learn the tale of that most tragic town.
The city through the centuries raised its head to the sky,
Through the centuries men raised its walls up on high,
The town where men stretched out their hands for a star,
The town that raised towers to Saturn on far,
Lost its pride and was crushed in the space of one hour,
Death took a great toll in the span of one hour.
Many women of beauty, like Kashmir's most fair,
Died in gardens of paradise — still they lie there.
The departed, entombed, shall rest in Heaven's law
In once lovely homes in the earth's ghastly maw.
Men whose homes were once filled with rich goods of all kinds,
Men whose stores were once filled with good things of all kinds,
Have been felled by misfortune and roll in the dust.
They perforce sold their sons for the sake of a crust.

People starve though the city is bursting with bread.
People thirst though the waters have everywhere spread.
In penury people put value on wealth,
But, death being near, on life and on health.
Those who perished were saved from misfortune and badness,
While the living are plunged in a sea of deep sadness.
All men knew misfortune. For children they keen.
The deaths of their brothers and sisters they've seen.
In mourning they bloody their cheeks with their nails.
They gnaw at their fingers to stifle their wails.
In the night-time disaster enveloped the town —
You have heard how the towers and walls were cast down.
Helpless children were left by their more helpless mother.
Inconsolable lovers forgot one another.
Till that day of doom none shared woe with another.
Till that day no man had to comfort his brother.
Today in disaster men lack clothes and bread,
And every one feels he were better off dead.
Since God in his wisdom created the world
And beyond it the planets in symmetry whirled,
Such tremors on earth there never had been,
A calamity such as mankind had not seen.
This misfortune is fruit of our own wicked acts,
For we did not repent for our unworthy acts.
To bring comfort to those who were not taken by death
The Emir, and his son were saved from sure death . . .

> (Slightly amended, from *Azerbaijan Poetry*, an anthology.)

There is no doubt in my mind that this is a brilliant and angry satire.

I fear that in a more frivolous spirit of satire I am now taking us forward to the 19th century to view Tabriz through the eyes of the most superior Englishman of his time, or so his contemporaries seemed to consider him. Tabriz had seen Cyrus the Great and Marco Polo. She had been under the rule of Medes and Persians, Mongols and Turks. She had known some of the greatest poets and philosophers of antiquity. She was now to receive, in 1892, the reflections of the Honourable George Nathaniel Curzon:

Tabriz, the capital city [of Azerbaijan], which occupies much the same position in North-Western as does Meshed in North-Eastern Persia, which is the residence of the Heir Apparent, the station of a British Consul-General, and the largest commercial emporium in Persia, deserves somewhat minute attention. Situated at the extremity of an extensive plain, which extends to the gleaming expanse of the Urumiah Lake, and a little to the south of the Aji Chai (*chai* is Turki for river), which irrigates the gardens outside the city, it is framed in a landscape of orange and red-coloured hills, while on the south rises the snow-covered cone of Mount Sehend, 11,800 feet above the sea.

Tabriz has enjoyed, or perhaps I should say suffered, an eventful history. Situated at so slight a distance from the frontier, it has fallen the first victim to invading armies, and has been successively held by Arabs, Seljuks, Ottomans, Persians, and Russians. What the rage of conquest or the licence of possession has spared, Nature has interfered to destroy. The city has been desolated by frequent and calamitous earthquakes. Twice we hear of its being levelled to the ground before, in 1392, it was sacked by Timur, whose path was strewn with ruins that vied with the convulsions of Nature. Five times during the last two centuries has it again been laid low. A reliable historian (Krusinski) tells us that 80,000 persons perished in the earthquake of 1721; and we hear from another source that half that number were claimed for the death-roll by its successor in 1780. It is small wonder that a city so relentlessly persecuted has scarcely ventured to raise its head, that its streets are mean and narrow, that it contains few or no public buildings of any distinction, and that the bulk of its dwelling-houses are one-storeyed and low. What is the use of building a lofty structure, only to find it toppling down upon your ears?

A fanciful tradition ascribes the origin of the name to the gratitude of Zobeideh, the famous wife of the Kalif Harun-er-Rashid, who, having been cured of a fever by its salubrious climate, is said to have called the spot Tab-riz, or Fever-expelling. This, in common with other far-fetched interpretations that excited the curiosity of the seventeenth-century travellers from Europe, must be not too respectfully dismissed. Tabriz is an Aryan word, derived from *tab* or *tap*, warm, tepid, and *rez, riz, resh*, a verbal root meaning to flow. It signifies, therefore, "warm-flowing", and originated from the hot springs in the neighbourhood. This word became the classical Tauris, which at the close of the third century after Christ was the capital of the Armenian King Tiridates III. Its predecessor, located by Rawlinson at Takht-i-Suleiman, was Ganzaca, or Gaza, the Kandsag of Armenian history. To Zobeideh we may concede the distinction of having, in 791 A.D., rebuilt and beautified the city, a service which has more than once in history procured for its author a founder's claim and honour. In Marco Polo's time it was a city where "the merchants make large profits". The Spaniard Clavijo spent nine days here in 1404 and nineteen days in 1405, on his journey to and from Samarkand; and so speedily had the city recovered from Timur's visitation that even then, though formerly much more populous, it contained 200,000 inhabitants, and "the finest baths in the whole world". A few years later it became the capital of the Kurdish dynasty of Kara Koyunlu, or Black Sheep; but they in their turn were expelled in 1468 by Uzun Hasan (Long Hasan), the chief of the Ak Koyunlu, or White Sheep, who made himself sovereign of Persia, and in whose reign the Venetian travellers, whose diaries have fortunately been preserved and given to the world, visited his dominions. Josafa Barbaro, who was at Tabriz in 1474, called him King Assambai (i.e. Hasan Beg), and left a long account of the city. Ambrosio Contarini called the King Ussun Cassan. A little later the anonymous merchant whose travels have also been published in the same collection (1507-20) said the city was without walls but twenty-four miles in circumference. As for the ladies, he seems to have found time in the intervals of business to appreciate their charms, for he leaves record that

The women are as white as snow. Their dress is the same as always has been the Persian costume — wearing it open at the breast, showing their bosoms and even their bodies, the whiteness of which resembles ivory.

On the other hand, less favoured or more exacting was "the most noble magnifico" Vincentio d'Alessandri, who in 1571 said —

The women are mostly ugly, though of fine features and noble dispositions. They wear robes of silk, veils on their heads, and show their faces openly.

All the writers of this and the succeeding epoch concur in eulogies of the great commercial wealth and importance of Tabriz. Tavernier, in the middle of the next century, said that "money trolls about in that place more than any other part of Asia". Chardin, however, in 1671, has left the most glowing account of its extent and features:

It is really and truly a very large and potent city; as being the second in Persia, both in dignity, in grandeur, in Riches, in Trade, and in number of Inhabitants. It contains 15,000 Houses and 15,000 shops. I did not see many palaces or magnificent houses at Tauris. But there are the fairest Basars that are in any place of Asia. And it is a lovely sight to see their vast extent, their largeness, their beautiful Duomos, and the Arches over 'em; the number of people that are there all the day long, and the vast quantities of merchandise with which they are filled.

The enthusiastic Frenchman went on to say that the city contained 250 mosques, 300 caravanserais, and a population of 550,000, and that

The Piazza of Tauris is the most spacious Piazza that ever I saw in any city of the world, and far surpasses that of Ispahan. The Turks have several times drawn up within it 30,000 men in Battel.

In the present century the most notable experience of Tabriz has been its unresisted occupation by the Russian army under Paskievitch in the campaign of 1827. The Governor was seized and handed over as a prisoner to the Russians, and the latter occupied the Citadel and captured the town without firing a shot. Nevertheless the "St Petersburg Gazette", in chronicling this achievement, stated that the garrison made a most obstinate defence, but that nothing could impede the ardour of the Imperial troops, who carried all before them, took numerous stands of colours, and finally wrested from the Governor the keys to the city. The colours, which had been specifically manufactured in the bazaar at Tabriz, and then artificially perforated with bullet-holes, were sent to Moscow and were enshrined in great state in the Kremlin. There were only eight gates in the city, but fifteen colossal keys, also manufactured for the purpose, were despatched to the same destination, and, I doubt not, are treasured as among the proudest trophies of Muscovite prowess. The city was restored to Persia upon the conclusion of peace in February of the following year.

Since 1805 Tabriz has been the capital and residence of the Heir Apparent, having been first chosen for that purpose in the case of Abbas Mirza, the selected son of Fath Ali Shah. Kinneir, about 1810, described it as "one of the most wretched cities in Persia", and as having only 30,000 inhabitants. Morier, in 1812, gave it 50,000. In the long reign of peace that has succeeded the Russian war, the numbers have gradually swollen, being reported at different intervals as from 100,000 to 140,000, until at the present moment they are said to be between 170,000 and 200,000. In 1886 General Schindler reported the town as containing eight *imamzadehs*, 318 mosques, 100 public baths, 166 caravanserais, 3,922 shops, twenty-eight guard-houses and five Armenian churches; but a good many of these figures, represent deserted fabrics, while the majority of the so-called mosques are *tekiehs* or public prayer-places; so that the totals give an exaggerated impression of the existing city.

Imposing and extensive as Tabriz must once have been, there are at this moment positively only two monuments of antiquity worthy of any notice, and both of them are in a state of ruin. The first of these is the Kabud Musjid, or Blue Mosque, so called from the magnificent specimens of enamelled faïence by which it was once encrusted. It was built by Jehan Shah, the last sovereign of the Black Sheep dynasty (1437-1468 A.D.). Earthquakes have shattered its walls; its dome has fallen in; and but few relics survive of the departed splendour; although these are sufficient to have drawn from a competent observer the remark that the Mosque of the Sunnis, as he calls it, from the tradition that it was raised in the days when the Sunni was the national faith, is the "*chef-d'oeuvre* of Persian, and, perhaps, of all Oriental architecture". The other relic is the Ark or Citadel, in the south-west part of the city, originally built by Ali Shah, and which once contained a magnificent mosque within the walls. It was converted into an arsenal in the first quarter of this century by Abbas Mirza, who employed a large number of English workmen; and here, in July 1850, was shot the Bab, or founder of the Babi heresy. A solid mass of masonry 120 feet high, and with walls twenty-five feet thick at the base, towers above the city, and is a relic of the ancient structure. Faithless wives used to be hurled down from its summit; but this method of execution was abandoned when one of these ladies, sustained by her inflated petticoats as by a parachute, descended unharmed on to *terra firma*.

The palace of the Vali-Ahd, or Heir Apparent, is the most elegant modern building in the city. The Europeans live in the Armenian quarter. Here are the residences of the Turkish, Russian, and British Consul-Generals, the last named having a charming and spacious house, a great contrast to the quarters in which I left him before his transfer from Meshed. France also maintains a Consul at Tabriz, whose business it is to foster such trade as she may possess, and to supervise the interests of the Catholic Nestorians whom she has taken under her protection. There was once a Belgian Consul; but a sinecure so complete could only end in withdrawal. As I have said, the interior of the town possesses no distinction: the houses are low, the lanes narrow and dirty; and size and business alone demonstrate the existence of a capital. Considering that it is the second city in the kingdom, the residence of the heir to the throne, and the seat of great wealth, and that there are in the neighbourhood abundance of the most beautiful marbles and building materials, it is surprising, in spite of the earthquakes, that

Ark (Citadel) in Tabriz.

more effort has not been made to embellish Tabriz. An inner wall encircles the building of the Ark, and a double outer wall, in no sort of repair, surrounds the city.

(From George N. Curzon, *Persia and the Persian Question.*)

In reading this passage aloud, which is what is really needed to gain the full effect, the reader should draw back the chin, draw in the cheeks and cultivate as closely as possible the appearance of a camel. The late Peter Sellers would probably have given an interesting rendition of it. Something of the text is lost, of course, in an oral rendition which fails to indicate such high points as the author's care to demonstrate (in an adjoining passage) the vagaries of the French spelling of "battle" when being translated. A little of the charm of the original is also lost here, through the elimination of footnotes in which the author is really able to wear his learning heavily. But let us not be ungrateful to the future Marquess and Viceroy of India: we have sweated his labour pretty thoroughly and, if it is slipshod at the finer points, there is nobody to beat him (fortunately) when it comes to hard slog!

But Tabriz means much that could never be gathered from George Nathaniel Curzon.

I have tarried long, and let my memory and imagination wander into many byroads, taking up each distraction presented by the association of ideas from each place, and like my mother you must wonder if we will ever reach my grandfather's house. And so I will stop playing and come to the road on which we will find it at last.

We used to arrive at my grandfather's house at about one o'clock in the afternoon. We approached the district called Varji, entering through twisted alleys with high walls, rather ugly from the outside although inside were hidden beautiful gardens and orchards. Perhaps the houses were designed in this way to trick the tribes attacking Tabriz from outside into believing that these houses were poor so that they would ignore them in the course of their assaults. Thus my grandfather's house did not look attractive from outside, but on passing through the entrance gate you could feel the cool and pleasant interior with the garden full of fruit trees. Going into the garden you could see the *cheshma*, which having wandered underground over many miles now came to the surface in Varji, to end in the famous area of large vegetable farms called Hokmabad — known in Tabriz by its local name, Homavar. I immediately wanted to strip off my trousers and dangle my legs in the cool, almost freezing, water, wash my face and arms, and relax after the long journey on so hot a day. While I was doing that my mother used to hold my shirt from behind in case I should fall in, which I loved to do as it gave me an excuse to swim. I would pretend that I was frightened when in fact I was not, and my mother would carry me off to change my clothes.

My grandfather and two older uncles were either in the village or at Davachi Bazaar, where they had a cloth and grocery shop, selling various goods to the villagers. My grandmother, a very kind and dignified lady, used to welcome us, and we had lunch usually about 2.00 p.m. which I eagerly awaited. Before lunch I would have already picked several apricots from the garden, or snatched one or two small cucumbers from the corner where they used to grow. My grandmother gave us delicious dishes, mostly made of different vegetables. Bread was cooked at home once every two or three months, stored in a room and used gradually. The bread was *lavash*, long and as thin as thick paper, a metre long and half a metre wide.

My younger aunt, Dilar, used to help my grandmother with the housework and cooking. They also had a manservant and several womenservants. My second-oldest uncle, Karim, was fond of horses and kept one at home and sometimes gave us rides on it, which was most enjoyable. I liked him most of all because he played with us a lot: he was the only older person who played with me and his two younger brothers. My grandfather had two brothers, one older and one younger than him, who lived in the houses adjoining his. There were doors dividing these houses. My grandfather was very well-bred and rather serious, and did not show much interest in children except for a brief smile and word of conversation. He thought our playing and running around the garden was pointless. We had a toy which was a round disc on a long string and could be made to go through the garden, twisting and turning and wandering off among the trees. "What is the use of that?" asked my grandfather. He did not know that it took me in my mind into the air, twisting and turning, and escaping from all the world. It was a great thing to do! I was surprised when I heard him ask what was the use of it. My young uncles, and sometimes Karim too when not too busy with his horse, would join in, chasing me as I tried to make the disc travel far enough to keep them at a sufficient distance. It was a great shock to the whole family, and especially to the children, when Karim was suddenly paralysed at about 25 years of age, and was taken to Tehran where after unsuccessful treatment over several months he died. My grandfather, too, died some five years afterwards, almost certainly from his grief, as he never recovered from Karim's death.

Villagers used to bring presents to my grandfather regularly. Once he had planned to take my grandmother to another city for a holiday while she was recovering from an illness. He intended to combine business with the holiday and so decided to go to Maragheh, to the north-west of Tabriz near Lake Urmiyeh. He wrote a letter to a friend asking him to prepare a house for them, sealed it in an envelope and stamped it. He came outside, looking for the servant to take it to the post-box. At the same moment a villager arrived with a donkey laden with presents — eggs, flour, chickens, butter and so on. My grandfather, remembering that he had sent the servant, Qurban, to his place of business, asked the villager, Nawruz-Ali, to take the letter to the post-box. Nawruz-Ali replied, as was customary: "Your servant be sacrificed to you. Let me unload my things." My grandfather insisted, "No, no, take the letter". So Nawruz-Ali took the letter and put it on the ground, and my grandfather shouted at him not to make it dirty. Nawruz-Ali said, "My lord, I wanted to untie the chickens and put the covering on the donkey" (to absorb its perspiration and prevent its taking a chill). "The poor animal has travelled a long way." Seeing my grandfather looking serious and rather commanding, he picked up the letter from the ground and went a few yards forward, but then returned to my grandfather saying, "Your troubles are my heart, my lord: let me take the eggs into the house in case the donkey should roll over them and break them." My grandfather shouted, "Don't talk too much: run and take this letter to the post-box." Nawruz-Ali was going away when my grandfather called to him, "Don't give that letter to anyone; don't show it to anyone. Put it quickly into the box and return." Nawruz-Ali said, "Am I a child, that I would let anybody take that letter from me? Do you think I am so crude? I will not even let the police touch it." My grandfather again showed him the way to go, and told him where the post-box was,

Nawruz-Ali, the peasant.

The village where Nawruz-Ali came from.

explaining several times. Nawruz-Ali disappeared, and my grandfather returned to the room, explaining to my grandmother what he had written to his friend and telling her to prepare and make ready for the journey. While they were talking Qurban arrived and asked, "Whose donkey is this in the garden? What are these things on the ground?" My grandfather answered, "Boy, go and take them in: they are presents from Nawruz-Ali Tazakandi", thus naming a village about 30 kilometres from Tabriz. Then Qurban took the chickens to the kitchen and opened the sack and told my grandfather that it was very good flour. My grandfather then ordered Qurban to bring lunch. We had lunch. Two hours went by, Nawruz-Ali did not return, and my grandfather became anxious. He called Qurban and told him to go to the post-office and find out what had become of Nawruz-Ali.

It was about half an hour before Qurban returned, without having found Nawruz-Ali. My grandfather was on the balcony, smoking, and worrying about his letter. While he was there, the police appeared at the door. As soon as they saw my grandfather they said, "Sir, the officer in charge asked me to beg you to come to the station, and bail out one of your subjects." My grandfather was very surprised at this, and after a few minutes' silence asked, "What has this poor man done that he has been taken by you to the police station?" But the officer said he did not know much about it, and my grandfather had better come himself. My grandfather did not say anything to my grandmother in case she might worry. When he arrived at the police station (he told me later), there he found poor Nawruz-Ali sitting among the prisoners and crying, and wiping his tears away with the end of his jacket.

After talking with the policeman in charge my grandfather brought Nawruz-Ali back to the house. As soon as Nawruz-Ali reached the garden, he squatted next to the wall and wept. My grandfather called him into a room and started to investigate what had happened. Nawruz-Ali wiped his eyes and said, "My dear Lord, may my life be sacrificed for you and for your children. Excuse me, it is not my fault, I am a simple peasant. How should I know what is a letter, and what is a postal-box, and what is the post-office. I have never seen any of these things in my life. For the sake of your children's health and your own prosperity, forgive me for this mistake. If I do not die and do live, I will recompense you for the error which I have made. What can be done? Perhaps this was God's wish, that this should happen." He moved forward and bowed down to kiss my grandfather's feet. My grandfather told him to sit down, and asked again what had happened. Nawruz-Ali said, "Sir, what happened to my donkey?" My grandfather said, "Don't waste time talking about donkeys, *tell me what has happened*." Nawruz-Ali said, "When I reached the post-box, I did not dare to put the letter in the box in case somebody should take it. After seeing one lady and one child bringing letters and lifting the cover and putting the letter into the box, I was heartened to take your letter and put it in the box. Then in order to be sure that nobody would steal it, I waited a few minutes to make certain the letter was safe. Then to my surprise I saw a man approach the box and, by fiddling with it, manage to open it. He stole my letter and the others. And then I rushed on him and snatched all the letters from him, and seeing that he resisted my attempt to save the letters, I punched his face and knocked him down so that he would not steal your letter. The policeman saw what I was doing from across the road and took me away. Sir, it was not my fault, I wanted to protect your letter."

Nawruz-Ali tended the donkey after dark and went back to his own village. He refused to eat anything in my grandfather's house. My grandparents went off to Maragheh, and when they returned to Tabriz they heard that after some weeks Nawruz-Ali had been taken from his village and sentenced to three months' imprisonment for the crime of having assaulted a public official. When my grandfather heard this, he stood for some time staring at the ground. He did not say anything.

3

I Live in Two Worlds

When I was a few months old my mother was unable to breast-feed me and had to entrust me to a nurse who was the wife of my father's cousin, Izzat. Izzat and his wife Humai used to live in our basement and whenever I was hungry and crying my father used to carry me downstairs, even at midnight, and ask Humai to feed me. Humai had a baby daughter called Fatima who was younger than me.

I was about three years of age when Izzat and Humai left the basement of my parents' house and bought a very small house in the outskirts of Tabriz, next to the North Gate. It was the last house on the border between the farmlands and the city. There one wouldn't imagine that one was in a city at all; it was rather like a village house, since most of it overlooked farmland covered by wheat and oats. The house was very pleasant and full of breezes and freshness. Besides its locality there was a world of difference between my nurse's home and ours. Our house was covered with soft and beautiful Persian carpets, whereas Humai's, both in the basement of my father's house and in her own house, had coverings of canvas and blanket. There was only an old, small *kileem* at the corner of her room and the rest was bare, consisting of bricks which would hurt my feet when I walked on them. (A *kileem* is another, cheaper kind of carpet where, instead of knots, the material is more akin to woven cloth. In fact some *kileems* can be extremely beautiful, and each tribe of those engaged in making them has their own specific design — among them the Bakhtiyari, the Qashqai and the Shahsevans. The most beautiful ones, such as those made by these three tribes, were much too expensive for Izzat and Humai to afford, whereas rich people used to give them as gifts.) We used to sit on the floor on cushions but whenever I fell on the floor while walking I hurt my knees and ankles. My ankles would hit the corner of a stone or brick, and the agony comes back to me very clearly even now.

My nurse's room in the basement at home was about one and a half metres below the level of the garden and I had to climb down — or when I was very small, roll down — the steps, which was actually very frightening; but I preferred to go to visit them in their new house where there were only two steps to descend. The basement in my parents' house was to be used in the Second World War as a hiding-place, with all the windows covered during German air-raids. When my nurse lived there, I always wanted to climb through the window of the basement to get into the garden and catch the light, but the window was so high and near the ceiling that I could never manage it. When we first visited my nurse's new house I was delighted to find that I could climb out of the only window onto the yard, which was hardly more than 12 square metres; the window was small, one metre by one metre, and divided into small panes, some of which were covered by newspapers and cheap paper instead of glass. The wind used always to make them shake and rattle. Our house had several bedrooms, large sitting-rooms and living-rooms and a huge kitchen which occupied two floors on the other side of the building, whereas Izzat's and Humai's only room was used as both a bedroom and a sitting-room. In the evening they used to put mattresses and bedding on the floor, and we used to sleep on them, all in one room. Separated from the rest of the room by a curtain, there was a place to pile the bedding at the side of the wall. In fact it became a good hiding place for Fatima and I when we wanted to play hide-and-seek.

There were hollowed-out alcoves within the wall in the lower and upper parts of their new house. Humai used to put sweets and dried fruit and the things we used to like on the top shelf out of our reach, but on the lower shelves there was a samovar and cups and glasses, and small boxes full of old keys and necklaces. It fascinated me most of all to open one of these boxes. I used to play for hours with the keys or ornaments. Fatima did not have any other dolls than those her mother made for her; I, too, used to play with them. Although my parents' house was full of expensive articles, I always preferred to play in Humai's house. There the world seemed under my feet and more under my control than in our own house. I was in fact free to handle everything without any obvious objections. I was even fond of trying Izzat's hat on my head, even though it covered my eyes and nose too, and this made him laugh.

I don't really remember when Izzat's family moved house. I was surprised when I visited them for the first time. It was a new world. The houses, streets, people and shops were very different from our environment. The distance between our house and Humai's was about one kilometre, but travelling on foot and at my pace it seemed much longer, as if I were travelling to another part of the country. However, I was excited and looked forward to reaching them. Sometimes my father used to take me by *doroshka*, a two-horse carriage. Town boys used to like to climb up behind the

Izzat, with my brother's children.

An alley next to Izzat's house.

doroshka and hold on by the metal bar as it drove, keeping their heads down under the perimeter so that if the driver turned back he would not see them, or even if he did could not easily reach them with his horse-goad. A stick with leather thongs was used to make the horses go faster, and this could prove very painful on the head or face; but if the boys were sufficiently concealed the thongs only descended on their back. Once I remember that I climbed on the back of somebody else's *doroshka* but had not gone far before, to my disappointment, my father's partner Haji Ali saw me and told me off by gently twisting my right ear. After that I never tried it again. The point was of course that having reached a certain economic and social status my parents and their colleagues could not let their children be seen behaving in public in the same manner as the children of the poor.

Humai's house was the northernmost house in Tabriz. It was situated next to the main road leading to the North Gate. In summer and winter there was a continuous traffic of mules, camels, donkeys, and flocks of sheep and cows, and (rarely) motor-vehicles. They used to arrive at early dawn and the bells on the camels' necks created a rhythm and melody all along the road and echoed as far as the horizon. Especially in the summer, we would all sleep on the roof of the house and I was usually wakened by the sound of camel-bells and the procession of the caravans. The sound of the bells, the sound of animals' feet and people's conversations, used to mingle with the pleasant morning breeze and lull me back to sleep until the sun shone on my bed and I would hear Humai calling me affectionately, "The sun is on your bed, Gholam-Reza. If you don't get up it will make you feel tired and give you a headache." We used to climb to the roof by a ladder which was about seven or eight steps. Humai did not allow me to climb the ladder alone. She used to say, smilingly, "If anything happens to you I cannot escape from your father's hand." Whenever she said that, I used to feel inside myself, "I do not belong to my father, I belong to you". When I was between the ages of three and six, I used to stay with Humai three or four days at a time or even for a week. I always returned home whenever I was bitten by insects, which caused my body to swell up here and there. It was never my wish to go back, but Humai was afraid that I would become ill and she would be blamed by my parents.

When we came downstairs from the roof the samovar would be boiling and the tea would be ready. We used to sit around the samovar as Humai served the tea. We had *sangak* — bread about a metre long and some 20 centimetres wide and much thicker than *lavash*. The samovar was similar to the one in my parents' house, but much smaller, and the taste of the tea was quite different: I did not realise that the difference was caused by the cheapness of the tea, though I did not find it any less pleasant. In my parents' house we would have cheese, eggs, fruit and fresh bread for breakfast, whereas at Humai's the bread was dry and stale and there was

A camel caravan.

very little cheese. Where in rich houses we put sugar lumps in our mouths and drank the tea through them, my nurse's family used raisins for the same purpose. During the Second World War, when the price of sugar rose spectacularly, this practice became commonplace. Children used to sing songs in the streets:

> Oh, Mother, oh, Mother,
> The tanks are coming,
> My heart is filled with thirst,
> Drinking so much tea with raisins
> Has brought pain to my teeth.

In fact, I preferred raisins to the sugar lumps, and I drank more tea in order to eat more raisins. Humai knew this, but did not say anything. She was a loving and affectionate person, who always had a sweet smile on her face. Whenever I was trying food which I had not known at home she used to say, "My dear, you are not used to these kinds of food", and then laugh while cuddling me.

I remember once she was cleaning a sheep's stomach in the yard, and I had not seen such a thing before. I sat next to her and asked her questions.

She did not tell me that she was going to cook it for a meal. She said she was cleaning it and would use it in the house, adding, "I know your mother has never touched these and you have never seen one." At the next mealtime we had pieces of white meat covered with soft skin. In fact it was rather tasty and it was only later that I found out the meal consisted of sheep's stomach.

Humai's house consisted of a small vestibule and pantry at either side of the single room. In the pantry she used to keep cases full of clothes, as well as the kitchen utensils she used outside the house in a small kitchen in the corner of the yard. She also stored left-over bread and some fruit and vegetables in the pantry. Half of the vestibule was taken up with the storage of charcoal, which was used for samovar tea-making all year round, and for the *korsi* during the winter. A *korsi* consisted of a low, square table under which a brazier was placed and fed with charcoal. It was the sole means of heating the house apart from an oil lamp. There was neither hot nor cold water in the house. Cold water would be brought in buckets from the neighbouring water-well, or from some *cheshma* far away. The source of cold water was therefore two buckets, one in the garden and one in the house, while the samovar supplied the hot water for washing clothes in addition to its normal function of tea-making. Seeing my nurse fetching water like this and comparing it with the water-reservoir and constant supply we had at home emphasised the sharp contrast between the two houses. I often wished I had been able to help her myself, for I did not like to see her wrapped with the veil and struggling with two buckets of water. Later on, when Fatima grew bigger, she would help her mother; but when I offered in my turn, the offer was refused.

I used to play with Fatima in the yard during the summer and in winter in the room inside the house. As summer gradually turned to autumn we used to climb over the wall and pick from the tree a kind of fruit called ida, which is grown in many parts of Azerbaijan and perhaps other parts of Iran as well. It needs the least attention and water of all fruits, and is likened to those natural geniuses (or genii) who produce immortal works of art having received the least possible cultivation or training. An excellent case in point is Samad Behrangi, writer of children's books, who was drowned before he was 30: that was in 1968, and the circumstances are mysterious, possibly connected with the repression of dissenting intellectuals by the security forces of the late Shah. He declared his own similarity to the ida tree with its need for so little water or care. And like the ida tree he brought forth very sweet fruit during his short life. He worked entirely for others, not for himself at all. In one of the chapters of his *Study of Educational Problems in Iran* he wrote:

Until we see an environment or society closely, until we live in it, mix with the people and hear their griefs and learn about their wants, it is vain and useless to

show ourselves sympathetic to that society and people, and even to write stories
for them . . .

Again in his last work, his masterpiece, *Mahi-ye Siya-he Kuchulu* (*Little
Black Fish*), he shows his philosophy and his vision that we should live for
others as well as for ourselves. Opposing the social oppression at the time,
he wrote:

> Now death can very easily call on me but as far as I can live I should not go
> towards death. If I once come face to face with death — I face it. That is not
> important. What is important is what effect my life or death can have on the life of
> others . . .

The words are his own philosophy, although in this story he has put them
into the mouth of the black fish who is speaking to itself just before being
caught by the fish-eating bird. When he visited me in my house with his
close friend Behruz Dihqani (later killed by the Shah's agents in the summer
of 1973), Samad answered my question as to what he was writing about:
"I am writing exactly what I see, not more, not less." In fact, his stories of
villagers in Iran proved his words exactly and recall Blake's statement in his
Jerusalem: "My Streets are my Ideas of Imagination."

The memory of Fatima and myself as children naturally brings back to me
Samad's wonderful stories for children, because he was so near to children
himself. Actually, when I used to play with Fatima sometimes I was rather
rough with her. Once, I remember clearly, I hit her hard and made her cry. To
my surprise Humai did not hit me back as I expected her to, and deserved.
Interestingly, children know when they do — and do not — deserve a
punishment. She kissed both of us and told me gently, "When Fatima is
grown up she will be a good sister for you." I felt really ashamed of my
behaviour. I don't remember ever hitting Fatima again. I loved Fatima, and
when we grew up I did not distinguish her from my own sisters. In fact, I felt
closer to her.

Fatima had bright and large blue eyes, brown hair and fairish skin, which
is not unusual in Azerbaijan. Her sister Marzieh, who was two years
younger, had dark eyes, dark hair and tanned skin. Fatima was seven years
of age when she started working in a match-making factory near their
house. Marzieh joined her there two years later. I missed Fatima's
companionship and I felt really lonely. I used to sit for hours and wait until
she returned from the factory. She used to get up very early, when it was still
dark, and rush to the factory while the factory hooter was still blaring out,
and not leave until the evening. When Fatima returned home from the
factory she looked pale and tired, and did not show any interest in playing
with me. She used to sit quietly, and I would be very anxious to make her

talk, smile or run around with me. We were moving apart, I felt, and I did not want this to be the case. I felt sad, but did not understand what was happening.

As we grew older the different environments of Fatima's house and my parents' house created a gulf between us. When Marzieh joined Fatima working in the factory I started to wonder why was it that they worked and I did not. I clearly remember that one evening Marzieh's face was very pale, and her normal smile and rosy cheeks were absent. It made me sad but I still did not understand. For the first time I felt alienated and estranged; indeed even before that occasion I had found they were ignoring me. I still loved them and wished they would return to playing and chatting as before, but they never did. The more Fatima and Marzieh worked, the less we saw of each other. I went to school and they went to the factory. Whenever they visited my parents' house, they remained quiet and rather shy, and reluctant to eat or wander around the house. It seemed as though an invisible wall was being built between us as the time passed. I wished I knew what had caused it, and could pull the barrier down.

I remember, too, that I would save my money to buy them presents at Nawruz. I once bought my nurse and her daughters stockings — at this time I was about 13. Humai was pleased and gave Fatima and Marzieh my presents. They accepted the stockings politely and put them on the shelf. I felt disappointed because they did not jump, laugh and embrace me as they would have done before. I did not know what to say, so I said, "Next time I shall buy you dresses." Humai said, "You are my lovely and kind boy and your sisters appreciate your kindness." But Fatima and Marzieh remained silent. The silence disturbed me and I felt myself as a stranger in their house, and when they came to my parents' house I would feel a stranger there as well. Humai's warm and loving attitude helped me to some extent but, nevertheless, this significant silence and distance existed between me and her daughters until they married and had children. When visiting Iran in 1964 I also called on Humai and her daughters. Fatima and Marzieh, to my excitement, called me *Agha-da-dash* (Big Brother) and received me very warmly. Even their children called me uncle. I felt happy and my early sweet memories of them were revived within me. I continued to visit my nurse and her daughters and two sons (born later on: Majeed and Hamid) whenever I visited Iran.

Fatima and Marzieh both married when relatively young, Fatima when she was 20. Her husband was a textile worker who then went on to build up his own small textile workshop, employing his sons. Marzieh's husband began by buying and selling cattle, and then went into the meat business, where he achieved considerable success. Both of them had beautiful children, of whom the girls finished elementary school, two of them subsequently marrying. No members of the families have as yet gone to secondary school.

My nurse, Humai, is still alive, but her husband, Izzat, recently died at a great age. I remember him well and liked him very much indeed. He was a builder and often used to work at my father's house or in the factory. He used to take Fatima and me to the National Park, and this was a most enjoyable treat for me especially as he used to let me ride on his shoulders and I felt myself on the top of the world. My father was too dignified ever to do anything of this kind. While he was sitting in the house, I was permitted once or twice to climb on his shoulder, but never on the street.

Izzat used to leave for work in the early morning, but being self-employed he sometimes found himself without any particular job and would spend his day at home or at the *chai-khaneh* or tea-house. Whether in or out of work I never heard him talk about money or have any dispute with Humai. I thought they both had a very good relationship. In contrast I well remember that in my father's house I heard constant discussions about how much profit they made out of carpets, how many losses they had, how many workers were on strike or absent and how far the price fluctuations would affect them. My father would always complain or worry about not being able to sell the carpets, and would warn my mother and everybody else to be careful how they spent money and used the things he had obtained for them, since the future was uncertain. Though Izzat was poor, and they did not have as much food and other things as we had in my parents' house, I felt that the most obvious and pleasant absentee in Izzat's was discussion about money. At my parents' house, too, the mullah would always be preaching about the eternal salvation or damnation of everyone, or what God would do when life was over. But Izzat and his family did not seem to be concerned about these things either. Perhaps they were too busy to worry about them. As the saying goes, "The busy bee has no time to worry." Even when men and women got together they talked about their daily work and children, and what they were going to do tomorrow. The stories that were told in the tea-houses opposite to Humai's house were from traditional epics, old heroic tales telling of peasants' insurrections against the feudal overlords and tyrants. These stories supplied the family with their chief topics of conversation, whereas the mullahs hardly ever came to such a poor district where they would not be likely to receive gifts and food of the value and delicacy to which they were accustomed in the rich districts. And where the old stories were retold, there would also be repetition of witty satires of Hafiz of Shiraz at the expense of the greed and rapacity of mullahs. So from every point of view the mullahs were wise in leaving the area alone — which was all to the advantage of Izzat, Humai and their neighbours.

There was always a sense of peace and pleasure in my nurse's home. They did not mention the price of things they bought. They had no bank account. They did not talk about profits, losses, bank drafts, defaulting workers and debtors. Nor did the gossip resemble the topics in my parents' district: who had married whom and how much dowry had been taken to her husband, what neighbour had bought that huge American Cadillac. There I felt suffocated in this inhuman and impersonal atmosphere. In my nurse's district money was important in order to buy the necessities of daily life, but it was not regarded as everything. The people were proud of their hard work and skill. The son of Humai's next-door neighbour was called Usta Hussein (skilled man) because he was a good carpenter. There were others who were well-known for their skill in making fine carpets — they made carpets in their houses for the carpet merchants, and often part of their sitting-rooms were taken up with carpet-looms. Usually all the family would work on the loom. Many women used to feed their babies, cook, wash clothes and sweep their houses and still had time to help their husbands make the carpet.

These people in Amir Khiz seemed more cheerful, hopeful and generous than those in the Shakkli district where my parents lived. In Shakkli, life seemed to be more tedious, and tiring. I felt that people watched each other's movements, clothes and appearances incessantly. Most disturbing of all were the disputes over distribution of inherited properties. Some argued, and some from time to time violently quarrelled over shares in villages, orchards, farms, gold and jewellery. They tried to cheat each other. Men took two shares and women one share of their parents' inheritance. In most cases the women were even deprived of their share by putting their finger-print on a document which they were unable to read. This was precisely the fate of my own sisters. When my father died I was studying in Britain. My brother Ibrahim had taken my sisters to the property registrar's office and asked each of them to put her fingerprint (because they could not write) on a document which declared that her share of our father's wealth was received therewith. This was done in exchange for a promise of the equivalent of £180, which in fact was not paid for a long time. Later, when my sisters learned of the purpose behind this action, they became upset and bitter, and repeatedly expressed their bitterness to me. Even my mother was made to sell her share of the house to her sons in exchange for a sum of money which she never received, and so she lived at the mercy of my brothers Ibrahim and Mohsen. Later, some three years before her death, her telephone was cut off because Ibrahim's wife accused her of using it too frequently. It is unlikely that this was the case; in fact Ibrahim's wife was herself often on the telephone to Tehran, where her parents and step-brothers lived. This action hurt me deeply as it cut off my link with my mother. When I last talked to her by telephone to Batul's house three months before she died, she talked of selling her jewellery to install a telephone, which would have cost about £1000. She did not know how to write and, later, desperately wished to get in touch with me two days before her death.

My own observations would lead me to conclude that this attitude to my mother was not a general practice. In Iran old people are usually loved and cared for by their younger family. They often live with their children and their children's families, and seldom live alone. This is generally the case in Asia and Africa. However, women have no economic and social independence. In comparison with Western women they are more protected and sheltered against social insecurity such as unemployment, but this security and sheltered position is often paid for with a loss of personality and dignity. My mother and sisters disliked their dependence on my brothers and their husbands. My mother often told me that she did not wish to live after my father's death. Initially, I thought she said this out of emotion and her love for my father — but later I learned that she did not want to be dependent on the mercy of others. No matter how rich my father was, my mother could not enjoy his wealth after his death because she was dependent on my brothers. Such provision as children's allowances paid to the parents and old age pensions are not common in Iran.

But difficulties between the generations over property are age-old. In the 14th century Hafiz of Shiraz wrote:

> Daughters are all at war and in dispute with mothers.
> Sons are ill-wishers of their fathers.
> The fools always drink sherbet made of roses and sugar.
> The strength of the wise is always made of the blood of their hearts.

(In fact, Hafiz wrote "liver". In the ancient world the liver not the heart was taken to be the seat of the emotions, which is probably why Prometheus in Greek legend had his liver rather than his heart devoured by a vulture each day only to grow again and be devoured once more.)

The only thing that frightened my parents' circle was death. The question of what would happen after death, and whether their destinations would be Heaven or Hell, haunted them. Mullahs used to make speeches about the horrors of Hell and the pleasant life in Heaven, where houris (beautiful girls) were in abundance, and honey and milk would run everywhere. Those who believed in Allah and followed his prophets would go to Paradise and those who disobeyed would abide in Hell after death and would burn and be tortured for eternity. This made the people cry, or rather howl. I had seen my parents crying and praying to Allah to save them from the fire of Hell or the tortures of the grave itself. They were especially worried when the mullahs (in order to get a bigger share of money) used to warn of those who have a lot of money but do not spend it on the ways of Allah. So they used to start paying *sadageh*, or alms, to the beggars in the streets, or to the poor. Naturally the mullah would be the first to benefit from this generosity born of fear. The mullahs would also make money in the countryside, in times of drought, by promising rain if the people would give them sufficient money. Not all of the mullahs were exploiters, however, and some of them were strong supporters of the people and bitter critics both of the oppressive ruling classes and of other mullahs who betrayed their religious calling in the ways I describe. At the beginning of this century one famous mullah of lower-class origin himself, Muhammad Baqir Khalkhali, wrote a remarkable work against the mullahs who cheated the people, a parable called *The Book of Foxes*. The Quran contains a verse "You shall not eat the property of the orphans", and mullahs often preached on that text. Well-meaning parents would leave their property to a mullah on the assumption that he would provide for the care and education of their children. A passage in *The Book of Foxes*, written in Azerbaijani, reads:

> Ozun "la Ta'akuloo" Hokmun verarsan
> Yatimin malini birdan yiyarsan.
>
> (You yourself issue the law "Thou shall not eat"
> And eat at one gulp the property of orphans.")

The book states its message as though the poet is describing the conduct of foxes and suggests that orphans left to the care of mullahs in such circumstances found themselves destitute.

Mirza Ali Mu'jiz Shabistari and Mirza Ali Akbar Tahir-Zadeh (who used the pseudonym "Sabir") who both also lived at the beginning of the century, wrote poetry in Azerbaijani satirising the reactionary clergy with their double standards and hypocrisy. They have influenced subsequent Iranian writers of prose and poetry and were influential in the Constitutional Revolution and the Democratic Movement of which I shall speak later.

"Sabir" was denounced by the landowners and mullahs as being an atheist (*kafir*) because of such writings. He defended himself in a reply to the people of Shirvan — a rural locality, now in Soviet Azerbaijan:

> I witness that God is Almighty and great.
> I possess faith, O people of Shirvan!
> I do not believe in any one religion.
> I am an old Muslim, O Shirvanis!
> I am Shia, not of these sorts.
> I am Sunni, but not these kinds.
> I am Sufi, not like these fools.
> I am a human being, lover of truth and justice, O Shirvanis!
>
> . . .
> Do not force on me the label *Kafir*.
> I believe in the Quran, O Shirvanis!
>
> (From Sabir, *Hup Hup Nama*.)

In my nurse's home there was none of this fear, as I have said. I never saw Izzat or Humai sit and listen to the speech of a mullah, nor did I hear them weep for the fear of Hell. Their friends were cheerful people. They made a lot of jokes, and in the evening we used to gather at the tea-house, and women stood at their gates or on the corner of the street and chatted late into the summer evenings.

Izzat was very popular among his neighbours. They called him Izzat Amoo (Uncle Izzat). He was a helpful person and often used to repair people's walls and roofs without charge, because they could not afford it, and also because he did not separate his neighbours' lives and happiness from those of his own family. I once remember that a woman who lived a few houses away from Izzat, Khadija, came to his house on a Friday morning. She talked quietly to Humai in the vestibule. Fatima and I were curious to find out why she had come so early on a Friday, which is a holy day for Muslims. Fatima and I were anxious to keep Izzat at home, hoping that he would take us to the farms nearby where we would have lettuce and *shingi* (a sweet plant grown near springs). Perhaps Fatima and I were curious to find out if Khadija wanted Izzat's help. She had lost her husband and had two children, and she, like Humai, used to spin wool for a wool merchant in my father's neighbourhood.

Humai came inside the house and Khadija stayed in the vestibule, as though she were too shy to come into the room where Izzat and we children were sitting and having breakfast. Humai, addressing Izzat, said that Khadija's room and kitchen had been damaged during the previous night's rain, and were in danger of falling on the children. "She is helpless!" All the houses in that area were built of clay: no brick was used for the walls and the roofs were covered by timbers and *kah-gil* (straw and mud).

Izzat listened to Humai while drinking his tea and looking at us. When Humai had finished Izzat thought for a minute, then said, "It does not matter, tell her I'll be there in half an hour and see what I can do". When we had finished our breakfast Izzat took Fatima and me to Khadija's house (or, rather, small hut). It looked twisted, and one side of the roof was much lower than the other and seemed as though it was falling down. Izzat looked at the building from the outside and then went in. He came back out immediately, looking sad, and blushing a little. "Khadija," he called. "Yes, Uncle Izzat?" she answered. "Take your children to our house and collect your things from within your own house and pile them somewhere next to your gate. This should be done immediately, and I shall help you. *The whole building is falling down.* I need to find one of the neighbours who can help me, and start rebuilding the roof and the wall."

Izzat took us back to his house and Khadija accompanied us, together with her children of about three and five years of age. We stayed with Humai and all played together. Khadija's children were very quiet and looked pale, but they joined in and seemed happy playing with us.

Izzat did not return before we were asleep. The following day he left home early. But he returned home at sunset. He had a water-melon and a *sangak* in his arms and a smile on his face. Addressing Khadija, who was sitting next to Humai's spinning-wheel while Humai was spinning wool, he said, "Khadija, the work is finished and your room is safe, but you have to wait another day or so before moving in. It is still wet. You and your children can stay with us. We have not much room, but we can manage. It is autumn and still pleasant to sleep on the roof. We will sleep there and you can sleep with your children in our room. Please look upon this as your own home. You are no trouble for us. In fact the children enjoy playing together and Humai likes your companionship."

"May Khoda (God) keep you healthy, Uncle Izzat! My children and I were homeless or dead without your help," Khadija said.

"May Khoda bless your husband!" answered Izzat. "He was an honest and a hard-working man. His sudden death, while emptying the cesspit in Haji Tavakkoli's house, made all of us very sad. First of all, when we heard the news, my friend and I rushed to Tavakkoli's match factory in order to rescue Yusef from the well, only to be told when we arrived at the factory that Yusef was working in Tavakkoli's house. When we reached Tavakkoli's house there was a crowd gathering at the door. Some of the workers in the area had tried to rescue him: but it was too late. Yusef had been overwhelmed by the gas in the bottom of the well, and had fallen unconscious, and by the time his helper called to Yusef's friends for help it was too late. I heard that no compensation was paid. God bless him! Your children are our children too. Children do not understand whether this house is mine or yours. They need a secure and happy place: besides, children become orphans more by the mother's death than by the father's."

Khadija seemed sad and, sighing, said, "I do not want compensation from Tavakkoli's. It is a humiliation to go and beg them for help. When my children grow up they will know where and how their father was killed. They miss their father and were made orphans by his death. He was our love, our bread-basket and livelihood. I do not know what could have been done without your help and that of the neighbours. Even the government of Reza Shah is not helpful. The other day I went to the police station asking where I should go for help. The police almost arrested me at the door of the police station, abusing me for wearing a *chador*. When this happened I forgot why I had gone to the police and was frightened. I hurried back home, and never thought of trying again. Mothers without husbands are helpless and are forced to beg in the streets. Then they are arrested by the police for begging and put in prison or in the house of beggars. The Shah does not want beggars to be seen in the streets of Iran. A few months ago an important Englishman was visiting Tabriz. The police went knocking at doors and telling the people to clear their shabby washing and rags hanging over their walls, sweep the streets, spray water on the pavements and put pots of flowers along the walls. But he did not know that I did not have money to buy bread for my children, much less think of flower pots. Uncle Izzat, they live in a different world and treat us like objects or tools rather than human beings."

After two days Kadija moved back into her own hut. The following Friday she came to see us. She brought with her a pair of colourful woollen socks which she had woven for Izzat. Izzat, looking at the socks in his hand, said, smiling, "I am glad that here everybody knows how to make something useful!"

When Izzat worked at my parents' house and my father was too critical of his work or did not seem appreciative of its value, it made Izzat upset and sometimes angry. This happened several times. I remember once, on a hot summer's day, Izzat was plastering some of the walls in the yard. In fact he was repairing the broken parts from the bottom. Most of the walls inside the yards in Tabriz are white and covered by plaster. Every few years they become swollen and crack in the middle or bottom of the walls. Izzat used to look after my father's house and repair it wherever it was necessary. He would start his work in the early morning and finish at sunset; so he used to work about ten hours. On this day everybody was asleep after lunch (as my parents did all through summer), while Izzat was working under the blazing sun. I was about 14 years of age and studying for an examination under a tree in the garden. I went to Izzat and asked if he wanted tea. He wanted cold water instead; so I took him water. Izzat seemed different to me from what he was like at his own home. He was working by himself and he looked very serious. Sweat was pouring down from his forehead and his cap was soaked. I felt disturbed and did not want to see Izzat so serious and seemingly unhappy. There must, I felt, be a reason for his being so distant from me. I tried to talk to him about anything — Fatima, Marzieh, Humai, and how he made plaster. He kept quiet. I felt upset and was near to tears. When Izzat realised I was upset he started to talk. "My son," he said, "there are things in the world which can wound one worse than a sharp sword: bad words and insults are some of those. This morning your father was unkind to me. He thinks I do not know how to work properly. The way he speaks to me is hurtful. I respect him because he is my older cousin, but everything has its limits. I cannot bear it if my work is regarded as worthless. My work is my personality and to insult my work is in fact to insult my whole life. He is sleeping now, and I am working under this blazing sun — I do not mind it, and I enjoy working — but when I remember that he does not appreciate my work I feel upset and rather angry. I have never answered my cousin back before, but now I am afraid I am losing my patience. I shall either refuse to work, or else tell him to mind his own business."

While Izzat was still talking my father came out of his bedroom going towards the toilets which were situated at the other end of the yard and near to where Izzat was working. As he passed Izzat he said, "*Khasta olmiyasan*" ("May you not get tired!" — a customary greeting to workers). Izzat kept quiet and said nothing. When my father came out of the toilet he stopped next to Izzat and commented, "It seems the wall is not straight." Izzat did not hesitate and answered, "It has not been straight from the start — you had better ask those who placed the foundation wrongly at the beginning." Whenever my father used to realise that "the smoke was too much to face" (as the Azerbaijani saying goes), he would back down and change the subject. Now, realising Izzat was upset, he did so, saying, "This afternoon the Ayatollah Dinavari" (the leading cleric in our district) "is coming to visit us. As soon as you have finished your work, or indeed before finishing it, help Gholam-Reza to climb the mulberry tree and shake some sweet mulberries down on a cloth — the Ayatollah likes sweet things. Also, go to the orchard and pick some ripe peaches, pears and large grapes — pile them all up in a big dish. Never mind washing them: Gholam-Reza will wash them. If the Ayatollah, who is very busy and usually has many landowner and business visitors in the afternoons and evenings, cannot manage to come to our house, then Gholam-Reza will take them to his house." My father then departed. A few moments passed in silence. Then Izzat said to me "My son, to tell the truth I do not want to pick fruit and fill the stomach of this parasite — I hate to see such individuals who do not work but only receive, and eat well. It is sad that your father believes in these hypocrites. Perhaps they need each other."

Izzat continued plastering the wall. I was frightened that my father would tell me off if I did not pick the fruit. Before I could say anything Izzat, realising my situation, announced, "Let us pick some fruit and eat at the same time." He got up and, with both of us laughing, started to lay a cloth on the ground for mulberries. By the time we had finished the task it was sunset, and still the Ayatollah had not appeared. I had to take the fruit to his house. When I arrived a group of fat and well-dressed people were leaving. As I approached the reception room the Ayatollah came forward wearing a white garment and without a turban on his head and said, "Oh, this is a blessing from Heaven! I love fruit. It is good for the health." Two of his women were also in the room. They all sat down around the fruit tray and began to eat. By the time I returned home Izzat had left for his house. My parents asked me to join them for dinner, but I excused myself, saying that I was not hungry. I went to the garden and then lay on my bed watching the moving stars and thinking about what had happened during the day. With the memory of Izzat's jokes about mullahs while helping me to pick the fruit, I felt relaxed and fell asleep, and when I got up the following morning the sun was shining on my bed and Izzat had already started his work.

My father's attitude to Izzat and the Ayatollah was not particular to him: it was characteristic of his class in their dealings with workers and clerics. And, equally, Izzat was in no way unique in his suspicion and dislike of the clergy. Nor were our times unique in these attitudes, although the literature of revolt against landowners and clergy which I noted a little earlier had flowered remarkably when Izzat was a boy. Parallel with the reactions of people like himself living in a non-literate culture there emerged the powerful literary assaults of the intellectuals. But throughout history the clergy, while teaching the people the value of a non-worldly or spiritual life and saying that in Islam "Allah resides with the masses", had in practice lived amid material wealth and sided with the landowners, businessmen and the rich as a whole. The great Persian poets, writers and thinkers — Firdausi, Khayyam, Sa'di, Hafiz as well as our writers of the present century — denounced these social parasites. When revolutionary figures such as Mazdak rose against feudalism and its accompanying oppression it was the clergy of the time who, in support of the Caliph, prepared the ground and sentenced Mazdak to death. Firdausi has recounted this in epic poems which are, in fact, a social history of the past and reflection of his own time. Firdausi, who was himself a *dehqhan* (small farmer), felt the burden of feudal duties and suffered deeply. His poetry is a cry from the depths of history, for justice and defence of human values. He revered Mazdak for his stand.

Mazdak, the leader of a great social movement which took place between AD 494 and 524, stood for social equality and defence of the peasants and the poor. His influence was so great that it made the Sasanian Emperor, Qobad, support his cause and identify himself with it. Historians have often dignified the pre-Islamic period of recorded Persian history as a Golden Age, but in reality it was, in common with many such myths, an age gilded rather than golden. It was a time of great cruelty while society was making its painful self-transformation from conservative aristocracy based on rigid rules and codes to a condition of feudalism with its very clear caste divisions. We have to imagine a time when declining and rising tendencies were working in opposition, often very painfully. Slavery still existed; the inhuman caste system which took its place, as often happens after the abolition or erosion of slavery, was being foreshadowed. Our castes never quite equalled the rigidity of those in some other countries, but they became cruelly separated, and deeply conscious of their individual identities to the detriment of all. In addition, there was a sudden incursion to the cities at this time — a massive urbanisation — through which the existing economy was hopelessly overstretched. A period of famine subsequently began, and Mazdak, crying out against the subjection of the people to starvation in order to protect those who had advanced themselves, won the attention and ultimate support of Qobad in his demand that the granaries be thrown open. By this time

Mazdak had won the support of the poor and those starving in large numbers — it is the king of the beggars who is the most successful of beggars to the king — and Firdausi was later to say that "every poor man became one with him, whether aged or a child".

The sort of people likely to be drawn into such a movement is obvious enough, and again history shows many parallels: there would be slaves recently emancipated and now reduced to the point of starvation by being cast out without the protection of an owner; peasants who had seen their customary privileges eroded more and more, to the point that they themselves could see little difference between their present condition and that formerly held by slaves. The fact that Qobad was induced to consider the position of women suggests that women, too, played a part in the agitation. Inevitably intellectuals and some religious leaders were captured by the cause, to say nothing of needing it to protect their own status and personal economic circumstances.

For a time Qobad and Mazdak worked in harmony. Qobad was choosing to please the people and the movement they followed in preference to the selfish and divisive motives of the nobility. Specific privileges of the nobility such as their harems were a particular target of resentment, and constituted such an obvious example of the grossest of human injustice in a time of starvation that they could only be defended by arguments of privilege, caste and above all force. But force overthrew Qobad, imprisoned him, put him on trial, narrowly spared his life and drove him into exile. He was only reinstated by a foreign army, to whose leaders he had to give recurrent rewards in money and territory. He was also drawn into endless wars in the north against the Huns (who were probably occupying Tabriz, among other places, at that time).

Mazdak's followers avenged themselves on the nobility by seizing their property and distributing it where they could, abolishing land ownership where they could gain control and breaking up the harems (which their enemies declared was to obtain the women for themselves). However, in addition to the nobles, they began to attract the bitter opposition of Christian and Zoroastrian priests who had their own interests to protect. Qobad had many others to reward in the power-game, and the crisis came, understandably, with his attempts to consolidate his own family's succession by confirming his son Khusraw Anushirvan as his official heir. Qobad turned on his old ally; Mazdak was ordered to be put to death, and was first conducted to a garden where he had been assured that all his followers were to be assembled to do him honour and to receive a presentation of royal gifts. What had really happened was that a deal had been struck between the rival priests and Qobad (supported by his new allies). If the succession was to be made secure, it was to be at the cost of Mazdak; but since an attack on Mazdak alone would lead to uprising and general disruption, Khusraw

Anushirvan was to prove his fitness for inheritance by designing the trap. All of Mazdak's people were promised the crucial honours and gifts which would finally symbolise their ascendancy, but once they had entered the great garden, they were systematically butchered by waiting soldiers. When the young heir conducted the prophet into the garden, he ironically congratulated him on his harvest — a forest of legs sticking out of the ground. The Mazdakites had been slaughtered and buried head downwards. Mazdak himself was then crucified or hanged, upside down, and then riddled with arrows.

The rise and fall respectively of Mazdak are the subject of two poems by Firdausi, which show how the memory of Mazdak's struggle against inequality was still cherished and honoured 500 years later. Firdausi himself had reason to know the ingratitude of rulers and the heady elation caused by initial hopes of their approval. Here is the first, "The Story of Qobad and Mazdak":

> To the King's Court one day did Mazdak walk.
> His words ran fast and certain like a hawk,
>   His mind discerning yet devoted too,
> His heart of courage endless as his talk.
>
> Outside, the Famine crawled along the globe.
> The Drought parched all, in rags or costly robe;
>   Throughout the sky no cloud, however small,
> Of rain or snow their heart-worn search could probe.
>
> The noblemen conversed in solemn ring
> Of food and water and no other thing,
>   When Mazdak spoke to them one single line
> "The path of hope is shown you by the King!"
>
> Then toward the King he seemed on wings to fly:
> "O pious King, in sheer sincerity
>   I would one question only put to you,
> And beg you to take note, and give reply."
>
> Farrokh Qobad, the King, sat deep in thought,
> And, giving answer, said that Mazdak ought
>   To speak the question that stood in his mind:
> And Mazdak spoke the question Qobad sought.
>
> "A man lies dying, bitten by a snake
> Whose poison threatens sure his life to take.
>   What fate deserves an owner who denies
> The antidote that could the venom break?"

Mazdak gave pause; the King in answer said
"His crime is murder once the man is dead:
   His keeping for himself the antidote
Took life, for which his own life's blood be shed."

Mazdak arose and left him; to the Crowd
Outside who wept despairingly and loud
   He spoke of his enquiry, and he said
"Return, and see your victory endowed!"

The Crowd departed, and at break of day
Returned, with anguish and despair in sway.
   Mazdak beheld them coming afar off
And ran indoors, and to the King did say:

"O King victorious, spokesman of your race,
When yesterday we spoke within this place
   So many doors long closed were flung ajar;
And may we now speak once more face to face?"

The King said not to leave his tongue unspurred:
For he had learned from what had then occurred
   And yet more would he seek, and speaking thus
Fell silent, and awaited Mazdak's word.

"A man lies chained by ankle-bone and feet,
And starving loses life he still holds sweet:
   What judgment will you now pronounce on one
Who, having food, yet gives him nought to eat?"

From the King's lips the air quick answer bore:
"If such a man with foodstuffs in his store
   Allowed the other die, how could he thrive
In fortune or in honour any more?"

Glad as a land in thirst which feels the rain
Mazdak in silence heard the King again.
   He kissed the ground, withdrew, and told the Crowd
"The granary awaits: go take the grain!"

They fled in concert, mighty caravan!
They found the city's grain, and every man
   Gets in, and gathers to himself the grain,
Shoulders it firm, and carries what he can.

Fear and dismay seized the guardians of the store
And to the King their tale of woe they pour:
   "The Crowd have all despoiled your granaries
On Mazdak's word, and left no pickings more!"

The King called Mazdak, urged by their vengeful minds,
Says Mazdak's speech his property unbinds,
   But Mazdak says he spoke but of their talk,
Questions he puts, and then what answers finds.

How he had spoken, and the King took note;
What the King said, repeated then by rote;
   How the King told him that the man must die
Who for the snake withheld the antidote.

"And, as from snakes", cried Mazdak, "must men die
When Famine's antidote's a granary?
   Thyself hath said it: profit-makers' food
Leaves poor men dead who should be fed thereby!"

The King sat dumb, with heavy heart like lead,
For Justice was what he and Mazdak said:
   And thoughts of what it means gave him alarm
At Wealth stored up to leave so many dead.

King Qobad questioned Mazdak in his turn,
And, listening, saw his mind with answers burn
   On prophets, and their teachings, judges, priests,
And heads of state: with logic none could spurn.

"Should he who hath not, die for him who hath?"
Many cried no! And were the Earth a bath
   Those who loved Mazdak soon could fill it up;
And swore the pathless way would be their Path.

Mazdak said he without a rag or roof
Was greatest in the Kingdom, and in proof
   Held none outweighed another, in that All
Made up Humanity, its Warp and Woof.

"He with thy most Wealth equals him with None!"
Mazdak whose Faith was shining like the Sun
   Would make it happen: those who would deny
Should stand accursed by God, th'Eternal One.

All would be one with him, young, poor, and old.
To those in need he'd give, from those with gold.
    The priests stood silent at his words and deeds.
The King fulfilled each word that Mazdak told . . .

The King placed Mazdak's Chair at his Right Hand:
Mazdak, who once to live had tilled the land,
    Now bore his Honours thick before the Court,
Though his beginning none might understand.

The World was swayed by Faith so Strong and Pure.
No person dared his noble Wrath endure.
    The Rich forsook their hoarded Wealth, and gave
The utmost that they had, to feed the Poor.

"Firdausi" is not a real name — it means "from Paradise", as my last name, "Tabrizi", means "from Tabriz" — and while he is never referred to as such, the poet's real name was Abulqasim. Although some confusion exists about his life — for example, a number of forged poems were long attributed to him, and the false biographical matter they included was given credence — he seems to have been a small landowner with very little money who was born about AD 934 in the village of Vazh, near Tabaran, part of the city of Tus, where he is supposed to have died and been buried about 90 years later. Modern scholars are doubtful as to whether his birthplace was indeed his place of death and burial, but this was the story with which I grew up. The legends which abound about him, many taken very seriously by former commentators, vary from his being of quite substantial means, to his being a strolling and destitute ballad-maker, and perhaps the most absurd of all is that he wrote his great epic the *Shah-nameh* (*The Book of Kings*) to obtain a dowry for his daughter. This last is scarcely credible as he began composing this work in about AD 975 when he was roughly 40, completing it around 1010, by which stage his daughter would hardly have been a candidate in the marriage-market! What seems certain is that he worked on his epic chiefly in his native town, with the support of patrons and friends.

    The origins of the epic itself stretch back long before Firdausi's own time, and he himself drew heavily on written sources, chronicles, poems and above all on the oral tradition in which so much of Persian identity has been preserved. The result is an extraordinary achievement, recounting the history of the Persian rulers, sometimes briefly, sometimes in complex and most exciting detail. The greater part of the epic is legendary — Zal, the father of Rustam, is suckled, nurtured and educated by a gryphon, for instance, and while this motif is found in innumerable cultures, from the Roman story of Romulus and Remus and the wolf to Thackeray's *The Rose and the Ring*, the emphasis on education is unusual, as is the reason for Zal's being exposed to death by the elements or the wild beasts. Zal was born with pure white hair, and his father decided on his destruction after undergoing the ridicule of others: the evil effects of prejudice, human vanity and herd instinct are characteristic of Firdausi's writing; his own life gave him all too much reason to despise the cruelty of court fashions and conformism.

The epic begins with the first ruler to produce a code of laws and establish some sort of kingly system, Kayumars, but the primitive note is struck at once by stating that he was clothed in the skins of beasts. Firdausi in one way had no obvious sense of time: his hero Rustam (and his horse Rakhsh) live in their prime through reigns apparently covering several hundred years, and Zahak's tyranny is said to have lasted for a thousand years. Much of this is obviously symbolic: the hero dwarfing the kings in age actually serves to signify that he towered over them in reputation, and a folk recollection of a peculiarly cruel tyranny acquires its force by presenting it as lasting a millennium. Similarly Rustam seems to be a giant, yet he is on perfectly ordinary terms of association with his associates, and this also has many counterparts in other mythologies (Irish, for instance). It is fanciful to think of Zahak's adviser, the wicked spirit Iblis who tempted him to kill his father, ultimately kissing him on both naked shoulders and thus causing two hideous serpents who lived on human brains to spring out; but again it is easy to see how well this could depict the horrific dimensions of a tyranny whose implications would mean far less in cold statistics of slaughter.

Obviously there would have lived strong men, and cruel tyrants, in the remote past: Firdausi's legends conveyed in clear, matter-of-fact language what were the true dimensions of tyranny or strength. Legend also credits Firdausi himself with being the victim of an evilly disposed vizier who poisoned Mahmud's mind against him. And while this could well be the outcome of someone else's interpretation of the epic rather than Firdausi himself making symbolic representation of his material, Firdausi would have known that Mahmud's rejection of him followed hostile advice from courtiers. In fact, quite apart from Zahak's case, Firdausi's epic consistently follows a pattern of incisive, realistic and at times bitterly satirical comment on court politics and treachery. Some of his use of such material would have come from folk memory — country folk throughout the ages have continued to live in cycles of hope and despair in their relations with courts — but it is a sufficiently urgent theme to suggest ugly personal experience.

Firdausi in a different way showed a remarkable awareness of historical development. His account of Kayumars's dress is one indication, and so is that of the achievement of his grandson and successor, who accidentally struck fire from stone in a fight with a hideous monster, and that of the next sultan's step forward, which is the discovery of reading and writing from a band of demons whom he had conquered and who offered him their knowledge in the hope of being spared. The role of the devil in advancing intellectual activity is much older than Faust. Perhaps the next achievement is tragedy, in the person of Jamshid, whose vainglory and complacency (after a successful reign of 700 years) leads to his overthrow, when he becomes a much more sympathetic figure.

> They say the Lion and the Lizard keep
> The Courts where Jamshyd gloried and drank deep . . .

Jamshid is ultimately killed by Zahak, who has taken to keeping the serpents away from his own brain by feeding them the brains of two children of the realm each day: but Jamshid himself is murdered by being bisected vertically. Again, this last point is not a sadistic wallowing in nastiness: it symbolises the division of the old Persian Empire as a result of the evil actions and self-enrichment of rulers. Zahak is ultimately defeated and imprisoned forever in a mountain cave (with the serpents for company) by a young hero called Feridun, who duly becomes Sultan. But, significantly, the first blow against Zahak is struck by a man of the people, the blacksmith Kaveh, when his sons are appointed for sacrifice to the serpents.

Zahak dreamed that a child called Feridun would be born in his kingdom and would take his throne. He could not rest by day or night and both harem and court were disturbed by his worries and woes. In order to calm his anxieties, Zahak ordered that an oath of allegiance be taken by the courtiers and members of the public alike. Kaveh, meanwhile, had lost 18 sons to the serpent of Zahak and now refused to give up his 19th and last son. He walked into the Sultan's court, protesting against the injustices committed by Zahak. He rescued his son and tore up the testimony of allegiance after he had first addressed the Sultan. Walking into the streets, he raised up his apron as a banner of freedom, or *drafsh*.

The epic continues with extraordinary achievements in narrative and symbol, vividly presenting individual dramas of counsel and diplomacy, divination and confrontation, while at the same time, especially in the context of Rustam, presenting powerful descriptions of battles and heroic deeds. The heroic drama and tragedy of Rustam, especially in the terrible conflict with his son Suhrab, whom he kills, has inspired East and West down the generations, as may be seen from Matthew Arnold's famous poem, "Sohrab and Rustum".

From heroic myth, probably drawn from some reality in the remote past, the *Shah-nameh* moves into actual history, dealing with persons like Mazdak who really existed and played a critical role in the development of Iran. Firdausi's narrative sharpens and his characters become much more clearly accessible as he comes within a few centuries of his own time. He knows he is now speaking of issues, as well as human behaviour, which have implications for his own day, although there have always been broad themes of contemporary relevance for him. The problem of fidelity in the service of a treacherous and murderous ruler is critical and ultimately fatal for Rustam, and prefigures the modern conflict for people whose patriotism is confronted by the destructive governments to whom they are expected to be loyal. In Rustam's case the state is the sultan, and hence he has to be loyal — though never servile — to the sultans but their successors will destroy his family. Mazdak, on the other hand, poses the new question of loyalty to the people, with the support of government if possible, but knowing the danger of destruction by it. These memories of this period were taken very seriously by the government of Iran in my lifetime, and the tradition of Mazdak in particular was regarded as being very dangerous. Zahak was presented as a figure inimical to true Persian royalty, and so on. Revenge as a motive stalks through Firdausi's narrative whether mythological or historical. It is natural that folklore should make so much of it since revenge, like folklore itself, depends on long memories.

Mahmud showed himself to be totally unworthy of Firdausi's hopes. The old version of Firdausi's own story assumes that all was going well until the epic had been concluded, when by fraud he was tricked into thinking Mahmud intended to insult him, but in fact it appears that Mahmud never truly responded to his overtures and the epic turns more and more against rulers in general and Mahmud himself. Firdausi probably revised earlier portions of it as this became increasingly clear to him, and we therefore find remarks about Zahak's liking for constant flattery from his attendant poets and historians being made to parallel Mahmud's behaviour. The epic, closing about a century after the death of Mazdak, is followed by a savage satire on Mahmud, but it now seems that this is a collection of various passages from the main text, and was probably assembled by admirers of Firdausi who wanted to remind readers of his reduction to poverty and wandering for want of support from Mahmud. The lines, however, are Firdausi's own, wherever they come. They consist of a proud denunciation of the empty and transient power of Mahmud, declaring in almost magical language how the power of the poet, both in his immediate effect and immortal reputation, makes him an impossible person to subdue. The tyrant has only shown his folly in making light of him. It is the poet's mind, and not the sword of the state, which is the truly powerful weapon, and the poet's art which will vanquish all the arts of government.

Firdausi and the followers who preserved his writing stand as testimonies to the role of intellectuals in Iran who knew that their destiny must be superior to any tyranny, however apparently omnipotent, if only they maintain confidence in their powers. It is because of this that the intellectuals and their enemies are both so much aware of the power of writing and teaching in more recent as well as past history. The old pagan tradition that the poet, especially through his use of satire, had magical powers and could curse his enemies, has in modern times become the awareness on the part of writers and the state alike that the public can be instructed and exhorted into protest if the satirist's pen does not fail. But Firdausi, both in his own experience of life and in his subject matter, bridges both sides of the satirical tradition: he reaches back into the old days of magic and forward into the political education of the people as individuals. And he is our own literary inheritance whereby the epic poet is not, as with Virgil, the defender of the work of the emperor or great king, but rather the vigilant and engaged critic of the injustices of government.

Firdausi can be regarded as the father of the modern Persian language and poetry. As he himself declared, he revived the language of Parsi or Farsi (Persian). He stood up against the invasion by Arab language and culture. Firdausi was not, as some have tried to project, a nationalist Iranian against non-Iranians or Arabs: he was not the enemy of any nationality. His opposition and anger were directed against tyrannical Arab caliphs or rulers who had trodden on Iranian culture, identity and freedom. He stood for justice and regretted that Iran was despoiled by the hands of dogmatic and ignorant rulers under the banner of Islam, much as Iran is ruled by the ayatollahs now. He made his language, poetry and name immortal by his love of humankind and his terrific sense of justice against any sort of cruelty and social tyranny. In his poetry and use of language Firdausi is, like Homer, a national poet, but in his universality of concern and humanity of outlook, again like Homer, he belongs to all humankind.

The Ghaznavid rulers of Iran, especially Mahmud Ghaznavi, the strongest king of the dynasty, spent most of their time at war and invading other countries. Mahmud took his army to India 17 times to plunder the wealth of that country. Though Mahmud brought back a great fortune from India this was not enough for his war machinery and he therefore had to put more pressure on the people by imposing heavy taxation. Thus during the rule of the Ghaznavids most villages were emptied of their inhabitants; there was a shortage of water; the price of land dropped and one famine followed another. The people in villages and cities alike were often starving. Firdausi lived under these conditions and witnessed the spread of cholera and other epidemics. He knew within his own time of the unnatural deaths of more than 30 monarchs, viziers and amirs (ministers) either at war or in prison, and could find exemplars from his own time for many of the characters of folklore and chronicle whom he was bringing to life in the *Shah-nameh*.

In the tea-house near Izzat's house stories from the *Shah-nameh* and comparable sources were told during the weekends and nights of Ramadan (month of fasting). But since the *naqqals* (story-tellers) who were doing the telling were themselves Muslims, they made Rustam a Muslim and a follower of Allah although (if he ever existed at all) he lived long before

Muhammad. This made the audience very excited and heightened their identification with the stories. Naturally the stories would not necessarily be told using Firdausi's own words, and could indeed be based on other versions of Rustam's adventures. The names of the leaders' sons, and peasants' sons too, frequently included Rustam, once his Islamic identity had been accepted.

Islam came to Iran in the seventh century. It attempted to impose a tribal system and tried also to bring feudal taxes into the framework of the Islamic laws. Iran was rather more advanced than Arabia at this time, but the new process, while taking a long time to develop, slowed down the processes of the existing feudalisation. The Abbasid dynasty became the rulers of Iran in collaboration with the indigenous aristocratic landowners. From then on, feudalism expanded and became more stabilised in many parts of Iran.

Around the time of Firdausi's birth three important events took place. In AD 909 the Fatimid dynasty established in the western domain of Islamic lands a rival regime against the Abbasids, who still clung to power in Baghdad. Two or three years later the Buyid brothers, who were from lower-class and working backgrounds, rose and established the Buyid dynasty in the west of Iran, threatening the power which Abbasids still sought to pre-serve in the east. When Firdausi was between five and ten years of age the Buyids moved to Baghdad and overthrew Mostakfi, the Abbasid caliph, and expanded the Shi'ite religion. The Fatimids, on the other hand, after capturing Tunisia, Syria and Arabia, became stronger and took over Egypt in 956, making Cairo their capital. The Fatimids, under the rule of Aziz, now overshadowed all the Islamic countries, and became especially active in Firdausi's native province of Khorasan. He witnessed all their political and religious activities, during which the ownership of Khorasan changed hands many times. Muslim rulers, like those of other religions, did not separate religion from politics and used religion as a weapon to defeat their enemies. Al-Qadir Billah, the Abbasid caliph (AD 991-1031), for example, in order to free himself from Buyid influence and stand up against the Fatimids (both of which were Shi'ites) used the conflict between Shi'ites and Sunnis. As I write this, the governments of Iran and Iraq fight a political battle under the cover of the ideologies of Shii and Sunni.

Between the lifetimes of Mazdak and Firdausi there had been more than 18 major uprisings of slaves and peasants against feudal nobles and the ruling system all over Iran. The nearest in time to Firdausi was that of the Qarmati movement in Khorasan, which both in spirit and destiny was essentially similar to that of Mazdak and lasted for 40 years, with great influence at the court of the then ruling Samaniyan dynasty. The movement influenced the whole of Iran and preached social equality and justice while condemning the greedy oligarchy. It was taken up by farmers, intellectuals and even government officials. Caliph Nasr-Ibn Ahmad (Nasr II) gave his support to the Qarmatis, just as Qobad had supported Mazdak. But when the movement became more forceful and seriously endangered the position of the nobles and army chiefs the latter backed Nuh-Ibn Saman (Nuh I) and rebelled against the Caliph, his father.

The Caliph was overthrown, the nobility crowned his son in his place and the Qarmati movement was brutally suppressed. Firdausi saw its persecution and suppression in his youth, and would also have seen opponents of the regime killed on the false premise that they also were Qarmatis. The situation resembled what in the 20th century was known in the USA as the "Red Scare" or McCarthyism. As late as Mahmud's reign the ruler was using the name Qarmati as a weapon against the people. It is said that there was a very rich man in Gaznin, and one day Mahmud ordered him to be arrested on an accusation of being a Qarmati. The accused, an intelligent man, summed up the situation: "I am not Qarmati but I am very rich. Take my riches and leave me alone." The fate of Mazdak was similar to the fate of Firdausi's contemporary, Hassanak, a vizier who was executed by the son of Sultan Mahmud (Mas'ud) under the excuse of being a Qarmati.

The suppression of the Qarmati movement at the beginning of the tenth century did not save the Samaniyan dynasty. Being afraid of the people, they employed many Turks in their army. The Turks were promoted to high ranks and increased their influence so much that in about AD 962 the Turkish Commander-in-Chief of the Imperial Forces, after an unsuccessful attempt to put his own candidate on the throne, withdrew to Ghazna and established himself by ousting the local family. He was succeeded by a trusted subordinate whose eldest son Mahmud wrested control of the city in 998 from his younger brother, the designated heir. When he died in 1030, his empire stretched from the borders of Azerbaijan and Kurdistan in the west, the Upper Ganges Valley in India, and from Khwarazm in Central Asia in the north to the Indian Ocean at Sind. He did not quite reach Tabriz, but had done very well for himself.

Whatever Firdausi's hopes of Mahmud, it was a courageous act to write in admiration of Mazdak, whose similarity to the scapegoat outlawed Qarmatis could have imperilled the life of the poet. Perhaps, after all, it was fortunate for the ageing poet that Mahmud took so little interest in his work. As Omar Khayyam put it (in Fitzgerald's lines):

> With me along the strip of Herbage strown
> That just divides the desert from the sown,
> Where name of Slave and Sultan is forgot
> And Peace to Mahmud on his golden Throne!

By the time Khayyam wrote this, Mahmud would have found Peace in the only way he would. But if Firdausi struggled without success to place true ideals before Mahmud, there were others who found easier ways of winning his favour. Similarly, at other courts such figures as the historian Tha'alibi, condemned Mazdak and advanced themselves accordingly. Firdausi was left to write:

> Nor salt, nor wood, nor oat are left for me;
> All is gone now, no single grain I see.
> In such dark days, with fear of tax to come,
> The snow heaps pitiless as ivory.
>
> The death-like Hail fell this year like no other;
> For me, compared to Hail, Death is a Brother.
> If food and wealth were shared in equal parts
> Then Life I would acknowledge as a Mother.

In these harsh and grim conditions, however, Firdausi did not lose his spirit of creativity and social criticism. Despite, and even because of, his sufferings, he created his everlasting gift to literature.

> I suffered much in thirty years' long span;
> By Persian language I remade Iran.
> Strong houses fall to ruin in the storm
> And sunshine in the lifetime of one man.
>
> I made a Castle with my might and main
> Which will withstand the strongest wind and rain.
> Since I have sown the seed of living words
> I shall not die, but henceforth must remain.

4

A Persian Canterbury Tale

The Characters of Chaucer's Pilgrims are the Characters that compose all Ages & Nations; as one Age falls another rises, different to Mortal Sight, but to Immortals only the same; for we see the same Characters repeated again & again, in Animals, in Vegetables, in Minerals & in Men. Nothing new occurs in Identical Existence: Accident ever varies, Substance can never suffer change nor decay.

(Blake, *Draft of Prospectus for the Engraving of Chaucer's Canterbury Pilgrims*, 1809.)

When I was about five years of age my parents went to Mashhad on a pilgrimage and left me with Humai and Izzat, who stayed in my parents' house to look after my sister Batul and myself. I rather resented my parents going to Mashhad and leaving me behind — so I kept misbehaving, refusing to eat and making life difficult for Humai and Izzat. However, they knew me and understood me very well and were patient and kind. I remember one evening I fell asleep and woke up to find that everybody had almost finished their dinner. They were having *abgusht* (meat stew with potatoes and chickpeas), and I became upset. Izzat asked me to join them as my dinner had been kept for me. "I do not want to eat," I said. "You have eaten the meat and now you are offering me the bones." Much to my annoyance, my comment made Izzat laugh. I did eventually eat, but Izzat kept repeating my words for years afterwards. Although he kept teasing me, I did not mind this because he was always good-humoured. I preferred to be teased by Izzat than by my playmates.

After four years or so my parents planned to return to Mashhad on yet another pilgrimage. Many relatives and friends gathered at the coach station to see everyone off and there was quite a crowd round the coach. Some had brought boxes of sweets or cakes, and others had melon, water-melon, grapes or nuts for the passengers. Some of the passengers were kissing their children goodbye and others were upset at leaving their relatives behind. In this chaotic situation I asked Haji Ali, my father's partner, to let me go with my parents. He did what I asked and lifted me up and pushed me through the open window of the coach into the seat where my parents were. I sat next to the window by my mother and kept quiet in case my father objected to my going with them. I was delighted and relieved to see that my grandmother was also in the coach with my parents, because I knew that she would look after me and protect me if I was naughty.

The coach departed about an hour before sunset and the tops of the buildings and streets were red with the setting sun. The coach passed through the main streets and left Tabriz as I eagerly gazed at the streets and buildings through the window. It was wonderful. Walls, trees and people seemed to be rushing past the coach. We stopped at the city gate and the driver picked up a villager who had a sheep standing in front of him and some chickens in his arms. The sheep was deposited in the middle aisle and the villager, with his chickens, sat at the back of the coach. The chickens were noisy, protesting against all being tied together. The sheep kept quiet, until the villager got off at a village called Bustan-Abad. Before arriving at Bustan-Abad, the coach crawled along a high mountainous road and through a mountain pass (called Shibly) and the frightened passengers offered the prayer "*Allah Akbari*" ("Allah is Great") in unison.

Bustan-Abad is not an ordinary village, but is the central gathering place for the surrounding villages — for two reasons. It lies on the main road between Tabriz and other major cities or towns like Sarab and Ardabil, and it also has hot springs. Bathing in this water is considered to improve one's health. There is a bath-house there on the top of a hill, which contains separate rooms, each with a small pool about two metres wide and two and a half to three metres long. The water circulates through the pool, so there is always clean water. Two or three people can use each room at a time. I have been several times to this place and it is very relaxing and refreshing.

Our coach did not stop at Bustan-Abad for long. The passengers stayed in the coach — but I managed to go to the toilet — just a hole in the ground surrounded with dirt. Our next stop was the city of Miyaneh, about 150 kilometres from Tabriz. It was late at night when we arrived. The shops and restaurants were still open and the city was lit by electric lights, but some of the shops and the tea-house where we had tea and food — my mother brought our food with her — were lit by oil lamps. We ate *kuku*, made with eggs, potatoes, butter and saffron, which she always made for journeys. We also had vegetables, from our garden, and a cheese similar to feta, together with homemade *lavash* bread. It was a delicious supper. A large, awesome picture of Reza Shah was hanging on the door and two smaller ones were hanging on the walls. It was the first time I had been in a tea-house on the road and I was fascinated to see how the food and tea was served, and how the local peasants sat on a platform in one corner of the tea-house busy chatting and slurping their tea. In another corner women, men and children were sitting round a table-cloth having their meal. My parents disappeared to pray in a back room of the tea-house while I sat next to my grandmother. I was glad to have this first opportunity to talk to my grandmother since leaving Tabriz. "I am glad you came with us," she said, and her words reassured me.

I did not sleep during the night, and watched the headlights of the coaches and cars moving through the twisting roads up and down the mountains. They flashed their lights while approaching each other as a sign either of greeting or of warning. I had no wish to be a driver on those roads. They were narrow and the passengers, especially the children, constantly had to be reminded to keep their arms and heads inside the coach; careless people often lost an arm or even a head when vehicles passed each other.

Before we arrived in Zanjan city the coach broke down on a mountain road called Qaflankuh. The driver and conductor spent a few hours trying to repair the coach, but they could not do anything. The driver was most upset, almost bursting into tears or perhaps even actually crying as he lay his head on the steering wheel and covered either side of his face with his arms. He had no money for repairs. My father and an Afghan man offered their help. The Afghan gentleman said, "We will pay all your expenses for the repairs — do not worry." My father, agreeing with the Afghan also gave some money. The driver, who had looked exhausted and desperate before, raised his head quickly and did not know what to say — but his eyes became bright and a smile appeared on his face. My father gave the money that he had collected from the Afghan, and two other people on the coach, to the driver. The driver took the money and said, "Thank you, you have saved my soul. I did not have any money to buy spare parts." Then he and his assistant went to Zanjan and returned after about six hours with the necessary parts. They set to work on the coach, but it took hours before we resumed our journey.

It was late at night when we arrived in Zanjan. It was a large pleasant city with well-organised restaurants and attractive bazaars. The shops in the bazaars were shut, but the bazaars were well lit and I could see long passages with their nicely curved and dome-like ceilings and roofs. We had *chilo-kebab*. I was so hungry and tired that I could have wished nothing better than to sit and eat while watching the comings and goings of the different passengers. In Zanjan they spoke Azerbaijani, and as I understood the people I felt at home. I would have liked to see the famous handicrafts and metalwork in the bazaar and perhaps spend a few more hours in the city, but the coach was due to leave in an hour or so.

In the restaurant my father, the Afghan and the driver were sitting at a table and chatting. When my father saw me returning from my walk round the place he invited me to sit down and have a cup of tea before we got back on the coach. While I was drinking my tea I heard the driver saying, "Being a coach or a taxi driver in this country is donkey work. You work day and night but at the end you are still in debt to a foreign company or Iranian businessmen. After 15 years working day and night I have not yet paid off the money for this coach, which will be old and useless by the time my debt is paid. You see we live an insecure life — our roads are bad and we have to change our tyres and suspension frequently — in fact we are constant consumers for the foreign factories. This morning if you had not helped me I could not possibly have afforded to replace an irreparable part. I thank you for your help — but this does not solve the problem. I do not expect my passengers to pay for my spare parts each time that I break down. Believe me I hardly spend any money on myself. I spend all my earnings on my wife and five children, and on my mother who lives with us. I love my family — the children are the source of my enjoyment, but some people ridicule me for having five daughters. When I drive at night through these narrow and twisted roads, especially in winter when it is more dangerous, the only thing which keeps me awake and vigilant is the vision of my wife, mother and children and the fact that I long to see them the following day or a couple of days later." At this point the driver looked at his watch, and facing my father and the Afghan man said, "I have had a tiring day, we had better stop overnight in Zanjan." Then he added, "I must say that in winter when the roads are blocked by snow we have to spend hours or days in this or other stopping places until the roads are open."

Some passengers slept in the coach and some, together with the driver, found accommodation in rooms behind the tea-house. My parents and grandmother preferred to have rooms though I would have liked to stay up in the tea-house and watch the passengers.

The following morning we were all in the coach. There was a new passenger — a dervish — who sat next to the driver and talked all the way until we arrived at Qazvin, a city 100 kilometres from Tehran. Usually these dervishes are welcomed by the drivers, who like someone to sit next to them and keep them awake or pass the time with their conversation or stories. Sometimes such companions sing songs, or the companion might be the driver's wife. But this cannot happen now under the ayatollahs. Women are not even allowed to sit next to a man in a city bus, let alone in a coach travelling from Tabriz to Tehran. This is meant to protect the dignity of women. Women have such an attraction that every man must guard himself from committing sin by indulging in illegal and unlawful thoughts of love, the ayatollahs argue. Rape by marriage (often girls marry against their will) is allowed, but to sit next to a woman in a bus is regarded unlawful and sinful!

The dervish kept talking and telling jokes and stories, which I could hear clearly two seats behind. The driver was happy and laughed at the dervish's jokes and stories and told him how his relatives and neighbours laughed at his having five daughters. The dervish then told him the following Azerbaijani folktale:

The Father of Seven Daughters and the Father of Seven Sons

Once upon a time there were two brothers. One had seven daughters and the other had seven sons. The father of seven boys, whenever he saw his brother, would ridicule him and say, "Hello, Father of seven bitches". The father of seven daughters used to feel ashamed, and hung his head and walked to his home.

One day the eldest daughter realised that her father was very depressed and upset — he was about to burst into tears. "What has happened, Father?" she asked. Her father replied, "Whenever your uncle sees me he addresses me as 'Father of seven bitches' and I am unable to answer him back."

The daughter said, "Father, don't worry. Tomorrow, when you see our uncle, answer, 'Hello, Father of seven dogs. One son from you and one daughter from me — let us send them on a journey and see which one can earn a better living.'"

The father of seven daughters became happy, and they had their dinner and slept. The following day the two brothers again saw each other. The father of seven sons said, "Hello, Father of seven bitches". The other brother lifted his head up and said, "Hello, Father of seven dogs. One son from you and one daughter from me — let us send them on a journey and find out which one can earn their bread better."

The following day each brother, according to his means, provided subsistence for the journey. The boy and girl got on their horses and went out of the city. They continued travelling until they arrived at a fork in the road, where there was a stone on which was written that he who took one turning can return, but he who travels on the other road cannot return, and he who has gone never returned. The boy said, "I shall go the way from which no-one can return." The girl answered, "No. I shall take this road, you had better take the road from which there is a possibility of returning." Her cousin accepted. They agreed to meet each other at the same spot after one year, and whoever arrived first should wait for the other. Then they each followed their own road.

The girl continued until she arrived at a city. She sold her horse and bought a man's suit and put it on. She went to a blacksmith's and became an apprentice. A few days passed and the blacksmith noticed that the appearance of his apprentice was not like that of a boy. But he did not say anything. Again a few days passed and the blacksmith was convinced that his apprentice was a girl. Then he could not keep silent and went and told the news to his mother:

> "Her arms suit a bracelet;
> Her neck suits a necklace;
> Her fingers suit a ring;
> Mother! my apprentice is a girl!"

His mother said, "Son, what are you talking about? Go and get on with your work and stop talking about this. How can a girl work for a blacksmith?" Finally his mother said, "Now if you insist, I shall teach you a way to find out the truth. When you return from work bring some roses with you. At night when we want to sleep, I will secretly put the roses under the apprentice's mattress. If he is a boy, boys are heavy and the roses will flatten under the mattress and will stick to the floor; if she is a girl then the roses will not be spoiled." The blacksmith accepted his mother's suggestion.

The blacksmith and his mother had a hunting dog in their house who was listening and had heard the conversation of the blacksmith and his mother. He went and informed the apprentice that Usta Halim Khan, the blacksmith, and his mother had a plan for her. The girl asked the dog what she should do. The dog said, "The solution is easy. At night turn so much this side and that side on your mattress that all the flowers will be flattened and stick to the floor." The girl agreed.

Night arrived. They had their supper and at bedtime Halim Khan's mother secretly put all the flowers under the girl's mattress. The girl, pretending not to know anything about it, went to bed. But during the night she turned this side and that side and all the flowers were spoiled. She got up early in the morning and went to sweep and swill the shop floor. Halim Khan's mother lifted the mattress and saw that all the flowers were spoiled. She told her son, "Did I not tell you this? Now give up thinking of this and get on working. These kinds of words are not good."

Again some time passed. The blacksmith all the time was watching his apprentice and again saw that the behaviour of his apprentice was like that of a girl. Finally he could not refrain from speaking to his mother about this once more and, as before, when he came home from work he said to his mother:

> "Her arms suit a bracelet;
> Her neck suits a necklace;
> Her fingers suit a ring.
> Mother! my apprentice is a girl, a girl . . ."

The mother lost her temper and said, "Son, give up these stories and don't talk behind people's backs." But Halim Khan did not give up. He said, "Believe me, my apprentice is a girl. I am not inventing stories about her."

Finally his mother said, "Since you insist I shall suggest another way to find the truth. Take the apprentice first to the mountain of ornaments for girls and afterwards take him to the mountain of swords. If your apprentice chooses the ornaments then you should know she is a girl but if your apprentice chooses the mountain of swords then he is a boy.

The dog again informed the apprentice about the conversation between the blacksmith and his mother. "What should I do in your opinion?" she asked the dog. The dog said, "Don't worry. When you arrive at the mountain of ornaments pretend that you are not interested in them and do not touch the ornaments. But when you arrive at the mountain of swords show excitement and take a few of them and put them on your waist while saying how nice they are."

The following evening Halim Khan said, "I am tired. Let us close the shop and go for a walk." First of all they went to the mountain of ornaments. Halim Khan went towards the ornaments and filled his hands and brought them to show to the girl. The girl said, "Usta, these are only good for little children, throw them away." Halim Khan threw the ornaments away. Then they went to the mountain of swords. The apprentice kept admiring the swords and looked excited at seeing them. She was taking the swords one by one and trying each with enthusiasm. She tried two or three of them on her waist and said, "Every young man needs these kind of things."

Then they left the place and returned home. Halim Khan's mother told her son, "Did I not tell you so; you had better give up all these nonsensical thoughts and pay attention to your work."

Some time passed. Halim Khan believed more than ever before that his apprentice was a girl and was wearing boy's clothes. Once again he could not restrain himself and spoke the same words to his mother. His mother said, "Boy, you yourself investigated and saw that it was not a girl. What else do you want? I'll show another way that might make you sure for ever. At noon tell your apprentice that it is too hot to work and that it is better to go swimming."

The dog again reported this to the girl. The girl asked, "Now what should I do?" The dog said, "It is not difficult to solve the problem. You let Halim Khan go into the water first. Then I will jump into the water and make the water muddy and also splash the face and head of Usta Halim Khan. You immediately take off your clothes and go into the water and come out soon afterwards and put on your clothes."

Noon came. Halim Khan said, "It is very hot today. Let us go swimming." The girl said nothing and got up and they went to a pool. First Halim Khan jumped into the water. The dog followed him and started splashing and throwing water on Halim Khan's head and face. Halim Khan suddenly realised that the girl had come out of the water and put her clothes back on and was waiting for him. He said, "Boy, why did you come out so quickly?" The girl replied, "I usually feel cold soon and cannot stay in the water long." In the evening they returned home.

Halim Khan's mother asked. "Ha, Boy! What happened?" Her son answered, "We swam but I did not learn much." His mother said, "I repeatedly tell you that your ideas are foolish. Now it is better to concentrate on your work . . ."

Some time passed. One day, early in the morning the girl had opened, swept and swilled out the shop and was waiting for Halim Khan when she suddenly remembered that a year had passed and she had to return to the road junction and then go to her father. So she got up, shut the shop and wrote on the door:

> "I came a girl and returned a girl, Halim Khan;
> I came honest and returned honest, Halim Khan."

Then she left and eventually reached the junction. She had all her wages with her. Her cousin had not yet returned. She waited the whole day. The following day she decided to go and look for him.

She walked and walked until she arrived at a city and asked here and there about her cousin. She was told, "The boy that you describe must certainly be the beggar who sleeps in the ashes of such and such a bath-house." The girl went and found her cousin and saw that he had buried himself in the ashes up to his neck. He had sold everything and spent all his money. He was a beggar. The girl went and bought clothes and a horse for her cousin and said to him, "Let us go back to our own city".

Now we leave the cousins here and go to Halim Khan and his mother. Halim Khan came to his shop and found it shut, with these words written on the door:

> "I came a girl and returned a girl, Halim Khan;
> I came honest and returned honest, Halim Khan."

Halim Khan stood rooted to the spot. Then he became very upset and went to his mother and said, "Mother, did I not tell you the apprentice was a girl? Now she has left and gone away."

Halim Khan bought some haberdashery goods, and started to search for the girl disguised as a pedlar.

The cousins, meanwhile, arrived at their own city, and each went to their parents. The girl gave her wages to her father and said, "Father, get up and go and get my horse back from my cousin." Her father went and said, "My daughter is asking her cousin to return her horse." The father and mother of the boy looked at each other but said nothing. The father of seven boys went and brought the horse. The following day the girl said, "Father, could you go and get my clothes from my cousin." The father went and said, "My daughter says that her cousin ought to return her clothes." The father and mother looked at each other's face and said nothing. The boy took off the clothes and gave them to his uncle, hanging his head in shame.

Meanwhile, Halim Khan travelled far and wide until he reached the city. He wandered through alleys calling out and selling his wares, in the hope that the girl would hear and recognise his voice. She did hear his voice, went and opened the gate and recognised Halim Khan. She invited him to her house and introduced him to her father. Halim Khan said, "I have travelled all this way for your sake. I wish to marry you."

The father and his daughter both agreed to the proposal and the wedding was held. The following day Halim Khan and his wife returned to his mother together.

This Azerbaijani story might have been told hundreds of years ago, but still prejudice against the female child is seen all over the world in varying degrees. I am reminded of the comment of one of our neighbours in Edinburgh when our third daughter was born in 1969. To her question, "What is your baby?" I answered, "A baby girl." "What a shame, another daughter!" she commented. I was surprised at this response and felt most upset by it.

When we arrived at Qazvin it was late afternoon, but the restaurants were still serving meals and tea. I was more eager to go to the bazaar and discover what the shops sold. The first thing I noticed was that not everyone spoke Azerbaijani, though some shopkeepers could speak Azerbaijani mixed with Persian. My father tried to make the shopkeepers understand with a mixture of Azerbaijani and some Persian words and phrases that he had learned during his previous journeys to Tehran and Mashhad. His conversation and bargaining with the shopkeepers in Tehran and Mashhad was most amusing and delightful to listen to. He used all the words, including Arabic ones, that he knew. This made even my mother laugh, who was very careful not to hurt people's feelings and especially those of her husband, and even when we were back home she kept teasing my father about how he had tried to speak in Farsi. My father would smile and say, "After all, Farsi is not my mother tongue and, besides, I did not have the chance to go to school and learn it when I was a child. I wish I knew how to write letters, at least in Azerbaijani." (Reading and writing in the Azerbaijani language, both in schools and outside in newspapers, was forbidden under Reza Shah's rule and that of his son, Muhammad Reza Shah; and still, under the ayatollahs, it is almost a forbidden language in schools and the mass media. Azerbaijani is spoken in Iran by more than ten million people. There are other minority languages such as Kurdish, Baluchi, Arabic, Luri and others, which have been treated in the same way.)

The food in the restaurants was good. Since I was very hungry the rice and *kebab* in Qazvin seemed especially delicious. There was another dish, which was served in Miyaneh and Zanjan as well, which I had not tasted in those cities. It was made of cube-shaped tender lamb with split peas and chips. The chips were also shaped like cubes. This dish was really delicious. My mother and grandmother also appreciated the food. My father tried to please us the most and did not seem to be attending to himself as much. He kept moving round — buying, serving tea or food or anxiously directing my mother and grandmother to the toilets and praying room. At home my mother was in charge of providing food and tea, but on this journey, and whenever we were out of the house, my father took on this role. He seemed very busy and obliging, and I remember him being at his best on this journey. He used his sense of humour and laughed much more — becoming one of us and sharing everything. Eating, drinking, chatting and laughing together is a social bond in Iran, and indeed in the East as a whole, and I took great delight in it. I disliked eating and drinking alone — and still do.

In Qazvin, as in Tabriz and other cities, there were many bazaars, each specialising in particular skills and crafts — blacksmiths', goldsmiths', coppersmiths', those selling hats, clothes, or carpets etc. I was attracted to the hat- and shoe-makers'. There were, again as in Tabriz, many kinds of hats to be seen. Perhaps Qazvin, being on the crossroads between the Caspian Sea to the north, Kurdistan and Hamadan to the west and Tehran to the south, had different types of customer with varying tastes in hats and shoes. There was an abundance of fruit also, as in Tabriz and Zanjan. Qazvin, however, did not have the beauty and attraction of Zanjan, which seemed a more orderly city, with trees lining either side of the streets and flower beds in each square. Qazvin seemed to be haunted by statues of Reza Shah, especially in the big squares, which filled the places with fear and terror. I was even terrified of his photographs in restaurants and public buildings. I was warned by my father not to make remarks about the Shah.

When the passengers were finally boarding the coach again it was late afternoon and the driver was saying goodbye to his friends and fellow drivers whom he had met in the restaurant and with whom he had shared a meal and tea. Both the driver and conductor seemed happy. The coach started, but the dervish was no longer sitting next to the driver. Perhaps he had stayed in Qazvin.

When we arrived in Tehran it was after midnight. The coach passed through wide streets, lined with tall trees, which seemed to welcome our tired driver. The streets were deserted except for a few nightwatchmen and policemen who were standing at the entrances of shopping centres or bazaars. Cars are forbidden to enter the bazaars, some of which have gates.

From the coach I could only see the bazaar entrances, which were situated on the main square next to a mosque. The city of Tehran seemed to me a huge and strange place. It was my first visit to such a big city. A few days later when I visited some public places I saw an enormous post-office building in a large square. Feeling so strange in the place reminded me of the time when Nawruz-Ali came with his donkey from his village to my grandfather's house, and my grandfather sent him to take a letter to the post-office, which Nawruz-Ali had never seen before.

The house where we stayed in Tehran belonged to Ismail-Zadeh and his wife, who were relatives of my grandmother. They had two bedrooms, a large sitting-room where we deposited our belongings, and a kitchen and bathroom, the toilet being situated at the end of the yard. The yard was large enough to play in and had a pond in its centre, but we did not swim because the weather was not suitable. I did not know how to communicate with the other children because I spoke no Persian, only Azerbaijani, but this did not stop me playing with them. Whilst playing in the street in front of Ismail-Zadeh's house I noticed that electric wires crossed over our heads like spiders' webs. We had these in Tabriz also, but in less abundance. The streets were cleaner than in Tabriz and were also asphalted.

Tehran wakes up at 5 a.m. and men in baggy trousers carry boxes of all shapes and sizes piled on their heads. They wake the sleeping people with a variety of song-like shouts to sell them their goods. Some offer milk, tea, warm bread or fruit, others newspapers. Men, women and children begin to appear from the houses or lean out of their windows to try and catch the passing traders.

Many of the shops in Tehran were very small and the goods were displayed outside. Some had mountains of melons and water-melons and others had rows of knives and forks spread out on patterned cloths. Carpet-sellers piled up exquisite Persian rugs or hung them on the walls to display them to the customers. Once my father was interested in two carpets and the shopkeeper showed him dozens of them in the recesses of the shop. They bargained over the price and finally, after copious quantities of tea, they came to an agreement. The carpets were to be sent to Tabriz by the shopkeeper. I found the Tehran bazaars just as fascinating as those in Tabriz.

Entering a bazaar is akin to entering a vast honeycomb. After passing the gateway one enters a myriad of dark, winding passageways which are covered by high, vaulted ceilings. Beautiful rays of light come streaming through skylights bathing the interior darkness. Along both sides of the narrow passages are booths and small cubbyholes, barely more than niches scooped out of the stone. Each shop has a variety of goods ranging from shoes and jewellery to tapestries and china. At first the bazaar appears to be laid out in random fashion, but there is an overall plan which in time one can easily grasp. What fascinated me most were the areas where skilled

A coppersmiths' bazaar in Tehran.

craftsmen were at work. I could stand for hours and watch a man decorating the large copper trays which were used at home for special occasions. From early Persian civilization, coppersmiths, weavers, goldsmiths and many other artisans have created and sold crafts and art objects in their workshops in the bazaar. Both the skills and the tools have been handed down through generations of the same family.

There is a continuous flow of people through a bazaar. You see women with bundles perched on their heads, men carrying heavy loads and donkeys piled high with various goods. For those who purchase more than they can possibly carry there are professional porters for hire. Of course, this remains the exclusive luxury of the wealthy. No one appears to be wandering aimlessly; everyone present has business to attend to and scurries to and fro with purposeful intent.

Buying in a bazaar involves a form of game between buyer and seller. Remembering my father's shopping, it seemed like a chess game. No article has a fixed price; the seller names the highest price and the buyer offers the lowest. After a long period of friendly argument (to Western eyes it might seem like quarrelling) and perhaps a glass of tea, a price will be agreed upon that satisfies both buyer and seller. If the prospective buyer decides to leave before a fair bargain has been struck the shopkeeper can be seen comically venturing after the customer while yelling in an attempt to entice him back. But unlike markets elsewhere the Iranian bazaar is not merely a place where goods are bought or sold. Many important meetings take place in the bazaar, ranging from marriage negotiations to political discussions. During the last and even the present century the bazaar played an important role in the formation of governments in Iran. At some periods its power was so strong that it could bring about the collapse of a government, and it played a crucial role in overthrowing the Shah in 1979 and bringing about the Islamic Republic in Iran. In other words the supporters of the ayatollahs on their rise to power were the big businessmen of the bazaars, and they have reaped a great deal of profit both from the Revolution and from the Iran-Iraq war. But life for the small businessmen is like that for ordinary people who suffer both from inflation and from the war which has claimed the lives of so many of their young men. The Shi'ite religion of Islam has always been closely connected with the bazaars, which have been the main financial source for its ayatollahs for centuries.

For example, in the 19th century, Nasir al-Din Shah (1848-1896) sold the tobacco concession to an Englishman, Major Talbot, in return for a personal gift of £25,000 to himself, an annual rent of £15,000 to the state and a 25% share of the profit for Iran. For these, Major Talbot received a 50-year monopoly over the distribution and export of tobacco. The arrival of his company in 1891 was met with a closure of the bazaar in Shiraz, in Iran's main tobacco-growing region, which rapidly led to a general strike of the leading bazaars, particularly those in Tehran, Esfahan, Tabriz, Mashhad, Qazvin, Yazd and Kermanshah. The strike was encouraged by a religious *fatwa*, or decree, against the use of any tobacco. Religious leaders in Iran and Iraq joined together in issuing the *fatwa*, and demonstrations took place in the streets of Iran. Both the opposition from the ayatollahs and the anger of the people in the street (and even of the royal harem, who refused to prepare the tobacco for Nasir al-Din Shah's hubble-bubble) forced the Shah to annul the concession.

This crisis paved the way for a fundamental change which culminated in the Constitutional Revolution of 1905-1909. In both cases, the religious leaders challenged the rule of the shahs, fighting the battle under the banner of Islam. The tobacco revolt was a rebellion by the businessmen who were being undersold by the imports from foreign traders, as well as becoming dependent on a foreign country. It was a popular uprising because it appeared that the Shah was bargaining the independence of the country to a foreign power, and hence the revolt was politically attractive. For this reason, intellectuals like Mirza Malkum Khan, former Iranian Ambassador in London, and his friend Jamal al-Din al-Afghani, played an active role against Nasir al-Din Shah. Malkum published a paper called *Qanun* advocating and describing the kind of laws which would bring about security and hence social progress in Iran. But the main intentions of the religious leaders and the intellectuals differed fundamentally. The intellectuals wished to free Iran from oriental despotism, whereas the religious leaders wanted to bring more profit and prosperity to the bazaars and their big merchants. The Constitutional Revolution of 1905-1909 incorporated both these components, but was more complex, as we will see later.

Looking at these big businessmen sitting in their well-decorated and finely appointed offices in the bazaar, in the manner of the head of a tribe, did not encourage an ordinary person or a small child to buy little things such as a torch battery or sweets from their stalls and emporia. Their attitude seemed like a big wall to which you could not talk. Small businessmen standing next to their scales or counter, or outside their shop, were much more approachable to a child like me. Once I approached a big businessman who was selling dried fruit and asked him to give me two rials' (two pence) worth of raisins. He said, "Go away, we don't sell for that money." I did not know he was a wholesaler. But a few yards away there was a small shop where they gave me raisins for my two rials.

There was a sense of pride mixed with religious arrogance in these more substantial businessmen which is really repulsive for a child to encounter. They gave the impression that it was their personal ability and divine Providence which had brought them to that position of prosperity. Later on, when my mother suggested I marry the daughter of one of the big merchants before I came to Britain, the first question he put to me, how high was my salary, made me cold and humiliated inside, and put me off the subject of marriage to his daughter completely. From the outset he made it clear that he could employ dozens of teachers like me in his office. In fact his response was a self-defensive one, stemming from his lack of education and his anxiety to show himself as good as me with my degree. I remember saying, "You may employ many teachers like me in your office but you may not possess the mind of any of them." He said he could employ doctors to come and visit him wherever he wished. "They run to my country residence like a servant when they know they will be receiving good money." Then he added, "With money you can do a lot of things in this world, but what can you do with your degree? At the most you will get a salary of 600 tomans a month, which is what I pay my secretary in the office." (1 toman is 10 rials.)

Many parts of these bazaars, sometimes the entire bazaar, were owned by these big businessmen, who leased them, sometimes for enormous sums, to their small competitors. In addition, they often owned extensive lands, including whole villages, outside the cities. Tehran was full of this kind of businessman, who came from different parts of the country, many from my own Tabriz and Azerbaijan. Now and then, when the bigger businessmen found that their goods were not bringing in the financial profits which they sought, and when they saw the small businessmen and street vendors lowering their own prices and flooding the market with cheaper goods, they would put pressure on the government to clear the streets. This would be particularly likely to happen when some foreign product — supposedly the monopoly of the big businessmen who increased their profits by selling it in Iran — was smuggled or even obtained perfectly legally by smaller business firms and marketed for a cheaper price; if the businessmen could not stop it entering the country, they made its distribution impossible, if they could, by putting pressure on the state to close down the vendors. I have seen policemen chasing young men who wanted to sell various Western products, while the persecution ceased when the victims agreed to buy from the bigger sellers and sell at the price they dictated. After the Revolution of 1979, the import of foreign goods by small vendors was outlawed, and the big businessmen were able to sell them at a huge profit.

The owner of the house where we were staying on my first visit to Tehran, Ismail-Zadeh, came from a small-business family, but he worked in an office, and his wife Azar was from an educated family. Both were kind to us. They seemed always very busy, running in and out. In Tehran some women did not stay in their houses as they did in Tabriz. Azar used to leave home early in the morning and return in the evening, then start cooking, cleaning and putting the children to bed. In comparison, I thought that women in Tabriz of that class had easier lives. The majority of such women in Tabriz stayed at home, and had only to run their houses, while their husbands would be the only bread-winner of the family. Women in Tehran had a double responsibility. I felt unhappy and insecure in that atmosphere where the woman of the house would leave in the morning: in my world I wanted my mother to be always available to me, a child. I knew that sitting beside my mother at home, or beside my nurse Humai (who of course, from the point of view of her own family, was a career-woman) I had a wonderful sense of warmth and happiness and joy which clearly the little girls in the Ismail-Zadeh household did not have, or lacked for much of the time. Even when their mother was at home, everything had to be done very rapidly, and there was obviously less time for fostering family affection.

When I came to Britain in 1960 I realised that many women work both at home as housewives and outside as employees in factories and offices. I thought the lower- and even middle-class women in Europe and Britain worked even harder than women of the same class in Iran. I wondered what freedom was gained by women in the West. Indeed, they seemed freer in social relationships, but seemed exploited at work, at home and in society, and I did not know why. I was rather puzzled. My sisters in Tabriz were repressed and exploited in one way, and the women in the West were exploited in another way. My sisters were not free to be exploited but the women in the West *were* free to be exploited. Women in my family in Tabriz seemed more secure economically than their counterparts in Britain. They did not seem to worry about jobs, prices, domestic expenses; their husbands were in charge of economic matters. Wives did not worry about economic questions. I found it quite different in Britain: housewives, while responsible for running their houses, had to budget and worry about how to spend the money for food and other necessary items. In the East women were haunted by mothers-in-law and in the West they were haunted by electricity and gas bills, price rises and questioning husbands.

My mother did not like Tehran life at all. She said, comparing it with Tehran, "Life in Tabriz is Heaven". She thought it was too complicated to live in Tehran: for one thing they bought in bulk for storage in Tabriz, whereas in Tehran they went out and shopped for necessities every day. My mother did not like the idea of having to ask for everything constantly. We in Tabriz had sacks of rice or split peas, or jars of cooking oil; in Tehran they used to obtain everything in small amounts.

When Ismail-Zadeh and Azar were out of the house, my father used to take my mother and grandmother and me with him sight-seeing. Once we went to visit a place of pilgrimage outside Tehran called Shah Abdul Azim. It was like a fairground, with a lot of sweets and other such things which we could obtain. It is believed that Shah Abdul Azim is related to Imam Hassan (the grandson of the Prophet Muhammad) and people go to his shrine for both pilgrimage and sightseeing as it is put in a poem:

> How nice, it offers two things:
> Pilgrimage to Shah Abdul Azim and seeing pretty faces.

It mattered little to me that it was also the place where the career of Nasir al-Din Shah had ended abruptly in 1896 when he was assassinated while preparing for the celebrations for the 50th anniversary of his accession to the throne. He was shot dead there by a bankrupt trader who had studied under Jamal al-Din al-Afghani. There was an ironic retribution there also, for after his capitulation to the religious forces unleashed over the tobacco concession, Nasir al-Din Shah had become anxious to placate the conservative interests and took hostile measures against any but the most severely orthodox forms of Islamic education. In practice, he embarked on a war against the intellectuals, and in theory he repressed modern education so as to ensure they would have no successors.

> I sometimes think that never blows so red
> The Rose as where some buried Caesar bled . . .

As we visited the place we saw some people sitting there having dinner and tea with family or friends, and some washing themselves in the pool, preparing for prayer. Others were sitting and telling jokes and making people laugh. I liked most of all the *kebab* and sweet that we had in a restaurant. There the *kebab* was wrapped in *sangak* bread with fresh mint, onion and *sumaq* (a kind of sour-tasting spice also used for *chilo-kebabs*).

Since we were going to Mashhad on pilgrimage, many friends visited us before we left Tehran, to ask us to pray for them at the shrine and wish us a good journey, giving us fruit and sweets for the journey. When we started our journey it was late afternoon. Passing through rather crowded streets and big buildings we arrived at the outskirts of Tehran, where we found large numbers of unfortunate poor people. The houses there were humble and streets narrow. The only things which stood out were the statues of Reza Shah to be seen in every square, the only substantially built edifices visible. The statues would seem isolated and separated from the people, standing on their own. The distance was psychological and political as well as physical, because I heard people say how much they hated him and his dictatorship. (My father used formally to curse Reza Shah every day. That was of course in private. Cursing Reza Shah in public could cost a man his life.) Not very far from the statues there were huts and houses made out of clay. Further on, a few kilometres outside Tehran, I noticed several tall chimneys. I asked my father what they were and he told me, "They are chimneys for the brick factories" and that the surrounding huts were where the brickmakers lived. Both men and women worked at the factories. I saw little children playing in mud next to their mothers who were laying bricks.

After a few hours' journey we passed a pleasant place called Damavand, which is the name of the highest peak of the Elburz mountains which run between the Caspian Sea and Tehran and the Persian plateau. Mount Damavand, which is to the north-east of Tehran, is 5,628 metres high, and forms part of a chain of mountains which continue until Khorasan, in the north-east of Iran. The mountains carry different names and normally are called after the names of places and cities that are situated next to them. The colours of the Elburz mountains vary in different places; in some places they are red, some places green and some places very dark, which gives a special beauty to the scenery.

We were travelling now across the uppermost part of the great Persian plateau, which cuts off the Caspian Sea in the north from the Persian Gulf and the Indian Ocean in the south. It is also a bridge from East to West, linking the steppes of Inner Asia to Asia Minor, and beyond it to Europe. Iran as a whole is said to be the combined size of Britain, France, Switzerland and the Italian and Spanish peninsulae, or, in American terms, twice the size of Texas. Our road lay between the Caspian coast, with its luxuriant vegetation, and the desert lands to our south, where so many of the population were nomadic, travelling from season to season up and down the mountains in quest of pasture for their goats, sheep and horses. As our journey went deeper and deeper into the east, we would encounter the mountains of Khorasan, much lower than Damavand and famed for its fertile valleys whose abundant supply of crops make it the "granary of Iran."

Khorasan, like Azerbaijan, is famous for the very many different peoples it sweeps together through its character as a crossroads. Our own journey was along one of the historic silk routes through which so much of Chinese trade had moved westward, and along which many invaders from Central Asia had also made their way. The sign that we were no longer travelling parallel to the south shore of the Caspian Sea came when we reached the mountain, valley and town of Gorgan, and commenced journeying northward. Gorgan itself remains in my memory for its warm people and for its numerous orange trees which even grew on the streets. Beyond Gorgan is the district of Turkman Sahra, very much a place of nomads — one-sixth of the population of Iran are nomads. I was pleased to find that the people whom I met spoke a similar language to Azerbaijani, which was quite comprehensible to me as both had their roots in Turkish. In Gorgan I had encountered an even less comprehensible dialect of Persian than in Tehran. The people in Turkman Sahra also impressed me by living in tents made from felt, as they had to be fit to stand both cold and humid weather alike.

The life of the nomads is most fascinating, and very active. They move every year between their summer pastures in the mountains to their winter pastures in the lowlands, in search of grass for their flocks of sheep and goats. Reza Shah's policy was to force them to settle permanently in villages; it met with very little success. This was also the policy of subsequent governments, cruelly interfering with the way of life of these people. Most nomads belong to tribes or nationalities such as the Kurds, the Lurs, the Bakhtiari, the Baluchi, the Turkmans and the Qashqai. Some tribes are descended from the very earliest inhabitants of the Persian plateau, others from central Asian invaders. Others, like the Qashqai, were brought in from outside Iran to serve as a military force. (The movement of Kurds and Turkmans took place during the reigns of Shah Abbas (1571-1629) and Karim Khan Zand (1750-1779); Reza Shah (1878-1944) also played an important role in this dispersal.) With these varied origins, it is fascinating to see these tribes with their different languages, different traditions and colourings. Their portable homes vary too. The Bakhtiari and the Qashqai have tents made of black goats' hair, while the Turkmans made theirs from felt, indicating that they came from a colder and wetter area than the others. They are a beautiful, vigorous and charming group of peoples; naturally I had little chance to talk to them then, but when I was 18 on a visit to Shiraz Bazaar I really had the opportunity to come to know the Qashqai and see how much linguistic ground we had in common. The Turkmans — the nomads I met in Turkman Sahra — also spoke a Turkish language, but the Bakhtiari spoke Persian.

We passed the cities of Bujnurd, Shirvan and Quchan before we arrived at Tus and Mashhad. Tus, which is the birthplace of Firdausi, is on the outskirts of Mashhad. We did not go to Tus on the first day, but we visited Firdausi's monument a few days afterwards. This journey was the first time I had heard of our great poet other than his name. There had been a school called after him in Tabriz: I had heard of it, and several years later attended it for a year. I had also seen a street named after him at Tehran: it led to a square where there was a fine statue — still there today — representing the poet as an old man with a long beard and a book under his arm, turbanned and wearing the long, flowing Persian robe of his time, with very sharp eyes and a face inspiring in its beholders thought, response and effect. Now at Tus we visited the great monument whose huge stone pedestal was covered with verses from the *Shah-nameh*: it had been placed there by order of Reza Shah in 1934 on the supposed millenary of Firdausi's birth. It suited Reza Shah to be identified with so great a spokesman for Iranian national culture and identity, although he naturally would not have wished to stress Firdausi's anger at the treachery of rulers against their people and the necessity for economic equality in the struggle against social injustice. But I did not think about Reza Shah as I looked at the tribute to the birth of Firdausi: I simply thought of this poet who so long ago had defended and enlarged the culture of my country. It strengthened in me, in ways I hardly understood, a sense of the richness of my inheritance in being Iranian.

(I had also passed through the birthplace of Reza Shah, or somewhere in that neighbourhood, when we had driven through the Elburz mountains about 500 kilometres north-east of Tehran. It was rather sinister country, and my father was not likely to have drawn it to my attention on account of its association with Reza Shah. The area is also an important location of many of the scenes in the *Shah-nameh*, on which evidence it has produced dragons, demons and ogres — in addition to Reza Shah.)

When we first arrived at Mashhad it was night-time and, from a few kilometres away, the city seemed to be lit up with millions of lights. The shrine of Imam-Riza, to which we were making our pilgrimage, was specially illuminated with the reflection of a golden dome, and when the passengers saw this scene from far away all 40 or 50 of us began to hail it with praise to Allah. I was rather excited and looking forward to seeing the city and especially the shrine, about which I had heard so much since early childhood. It is more than a simple journey for Iranian families to visit the shrine of Imam-Riza. All my mother's words were in my ear. She used to say at home, almost every day, that if you had a wish or a desire you should go to the door of Imam-Riza and ask him to grant you your wish. So when we were approaching Mashhad she whispered, "You can get from Imam-Riza whatever you ask." I did not know what I could ask for, but it suddenly came to my mind, "What about a bicycle?" which I had wished to have for

Women from the nomadic Turkman tribes.

many months. I think that in mother's mind was hope for the cure of Ismail, who had contracted tuberculosis by this time, as well as general prayers for the well-being of the children, beginning with her stepdaughters Sakineh and Khanum Sultan.

Some of the passengers on the coach burst into tears at the sight of the lights of the shrine. They were from many different cities — Tehran, Tabriz, Zanjan, Ardabil — and some villagers were also with us who had saved for years in order to make this pilgrimage. But the desires and hopes of the people differed: a woman from Ardabil was going to pray that her son, a soldier, might return safely from military service; while other peasants were hoping that their prayers to Imam-Riza would bring to them the offer of some land for cultivation. A man from Zanjan was taking his wife, who was ill and could not bear children, in the hope that she would become fertile and produce them. I was the only one who wanted to have a bicycle, but I didn't know how Imam could provide me with this bicycle. That was a mystery. As the days passed, I imagined that he might order some of his servants to deliver the bicycle to our house in Mashhad, especially when my mother, after visiting the shrine several times, told us that she had received a letter of acceptance from Imam-Riza. The practice existed at the shrine by which letters were sent from the top saying that devotees should be happy and their prayers would be granted. My mother had such a message fall from on high into her lap, and took it as a direct sign from Imam-Riza that all would be well with the cause of her petition. But to my disappointment I never received my bicycle!

Imam Ali Ibn Musa al-Riza was the eighth Imam (or religious leader) of the Shi'ites, and was brought to Mashhad by Ma'mun (who reigned from 813 to 833), the son of Harun Al-Rashid, Caliph of Baghdad. Ma'mun had been Governor in Khorasan, but was attacked by his younger brother from Baghdad and defeated. Now Ma'mun sought to make Imam-Riza Caliph of Baghdad, but the Iraquis rejected him and Ma'mun was forced to journey to Baghdad to take charge. Imam-Riza died suddenly, and it was believed (not necessarily correctly) that Ma'mun had got rid of an embarrassing favourite by having him poisoned. No doubt Ma'mun himself, either sincerely or hypocritically, began the cult of the lost heir.

People went to Mashhad for a mixture of holiday, business or pilgrimage, or any one of the three; some even went there to find concubines and wives. But all who went there went under the name of pilgrims, to do honour to the place. For a child, who took no part in long hours of prayer, or sitting and reading prayers, which was boring, the whole thing was very much a cross between a museum and an amusement park, with the fantastic domes, the chandeliers, the mirrors, the great dinners served in public — a sort of entertainment for children. Huge pools with hundreds of pigeons playing around in lovely sunshine surrounded the tall trees and flower gardens. Hot

The entrance to Imam-Riza's tomb in Mashhad.

puddings and sweets were served to us at the huge gate before the gardens of the shrine, or sweets were distributed by the pilgrims in recompense for the granting of their wishes (or in hope that they would be granted). So each day, whenever my mother and grandmother asked me to visit the shrine, all that persuaded me to go were the pigeons and sweets; and I had not completely given up on the bicycle, though I was finding it increasingly difficult to work out how Imam-Riza was to deliver it.

Going to the tomb of Imam-Riza itself meant being pressed up against the metal silver of the bars around it, through which so many people had pushed paper money. I wondered how a person so long dead could be of any help to us. I found it even more alarming, if not sickening, when people would arrive with a coffin which would be taken around the tomb in a circle, while the parents and mourners followed, asking that Imam-Riza cleanse the dead man of his sins. On the other hand, it was impossible not to be impressed by the pure gold or silver of the gates: the tomb itself was about the size of an ordinary Western suburban reception room, but the entire building, almost all of it constructed of white marble, was the size of my university in Edinburgh. Some of the rooms were covered in costly carpets; most walls were bare marble, which would be pleasantly cool after the hot summer sun. I could hardly have failed to be impressed by the golden domes and colourful mosaic exteriors of the building housing the tomb.

All sorts of reasons had contributed over the centuries to the cult of Imam-Riza, beginning with Ma'mun who either deeply mourned his ill-fated successor-designate or wished to conceal his own guilt in his demise. There were the Shi'ites who venerated him as a Shi'ite holy man, martyred by his enemies (Ma'mun personally believed that the Quran was written by men, not a work "uncreate", as most Shi'ites believe, and hence they would be glad to believe the worst of Ma'mun.) There were the Persians of Khorasan, who had been involved by then in a series of military conflicts with Baghdad, who saw Imam-Riza as a holy man whose rejection by Baghdad was responsible for his death, although as he was from the region of Iraq, he should have received acceptance at its hands. There were the Mongols, who found the cult useful for the consolidation of their hold on Khorasan when, with the passing of the centuries, they acquired it. Even in the recent past, the various Iranian rulers have found it advisable to show their respect for it. Reza Shah had added much exotic architecture to the shrine, stressing his own similarity in name: the very fact that he and his predecessors often fell foul of the holy men made him and them all the more anxious to show their credentials with so popular a figure, who, being dead, was less likely to question their actions than the mullahs and ayatollahs. And the obvious presence of Imam-Riza as a symbol of Iranian unity over the thousand miles from Tabriz to Mashhad, as opposed to the perfidy of Baghdad in rejecting its own truly descended Imam and thereby causing his death, gave even stronger motives for the furtherance of the cult. Ruler after ruler had increased the extent and magnificence of the adjoining buildings to the tomb and its attendant shrines and, as could be seen by all those pieces of paper money pushed through the silver bars of his tomb, Imam-Riza had become an exceedingly rich corpse over the centuries. He could well have afforded to give me a bicycle.

The whole story of Imam-Riza and his posthumous cult is a perfect example of the intricacies of politics and religion. Ma'mun, aware that Baghdad bitterly resented being ruled from Khorasan, decided on Imam-Reza as someone whose religious situation would surely make him acceptable to the devout Shi'ite population of Baghdad. But Baghdad's regional loyalties proved stronger than the appeal of even so distinguished a representative of the Shi'ite religious culture. Ironically, once Ma'mun arrived in Baghdad after Imam-Riza's death the rebellion ended. It is possible that Imam-Riza would have been able to rule in accordance with the wishes of Ma'mun after his powerful protector had pacified Iraq, but the chief reason for appointing him disappeared when it became clear that his status would not make him an automatically acceptable ruler. The belief persisted down the centuries that Ma'mun grew to resent Imam-Riza as a potential rival to himself, but this actually makes little sense, since when Imam-Riza died he had conspicuously failed to win the support of the region he had been chosen to rule. We will never know whether Ma'mun poisoned him or not; it may simply have been that Imam-Riza died suddenly and, as often happens throughout history, his sudden death gave automatic rise to suspicion of poison. In any case, politics raised Imam-Riza to his elevated position and politics subsequently kept his name alive and greatly enlarged his cult as time went on.

A great deal of Iranian history flowed under the surface of my family's journey to the shrine. I did find in Mashhad that the local inhabitants made relatively little use of their own proximity to the shrine. Most people to whom I talked admitted they never went to visit it more than once a year. On the other hand, it was of enormous advantage to them, both in focusing attention on so remote a part of Iran, and in bringing in extensive and consistent income through the endless stream of pilgrims.

Western Christian readers may find interesting parallels between the cult of Imam-Riza, as a religious leader rejected by his own people as a result of which he was supposedly killed by an alien ruler, and the Gospel narratives of the life of Jesus Christ. Christians have consistently spoken of Christ as having been rejected by the Jews, his own people: in fact all of his initial supporters were Jews, and while the majority of Jews did not accept him as the Messiah, only very few had any responsibility for his death. It is a truly dreadful thought that the hideous history of Christian persecution of the Jews has so consistently been undertaken in the name of punishment for this supposed rejection, mingled with allegations of blood-guilt on the Jews for Jesus's death. This persecution culminated in the Nazi atrocities of the Second World War. The subsequent Western burden of guilt has continued to the present day. It has played a part in their condoning Israeli treatment of the Palestinian Arabs.

Of course, the cult of Imam-Riza has been used in various ways. The anti-Iraq element, or, on its positive side, the emphasis on the unity of a far-flung Iran, was what particularly appealed to politicians. Even after our pilgrimage I have seen further workings-out of this; the late Shah, who was overthrown in 1979, gave additional golden doors to parts of the shrine in place of their gates, with an inscription that these were His Majesty's gift. On the other hand the mullahs were if anything inclined to stress the lessons of the story as a warning against secular rulers. I often heard them narrate their version of the circumstances of Imam-Riza's death. He and Ma'mun were sitting together, and grapes (which had been dipped in poison) were brought in. Ma'mun offered the grapes to Imam-Riza. Imam-Riza knew they were poisoned, and refused. Ma'mun insisted. Imam-Riza could not withstand him, and said, "This is my destiny. I have come from Allah, and I am returning to Allah." Imam-Riza then went to his house and asked his servant to bring a big bowl, into which he quickly vomited his liver, corroded into pieces. This story, whether told in our house or to crowds, would make us very sad, and very angry towards Ma'mun and the Baghdad caliphs, and suspicious of rulers in general.

Later on in my life, when I was away from Iran, my sisters told me that my mother used to talk about the similarity of my name to that of Imam-Riza, and speak of his having died in a strange land. She would grow anxious about me, and used to pray to Allah, "Oh Allah, for the honour of his name, make my son healthy and successful and do not let him suffer through poverty in a strange land."

While in Mashhad, we stayed in the rented house of my father's uncle. It had two rooms with one kitchen and one vestibule. There was also a little yard, surrounded by vines, with a pool in the middle. It was a very pleasant place for me to play by myself, or sit and chat with my grandmother while my parents were at the shrine and my father's uncle's wife (an old lady) was busy in the kitchen. My father's uncle sold sweets in front of cinemas and schools: Sadeq, my father's cousin, used to make them in a workroom a few doors from the house. The sweetmeat was a kind of toffee made with a mixture of chocolate and milk. I called my father's uncle "Great-uncle" — I did not know his name — and called his wife "Wife of my uncle". They were both about 60 years of age.

Great-uncle used to take the sweets around every morning and evening. One day I insisted he should take me with him. After passing a few alleys, we came to the main street, which was facing the big gate of the shrine. We went to a cinema where Great-uncle started selling sweets. Before we had arrived at the cinema it started to rain and he immediately put his handkerchief over the sweets and put the sweets next to the wall, took off his coat and placed it over me to prevent my getting wet saying, "If you catch cold, your father will tell me off." The coat was so long that it was like an overcoat for my eight-year-old size and its sleeves were hanging over my hands. I was very pleased with what he did, and I felt proud that he had put his coat over me. But when he was busy selling sweets and crowds were gathering, I lost him. After looking here and there and not finding him, I decided to return home by myself. In fact the big gate of the shrine and the clock over it helped me to find my direction. I went directly to that gate and from it I found the house. After an hour or so he returned, shocked and worried. When he found me in the house he was relieved and delighted that I had found my way back, and admired the way I did it.

My respect and love for Great-uncle increased during our stay in Mashhad, because he introduced me to children of the area and also walked with me round the city, which my parents would not bother to do. But my father took me to the fruit market and the bazaar several times, and I remember we bought plenty of grapes and melons. Although we had sweet melons in

Tabriz, I thought I had never tasted melons so sweet as those of Mashhad. I well remember that I ate so many that it affected my tongue and my lips, which became almost burned by the sweetness: but I did not tell my parents what had happened, and did not mind.

One day I asked Great-uncle to take me to Sadeq's factory to show me how they made the sweets. So he took me to there, where we found Sadeq was making the sweet mixture in huge bowls and pouring it out into tin trays. Some of them were cold and ready to be sliced, so he cut them into cube shapes by a hand-operated machine. He offered me some sweets: of course I had already had plenty from Great-uncle, so it was not quite so great a privilege as Sadeq might have imagined, but I was pleased just the same. At the time I thought it was a great job to be a sweet-seller and to make people happy by what one sold, and I had great admiration for Great-uncle for all the happiness he must bring. It often happened that children did not have enough money, and Great-uncle never refused a child, and gave them a full measure however little they had.

I had thought, before I met Great-uncle, that he was much more prosperous than in fact he was. It was not that we did not have some relatives who were poorer than my father, for example Izzat, and I had already seen the tragic proof of the difference in income creating class barriers within the family. But I had heard that Great-uncle was a substantial businessman, who traded extensively with Russian Turkestan, travelling for a long time to and from Ashqabad. Ashqabad was not far from Mashhad, only a little over 150 kilometres, much nearer than the distance from Tabriz to the nearest point on the Caspian Sea or from Edinburgh to Aberdeen. But after the Russian Revolution the border gradually closed. British forces attacked Ashqabad after the Revolution, using the support of the powerful Alam family, the most prominent family in Khorasan (Asadullah Alam, from the younger generation, was subsequently Prime Minister under the last Iranian Shah but covertly also protected Ayatollah Khomeini in 1963 — it was a family long skilled in planning ahead to allow for possible political vicissitudes). The Russians repulsed them, but no longer trusted their southern neighbours, and the extensive coming and going between Russian Turkestan (Turkmenistan) and Iran ended.

After Reza Shah came to the throne in 1925 he specifically forbade all communication with the USSR, all the more because refugees from Iran had fled there. Great-uncle was no longer able to trade and sojourn in Ashqabad, and was forced to live in much poorer conditions working as a street-vendor for his cousin Sadeq. For family as well as financial reasons Great-uncle was anxious to entertain and please my father, but while Father bought presents for the house, Great-uncle was a man of such powerful personality that I do not think he would have accepted any cash payment for his hospitality, and I saw no sign of anything of that kind. I had wondered why Great-uncle never visited us in Tabriz during my childhood, in view of the close links among Eastern families, much closer than is known in the West. But I now realise Great-uncle would have been much too proud to bring his poverty into the house of my wealthy father, and in fact I have since noted how difference in income cuts off members of my own brothers and sisters from one another apart from meetings at Nawruz.

About a year after we returned to Tabriz I heard that Great-uncle's wife died, and again a year or so after that I heard he himself had died also. But five or six years after that, Sadeq realised that he in his turn was dying, and returned to Tabriz to die there. It was from Tabriz that Great-uncle had started out at the beginning of the century: but his poverty, and not the journey, prevented his ever seeing it again once he had lost his main source of income. When members of a family go from one Iranian city to another far-distant one as Great-uncle had done, those who remain behind tell glorious stories about how well the emigrant has done and how much property and wealth he has accumulated. Those who really do make money and keep it will return to their native city, but those who are less fortunate never come back, wishing to save their faces and not confront the great stories of their success with the tragic reality of their material failure. So children like myself assumed that a far-distant uncle must be rich, although no doubt our parents and older relatives would have a much clearer idea of the reality, deducing this from the failure to visit if not from actual concrete information. In material terms, Great-uncle was a failure. To me he was and is one of the kindest and finest people I have ever known.

We took a more southern route on our return: it would bring us home by the south instead of the north side of the Elburz mountains, and it gave me my first sight of Nishapur, about 40 kilometres from Mashhad. It was here, somewhere between 850 and 900 years before our visit, that Omar Khayyam was born.

> What, without asking, hither hurried *Whence*?
> And, without asking, *Whither* hurried hence
> Oh, many a Cup of this forbidden Wine
> Must drown the memory of that insolence!

In the eleventh century Khayyam lived in a society that was suppressive and potentially destructive to human thought. Local rulers had, for the time being, apparently succeeded in stifling all philosophical and political activities. They employed, first, the Ghaznavid and then the Saljuq Turks as tools for this policy of suppression. Khayyam and his famous contemporary, the philosopher Muhammad Al-Ghazzali (who was born and died in Tus, 1059?-1111) had been the final flowering of that vigorous growth of freedom of thought which had sprung up in Iran, particularly in Khorasan, since the eleventh century.

Now both Ghazzali and Khayyam, during the succeeding period of repression, had to submit to an oppressive authority in one way or another. A letter from Al-Ghazzali to Sultan Sanjar (1087?-1157) of Khorasan has come down to us in which he says:

> I have sat in a corner for twelve years. I avoided the people. Then Fakhr al-Mulk, God bless him, insisted that I go to Nishapur. The present day, I answered, cannot stand what I say. For if anyone teaches philosophy at this time all the doors and walls rise against him in enmity. "The King is just," said Fakhr al-Mulk, "and I would support you. . . . Nowadays the situation has changed so much that I hear certain words which, if I had dreamed them, I would call confused dreams . . . Please excuse me from teaching in Nishapur and Tus so that I can live in my own safe corner because the present time cannot endure my words."

Khayyam, who was a more progressive thinker than Ghazzali, sensed the danger of reactionary power to an even greater extent. Al-Qifti (1172-1248) described Khayyam's dark days in his *History of Philosophers*:

> His contemporaries began criticising him and talked about his religion and beliefs so that Khayyam became terrified. He silenced his tongue and pen and left Nishapur for the pilgrimage to Mecca. After his return from Mecca he tried to hide his thoughts and became a devout follower of religion to all outward appearance.

From these examples we can gain some idea of the atmosphere of the time and the naturally pessimistic reaction of the philosophical thinkers towards this atmosphere.

Khayyam's revolt against the existing philosophical system shows itself in his work in two ways: one is his satire of the whole universe and its doubtful creator and the other is his philosophy of materialism formed in opposition to the selfishness of "spiritualism".

What do we mean when we say that Khayyam is a materialist philosopher? In Khayyam's time the accepted philosophical doctrine taught that the source of all life is the spiritual world. Love of God and the spiritual world was regarded as good, and love of the material world and bodily desire were considered evil. Orthodox religion and philosophy, while living amid wealth and worldly riches, taught self-denial and the love of God. Orthodox Islam, like orthodox Christianity, advocated self-restraint, warned of "Hell" on the one hand and on the other hand promised "Heaven" in the afterworld. Opposing these abstract teachings, Khayyam wrote:

> They say there will be a heaven and houris within it,
> There will be wine, milk and honey.
> Then if we have already chosen wine and a mistress, there's no need to worry,
> Because the end of the affair will be just this.

. . .

For how long shall I lay clay bricks on the sea,
I am fed up with the idolators of the synagogue.
Khayyam, who said there will be a Hell?
Who went to Hell and who came from Heaven?

Rejecting the idea of predestination — that some are born for "Heaven"
and some for "Hell" he wrote:

I do not know at all whether he who moulded me
Made me one of the inhabitants of Heaven or Hell.
A bowl of wine, a beautiful woman and music in a garden,
Give me these in cash and you can take Heaven in credit.

Khayyam stressed the importance of the material world. It is necessary
for human existence. He regarded abstract religious teachings as a cunning
deceit to deprive humanity of the pleasure and enjoyment of life. Attacking
the hypocrisy of the ruling system and its use of the prohibition of wine as a
means to vilify its opponents, he remarked:

If you do not drink wine do not speak about drinkers sarcastically.
Do not lay a foundation of deceits and tales.
Do not be proud for not drinking.
You devour one hundred mouthfuls, so that my drinking is nothing in comparison.

Although Khayyam was philosophically a materialist, morally he was a
spiritualist and humanist. He asserted the importance of the material world
but criticised selfishness. The material world is not evil but evil can exist in
the nature of human relationship with the material world. The man who sits
with his mistress in a garden and drinks wine is not committing a sin. But
he who forbids drinking while accumulating his wealth at the expense of
others, is sinful:

For how long will you spend your life in selfishness
Or worrying about having this and not having that?
Cease your greed for this world and live happily.
Cut yourself away from good and evil,
Take wine and a mistress
For these few days would pass quickly.

In the following century, the twelfth, perhaps some years before Omar
Khayyam died in Nishapur, it was again the birthplace of a poet, Farid ud-
Din Attar whose poem *Manteq al-teir* (*The Conference of Birds*) is at last
becoming widely known in the West.

Attar (1120-1215) was more directly concerned with spiritual questions

The tomb of Omar Khayyam in Nishapur.

in *The Conference of Birds*. He does not neglect the material world but in this poem he depicts human qualities, embodied as birds, seeking a figure of salvation which they ultimately find in their collective identity.

He sees the five senses and the material world as a vehicle for the human imagination. Where Reason is limited, Love is unlimited:

> Give up the intellect for love and see
> In one brief moment all eternity;

Every man is imprisoned by his five senses and natural impressions unless he frees himself from this cocoon. Excessive devotion to self prevents one from attaining the larger Self beyond individual obsessions and attachments: such excessive self-love may be bound up in a person, a possession, a house, a jewel, or some other object which cuts off the votary from full realisation of his place in the spiritual universe, and humankind as a whole:

> The Self is like a mail coat — melt this steel
> To pliant wax with David's holy zeal,
> And when its metal melts, like David you
> Will melt with love and bid the Self adieu.

And again, in his *Musibat-nameh* (*Book of Laments*), Attar especially revolts against God's injustice and opposes the cruelty and social injustices of his own times. The following is my translation of a poem from the *Book of Laments*:

Once there was a poor wanderer
For whom it was easier to die than live:
He had nothing to satisfy either his hunger or thirst;
He had neither anything to eat nor anywhere to sleep.
Anyway, once, in utmost humility and resignation
He went in distress towards Nishapur.
On his way he saw a whole field blackened with cows.
Like one's heart blackened with sin and cruelty.
He asked, "To whom do these cows belong?"
He was told that they belonged to the Amid of the town.
He left there dazzled.
He came to another field, also blackened,
The whole field was full of horses;
You would say that horses had taken over the world.
He asked, "Whose horses are these?"
And was told that they belonged to the Amid of the town.
He walked for a little while, the unfortunate —
And saw another field covered with numerous sheep.
He asked, "To whom does such a big flock belong?"
He was told that it belonged to the Amid.
He walked a little further until he reached the town gate
[Where] he saw numerous Turks [slaves] . . .
"Whose slaves are they?" asked the bewildered man . . .
"They are men selected by the Amid" [he was told].
The wandering man thought to himself, listless,
Who could not afford [even] half a loaf of bread;
Something boiled up inside him
And fury overtook him.
He tore off his ragged turban
And threw it towards the sky.
"Take this too," he yelled [to God],
"So that you can hand it also to your Amid.
Now that everything is destined to belong to him
It is fit that he has this headgear too."

But Farid ud-Din Attar, while making his narrative and his fables as captivating and diverse as the characters and discourses of Chaucer's *Canterbury Tales*, with its comparable (though in this case unconcluded) pilgrimage and discussions or stories among the participants, takes care to point out many direct lessons which have all too much relevance to the history of Iran from his time to ours, and indeed to the world as I have seen it. Let him conclude this narrative of my childhood pilgrimage to Khorasan with one instance of his timeliness:

At public prayers a great lord cried: "O God,
Have mercy on me now and spare the rod!"
A crazy dervish heard his prayer and said:
"You dare to call His mercies on your head
When behaviour seems to say 'The earth
Can hardly hold a person of my worth' —
You've raised a palace up against the sky,
Embellished it with gold to daze the eye;
Ten boys and ten young girls await your whim,
What claim have you on mercy or on Him?
Look on your life, on all that you possess —
There isn't room for mercy in this mess!
If Fate gave you my daily round of bread,
Then you could call down mercies on your head.
Shame on you, man! Until you turn aside
From power and wealth and all your stinking pride,
There's nothing to be done — turn now, and see
How like a hero you can still break free."

(From *The Conference of Birds*.)

5

My Return to Azerbaijan

Returning from Mashhad to Tehran we took the road which ran south of the Elburz mountains and passed through Shahrud, Damghan and Semnan. But returning from Tehran to Tabriz we took the coastal road along the Caspian Sea. We stopped at Rasht city for a few hours.

Rasht seemed very pleasant and green — full of orange and lemon trees. It had wide streets and attractive bazaars. The people there spoke Gilaki and Persian and had a sweet accent. The people in the shops and restaurants were very helpful and kind. Women worked in some shops and restaurants. In a restaurant where we had fish a pretty Russian girl with long golden hair served us. My parents did not approve of the girl's serving in the shop but they did not say anything. More women could be seen in the streets without a *chador* than in Mashhad, Tabriz and even Tehran. They wore colourful headscarves and dresses. Rasht did not seem to be a religious city; at least I did not see any mullahs in the streets.

Rasht is famous for its rice and my father bought a sack of it which we took back with us to Tabriz. From Rasht we proceeded to Ardabil, an ancient, historical city. In contrast with Rasht, it seemed dominated by religion. I hardly saw any women without a *chador*. Ardabil was the city of the Safavids (the dynasty who ruled Iran from 1500 to 1722), the city of legends.

We stayed in the city and its surroundings for a few days. The heroes of my childhood stories were reborn and came to life by seeing the Ardabil, Talish and Sabalan mountains with their mysterious and beautiful valleys. Sabalan had snow on her peak and hot water on her slopes and in her valleys. The honey of Sabalan is famous all over Iran and I almost lived on honey and *sangak* bread. The honeycomb melted in my mouth and was the colour of sunflowers. My mother was terribly worried about my eating so much honey, and on the last day of our stay there, when we were on our way to Tabriz (and even after we had returned home) she poured yoghurt into my stomach believing that it would counter any detrimental effects of the honey, which she thought likely to cause spots all over my body. In fact I did have some spots, but not as many as my mother had feared: I had them all over my forehead. Children were usually discouraged as much as possible from eating two things — honey and cheese. It was said that cheese made one unintelligent.

The most significant and deep memory which had excited me by seeing Ardabil, Sabalan and Talish mountains was the heroic story of Babak Khurram-Din, or Khurrami, who defended the people of Azerbaijan and fought against the caliphs of Baghdad. (Babak was a follower of Mazdak's ideas and his followers called themselves Khurram-Dinan — the people of happiness or the followers of the religion of happiness. The name 'Khurram' is said to be taken from the name of Mazdak's wife who, after the execution of her husband by Anushirvan (the son of Qobad), continued to spread the message of her husband.)

Ardabil-Mughan and the shores of the Aras river (now the border between Soviet and Iranian Azerbaijan) were the lands of my childhood hero — Babak Khurram-Din. I remember that Izzat used to sit by the field next to his house with his face towards the red mountain of Own-Ali saying, "Babak revolted against the Abbasid caliphs and fought against the strong army of Baghdad for 22 years. It is said the Abbasid's dominion was so vast that the sun never set on it." The story he told me went like this:

Harun al-Rashid had the most sophisticated, entertaining and beautiful court in the world. He copied the emperors of Persia and their court style. In the Abbasids' realm there lived numerous nationalities, who were often discontented living under the suppressive and unjust system. Whenever any chance was created by changing circumstances they revolted and demanded liberty and independence. One of the revolts which disturbed the pleasure and sleep of the Baghdad caliphs was the revolt of the Khurramiyan in Azerbaijan. The movement under Babak's leadership fought against three caliphs: Harun al-Rashid, Ma'mun and Mu'tasim. Babak's struggle against these caliphs took 22 years. (Here, when Izzat was telling his version he used to become excited and often repeat, "The determination of the people of Azerbaijan is great and unmatchable . . .".)

At the beginning of the ninth century Azerbaijan was under attack from different directions: by the Khazars from the north, the Byzantine Empire from the west and the forces of the caliphs from the south. Azerbaijan had to either fight against these forces or accept defeat. The people wanted to fight against their enemies and were looking for a leader. Babak, the son of Merdas (a shepherd), who was born in the village of Bilal-abad, accepted this responsibility.

Meanwhile, there was a deep conflict within the Abbasid Caliphate, particularly between the Arab and Iranian aristocrats. There was great rivalry concerning the future successor to Harun al-Rashid: The Iranians supported Ma'mun, who was born of an Iranian mother, and the Arabs supported Amin. Ma'mun had Amin killed by an Iranian army leader and assumed power. The Iranians dreamed of the old Sasanid period and the Persian Empire, and wished to revert to those days. For this reason the Iranian aristocrats encouraged famous Iranian army leaders such as Maziyar and Afshin, who served Baghdad, to disobey their orders from Baghdad. In spite of the conflict between Iranian and Arab leaders, neither party showed any interest in the revolt in Azerbaijan. In fact, the Iranian aristocrats helped the caliphs to overcome their enemies. Although Baghdad and these Iranian army leaders regarded each other with deep suspicion, Mu'tasim managed to persuade Afshin, who was a remarkable army commander, to fight against Babak. It was Afshin who finally, by sheer trickery and the help of a traitor, succeeded in arresting Babak and his brother Abdullah.

I had several friends who were called Babak. One whom I got to know in later years was a very politically conscious person and supported the Tudeh Party (the Communist party of Iran). The story of Babak was told to children in their homes and to adults in the tea-houses of Azerbaijan. The names of Ardabil, Mughan and those of mountains such as Sabalan and rivers like Aras were legendary names to me. When we arrived at Ardabil and I saw the Sabalan mountain covered by snow on the top and hot springs in its foot, I thought I was sitting next to Izzat and listening to his story of Babak. My imagination was translated into reality. Further north were the Talish mountains where Babak lived, in an area called Bazz.

As the story relates, Bazz was Babak's fortress from where he fought against the caliphs' armies. Babak defeated the army of Harun al-Rashid and Ma'mun and now was fighting against the army of Caliph Mu'tasim under the command of Afshin. Each caliph had promised to give the governorship of Azerbaijan to anyone who would put an end to Babak and the Khorramiyan movement. Azerbaijan was regarded as the flower of the Abbasid realm. Harun al-Rashid had given it to his beloved wife Zubaideh Khatun. My history teacher, once commenting about this, said, "Azerbaijan is not an object to be offered to army chiefs or a king's favourite wife."

Zubaideh used to spend her holidays in Tabriz. It is said that Zubaideh Khatun had once been suffering from a fever and was cured after she spent some time in Tabriz. From that time the city was called *Tab-riz* (the place where fever drops or is cured). I wonder how far this theory is correct! But my schoolteacher also once said, "People do not name or change the name of their city for the sake of a caliph's wife." However, the story I heard as a child tells how Zubaideh Khatun lamented and shed tears about missing the beauty of Azerbaijan and the lovely days of her engagement in Tabriz. Zubaideh, sitting in the harem next to Harun, said to him, "Alas, those happy days of our engagement past. How dear to each other we were in those days. How can I forget those days and not regret? It was at the beginning of our engagement that you gave me Azerbaijan as a gift. Once we went on a journey and walked round the Caspian Sea and returned to Tabriz. While in Tabriz you ordered a spring to be diverted to the front of my summer palace and you named it after me, 'Zubaideh Khatun spring'. This year whenever I drink from that cool and sweet water it reminds me of our deep love for each other. I miss that love and those days, the days without sorrow and worry. I will never forget those bunches of flowers that you used to gather for me while we were walking in the Tabriz countryside . . . Have you forgotten those lovely days and nights?" "How is it possible to forget those sweet memories?" answered Harun al-Rashid.

Zubaideh Khatun had a great influence over Harun al-Rashid and could bewitch him with her beauty and charm. Whenever she wanted to get rid of anyone she disliked she used to use her power over Harun with great might. She wanted to get rid of Jafar Barmaki, the vizier who was supported by the Iranian aristocrats and other influential persons. He had married Harun's sister Abbaseh, but Harun did not let them sleep together in case they had children who would succeed Harun. Jafar used to see Abbaseh secretly and they had two sons who were brought up in secret and kept away from the Caliph. Zubaideh Khatun knew all about this and was worried about Barmaki's influence. One day, Harun was lying with his head on Zubaideh's lap and his arm around her waist. "My darling," he said, "I repeat that God is in Heaven and Harun is on earth. As God has not a partner, so in our kingdom there is no rival for me. No matter whatever the vizier wishes. His station will not exceed that of my dog . . ."

(Here, Mohsen once commented, "Exactly like our country, Iran, where the prime minister is lower than the Shah's dog. It is a shame." "The prime ministers are proud of being even the slaves of the Shah, let alone his dogs. I respect dogs more than those hypocrites and traitors," Ismail added.)

Zubaideh seemed content and said, "I beg the Almighty God for unsurpassed glory for my darling leader. For this reason I have not been able to talk to you about things which have been disturbing me. May I talk to you now?" "What things can cause disturbance in the heart of my darling?" asked Harun. "Jafar!" answered Zubaideh. "Jafar?" asked Harun. "Yes, Jafar," Zubaideh answered. "The same Jafar that you call 'brother'. For years he has been wanting the Caliph's throne. I have no doubt that if he has the opportunity he will make you, the Caliph, and our son Amin, both blind. Do you remember one day when he was sending me to Tabriz and what he said on the way? He said, 'Anyone who trusts his enemy has turned against himself and he who makes enemies happy has killed friends.' Let me tell you frankly that the free hand you have given him has annoyed many of our sincere friends and they have begun to turn away from you. I have even

heard that Abu Nuwas, your special companion, is thinking of going to Egypt
. . . only your palace guards obey Jafar. Is this cunning Iranian worthy of so
much trust? I take oath to Holy Mecca that if they can they would raise the
banner of Blacksmith Kaveh. They have God's plans and thinking mind.
Have you not noticed what remarkable skill they have in playing chess?
Ma'mun, who defeats Abu Hafiz, his chess teacher, has inherited this talent
from his Iranian mother . . . In the chess game of politics you have to be very
careful with Iranians, otherwise we will face great troubles. I tell you this,
that sharing a mother's milk makes two people brothers. Thank Heaven that
the Amin's milk has been separate from that of Ma'mun . . ."

(Here, the storyteller, to the great amusement of his listeners, used to act
as the Caliph — laying his head on an imaginary queen's lap and remaining
silent for a few seconds. Then, to our excitement, he would continue.)

This silence gave Zubaideh, the Queen, encouragement and excited her.
The atmosphere seemed favourable to tell the Caliph about all the people
she disliked and to denigrate them. Now, after having spoken against Jafar,
it was the turn of Alkindi, the great philosopher and influential intellectual
in the court.

(Once, I was telling this story of Harun and Zubaideh to my father and
Ismail. When I reached this point in the story my father said, "Reza Shah is
persecuting the poets and philosophers and so far many have lost their lives.
I wonder if, like Harun al-Rashid, he also is under the influence of his wife?"
And Ismail commented that the priests or mullahs must have had a hand in
the plot against the philosophers and intellectuals, as they wanted to see the
world without a sun and society without thinkers.)

"Does my Crown know," continued Zubaideh, "that if that student of
Plato is not dismissed from the court the Iranians will dominate us? This
unbeliever-scholar has nothing to do except fill the mind of Ma'mun with his
dangerous and untrue thoughts. I myself have heard him several times
saying to Ma'mun, 'The Caliph is making a great mistake when he massacres
the Khurramiyan. If things progress like this, then who is going to pay taxes?
Perhaps the dead will be taxed! With an empty treasury what will happen to
the Caliph's kingdom?' Alkindi was acting as though no one in the court
was more sympathetic to the Caliph than he."

Having said this, Zubaideh's heart was still full of her complaints, plans
and plots — and she wished the night would never end, as she spoke of her
journeys to Tabriz and of Marajil, Ma'mun's mother.

The Caliph did not like to hear all this, especially during such a night, but
Zubaideh being his most beloved wife, he had to listen. On the other hand,
he knew that there was no end to Zubaideh's complaints and jealousy. So
the Caliph turned to Zubaideh and said, "My beautiful angel — I have a
request." "I am obedient to the Leader of believers," answered Zubaideh.
"Why don't you want to talk about us and make me happy with your sweet

words? It is a pity that my beautiful darling would make the pleasant atmosphere of our bedroom cold and sorrowful by these words. Do you remember our engagement days? I used to take you personally to the Tabriz countryside. Have you forgotten the poems that you used to sing for me there?" "No, I have not forgotten."

(As the story was being narrated in the heart of my family one winter night, I recall at this point my brother Ismail ironically sang:

"When we step on Tabriz
The heat makes our love rise;
When we step on Tabriz
We forget all our troubles.

For Babak and his people Azerbaijan was the motherland of culture, creation, living and joy, but to the Caliph and Zubaideh it was just a holiday resort," he added. "The court of Harun must have been covered by beautiful Persian carpets," Ibrahim remarked — and all burst into laughter. "Why don't you sell him some of yours?" Ismail muttered.)

The night ended but Zubaideh's hate for Jafar and Alkindi never ended. On another occasion I heard my teacher defend Alkindi against the argument he should not have worked in the court of Harun al-Rashid. Ismail agreed with him: "Philosophy has been part of life in Iran and philosophers have had links with the people, and often were forced to work in the court."

Alkindi was sympathetic towards Babak and was also a follower of the ideas of Mazdak. He had sent books to Babak and had even visited Babak secretly in his Bazz stronghold. On a very cold winter night, so it is told, Abdullah and Maavieh, two of Babak's brothers, had helped Alkindi, who was an old man, to climb the mountain to Babak's tent amid heavy snow. Babak welcomed him at the tent: "Hail to you, great philosopher!" "Hail to you, great leader," answered Alkindi. "If I am not mistaken, you are Alkindi from the court of the Caliph?" "The great leader is not mistaken," replied Alkindi.

The philosopher seemed exhausted by the cold and looked through his greenish eyes directly into the eyes of Babak. Drops of ice were hanging from his eyelashes. His chin, covered with a beard, was trembling and the few teeth that he had left were chattering against each other. His pock-marked face was weary.

(Here, my mother once said, "Poor old man — why did he trouble to climb the mountain in such a cold winter amid snow? Why did Babak not go and meet him somewhere near the foot of the mountain?" "Perhaps the initiative, as usual, came from the philosopher and Babak was taken by surprise," Ismail responded.)

Babak took the old man's arm and brought him next to the fire, inviting him to sit on a block covered with white sheepskin. "Please sit down. It is warm here — and take off your cloak," said Babak. The philosopher tried to take off his cloak but he was not able — his fingers were frozen. Babak helped him and draped the cloak over a large jar. The old man was aware of the smell of hide and felt in the tent. He understood that Babak was not brought up in palaces. He was a lion, bred and brought up among mountains and fields. Babak's headquarters seemed to him full of wonders. Here there were no perfumed woods as in the court. Instead, burning in the fireplace were thorns and bushes.

Babak also sat on a block of wood, facing the philosopher. The old man's tongue could not yet move and speak because of the cold. His eyes were full of wonder and questions: "This is the great hero, Babak, who has stood against the storm of the Azerbaijan mountains and has fought against the unlimited army of the Caliph?"

Babak, being aware of the value of knowledge and the learned, told himself, "The Caliph is helped to rule by the intelligence and wisdom of these learned men. Six thousand learned men from various nations are gathered round the Caliph. The Caliph has not only usurped the lands of these nations, he has also plundered their brains and spiritual treasures. The knowledge of a learned person is equal to a thousand swordsmen. The ruler who prefers to use his sword rather than his intelligence and insight will face defeat."

The warmth of the fire eventually brought the philosopher round. Sometimes he rubbed his hands together and sometimes he touched his beard, which was now free from ice . . . the servants brought food . . . in Alkindi's eyes Babak seemed more dignified and awesome than his fellow philosophers. The warmth and food broke the silence of the philosopher and he started the conversation with a smile: "If wisdom and imagination ruled in the world, then swords would have never been used."

Babak nodded his head in agreement: "Unfortunately the rulers' ambitions and whims supersede their wisdom and imagination."

The philosopher wanted to learn more about the outlook of this mountain leader and so he asked, "Among the leaders in history which one is dearer to you? Ispartakos [Spartacus], who was the leader of the oppressed? Or what about Alexander Magdooni [of Macedon]?"

"I hate all cruel conquerors," Babak answered, and continued in a serious tone, "Caliston [Callisthenes], Alexander's companion, has called him 'guardian of the world', but in my opinion Alexander enjoyed destruction more than construction. He cannot be regarded in the lands of the Orient as a blessing. Alexander set the libraries on fire. He burned the holy book of Zoroastrians. Is it possible to approve of this kind of destruction? What did Alexander offer to the people of the East except torture, hunger and

Babak's mountain stronghold.

deprivation . . . ? Caliston is mistaken with regard to Alexander. He was neither the guardian of the world nor a learned man or prophet."

(My teacher once said, "The West has painted aggressors as great heroes in their history books and films and does not respect the feelings of other people. Even Reza Shah is depicted as a great hero by some Western Orientalists." When I came to Britain in 1960 I read several books in English about the Persian royal family and Reza Shah. I compared my childhood impressions of Reza Shah with what the books said about him — and I found a gulf between reality and fantasy. In fact I found many "Orientalists" to be unsympathetic and cynical in their attitudes towards the peoples and their culture. I wondered why, if they were so prejudiced against other peoples and their culture, they should bother to study such subjects at all and regard themselves specialists of a culture or society without even being able to speak the language of the same people.)

Alkindi liked intelligent and enlightened people. Babak, right from the first instance, had made a good impression on the philosopher. If he could, he would have preferred to stay with Babak rather than the Caliph. The philosopher seemed to regret having mentioned the name of Alexander. Babak sensed this, and changed the subject by offering a cup of drink.

After a while, Alkindi started talking again: "Does his Leadership think that he will be able to stand against Islam and the Muslims' Caliph?"

Babak, with a meaningful smile on his lips, looked at the philosopher's face with his oak-coloured eyes and, seeing him waiting for an answer, said, "My great philosopher and honourable guest ought well to know that I have not been and I am not against Islam or Arabs. I do not know whether you know that there are many Muslims among my close friends, who carry out their religious duties freely. Many of the Khurramiyan have even helped them to build their mosques. Our struggle is against oppressors and plunderers, not the ordinary poor people. Our struggle is against those who use the Quran and Islam as a means for domination and oppression. I tell you frankly, I am fighting against the Abbasid caliphs, not against Arabs or Muslims . . ."

The philosopher interrupted Babak: "Is it possible for the Leader to clarify what he means by plundering, oppression and disregarding human lives? What is the difference between the Caliph's army and the Khurramiyan army, who both have sent human beings into a whirlpool of destruction? Both armies kill and destroy cities, villages and crops. Both offer only destruction, calamity and tears. Ma'mun wants to expand and strengthen his kingdom under the name of Islam and you want to do the same under the ideas of Mazdak."

When Alkindi had finished, Babak seemed hurt. He stood up and said, "Does the great philosopher not see any difference between the war which is for selfish ambition and greed and the war which is for the defence of human dignity and the right to live freely on one's own land? What can one do when a great thinker like you considers us as fighters and interested in killing? I can understand how much money our enemies have spent in order to change opinions against us. They have spread unjust rumours that we enjoy killing . . . but lies and cunning will not last for ever. The people cannot be fooled for ever. Victory and success will come with the truth — and this will be achieved by human beings. Everyone has a duty to struggle against lies until their deathbed. By casting out lies from the world the rule of truth will start. On such a day all wars, killings, oppression and exploitation will disappear and will be replaced by peace and happiness for all . . ."

The philosopher felt himself weak in the face of Babak's analytical mind. "Truly this man of the mountains must be an extraordinary person," he said to himself.

When Babak's army was defeated he was imprisoned by Afshin and brought to the court of Caliph Mu'tasim. Alkindi was sitting on the left of the Caliph and thought back to his meeting with Babak and felt sad. He, in fact, advised the Caliph to spare Babak's life, but Sheikh Ismail (the court priest) encouraged the Caliph to kill him. The event of Babak's execution was related by Muhammad Awfi in his *Javame al-Hikayat* (his collected stories):

Ibn Sayyah related, "when Babak Khurrami was imprisoned, I and a few others were his defenders. We were about to go to the Caliph and Babak was advised that if he were taken to the Caliph and if he were to be asked by him, 'Are you Babak?', he should say, 'Yes, Oh Leader of believers, I am your slave and have sinned and hope that you, Leader of believers, will forgive me and will not kill me.' When Babak was taken to the Caliph, he was asked, 'Are you Babak?' Babak answered 'Yes' and kept quiet. We looked meaningfully at him and pressed his hand to tell him to say what he had instructed him to say. Indeed, he said nothing. He neither grimaced nor did the colour of his face change".

Khaja Nizam al-Mulk, the famous vizier of the Saljuq Turks wrote of another scene from Babak's execution, which might show the wonderful spirit of this revolutionary shepherd. It must be added that Khaja Nizam al-Mulk, who belonged to an aristocratic family and also believed in a strong central government, was hostile to these movements. Nevertheless his record is interesting:

When one of his hands was cut off he dipped his other hand in his blood and rubbed it on his face. Mu'tasim said to Babak, "Oh dog! What is this action?" He answered, "There is a logic in this. You wanted to cut off my hands and feet, and people's faces are red because of their blood. When the blood disappears from the face it becomes pale. I have made my face red with blood, so as soon as the blood has drained from my body you ought not to say that I was pale because of fear."

(Quoted by Ehsan Tabari in *The World Outlook and Social Movements in Iran*.)

After this the Caliph tortured and killed Babak and hung him in a place which was later called "the tomb of Babak". For many years the body of this hero remained there. Later on Mazyar, another of his heroic fellow countrymen, was hanged in the same place. Caliph Mu'tasim, in order to silence the people of Iran and extinguish any spark of revolt, ordered that Babak's embalmed head be taken and displayed all round his kingdom.

Babak met the same destiny as Mazdak, yet the revolt in Iran never did die down. From the medieval age up to the Constitutional Revolution of 1905 many movements took place. Khusraw Gulsurkhi, the Iranian revolutionary poet, who was executed by the Shah in 1974, wrote about Babak in his *Selected Poems*:

Where is the redness [fire] of the cries of Babak Khurram?
Where is a free Kaveh once more?

. . .

A revolutionary eagle flies within me,
It has never uttered a word of weariness,
It has never kow-towed to authority,
Don't ask me to climb down,
Let no one see the pale face of Babak . . .

It was the middle of winter when we returned to Tabriz. Everywhere was covered with snow and everything was frozen in the garden. It was 20 degrees below zero!

Humai and Izzat and their daughter Fatima were in my parents' house. I was so pleased to see them. I had particularly missed playing with Fatima. My parents had brought them presents: material for Humai to have a dress and *chador* made and Izzat a suit. Fatima had golden earrings, which she loved.

Humai wore a cotton *chador*, decorated with pretty patterns of flowers. She liked it, but I, as a child, had mixed feelings towards the *chador*. On the one hand I liked it when I used to lie in my mother or nurse's bosom and was covered by such soft material. In summer I used to sleep under it and cover myself from the hot sun or flies. However, I also associated the *chador* with several unpleasant experiences. My mother and sisters used to disappear behind their *chador* whenever a strange person — cousins or male friends — visited us. This sudden transformation disturbed and annoyed me because as a child I did not like to be separated from them, especially so suddenly and unexpectedly. I disliked it even more when I used to walk in the street with my mother or Humai (also at times with my sisters) all heavily veiled in black outdoor *chadors*. I still remember how my mother and sisters were terrified to go out with a *chador* during Reza Shah's rule. This was forbidden, and the police used to unveil women by force and sometimes even hit them. Imagine a mother being treated like this in front of her child. I remember one occasion when I was going to the bath-house with my mother. We had come out of our house and were walking towards the main road. Just before we reached it my mother suddenly let go of my hand and ran away, leaving me behind. I was surprised and frightened. Looking around I saw a policeman approaching. I was terrified and ran back home and waited for my mother. After an hour or so she returned and explained how she had seen the policeman and ran and sheltered in the house of one of the neighbours. She still looked pale and shaken. I felt angry inside against the police but I did not understand the situation. To a child its mother's reaction to the surrounding world and events is very important; it can create security and peace in a child or disturb and destroy him. I was disturbed by seeing my mother being frightened.

Looking back (although I have always been against the *chador*), the way in which Reza Shah, during his reign from 1925 to 1941, tried to forbid it being worn seems as crude and cruel as Ayatollah Khomeini's imposing its use on Iranian women since the 1979 Revolution. Both policies (indeed both regimes) seem to me to be two different sides of the same coin. I, as a child, was terrified by Reza Shah's police and Iranian children today are terrified of Khomeini's *Pasdar* (revolutionary guards). Much later, when I was arrested by the SAVAK, I did not think about imprisonment, torture or even death. I thought about my mother. I did not want her to see me in a situation which might terrify her or fill her with grief. This was the weakest spot within me. I tried to hide all bad news from my mother, and even my nurse.

To explain to you the things which were happening around me at this time, but of which I saw very little and understood practically nothing, it seems appropriate to give a brief outline of the historical background.

It was a time of great change in Iran — and the rest of the world. I do not really remember my parents speaking about the events at the time, though I am sure that what they said to each other was bitterly critical of Reza Shah. I am indebted to one of my former students at Edinburgh University, Dr Najileh Khandagh, whose PhD thesis "The Political Parties in Iran 1941-1947, with Special Reference to the Democratic Party of Azerbaijan", has provided the basis for the account which follows.

By the 1930s, Reza Shah had established himself as an absolute ruler and tried to consolidate his position financially by improving the tax system, monopolising foreign trade and establishing a state bank to replace the existing British-controlled bank. The country's wealth was being accumulated in the hands of a small minority, among which Reza Shah was the leader. At the time of the coup d'état which brought him into power in 1921, and in 1925 when he declared himself as the Shah of Iran, Reza Shah possessed neither land nor money; but by the time of his abdication he was one of the wealthiest Iranian landowners and one of the richest men in the world.

Also by the time of his abdication, all the major landowners, tribal leaders and politicians who had opposed him, and all the leaders of political parties such as Taqi Irani, had been killed, imprisoned or expelled.

During his reign Reza Shah wished to reduce the British influence in Iran, although it was this that had placed him in power. In order to do so he received the support of Germany. German industry and commerce was introduced to the Iranian economy on an increasingly large scale and Germany became the main recipient of Iranian exports in the pre-war years.

By 1939, Germany's importance in Europe had risen dramatically; it had also established a secret fifth column within Iran. Encouraged by Germany's strength, Reza Shah entered into an agreement which allocated to Germany an increased measure of raw materials and the right to build a railway through Iran, as well as to use Iranian air space. By 1941, Germany's influence in the Iranian governmental institutions and even its army was widespread. Furthermore, Germany commanded emissaries and agents, especially in the north, who were capable of carrying out terrorist activities or sabotage operations in Soviet Azerbaijan.

In order to fully utilize Iranian territory against its enemies, namely Britain and the Soviet Union, Germany wished Iran to enter World War II and therefore put forward this proposal on 17 August 1941. Despite the promise of arms, Iran claimed neutrality, which led Germany to plan a military coup within Iran which would bring its policies into line.

After the invasion of the Soviet Union on 22 June 1941, the Soviets warned Iran three times of the danger of German espionage activities. On 16 August the Soviet Union and Britain handed a formal note to the Iranian government, demanding the suppression of German activity in Iran. In return they promised to respect Iranian independence and neutrality, and to work towards developing friendly relations. They conceded that Iran might keep those few Germans who were doing genuinely important technological work. The following week Iran replied that the number of German residents in Iran was not as great as was supposed and the Iranian government believed that the expulsion of Germans from Iran without any logical reason was against the neutrality of the country.

The Soviet Union and Britain were not satisfied with this reply. They were unable to make Reza Shah understand the immediate danger, both for himself and for them, and could no longer afford to allow this danger to develop unchecked. They had no choice but action. At 4 a.m. on 25 August 1941, Allied troops crossed the border and attacked Iran by land, sea and air. The British entered at three points from the Persian Gulf to the Turkish border. The Soviet Union struck in three areas, in the north-west pushing towards Tabriz and Bandar Anzali, and in the north-east advancing towards Mashhad.

Reza Shah knew that he could not rely on immediate German assistance, but he continued to believe in Germany's final victory in the war. In an effort to maintain his political position for such an eventuality, he commanded his troops to resist. But this action effectively sealed his own fate, for the Iranian army quickly disintegrated and the Allies managed to occupy all the important centres in the south (British) and north (Soviet) of the country.

On 16 September 1941 Reza Shah was forced to abdicate, partly due to Allied pressure and partly on account of a lack of popular support. He was deported to Mauritius, then to Johannesburg, where he died in 1944. His son Muhammad-Reza Shah took his place.

Although my father and his friends opposed the Soviet/British invasion of Iran, nevertheless they seemed pleased that Iran was freed from the dictatorship of Reza Shah and the influence of Nazi Germany.

Besides my memory of my mother's escaping from the police, I have three other memories of this time. The first two come from before the fall of Reza Shah and convey something about him, while the third memory may be from just before or just after his last days in power.

There was a police officer in our district called Kazim Khan. He was well known for his loyalty to Reza Shah (and was very strict towards the women who wore the *chador*). He was a fearful character. He used to put on his uniform, and decorations, and stand outside the alley which led to his house. He was truly a symbol of Reza Shah's dictatorship and a manifestation of his policies among the people.

One hot summer's day, perhaps just before the end of Reza Shah's rule, Kazim Khan, as usual wearing his uniform and well armed with a long sword and pistol, was standing in our district at midday. My father and I were walking past and my father, greeting him, said, "Kazim Khan, why are you standing under such a hot sun? Do you think Reza Shah is watching you from above?" There was no response from Kazim Khan except a grim look.

My father used to mention the names of three people in his conversations with his friends: the pro-British Sayyid Zia Tabatabai, who led the coup d'état against Ahmad Shah and became prime minister in 1921; Davar, Reza Shah's minister of justice and Mukhtari, his terrifying police chief. It was said that Mukhtari (indeed, by Reza Shah's order) had eliminated a number of intellectuals, poets and political thinkers. I remember I had heard of the assassination of Mirzadeh Ishqi (1893-1924), who was an outstanding literary and political figure. I had learned about him from different people, notably my history teacher, Mr Rezai. He used to say that Ishqi was one of the most outspoken and revolutionary poets of the Constitutional Revolution era. He also used to mention Mirza Muhammad Taqi Bahar (the Poet Laureate, 1880-1951), who came from Mashhad and was a close friend of Ishqi. Bahar later gave up his court career and, with profound conviction, entered the service of the Constitutional Revolution.

Ishqi was born in Hamadan, in the north-west of Iran near Kurdistan. His father, in fact, was called Abulqasim Kurdistani (Abulqasim from Kurdistan). Ishqi knew Farsi, Turkish and French. He started writing poetry at an early age and was editor of a famous newspaper, *The Twentieth Century*.

Mr Rezai explained how Ishqi had opposed the 1919 treaty between Britain and the pro-British Vusuq al-Dowlah (Prime Minister 1918-1920) and Sayyid Zia Tabatabai. He wrote against Reza Khan's rise to power. One of Ishqi's poems became famous and is widely believed to have cost the poet his life. It is a humorous satire in which the figure of His Excellency Jonbol (John Bull) appears with a donkey, which represents the Republicanism of Reza Khan. The poem appeared in the last issue of Ishqi's newspaper, with a cartoon on the front page depicting His Excellency Jonbol mounted on the donkey of Republicanism drawing near to a jar full of syrup which Jonbol intends to eat. The caption warns that Jonbol has already feasted on the goodness of the country and now wants to plunder Iran further using the popular guise of Republicanism.

The poem tells the following story:

There is a village in the vicinity of Kurdistan called Qasim-abad.

The events which I relate happened in that village.

There was a village headman called Kaka Abdin.

He was in charge of the people in that area.

He had a huge jar of syrup which he had saved up and acquired by his own effort.

There was a bad thief called "Yassi" who continually troubled the people in the village.

He was Kaka Abdin's neighbour.

Heaven save us from inconsiderate neighbours.

Whenever Abdin left his house

Yassi would quickly enter his door

And sit by the jar of syrup.

He kept sweetening his mouth with that syrup.

As this action was repeated so the syrup decreased, until one day the village headman noticed how much of the syrup had gone.

He carefully examined all round the jar until he noticed a strange footprint round the jar.

He followed this footprint here and there

Until he reached the gate of Yassi.

He called Yassi from his house and demanded "Why do you trouble your neighbour in this way?"

That cunning syrup-thief Yassi stretched his neck out of the door.

Kaka asked him:

"What right have you to eat my food?

I have saved the syrup for my own use."

The culprit was just about to deny everything when Abdin said,

"Look on the ground, and see clearly your own footprints."

Realising that the game was up, Yassi could do nothing but say he was sorry.

"Yes, I did it Kaka, but excuse me.

Forgive me for the sake of Hazrat Mola[1]

If I do such a deed again

Then banish me from this land".

Soft-hearted Abdin out of pity forgave the crime and Yassi felt ashamed.

However, some time after this conversation

Greed overcame Yassi once again.

With nothing sweet to taste, he lost control.

His sweet tooth stole his patience and calm.

Aware that he had made a bargain with Abdin not to steal his syrup again

That wicked person pondered and then decided to use a trick.

He went and mounted a donkey and rode the donkey into Abdin's house.

He put his hand into the jar and ate as much syrup as he wanted.

He satisfied his greed while on the back of the donkey and, still mounted, made his way out of the house.

Kaka returned and went to the jar to check the syrup.

He soon saw that something was amiss.

[1] Imam Ali — the cousin and son-in-law of the Prophet Muhammad.

The syrup in the jar had gone down.

He carefully checked round the jar but only saw the donkey's hoof prints.

He lowered his head into the jar and clearly saw Yassi's hand print.

Abdin was amazed. He didn't know what to make of it and who to blame — the donkey or Yassi.

He talked to himself and lamented.

"Oh God, who has done this?

If it's the donkey, he hasn't got a hand to leave marks in my pot!

If it's Yassi, then Yassi hasn't got hooves!"

Abdin hit his head with his hands and shouted out his bewilderment.

"The hand prints are the hands of Yassi and the footprints are those of a donkey. I can't figure this out!"

I am telling this story so that present-day children can understand that if someone wants to mislead others about what he is doing, he changes his feet into hooves.

Anyone who has goods in his house

Also has a neighbour like Yassi.

My dear friends, our Yassi is none other than His Excellency Jonbol, that is, the English.

Jonbol always does the work of Yassi.

He does it through diplomacy.

He sees our country as desirable and has cheated us.

He thinks that Iran can be plundered and eaten like syrup.

England had made a treaty with Vusuq al-Dowlah, then saw that it was not fruitful.

The Vusuq government accepted a bribe from England but failed to carry out England's plans.

When England became disappointed in Vusuq

She caused a coup d'état which disturbed Iran.

This was done through Sayyid Zia . . .

The coup d'état did not make England's mouth sweet, nor did this henna make her hands colourful.

England soon realised that what is done openly is immediately spoiled by the nation; recoiling from the name of England, the people quickly disclosed her aims:

Accordingly England decided "I had better succeed in such a way that my name is kept out of it."

Pondering for some time, England chose the path of Yassi.

She decided that "I had better put forward the idea of Republicanism for discussion

And thus take the bridle in my hand.

I can use the people who want a Republic like a donkey and do better than I have done before.

When the idea of Republicanism is raised, Iranians follow like donkeys, so I will put hay in their path and everyone will come under my control.

If everything goes well I shall ride on them, lure them all away and empty the jar of syrup. Republicanism is the latest thing, the sign of modernity appears on its forehead."

England secretly plays the part of Yassi of Iran. She eats the syrup while the donkey is blamed.

For this reason she cooked up something with the "Socialists" and thought it
   better to go into one sack with them.
She mounted on the donkey to steal the syrup and receive five million pounds.
She put the sign of Republicanism on the donkey and secretly stretched her hand
   into the jar of syrup.
Suddenly the intelligent Iranians became suspicious of both donkey and rider.
They started to protest: "What sort of Republic is this? What an odd appearance!
   The feet are Republican and the hands are English!
Catch the thief! Catch the thief, Oh Police!
My people, this Republic is false."
Suddenly the people hissed it away.
The donkey became scared and ran off.
The donkey neither succeeded with money or force.
The syrup remained and the gentleman became pale.

Before his rise to power and before he made himself a shah, Reza Khan
(as he was known at the time) had put forward the idea of Republicanism,
but later gave up the idea. Many times I had heard my father and others say
that "England had put Reza Khan in power".

Another person I remember people talking about was Dr Taqi Arani. He
was a physics professor, born in Tabriz, brought up in Tehran and graduated
from a German university. He was one of 53 intellectuals who were arrested
and imprisoned by Reza Shah's police in 1937 for having an interest in
Marxist theory and discussing the ideas of Socialism and Communism.
They were put on trial according to Reza Shah's law of 1931 which forbade
this. Arani's defence and his challenge of Reza Shah's laws were well known.
At the trial, I heard, he had compared the tribunal to the Nazi kangaroo
courts, and declared that the 1931 law violated the constitutional right of
free expression. Arani received a sentence of ten years' solitary confinement
and died in prison after 16 months. Many believed that he was murdered by
Ahmadi, the prison doctor of Mukhtari's police. Arani, besides being a
successful scientist, was a philosopher, literary critic and founder and editor
of *Donya* (*The World*) magazine, which later became the ideological journal
of the Tudeh Party (the Communist party of Iran). Dr Arani became the
spiritual leader of the Tudeh Party, which was formed in 1941.

At the same time I had heard Muhammad Kamali (Baji-jan's husband)
talking about the Lahuti movement against Reza Khan in 1921. In Tabriz,
Major Lahuti, the commander of the local gendarmerie, had rallied his
troops to challenge Reza Khan (1921-1925). Lahuti was also a revolutionary
poet in his own right. Muhammad Kamali had a copy of his book of poetry
and used to read for us. I only remember the following lines:

   I am writing for the happy moment of the red wine,
   When from the East Revolution rises with the red sunshine.

Happy that day from the blood of the rich
The ocean of Revolution becomes full of red bubbles.
Happy that moment that, with the power of the Hammer and Sickle,
The peasant puts the red rope on the king's neck,
It is obligatory to wash in the blood of priest (mullah), police and king
In the religion of Revolution according to the holy script of the red book.

Lahuti was from Kirmanshah, in the north-west of Iran and part of Kurdistan, and rose against Reza Khan but did not succeed. He escaped first to Turkey and then to the Soviet Union.

My third memory may be from just before or just after Reza Shah's last days in power. It must have been between our return from Mashhad and the arrival of the Allied forces, when I first became aware that Iran under Reza Shah was threatened (with subjection by the Nazis, with Reza Shah's help or, if necessary, without it).

My memories of the Second World War, though limited, are very distinct. We lived in the basement of our house during this period. At night we would light an oil lamp and draw thick black curtains. We had been told that the Germans might attack at any time. Either the Turks or the Germans dropped bombs in several places in Tabriz: their aim was to cut off the supply line between the south of Iran (the Persian Gulf) and the Soviet Union. I remember, too, a stream of trucks loaded with supplies heading towards Jolfa (a border town between Soviet Azerbaijan and Iran) and then to the battlefront. These trucks passed day and night along the banks of the Mehran rud (Mehran river) which passes through Tabriz. The left side of the river was allocated only for these trucks.

There were Russian soldiers in Tabriz at this time. I even saw some women soldiers. The relationship between the people of Tabriz and the Russian soldiers was friendly. The people offered them cigarettes and fruit and sometimes food. The soldiers seemed to have a hard life: I could not imagine where they slept. There were some people, however, who supported the Germans. Swastikas were to be seen here and there in the city. There were ideological followers of Nazism in the Iranian army, and Reza Shah himself was said to be sympathetic with Germany.

Both the German and Allied planes used to drop propaganda pamphlets on Tabriz. Sometimes the pamphlets did not succeed in scattering as they were meant to and once a bundle of papers dropped in our garden. As soon as the children saw these planes appear in the sky they would rush out of the houses and wait to catch the floating papers before they touched the ground. This became a popular game during the war and continued for several months.

Bread and water were soon in short supply but the people helped each other. My father opened our door to those who needed water and sometimes he gave bread and charcoal to the poor. The workers and the poor suffered the most during the war. My father hated the war because he lost his carpets in the Baghdad depot. It had caught fire, we were told. Many merchants, however, made fortunes during the war.

My great ambition was to see one of the German planes shot down, to get inside it and try to fly it. I had dreamed several times that a plane had crashed in our orchard and the pilot and the plane had both survived unscathed. Then I intended to climb inside the plane. I felt pleased that our home was not damaged and my family was safe. The war influenced my games as well as my dreams; like other children, I made toy guns, planes and soldiers and played war games.

The adults would talk constantly about the war and would tell each other that the German army was advancing. This caused mixed feelings: some wanted the Germans to win and some wished for a Russian defeat over Germany, but the majority wanted peace, especially as Iran — unwillingly — had been turned into a bridging supply route for the Allies. Ordinary people suffer the most during any war. The peoples of Iran and Iraq, for example, have suffered the most during the past eight years of the current war with each other.

After we returned to Tabriz from Mashhad my brother Ibrahim and I were sent to the *maktab* (a traditional and religious school). I had already completed my first year of primary school at Mulavi school at Davachi Bazaar, but for my brother this was his first year at school. My father had decided to send us to the *maktab*, as I learned later, in order to make us learn the Persian language, to understand the Quran in Arabic and to give us a sound knowledge of our religion.

The *maktab* was about two kilometres away from my parents' house and we used to leave home at 8 a.m. and not return until 5 p.m. We walked there and back: my brother always dawdled and every few metres I used to turn back and urge him to walk a little faster otherwise we would be late. Sometimes we chatted or shared the dried fruit which our mother had put in our pockets. Otherwise we both walked solemnly and thoughtfully, stopping perhaps and gazing into a *cheshma* in the bottom of a well which was on our way. There were many openings to this *cheshma*, but most of them were covered by a large stone. The depth of the shaft to water level was not deep; at least not as deep as the *cheshma* at the Davachi Bazaar on the way to my grandfather's house. In the *maktab* itself, the *cheshma*, as in my grandfather's house, ran close to the surface and in order to keep it clean and prevent the children from falling in it was enclosed by a room-like place which Mirza Ibrahim, my teacher, and his family used as a cooling room. The room was almost always kept locked and I was always curious to find out what was kept there. Once or twice it was accidentally left open and I peeped inside and saw only some fruit and food stored in the corner.

The road between my parents' house and the *maktab* was made up of dozens of twisting alleys. Each alley had something interesting to look at or watch for hours. At the beginning of our journey, just a few minutes walk from our house, there was a huge fruit shop with all kinds of fruit either obtained direct from the orchards or from fruit markets. There were various colourful grapes, many kinds of peaches (red, white or green, small and large), all kinds of melons and water-melons, red, black and yellow cherries — all these, in the mild morning sunshine looked most appealing and tempting for a child. The coming and going of the customers and the arrival of mothers with baskets to buy fruit and vegetables always caught the attention of Ibrahim and me. We would stop and watch them for a few minutes every day — and sometimes longer, which made us late for school.

Another shop which we found fascinating was a large grocery shop. In the afternoons we would stand and watch as the milk was delivered there, carried by mules and camels from the surrounding villages. We were interested to see how large containers of milk were lifted down from the mules and camels by strong-looking villagers who wore special hats and clothes. The containers were carried into a yard next to the grocer's shop. Once, while Ibrahim was standing across the road and watching this, I peeped inside the yard to find out what they were doing with the milk. I saw a few huge pots standing on wood-burning fires and the milk being poured into the pots and then stirred. In other corners of the yard, piled high, were stacks of blue earthenware bowls. I later discovered that they were yogurt containers and that the grocer made yogurt from the milk. In fact Masha Quli's (the grocer) yogurt was extremely popular in the district.

Our day at the *maktab* started at about nine o'clock, and we sat on the floor in a room waiting for Mirza Ibrahim to come up from the ground floor where he and his family lived. The house had two floors: the ground floor comprised two bedrooms, a sitting-room and kitchen; on the first floor were a large room which was used as our classroom and a smaller room where bedding was stored, as our teacher had a rest at midday. In front of the building there was a fairly large yard completely enclosed by a high wall, with the gate situated at the corner of the yard. We used to enter the yard, walk along and go into the house, passing through a vestibule before climbing the twisting steps up to the classroom.

The classroom had a large window which was overshadowed by a tall mulberry tree. Mirza sat on a stool next to the window with a desk in front of him and a stick on his right. All the walls round the room had a number of cavities which were used as shelves for books and other things. The students sat on cushions around the room, leaning against the wall. My mother had made our cushions, as we all had to provide our own. My brother and I used to sit next to Mirza's desk, and so were under constant surveillance.

There were 25 boys in the class and only one girl (Miss Taj), who was older than us and a neighbour of the teacher. I remember her as being a very pleasant girl who would sit, without her *chador*, in front of the window. She left the *maktab* before we did. The other students came from a variety of backgrounds. One was called Gholam and his father worked in his brother's butcher's shop. Gholam always sat next to the door: he must have felt cold in winter because of the draught (the stove, which was wood-burning, was in the middle of the room). I felt sorry for him because Mirza did not treat him kindly. He used to call us one by one to sit in front of his desk and show him our homework, read some passages and receive a fresh lesson. But when it was Gholam's turn Mirza used to call him Mr Gulat (a sarcastic way of addressing a person and somewhat belittling). This made me unhappy and rather angry, especially when Mirza used to hit Gholam with the stick, as I liked Gholam. He was a kind and gentle boy but did not wear smart new clothes and his shoes were always torn.

There were also two brothers, Ali and Hamid, whose father had a drug-store and lived in the neighbourhood. Mirza treated them politely, as he did another boy, Ismail, who was older than me and wanted to be a mullah. I did not like this boy because he tried to impose his opinion and personality on me. In fact one day I fought with him outside the *maktab* and if Ibrahim had not bitten Ismail's toe from behind, which hurt him badly, I would not have matched him. Later on he left me alone and appeared to respect me.

We had five hours of classes and plenty of breaks. We took our lunches with us to the *maktab* and would eat them in the yard during the summer and in the classroom in winter. We would take meat, cheese, fruit and bread; one or two other students did the same but the rest either went without a proper lunch or would go home for it. I never saw Gholam eating a proper lunch. Our teacher would eat with his wife and son. We often knew what Mirza was going to have for his lunch either by the smell of cooking or by actually seeing his wife preparing it in the yard.

The middle of the yard was full of different fruit trees — fig, plum, mulberry and apple. There were also vines, which hung over the surrounding walls — often laden with grapes. Between the walls and the middle part of the yard was a paved area where we played and ran about, and there was also a small playground at the bottom, next to the *cheshma* and small toilet.

Mirza did not like the students to use his toilet and so we were only allowed to use a pit for urinating. He was afraid that the cesspit would be filled too quickly if everybody used it for other needs besides urinating, so when we needed to go to the toilet we were sent home. One afternoon my brother Ibrahim urgently needed the toilet and Mirza duly sent him home.

Since my grandparents had recently moved nearby Ibrahim decided to go there. By the time he reached the house he had dirtied himself and my grandfather, treating him kindly, had asked him his reason for leaving school. When Ibrahim told him he said, "My heavens, I, as a grown-up person cannot control myself for a few minutes, let alone a child — Mirza must be a fool." This incident made me angry, too, as I did not like to see my brother in that humiliating situation.

We attended the *maktab* for almost three years, by which time I had learnt how to read the Quran and read and write the Persian language. But Mirza's treatment of Gholam and his sending my brother home to go to the toilet, as well as a number of similar things had filled me with anger against him. I was looking for an excuse to leave but did not want to do anything silly and give him the chance to humiliate me either by punishing me in front of my classmates and my brother or by telling my father.

Nawruz was ahead and Mirza was expecting his New Year present from the students as well as his monthly fees. He liked three things (besides money) most: tobacco for his pipe (usually a western-type pipe but with a longer stem), henna for his beard (for dyeing it red or brown) and all kinds of dried fruit. Two weeks before Nawruz my parents prepared a tray of dried fruit and told my brother and I to take it to Mirza and then ask for permission to leave the school at midday as my father was going to take us to a bath-house. We took the tray, which was covered with a white tablecloth and tied.

On our way to the *maktab* we passed a *dalan*, a short, covered passage which connected one alley to another. Both sides of this passage were surrounded by quiet gardens and walled houses. Why, I suggested to my brother, should we bother going to the *maktab* for such a short period and then return home? It would be better to sit near this *dalan* and see what Mirza's present was. My brother agreed with me, so we opened out the tablecloth and found all kinds of dried fruit on the tray. We decided to try just one of each kind and then take the rest to Mirza. Of course, by the time we had done not much was left on the tray except raisins and nuts — which we could not possibly give to Mirza as a New Year present. After some deliberation we decided it would be better to divide the rest and fill our pockets and return the tray and cloth to our parents with thanks from Mirza. So this is what we did. We went to the bath-house with our father and did not worry at all about what had happened. In fact I felt pleased that Mirza had not received the present.

A few weeks passed. One evening my father returned home as usual and we had our dinner. He then called me and asked about Mirza's Nawruz present. I soon realised that he must have met Mirza in the street and learnt that he had not received the present. As a result of this episode I was punished by my father; in the *maktab* I also found that Mirza's attitude towards me had changed. He treated me in similar sarcastic manner to that of my classmate Gholam.

By this time the summer holidays were approaching. One day, making some excuse, Mirza tried to hit me with his stick in front of my brother and the others, but I grabbed hold of his stick and broke it by twisting it. This cheered up the students but made Mirza very angry. I immediately packed together my books, took up my cushion and walked out. My brother followed me. We did not return to *maktab* again, but were sent to a newly opened semi-religious school called Elmieh. This school was a modern one and had been opened by a leading ayatollah in Tabriz when the Democratic Party of Azerbaijan, headed by Pishavari, formed a government in Azerbaijan in 1945 and the Persian language taught in school was replaced by Azerbaijani.

There were several teachers at Elmieh School in addition to the headmaster, Mr Naqavi. The building was fairly new, with several classrooms, and catered for both primary and secondary level. But the medium of instruction, contrary to the state schools, was still Persian. I was in the fourth year primary and there were about 40 students in our classroom, mainly from a commercial middle-class background. There were hardly any students from poor families. The school was private and charged monthly fees.

Elmieh School was situated at the entrance of the Jami' Mosque and next to the *karvan-sarais* full of sacks of dried fruit where I used to stop and play on my way to visit my grandparents with my mother. Most of the students there were well-dressed and looked healthy with rosy cheeks. Some of them were so handsome that they had attracted the attention of some other students and our Quran teacher, Mr Ahrabi. The Quran teacher's special attention towards the good-looking students had aroused the jealousy and anger of other students in the classroom. The teacher was not so friendly with me, though I considered myself just as handsome — yet I did not wear nice clothes.

The students had discovered that Ahrabi was afraid of mice, so one day one of the students, Mustafa, who was rather taller than the rest, brought three mice into our classroom in his pocket. When Mr Ahrabi was sitting and talking in his customary self-satisfied manner, Mustafa freed the mice and let them run under the desks in the middle of the classroom. Some of the students, being aware of Mustafa's plan started shouting, "There are mice! There are mice! Catch the mice!" Meanwhile two of the mice darted in front of the teacher's desk. As soon as he saw them Mr Ahrabi jumped up and fled the classroom. All burst into laughter.

After half an hour Mr Ahrabi returned, with a long stick in his hand. His face was red and he was pretending that he was not afraid, but he was upset because the class had been interrupted and intended to find out and punish the student who was responsible. He asked everyone but no one gave away Mustafa, who was looking rather pale. Mr Ahrabi seemed frustrated and angry. In order to save his face he made the monitor, Babak, a scapegoat by dismissing him and replacing him with another student, Mr Golabi, who only kept his job for a few days because he could not control the class. Babak was asked to resume his responsibility. At first he refused but the rest of the class made him change his mind.

Mr Ahrabi ended up in a special religious school training to be a mullah and some years later I saw him in the robes of a mullah. Many of the students in this class later became merchants and some went to university or became civil servants. Mr (later Dr) Golabi became a successful lecturer at Tabriz University and after the Iranian Revolution of 1979 he turned out to be the right hand of the Ayatollah's regime in the University and the city of Tabriz. He took an active part in the dismissal of both students and teachers from the university and administered important appointments in the Town Council. It is said that he also had a friendly relationship with the Shah's regime.

I met him at the University of Tabriz in 1978, almost 33 years since we were at Elmieh School. He was very polite and courteous to me and we both participated in the university's pre-Revolutionary meetings. I was on sabbatical leave, six months before the Revolution, and took an active role in the meetings of staff and students.

Then, one day, there was a rally at the university for the public and students in support of the Revolution at which I was asked to speak. When I arrived half an hour beforehand I saw Dr Golabi with some students at the platform. I was told by one of the students that my speech had been cancelled. I felt upset and rather angry and asked Dr Golabi for an explanation. He said, "You use the words 'workers', 'peasants' and 'masses' in your public talks and the people do not like this." It was the first time that I had clashed both intellectually and politically with him. Hearing his comment and also finding out that he was mainly responsible for the cancellation of my speech, I asked him, "What do you mean by the people who do not like the words 'workers', 'peasants' and 'masses'? If the people have made the Revolution — or it is for the people — then how can you exclude workers, peasants and masses from this great event?" In answer to my comment, he said, "True Muslims and believers have to decide who should talk and who should not in public meetings." "You are Fascists — Hitler also believed he was a true Christian," I said in wrath. I departed from Dr Golabi but I did not change my opinion of him and the regime that he is still supporting.

Two events stand out in my memories of Elmieh School: one was when Sattar (my youngest uncle) was punished with the stick (used on his feet) in front of all students in the middle of the schoolyard. I did not know exactly what his crime had been to deserve this awful punishment, but I knew that he used to come to school late. The other event was my fight with one of the students, Hassan, who used to boss everybody and many were scared of him. One day, when I was sitting reading he came up and annoyed me by pulling the book out from my hand. I became angry and suggested, in the presence of other students, a fight outside school that afternoon. When we came out of school, Hassan and I met in a large square away from the traffic. A large number of students formed a ring round us. The fight began and I received a few punches from my rival, but before he could knock me out I managed to trap his head under my arm so hard that he could not breathe and became scarlet. I asked him to apologise but he was unable to and the students eventually separated us. After that Hassan kept quiet in school and above all treated me politely — and we became friends.

Elmieh School closed after two years when the ayatollah who sponsored it died, and my brother Ibrahim and I moved to yet another school called Muhammadieh and were joined by Ismail, who had been attending a state school. This was a private school set up by businessmen; it was not as exclusive as Elmieh School and the syllabus was half religious and half modern. Ironically, Mr Ahrabi also moved to Muhammadieh School when Elmieh school closed. In this school I was preparing for the final (sixth) year of primary school and most of our lessons were taught by Mr Najiyan, the headmaster, and his brother Mr Akbar, so I did not have any class taken by Mr Ahrabi.

We had to take the final examinations in June at the Department of Education or in one of the schools other than our own. There was intense competition among the students. In my class there were students from all different backgrounds. Some, like me, had come from Elmieh School and the rest were from poorer families. One of the students, whose name was Hashim Tutunkar (tobacco grower), used to get top marks in every subject. I tried hard to catch up with Hashim but I did not succeed. I developed a special respect towards him; he was polite, serious, well-spoken, friendly and intelligent. All these qualities impressed me but I did not know whether he came from a poor or middle-class family. He did not appear to be from either.

Only ten students from my class took part in the examination, which was held in the girls' secondary school in the town centre. There were many examinees, including adults, from all over Tabriz. Hashim gained top marks overall. I was so impressed by Hashim's marks when I went for my results that I did not bother to ask who had come second and third after Hashim and walked out of the Education Department.

When school closed for the summer holidays I worked at my father's factory and his office in the bazaar. One day, I was returning from the office when I saw Hashim going in the opposite direction. I greeted him and was very pleased to see him. He was carrying a bundle of cotton for weaving socks. Looking pale and sad, he said to me, "I shall be unable to come to school next year. My father has recently died and I have to work to support my mother." I felt frozen to the spot and as if the entire ceiling of the bazaar had collapsed on my head. I did not know what to say. He realised I was upset and said, "Perhaps we will meet again someday." I did not see Hashim for a few years until one occasion when I recognised him at a coach station, but he did not see me. He looked much older and pale. I still feel deeply angry against the circumstances which prevented Hashim from continuing his studies.

6

I Live Under the Democratic Party of Azerbaijan

Sahand O mountain of pure snow,
Descended from Heaven with Zoroaster
Fire in your heart, snow on your shoulders,
With storms of centuries
And white hair of History on your chest . . .[1]

(Yadollah Amini (Maftun).)

I had been sent to Elmieh School by my father when the Democratic Party of Azerbaijan formed an autonomous government in Azerbaijan, which lasted from 1945 to 1946. My father did this under the influence of the ayatollahs and mullahs, who opposed the Democratic Party. They maintained that Islam was in danger, but in fact the interests of landowners and merchant families upon whom they were dependent were possibly more threatened by the social reforms.

Most aspects of the education system at Elmieh School differed from the state schools but I was able to learn much from the history teacher there and, indeed, from what was happening every day in the world outside school. The atmosphere in the school and my home was similar, but in society as a whole it was very different. There was a new openness; many things were happening all at once and for a child like me it was a new life and a significant experience. I used to take part in demonstrations and peaceful processions of musicians, artists, schoolchildren, workers, peasants

[1] Sahand is a mountain south of Tabriz and is one of the highest mountains (about 4000 metres high) in Azerbaijan and Iran. It has a volcano underneath and snow on its top and has been a source of inspiration for poets and revolutionaries.

and teachers, as well as other kinds of public performances. The women also participated in these processions and my sisters used to come outside to watch them. It was like a festival and a spring of fresh happenings. The police were replaced by youth organisations in every district of Tabriz. The young people who guarded their own area were called *Fidais* (volunteers or sacrificers). They were respected and loved by the public and I do not remember ever seeing them acting violently or interfering with people's private lives. Women now went out in the streets with or without a *chador*, men wore any clothes that they could afford; even mullahs were free to preach and wear their special religious garments.

I remember most of what happened during this time but there are a few events which I recall vividly. Firstly, the national revolutionary leaders like Sattar Khan, Baqir Khan and Sheikh Muhammad Khiyabani were reintroduced to the public and the writers and poets of Azerbaijan were highlighted. Many meetings were held by women, and educational and health films were shown. New schools were being built; the University of Tabriz was established; a radio station was opened; pipes were laid for fresh water and young men and women were trained as nurses and first-aid personnel and then sent out to the villages.

I remember Sattar Khan's statue being erected in the middle of the city's public garden (called Gulestan Baghi, or the Garden of Flowers). He was introduced to the schoolchildren and special attention was paid to the role of ordinary people in the history of Iran in general and Azerbaijan in particular.

The district where Izzat and Humai lived was called Amir Khiz (Amir- or leader-producing area). This is the district from where the two important leaders of the Constitutional Revolution (1905-1911), Sattar Khan and Baqir Khan, came. As in my childhood I had heard a lot about Babak, so had I also heard about these men from Izzat and his neighbours, who had seen them in the flesh and in action. They talked of Sattar Khan with great pride and patriotism. He was known as "*Sardar Milli*" (the national leader).

I had heard how Sattar Khan had defended Tabriz against anti-Constitutionalists and fought against the army of the despotic Muhammad Ali Shah and his feudal supporters such as Rahim Khan. In fact I knew the grandson of Sattar Khan and we went to the same school. But he was not all that clever, which surprised me because I expected Sattar Khan's grandson to be very intelligent and know all the details of his grandfather's life. I was disappointed when in later years I put questions to him about Sattar Khan which he could not answer. However, I liked him and enjoyed walking back home with him.

Sattar Khan rose to prominence in 1908, when he heard that Muhammad Ali Shah had closed the Majlis, or parliament, and ignored all the achievements of the Constitutional movement. After the subsequent coup d'état he invited the people of Tabriz to resist and defend the Constitution.

Tabriz was divided between Royalists and Constitutionalists. My parents' district was predominantly Royalist. My father said that he did not take sides, "I was neither Royalist nor Constitutionalist." But Amir Khiz, Izzat's district, was the heartland of the Constitutionalists. In June 1908, after the bombardment of the Majlis, and Muhammad Ali Shah's coup d'état, Sattar Khan rose in Tabriz. After eleven months of struggle, he not only brought back the Constitution to Tabriz but also saved all of Iran.

I remember my history teachers at both Elmieh School and, later, Nizami Secondary School taught us the background of the Constitutional Revolution of 1905. They used to say that in order to understand the Constitutional Revolution one had also to understand the society of the Qajar period.

When the Qajars came to the fore, at the end of the 18th century, the Iranian population was made up of a mosaic of ethnic, cultural and linguistic minorities. Geographically, Iran is split by three mountain ranges bordering a central arid plain, making communication between communities a rare occurrence — save for the factional feuds which occurred regularly at this time. The bellicose nature of the tribesmen is aptly summed up in a quote from a tribal chief: "I against my Brother. I and my Brother against my Cousin. I and my Cousin against my Tribe. I and my Tribe against the World."

When Agha Muhammad Khan made the first moves towards Qajar supremacy, he did it through forging alliances with tribes or conquering rebellious factions himself. He was at heart a tribal leader and respected the tribal system, but in attempting to bring the whole country under one ruler he was trying to create a united society out of what had been a geographically, culturally and economically diverse one.

After his assassination, however, and with the eventual accession of Fath Ali Shah in 1797, his policy was reversed. Fath Ali Shah and his successors, Muhammad Shah (1834-1848) and Nasir al-Din Shah (1848-1896), disregarded the tribal aspect in favour of the ancient traditions of the Imperial Shah of Shahs. They tried to protect their position by creating an effective army and state-wide administration and legitimise their dynasty by imitating the court manners of previous emperors.

They failed in all these respects. The administration involved the deputising of provincial governors to collect taxes and run particular regions. The scheme floundered as the Shah failed to realise that a governor was completely powerless outside his own village.

The creation of a viable army collapsed for similar reasons. Each province was required to provide a regiment of cavalry which would understandably be headed by a tribal chief, who naturally held the interests of his tribe much dearer than those of the Shah. Tribal life continued in the provinces whilst the Qajar court lived the luxurious lifestyles of its ancient predecessors. They remained in power by a policy of "divide and rule". To outsiders looking on, the period of Qajar supremacy seemed to be a period of absolutism. In fact it was not as a result of their strength that the Qajars retained the Peacock Throne, but merely of the inevitable weakness of the disunited society of the country. (This was also the case with the late Shah, whose strength was the result of social disunity.)

Iran began to be influenced by the West early in the 19th century. Military pressure in the north from Russia resulted in the treaties of Gulistan (1813) and Turkmanchai (1828) — both embarrassing to Fath Ali Shah and resulting in an indemnity payment of some £3,000,000 to the Tsar, as well as the imposition of certain conditions by the Russians. The Russian dominance was soon followed by British offensives — eager to halt the Russian advance they extracted the Treaty of Paris (1857) which too resulted in Iran making a number of concessions.

These concessions gave foreign merchants an almost free hand to exploit Iranian resources and manpower, and to remain exempt from any tariff duties, local travel restrictions, and the jurisdiction of the Sharia Courts. The Qajars were defenceless against the economic penetration by the West, an example of which was the notorious Reuter concession by Nasir al-Din Shah in 1872. This involved the profits from customs' duties going to this British firm as well as the right to finance a state bank and exclusive mineral rights within the country. This particular concession was later withdrawn as a result of national and international pressure, but the Shah continued to permit Western exploitation of Iran's resources. As we saw earlier, this began to disrupt the traditional bazaars within Iran, as cheap manufactured goods from abroad flooded the market. On the one hand, a number of the bigger merchants grew wealthier, but on the other, the traditional smaller traders and craft workers began to decline. All this helped to unite the traditional forces in the bazaars, who were closely backed by certain progressive and religious leaders (whose livelihood depended on the bazaar).

Meanwhile, Nasir al-Din Shah was continuing to permit the rise in foreign interest in the country, purely as a means of obtaining some cash. It was at this time that Nasir al-Din Shah sold the tobacco concession to Major Talbot (described in Chapter 4) which had led to the strike of leading bazaars and other opposition. This came to be known as the Tobacco Revolt.

I remember my history teacher covering this period and talking about Mirza Taqi Farahani (known as Amir Kabir), vizier of Nasir al-Din Shah and founder of the famous Dar al-Funun (Abode of Learning) college in Tehran, and explaining how he was sentenced to death by Nasir al-Din Shah in 1852. At this point he became emotional and tears appeared in his eyes. He took his handkerchief out of his pocket and wiped away his tears.

Nasir al-Din Shah's policy proved to be a mistaken one, as the effects of improved communications, such as telegraph lines built by foreign investors, were for the first time permitting anti-dynastic feelings to unite across the country. It was ironic that the Western infiltration which the Qajars had seemed so eager to allow, apparently to protect their position at the head of society, in fact set the wheels in motion for the downfall of their dynasty. The state was in no way weakened by the increase in foreign influence, but society was greatly strengthened in that it was galvanised into united action against a common enemy — the foreign menace. (We saw a similar thing happening at the fall of the Shah in 1979. The clergy (ayatollahs and mullahs) were united with the bazaar merchants against the Shah and his Western backers.)

The assassination of Nasir al-Din Shah in 1896 brought Muzaffar al-Din Shah to the Peacock Throne. He immediately threw Iran's gates wide open to concession hunters and appointed a Belgian, Monsieur Naus, Director of Customs. His liberal policies, he hoped, would satisfy his political opposition. However, they merely encouraged the formation of clandestine societies sworn to the overthrow of despotism. Many such societies sprang up, such as the Revolutionary Committee, the Society of Humanity, the Social Democrat Society and the Secret Society. The Secret Society was organised in Tabriz by twelve young radicals. There was a close link between Tabriz and Baku. The Social Democrat Party of Iran was formed in early 1904 in Baku by a group of immigrants who were active in the Social Democratic Party of Russia, headed by Nariman Narimanov, who was an Azerbaijani schoolteacher. He later became the president of the Soviet Socialist Republic of Azerbaijan.

By 1905 Iran was moving rapidly towards a political revolution. The traditional middle class was now economically, ideologically and politically alienated from the ruling dynasty. The actual revolution took place in three stages — each one becoming more decisive than the last. After a bad harvest, and a sudden disruption in trade caused by the Russo-Japanese War, some 200 shop-owners staged a peaceful march. They demanded the removal of the Belgian, Naus, and the repayment of loans. The Shah agreed to these terms, but failed to keep his word.

The second protest was more vehement and resulted in a Tehran general strike. Again Muzaffar al-Din Shah gave in and then failed to honour his promise.

In the summer of 1906 a preacher was arrested for denouncing the government in public. This infuriated the secret societies and they marched on the police station. In the disturbance which followed, a theology student was shot dead. The following morning a larger mob set out with his body for a public funeral in the central mosque. They were met on the steps of the mosque by Cossacks and a bloodbath ensued — 22 dead and more than a hundred injured. The Qajars now found the religious leaders openly denouncing them. Islam, the most powerful unifying force, had turned against these despotic rulers. (The opposition of religious leaders to the Qajars should not be interpreted as their support for the Constitutional Revolution. In fact, leading religious leaders, except for a very few, were mostly against the Constitutional laws. For example, Ayatollah Sheikh Fazlullah Nuri, to whom Ayatollah Khomeini refers frequently, was fanatically opposed to the Constitutional laws.) Muzaffar al-Din Shah had no choice and on 5 August 1906 he signed a proclamation convening a Constituent Assembly.

The power of the Shah had finally been reduced and the rift between state and society was dramatically reduced in size.

When Muhammad Ali Shah ascended the throne in early 1907 he was determined to rejuvenate the power of the Qajars. He tried to reinstigate tribal rivalry and even proposed that he should have the right to select the entire National Assembly. His proposals were met with public protests in cities throughout the country. His premier, Amin al Sultan, was assassinated and he himself had to retire meekly before the National Assembly.

In the meantime, however, the Liberals were pressing ahead with ambitious reforms — trying to reduce the power of the traditional middle class in the Assembly and distribute it more evenly amongst the provinces. This, understandably, did not meet with the complete approval of the bazaar merchants in the city and the Shah now found himself with increasing support. The traditional middle class opposed both the Shah and foreign powers until they achieved what they wanted. The people in the street did not matter much to them.

In June 1908 the Shah, supported by a Cossack division and reactionary mullahs staged a successful coup d'état. Martial law was imposed in Tehran and civil war broke out. The slums were hotbeds of reaction, while the middle-class regions had become the bastions of revolution. The initial successes of the Royalists soon turned into defeat as the provinces rose in revolt and two rebel armies converged on Tehran. The Royalists fled the city and the Shah sought asylum in the Russian legation. The civil war was over. So was the despotism of the Qajar period.

Muhammad Ali Shah was deposed and his twelve-year-old son Ahmad took his place. Cabinet posts were distributed among notables who had supported the constitutional movement only for their own limited interest.

The Shah remained as the nominal monarch, but power had finally been wrested from his grip. August 5th, 1909, saw the calling of the Second National Assembly. The revolt of traditional bazaar merchants against the feudals had ended with the merchants having one foot on land and one foot on commerce. Feudalism was far from defeated. With regard to a National movement against Tsarist Russia and Britain, the latter ended up with more influence and power than ever before — having friends among feudals, intellectuals, traditional bazaar merchants and, above all, religious leaders.

When I used to go to collect the children to come and work in the factory I used to think about Sattar Khan, Baqir Khan, Haydar Amu-Oghli and Sheikh Muhammad Khiyabani, who were popular amongst the workers. Mir Taqi, a senior carpet-maker, used to bring literature about these people to the factory and read it during his lunch break.

The story of Sattar Khan's constitutional achievements was a great contrast to my childhood experience of Reza Shah's dictatorship. But during the government of Firqa-yi Dimukrat-i Azerbaijan (the Democratic Party of Azerbaijan) I came to know these national figures through my own experiences.

One thing I clearly remember about Sheikh Muhammad Khiyabani (1879-1920) was the appearance of his monument with a picture of him at Siqat-al Islam school (Siqat al-Islam was one of the progressive religious leaders in Tabriz who fought for the Constitutional Revolution of 1905). It was surrounded by flowers and the people visited the place. I too went there a number of times. When the Democratic government fell, this memorial and the statues of Sattar Khan and Baqir Khan disappeared. I do not remember any statue of Haydar Amu-Oghli but I remember seeing handsome photographs of him wearing a cossack hat.

My history teachers had told me about Khiyabani and his uprising against the unpopular British treaty of 1919 with Vusuq al-Dowlah's government (1918-1920) and especially how Britain had helped Vusuq and his succeeding governments to suppress the Khiyabani movement and other democratic movements such as the Jangali movement of 1917-1920 led by Mirza Kuchek Khan and Haydar Amu-Oghli in Gilan.

In order to give a more detailed picture of this important figure, Khiyabani, and the historical context in which he defended the Constitution of Iran I will include in the next few pages some of Khayabani's speeches and articles, translated by Dr Tabatabai whose PhD thesis on Khayabani I had the honour to supervise in 1984.

Khiyabani's struggle was in line with the Constitutional Revolution of 1905-1911 and he made clear his concern for the practice of Constitutional law from his very first article in *Tajaddud*, the newspaper which he published. In one article, published on 5 May 1917 he declared:

> With the example of the rebellion in the neighbouring country, it is impossible for the Iranians to surrender to the despotic regime which we have been facing. Now what have we to do? First of all we must realize that this freedom and our Constitutional Laws have been achieved by our good and brave patriotic fellow countrymen and women. By sacrificing their valuable lives they have helped to keep our freedom alive. We should like to ask our government, which came to power as the result of direct election, to act in accordance with the Constitutional Laws . . .

In another article three years later Khiyabani revealed his love not only for Iran in general but for Azerbaijan in particular:

> While Azerbaijan is living and its freedom fighters are alive the 'Constitutional Law' will not be left defenceless . . .
>
> (*Tajaddud*, 16 April 1920.)

Khiyabani wished to see the people of his country truly and democratically represented. To this end he wished to see the parasitic and reactionary elements of the society eliminated:

> Law-givers of the present time must believe in the principle of democracy. Democracy should not be entrusted to the aristocracy. We want a parliament which is created by the sincere wishes of the people and which knows their needs and problems; not a parliament which is used as a net of hypocrisy and treachery in the government of Tehran . . .
>
> (*Tajaddud*, 11 May 1920.)

With the outbreak of the First World War and its subsequent circumstances for Iran, the country had suffered a collapse of political structure; but by the end of the war the revival of political activities was once more encouraged.

Iran's declared neutrality in 1914 had been ignored, and Britain and Russia continued to keep their troops in Iran and interfere with the country's internal affairs. The third Majlis, which was elected in June 1914, failed to meet. The balance of rivalry between the British and Russians was interrupted with the 1917 Russian Revolution, which on the one hand had led to a further state of anarchy in Iran and on the other hand had helped the growth of nationalist feelings and movements in different parts of the country. The subsequent treaty between the British government and the Iranian premier Vusuq al-Dowla was forcibly abandoned under internal nationalist pressure. It was in this context that the nationalist uprising of Khiyabani in Azerbaijan gathered momentum.

In spite of the accusations made by the aristocratic and pro-British forces, Khiyabani was a patriot and nationalist in his tendencies and policies. He refrained from obtaining foreign support, despite the fact that it was so readily available in neighbouring revolutionary Russia. He also refused to follow a separatist policy, even though his influence and authority was restricted to Azerbaijan.

Despite his significant role in the modern history of Iran in general and Azerbaijan in particular, he remains an ambiguous character. The following quotation from Khiyabani provides a general picture of the ideas of a man who left a great mark on the history of my motherland and influenced a whole generation from whom I had much to learn:

We are looking for a common source of light to cover all our country. To create such a light, no doubt a clear and progressive policy is a must . . . It is the aim of our uprising to cease anarchy and disorder, and to cut off the hands of the traitors . . . thieves . . . criminals . . . Our policy is not confined to Azerbaijan; it is not our aim to have a separatist programme . . . We know that our voice is now kept unheard beyond Tabriz but we shall carry on our activities until the establishment of a lasting democracy throughout Iran . . .

(*Tajaddud*, 23 May 1920.)

Mushir al-Dowla, the governor of Azerbaijan, eventually offered a peace talk to Khiyabani. Khiyabani accepted his invitation. However, while the talk was in progress between government representatives and Khiyabani's group, Mushir al-Dowla, backed by the British army, attacked Khiyabani's forces. Khiyabani himself was shot dead in his own house.

Khiyabani's monument was about twenty minutes' walk from my parent's house. Most of the people in our district, including my father, had visited the place. Sayyid Jafar Pishavari, who was elected leader of the Democratic Party and government of Azerbaijan repeatedly mentioned and highlighted Khiyabani's uprising of 1919-1920. Pishavari delivered a speech on the occasion of the unveiling of Khiyabani's statue in 1946, in which he declared:

If there is a pride for Azerbaijan the Azerbaijanis themselves and their pride secure this. . . . The Sheikh was a great thinker . . . The uprising of Khiyabani, no matter how it ended, has a great importance in Iran. Our movement is the continuation of his uprising . . .

About this time, my parents used to take us to the newly built schools to watch educational and agricultural films. For the first time I saw how the peasants lived in the villages of Azerbaijan. Azerbaijan is one of the most fertile parts of Iran. It is sometimes called the country's "basket of grain" and "land of various fruits". Despite this, the peasants have lived and suffered under suppression and deprivation for centuries. The large landowners and feudals treated the inhabitants of their villages as objects and their property. The villagers would be bought and sold along with their villages and lands. The most fearful force in the villages was the gendarmerie, which acted as the arm of the landowner. They would arrest, punish, imprison and kill peasants according to the wishes of their landowners. If a peasant failed to provide the landowner with grain, butter, eggs and other dues, then he would be punished. The government would take their sons as soldiers and landowners their products for their own profit; and the gendarmerie served both these forces. The peasants were frightened and would shiver at the very name of gendarme.

Once I remember I was staying with my mother's relative in her village. It was summer and her huge brick-built house towered above the other buildings, which were no more than humble huts. The peasants lived with their animals in the same room or area. They seemed poor but they were kind and hospitable. The village headman informed Mrs Badir, my hostess, that a few peasants had failed to pay their debts and had not brought the required amount of wheat. Mrs Badir ordered the village headman to summon all these peasants to her house. In an hour's time, they were all brought before her like slaves. They entered and bowed to Mrs Badir and her sons, and were ordered to sit by the door. Mrs Badir asked why they had not paid their debts and brought the grain. There was silence for a few minutes. She repeated her question more forcefully and threatened them with calling the gendarme. They were frightened and responded immediately by giving their excuses: their crops had failed; one man's wife had given birth to a child and could not work; another said his father had died and he had to sell his cow to pay for his funeral; yet another said his cow had become ill and died and he could not work without the cow.

Mrs Badir's youngest son, Kaykavus, was a captain in the army and wore a very showy uniform. He came to his mother's assistance and retorted, "What you say are your personal problems. You must pay your debts, otherwise . . .'

To my horror the younger men began to cry and the old men bent their heads. The younger men begged Mrs Badir and her son not to call the gendarme and promised to sell their animals and pay their debts; but the old men sat pale with their heads still bent.

A British visitor to both Iranian and Soviet Azerbaijan in 1945, Mr Philip Price, MP, observed the contrasting conditions of the villages there. In an article in the *Manchester Guardian* (Tehran, 20 December 1945) he wrote:

> The centre of interest today is Azerbaijan, in the northwest. This is the Iranian province bordering the Caucasus. It is inhabited by people who are the same in speech, religion and history as those who live in the adjoining territory of the Soviet Republic of Azerbaijan, in the eastern Trans-Caucasus.
>
> Now Soviet Azerbaijan has made tremendous progress, culturally and economically, since the October Revolution. I have recently spent some time there and was able to compare the state of the Moslem population today with what I saw 33 years ago when I was there last. Then they were priest-ridden and backward, the women veiled and subjected, education virtually non-existent. Now I found Moslem Azerbaijanians in all the Government offices, in the educational, scientific and research institutions, and staffing them up to 75 per cent. Such has been the effect of 25 years of union with the Soviets.
>
> Here [in Iranian Azerbaijan] the peasants can see that north of the border the feudal magnates have gone, irrigation works are in full swing, and the tractors plough the land on collective farms, where the peasant reaps the benefit of his

labour. Meanwhile they scratch the land with primitive ploughs, as I saw with my own eyes the moment I crossed the borders into Persia, and have to deliver anything up to 50 per cent of their produce to absentee landlords who live in fine houses in Teheran.

Sabir, a famous poet from Azerbaijan (1862-1911), wrote at the beginning of this century about the miserable conditions of the peasants. When the people of Iran heard the news that their country was to have a Constitution, one old man fell on his knees in the fields and exclaimed:

> Great Allah be praised; over Iran, our prison,
> The dawn of the Constitution has at long last arisen.
> The very foundations of evil have suffered a blow;
> No more will the village elder plunge us in woe.
> The foul flame of tyranny has been put out.
> Iran will again be a paradise, no one can doubt.
> The wanton authorities have been bridled at last.
> And the peasants' sufferings are a thing of the past.
> The ploughman will never be beaten again any more,
> He will not be insulted, maltreated again any more.
> The landlord won't squeeze us out any more,
> No, from now on he will never curse and shout any more!

No sooner had he finished, than a *farrash* (official) sent by the authorities appeared on the scene and, in full sight of his family, tied the old man's hands and bade him go to the landlord on foot, while the official himself rode after the peasant on horseback.

The landlord came out holding a whip in his hand and thus addressed the peasant:

> Yeah . . . a whole month has gone by since the day
> When the wheat was threshed and stored away,
> And where have you been, you worthless old lout?
> You took all the crop for yourself, no doubt!
> And what did you bring your landlord, eh?
> All the fruit from your garden you hid away.
> Neither barley nor wheat have you given your lord,
> Neither peas nor beans have you given your lord.
> You ought to be pinched a little, peasant,
> To teach the rest of your people a lesson.

The first thing that Pishavari did was replace these village gendarmes with *Fidais*, as he had in the towns. My grandfather called these *Fidais* thugs! In the absence of gendarmes and landowners the peasants began to act freely and formed their units of support to the Democratic government.

During a single year of Pishavari's government in Azerbaijan, the faces of villagers had been transformed (but my grandfather did not receive as many presents from the villagers as he did before). Health, education and above all land reform were introduced to villages. This government policy combined with the absence of fear of the gendarmerie gave even the poorest peasants a new personality and hope that I can vividly remember. Many peasants still remember those days and continue to talk of them with pride and enthusiasm.

I remember Pishavari in Tabriz. The Pishavari government started to build new schools on old and delapidated burial grounds — despite protests from the mullahs who said that it was dishonouring the dead. But the dead could surely not rest in those neglected places! During the school building programme I remember the powerful lamps at every corner of the graveyards turning the night into day. The building workers worked three shifts a day, for it was a 24-hour programme. I was astonished to see the work completed so quickly. Three schools were constructed, two primary and one secondary, made of brick and with tin roofs which gleamed like silver under the sun. One primary school was for girls, the other two were for boys. The secondary school was called Razi School (after the famous Persian scientist and physician Zakariyya Razi, known as Rhazes in the West).

Razi School was mostly attended by poor and working-class children. I did not study there but did visit it in later years, when I taught in one of the neighbouring schools called Taqi Zadeh, which was also built on the ruins of a graveyard.

It was situated in front of the Davachi Bazaar, which had a huge door like the one at the *karvan-sarai*. Tea-houses, charcoal and firewood shops were in its neighbourhood. A few yards away from the school there also stood a very large bakery which sold *sangak* bread. Bread plays a significant part in the daily diet in Iran and is a necessary accompaniment to every meal. I used to go in the mornings and evenings to buy fresh bread for my parents. *Sangak* was sold in metre-long thin strips and was crispy and brown, delicious hot although you had to avoid the odd stone from the oven which sometimes stuck to the cooked bread. I often used to eat the end of the *sangak* on the way home; between meals I would sometimes make myself a snack of *sangak*, fresh herbs and cheese, while warm *sangak*, with ice-cold butter and thick, dark honey was a rare and special breakfast treat.

The bakery itself was a source of interest and delight to me. In the front of the shop was a scale suspended from the ceiling. A man stood behind the scale and weighed the bread as it came out of the oven. Next to the scale was a platform on which the people spread the hot bread to be cooled before weighing, because they thought hot bread was heavier. The oven was situated in a large area behind the counter and separated from it by a door. We used to go inside and often queued up to receive the bread from a man who stood in front of the oven to remove the bread and keep an eye on the oven's temperature. When I was younger the oven was heated by wood or *khar* (a kind of thorny bush brought from the mountains), but later it was fuelled by diesel oil.

The *shatir* or baker stood to the left of the oven, taking dough from huge pots and flattening it on a wooden board connected to a long wooden handle. After shaping the dough into a square with his fingertips, the *shatir* lifted the board with the dough still on it, placed it inside the oven and manoeuvred the dough onto the bed of hot stones in the oven by twisting and turning the long handle. He then withdrew the board from the oven and placed the flat end on a stone which stuck out of the wall and the long handle on a V-shaped piece of wood two metres below on the ground.

While the *shatir* started on another piece of dough, his companion, the *vardast*, took a stick with which he reached for the bread in the oven and, sliding it gently underneath, loosened the bread from the stones and carefully withdrew it. He then quickly put his hand to the oven door and pulled out the bread. This process was repeated over and over again, as the oven was only able to bake 10 to 15 *sangaks* at a time.

Watching all these processes with the noise, heat and hustle and bustle was very interesting for a child. But there were other reasons why I was always willing to go to this bakery or another one near our house. I met and chatted with my classmates or friends there. If no one I knew was around I also used to read my school books. Sometimes I stayed there for a couple of hours and found it pleasant to sit by myself, think for myself and observe the other people from a corner of the basement bakery.

Apart from the workers at the front of the shop there was another man who toiled at the back, often covered in flour. He made the dough, in two or three large mixing pots. He first poured water into these, before adding flour from large sacks. He mixed the dough by hand, continuously thumping it across and against the sides of the pot until it was finally ready to be passed on to the baker. It was then usually left for a few hours to rise. If bread was cooked from dough which had not risen sufficiently then the customers would complain, especially my father, who would grumble that it was not tasty and was indigestible.

During the government of the Democratic Party of Azerbaijan, the bakeries were well organised and bread was plentiful; sometimes in the past greedy bakery owners had hoarded flour to create an artificial shortage and so put up prices. Kaviyan, a member of Pishavari's government, made routine checks on the Tabriz bakeries to make sure this did not happen. One day he arrived at a bakery to find queues of people waiting for bread, the staple diet of the poor. He called the shopkeeper to account for his delay. After listening to his excuses, Kaviyan said that he was going to check the other bakeries. By the time he returned he wanted to see bread on sale for both the waiting customers and future customers. If there was no bread then he would bake the owner and the baker in their own oven! Needless to say, the bread materialised. News of this event quickly spread and made a great impact on the community. The Pishavari government would not tolerate two types of people — professional criminals, and those who tried to artificially increase prices.

There was a man in Tabriz called Qarni Yirtik Kazim (stomach-torn Kazim) who was terrifying: he used to rob people's houses and attack both the public and police. No-one dared to challenge him. One day, I remember, the news broke out in the city that Qarni Yirtik Kazim would be placed on trial by the Pishavari government for raping a woman. At the trial he was sentenced to death and later hanged. There was great relief among the people of Tabriz and from then on other minor criminals did not dare to harm the public.

I remember also when the health service became free. The workers in my father's factory and the poor people in Izzat's area now had access to doctors and hospitals without worrying about the cost. Young girls and boys were attending six-month courses to become nurses and first-aid helpers in the villages. They were very proud to graduate from this course: there were several from my parents' district who had attended this course and had received a diploma or certificate, which they then showed to other children.

Two of these girls were the daughters of a man called Mirza Hussein Vaiz. Although their father used to wear priest's garments and preached in public, he was different from other mullahs. He was a progressive man who supported the government of Pishavari and an outstanding supporter of women's emancipation and education. Mirza's daughters were well known for their political and progressive views. They did not even wear the *chador* and were educated. They organised meetings for women, especially from the working and middle classes. After the fall of Pishavari's government, I heard that Mirza's daughters had been imprisoned and Mirza was forbidden to preach in public. He was placed under house arrest and without income — probably relatives and friends helped him.

Years passed and I did not know what had become of Mirza and his daughters. I had not forgotten them and often wondered what had happened to those sparkling, outspoken and revolutionary girls. Eventually I came to Scotland and there occurred one of those astonishing coincidences which sometimes happen in life. One day in June-July 1969 I was asked by the British Council in London to act as interpreter for a visitor from Iran. I eagerly accepted the job, firstly because the visitor, a Colonel Rezvanpour, was from Azerbaijan and spoke my mother-tongue, and secondly because the fee would be a welcome addition to our income!

The colonel arrived in a chauffeur-driven car which had been placed at his disposal. He looked spruce and handsome and was in early middle-age.

Speaking in Azerbaijani, he told me that he was originally from Tabriz and had been in the police force for twenty years.

The first day the car took us to see Sir Walter Scott's house, at Abbotsford. The second day we visited the Police Training College and watched the graduation ceremony. I interpreted for the colonel, the police chief and members of the college. We had lunch and enjoyed good hospitality. Afterwards we visited Saughton Prison in Edinburgh. The colonel was eager to see everything: single cells, shared rooms, workshops and recreation centres. He was surprised to find no "interrogation" room. He asked many questions about punishments and whether, where and how the prisoners were tortured. It was a dreadful experience to stand on the cold and black stones of a prison cell and interpret these kinds of question. I could not help thinking about the impression the colonel must have been making on our host and wondered, desperately, whether I could misinterpret some of his questions. I was also acutely aware of the significance this all had for the situation in Iran. I felt sick and wanted to leave.

I was particularly sickened on two occasions. Once was when he was discussing and telling his surprised host about the methods of torture in Iranian prisons. The colonel turned to me and said, "They do not know how to torture — if I were them I would know how to handle these prisoners, especially the political ones." I had long opposed the Shah's treatment of political prisoners, but had to contain my anger and listen politely. The second occasion was when we were visiting the prison workshops. The combination of the colonel's self-satisfied, pompous demeanour and fatuous questions on the one hand, and the angry, contemptuous faces of the prisoners as they overheard our conversation on the other made me feel nauseated. By the time I had taken the colonel back to his hotel and returned home I was physically and spiritually so exhausted that I felt as if I myself had been under hard labour and mental torture for days.

On the third day, on our way to visit some cultural centres, the colonel began, as usual, to tell me about his adventures and the important posts he had held in Iran. Suddenly I pricked up my ears. He said, "As a young officer, I became a member of the Democratic Youth Organisation in Tabriz and gave the names of members to the police. So they were arrested and the organisation was destroyed." He particularly mentioned how the daughters of Mirza Hussein Vaiz had been arrested, imprisoned and tortured. "I personally tortured them," he told me, proudly. Hearing this, I did not know what to do. I wanted to strangle him on the spot. I was afraid of the driver and thought of the consequences. My body was at first as hot as fire, then I felt cold and began to shiver inside. I kept quiet and tried to keep my feelings hidden. I had my mother, sisters, brothers and many relatives in Tabriz. This man could easily have harmed them. Nobody could have learned and understood the reason.

I remained quiet. He, however, was still talking, explaining what he had done to the daughters of Mirza and how cheeky, shameless and courageous they were: "One day I asked the guard to bring the two sisters to my room in the prison. I asked each of these sisters to confess their guilt and errors against the Pahlavi royal family. I invited them to announce their loyalty towards Muhammad Reza Shah (the son of Reza Shah), stop their political activities and be released from the prison. Otherwise they would have to face more imprisonment and torture. But before I finished my talk the elder girl jumped up and slapped my face and the younger girl shamefully sat at the corner of the room urinating on the ground and saying, 'I am urinating into your Shah's mouth'. The elder sister's unexpected courage and her younger sister's shameful performance made me so angry that I started torturing and cut off an ear from each."

After hearing all this I began to think about and question his visit. Who had invited him to the UK? If the British Council had invited him, what was the connection between a police chief and the British Council, which is known to be a cultural institution? Who had paid his expenses and arranged this trip? Why was such a person treated as a VIP? Many other such questions flooded my head. I had to control myself and remain patient.

One day, just before his departure, his wife joined him in Edinburgh. They asked me to take them shopping and his wife asked my wife to accompany her to Princes Street, to help her in the choice of purchases. My wife politely went out with her once and thereafter hastily excused herself because she had to look after our children. So I found myself trapped in yet another embarrassing episode. They both handled things in every shop and were like petulant children — opening packages and complaining about the colour, size and price of the goods. In Marks and Spencers they seemed to think I could bargain for them over the price of the underwear. I was exhausted.

At four o'clock in the afternoon we were sitting having tea at the hotel. The colonel asked me if I knew how to change sterling into Iranian currency and then transfer it to Iran; he also wanted me to telephone a company in London and ask for an extension to his stay. Regarding the exchange of currency, I suggested he should go to the National Bank of Iran in London and they would arrange the transaction. (While saying this I was wondering how and from where he had got several thousand pounds. In those days, even one hundred pounds was a lot of money for a university teacher like me.) Regarding the colonel's request for an extension of his stay, I asked to look at the file that he was carrying so that I could find the telephone number of the company he wanted me to contact. He seemed reluctant to hand over the file and searched for the telephone number himself. However, he could not read English and recognise which letter was which, and in despair gave me a letter which he had received from the company which showed its telephone numbers and address.

When I had read the letter, a copy of which I include in this chapter, I asked the colonel how he came to know this firm. Answering my question, he proudly said, "I am the chief of police in Arak and this British company has a factory in the city. I have helped the company control the workers and punished and put the wind up them for going on strike. In return for my looking after this company they have invited me and my wife to visit Great Britain and their company in England." "Don't you think it is rather immoral and indeed unpatriotic to support a company against workers because of a holiday and money?" I asked him. "Nowadays, who thinks about the workers and the country?" the colonel answered. He then concluded. "The Shah and his Prime Minister Hovida are willing and, indeed, flattered to be asked to do such favours for foreign companies. They do this and many other things, so why should I not do also?"

The colonel and his wife concluded their stay with a visit to a psychiatrist in Edinburgh (because he was complaining of nightmares and insomnia). They then left Edinburgh, but his story of the torture of Mirza's daughters never left me. I never heard of the girls again.

Pishavari's government did not interfere with the religion and traditions of the people. I remember the government even had its own official priest, called Mullah Fatali, who preached in the barracks to the soldiers, and in the streets to the public. During the month of Ramadan he had told the soldiers and the workers that they were, from the religious point of view, allowed not to fast when they had to work, or could fast for only half the day. This was greeted with strong reaction from the traditional and fundamentalist mullahs, who regarded Mullah Fatali as an improper priest. Even my father did not approve of him, but I liked him as he used to mix with the public and was very informal and energetic. However, I did not, at the time, understand my father's cynicism and a particular mullah's opposition to Mullah Fatali. I remember this mullah used to ride a motorbike while wearing his loose cloak and turban. As he sped along the road the wind used to lift up his cloak and cause it to billow out. From a distance he looked like a huge samovar sitting on the bike, and I was both amused and fascinated by this image.

Mir Taqi, a master workman in my father's factory, was the source of my information about Pishavari. Mir Taqi had a friend called Mir Jamal who used to visit Mir Taqi in the factory bringing with him an Azerbaijani newspaper in which most of the news about the Democratic Party of Azerbaijan and Pishavari's speeches were published. Mir Jamal, who used to work in the newspaper office or was a journalist, would sit next to Mir Taqi and read to him from the paper and I used to stand at the carpet loom and listen. Both were very kind to me. Several times I asked questions,

Letter from Colonel Rezvanpour.

which Mir Taqi tried to answer, relating to what Sayyid Jafar Pishavari had said in his latest speech to the City Assembly or at public meetings. I remember one of his speeches well. It was about why Pishavari and the City Assembly decided to form the government of the Democratic Party of Azerbaijan.

The rejection of Pishavari's credentials (he was elected as representative from Azerbaijan) by the 14th Majlis forced him to return to Tabriz from Tehran in September 1944 and form the Democratic Government of Azerbaijan. This decision was viewed as a protest by the people of Azerbaijan against the central government. Pishavari and his committee members met on 5 September 1945 and decided on the following points under the title "These are our Mottoes":

1. While the Democratic Party respects the independence and territorial integrity of Iran, it also seeks autonomy for Azerbaijan so that it might improve its culture . . .

2. In order to achieve this, a provincial body should be elected to begin work immediately. It would be active in cultural, economic and medical spheres . . .

3. The Azerbaijani language is to be taught up to third-year level in all primary schools, and thereafter both Azerbaijani and Persian, as the state language. The establishment of the National Academy of Azerbaijan is one of the essential aims of the Democratic Party.

4. The Democratic Party will try very hard to improve industry and to increase the number of factories in Azerbaijan. It will also aim to reduce unemployment through encouraging and expanding hand and machine industry.

5. The Party considers increase in trade as a very serious and essential concern . . .

6. One of the essential aims of the party is the development and improvement of Azerbaijani cities . . . One of the immediate aims is to supply Tabriz with piped water.

7. The Party recognises that the wealth and well-being of the country depends on the peasants, and therefore will be responsive to the movement among them . . . The Party will try to solve their problem in a way that satisfies both peasants and landowners. The latter will be given security and will be encouraged to do their best for the improvement of peasants and their own lands. The lands of the state and those landowners who have left Azerbaijan will be distributed amongst the peasantry . . . Beside these, the Party will try to provide land and agricultural equipment for the peasants of Azerbaijan through simple and easy methods.

8. One of the most urgent duties of the Party is the fight against unemployment . . . Immediate alleviation of unemployment would be effected by building factories, increasing trade, and constructing a railway network and new roads.

9. Concerning the election laws a great injustice is done with regard to Azerbaijan. The Democratic Party of Azerbaijan will try to achieve the right to have members of parliament according to population. This, approximately, will form one-third of the parliament. The Party supports absolute freedom of

election for parliament. The election should take place on the same day throughout Iran.

10. The Party promises to fight against corruption among civil servants . . . At the same time we will encourage and appreciate honest government employees. The Party will especially prevent corruption by improving living conditions and increasing wages . . .

11. More than half of the tax raised by the central government will be spent by the Party on internal improvements within Azerbaijan, and they will try to reduce the amount of indirect tax demanded.

12. The Party wishes friendly relations with all democratic countries, especially the Allied Powers . . .

My father used to take part in the meetings between factory owners and the government. At home he would tell us that Pishavari's government looked after his workers better than he did: "In fact the government is doing what every factory owner should do. The workers are sent to health centres for examination. They are sent to bath-houses free of charge. At least they are now free from lice and dirt. They are better clothed. The government insists that workers should not work more than eight hours and they must have centres for sports and recreation." We used to tease our father by saying, "You like Pishavari so you like Communism." He used to answer gently, "I am not in love with the eyes or eye-brows of Pishavari, nor do I understand his ideology, but I see reality and what he is practically doing for our people."

While my father admired the Pishavari government for these actions, he did not like its support of trade unions, interference with wage levels and the restrictions on employing young children in factories. My father was well aware that without young children the carpet factories would grind to a halt; besides, he argued, employing adults for the same job would be costly. Child labour formed the basis of essential work in the carpet factories. In fact Pishavari realised that it would be impossible to stop child labour being used all at once; so rather than forbid children from working he stressed the importance of their receiving an education, suggesting that it would be better to send the children to schools, which were free for all levels, than to factories. This, indeed, was not met with approval by factory owners like my father. However, my father co-operated by sending the children and even adults to evening classes so they could learn to read and write. I remember how the children in the factory would bring their books with them and look at them during their lunch break; they seemed very happy and proud to be receiving an education. Some of them even used to ask me to help them with their reading and arithmetic. Mir Taqi was also very helpful and encouraged many to go to evening classes. This meant they had to leave the factory at a certain time and not work more than eight hours. For this reason and others almost all the workers eventually joined the evening classes. One of them, Habib Farsh-baf from Qara-Dagh of Azerbaijan began to write poetry. Here I quote part of one of his poems:

> Thump, thump. Noise is coming from making carpets;
> The factory is too hot and dusty to breathe.
> The pale fingers are cut
> And make red lines on the frame.

During working hours all the workers talked among themselves about what had happened at the evening class. Their stories were often humorous. They made jokes and imitated teachers and their fellow students, then all laughed together. They used to argue about whether or not the girls should share the same classroom with boys. Mir Taqi said, "If we work together in the factory then we should be educated together too." This pleased the girls and they giggled and whispered to each other.

Pishavari's government was in favour of co-education, but in order to avoid the inevitable attacks and accusations by religious fanatics they did not press the issue. However, meetings for women and the formation of women's associations were strongly encouraged despite opposition by the majority of mullahs. I attended several of these out of curiosity. One was at Surkhab Qapisi and was called Qandinlar Jamiyyati (Women's Association); I used to peep in on my way back from my father's office in the bazaar and see a large gathering of women in the yard, standing and listening to a woman speaker. I do not remember my mother or sisters ever taking part in these women's associations; even if they had wanted to my father would not have approved. The mothers and sisters of the workers in my father's factory were often involved. In fact some of them were elected as leaders of their local associations. I remember seeing the suntanned, lovely smiling faces of old and young women in colourful skirts, shirts and scarves waiting to get on special buses to take them to work or meeting places. They looked cheerful and proud. Some of them used to wear medals as a sign of distinction. These medals were awarded by the government, to both men and women, as a mark of their service to the community.

As the list of Pishavari's aims had stated, his government was against unemployment. So much work, especially building work, was created that there were shortages of labour. People used to go to Pishavari to see him in person and tell them about their problems. Once Pishavari visited our district and the people quickly surrounded him and were asking questions. When he started to leave a young man shouted, "Comrade Pishavari!" Pishavari stopped, turned back and, seeing the young man, said to his ministers, "Let the man come forward and say what he wants to say." The young man stepped forward and, facing Pishavari, said, "You say there is a job for everybody — yet I have been without a job for weeks." Pishavari replied, "I am not supposed to be looking for you — you ought to come to our relevant departments and ask for a job. What can you do?" The young man said, "I can drive, build and work as a joiner." Pishavari called over to one of his companions and said, "Take this gentleman and give him a lorry and send him to bring grain from Ahar (a city about 100 kilometres from Tabriz) to Tabriz."

Under Pishavari's government the relationships between different ethnic and religious groups improved along with the communication between cities. The different tribes and people from cities throughout Azerbaijan used to visit Tabriz in groups and take part in celebrations and street processions. The Democratic Party of Kurdistan, which had also formed its own autonomous government under the leadership of Qazi Muhammad, used to send a group of supporters and traditional dancers and musicians all clad in their colourful national costumes. Armenians and Assyrians, who constituted the largest religious minority in Tabriz, were encouraged to participate in the building of industrial units and offer their views on the establishment of cultural centres. They also had representatives in Pishavari's government.

One of the most striking features that I remember from this time was that I came to learn about some great poets and writers of Azerbaijan and other parts of Iran. Azerbaijani culture had been devalued and suppressed by the central government since the coup d'état of Sayyid Zia in 1921 and the rise of Reza Shah. Pishavari and his minister of education, Mr Biriya, encouraged teachers to introduce the poets and writers of Azerbaijan to the people. Newspapers, literary magazines and radio programmes were all allocated for this purpose. I remember dozens of plays being staged in Tabriz, as well as other cities and villages of Azerbaijan.

Among the poets I came to know, Mirza Ali Akbar Sabir (Tahir-Zadeh) (1862-1911) and Mirza Ali Mu'jiz Shabistari (1873-1934) were popular. Here I will quote a poem from each of them:

My friend, in what state is your glorious city today?
God be blessed, it's the same as it was in Noah's day.
Have you new schools for the young of your country to learn in?
No, we've only Madrassahs, which stand since the year Adam was born in.
Do the citizens in your land read newspapers every day?
Some literate madmen do, but I don't, I must say.
Now tell me, my friend, are there libraries in your town?
Young people opened a few, but we turned them upside-down.
Are the hungry helped in your country by other men?
God sees their sufferings himself — why should we help them, then?

Do you take care of widows and women that are in need?
To the devil with them — can't they marry again, indeed?
Is the need for unity talked about in your land?
Yes, it is, but for eloquence's sake, you must understand.
Is the nation split into Shi'ites and Sunnites still?
What do you mean? For such words, young man, you ought to be killed.
Well, there is nothing else I can say to you, so good-bye.
Good riddance! I wish you to fall in a pit and die!
Just look at him! Look at his face — what a loathsome sight!
The way he talks! Why, he can't even put his cap on right!

("Questions and Answers" by Sabir.)

Allah be praised, at last our nation is glad:
Nakhichevan in a crimson gown is clad.
Just Soviet power has been established,
The exploited masses are ruling the land.
The Shah is mated, his viziers dismounted,
The elephant tramples on the khans uncounted.
Buds are unfolding, the season of flower has come,
The nightingale's singing his song of love.
The people everywhere feast and rejoice.
Other regions envy Nakhichevan for its choice;
Tabriz, Khamina, Shabistar show their envy
Together with Azerbaijan in one voice.
Not in vain is our envy, its cause is clear:
While they're having a wedding, we're mourning here.
And yet, Mu'jiz, do not weep bitter tears:
The day of delivery for us, too, is near.

(A poem by Shabistari.)

Another important personality and thinker about whom I had heard was Ahmad Kasravi (1890-1945), who wrote famous history books on the Constitutional Revolution, on the 18-year History of Azerbaijan and on the 500-year History of Khuzistan. He was born in Tabriz and lived in a district called Hukm-Abad. He was a companion and also a critic of Khiyabani.

I remember two news items about Kasravi which had been widely discussed in Tabriz. One was about how (as a judge in a court of law) he had passed a verdict in favour of a peasant against Reza Shah. The peasant had complained to the House of Justice in Tehran that Reza Shah had confiscated his land (as he had the land of thousands of other peasants). After examining the case, Kasravi ruled against Reza Shah and declared that the land should be returned to the peasant. Reza Shah, on hearing the verdict, ordered Kasravi's dismissal saying that, "Kasravi should be dismissed and should wait until he is called again". Kasravi replied thus: "He should wait for me rather than I wait for him . . ."

At a later date people talked about how Kasravi had claimed to be a prophet. Kasravi had once started training to become a mullah, but gave it up and began instead to criticise religious hypocrisy, especially Shi'ite rituals such as beating oneself or cutting one's head with a knife or sword. I remember that he was imprisoned and put on trial in 1945. While he was before the court a man named Sayyid Hussein Imami, who was connected with a fanatic Muslim group called Fida'iyan-i Islam entered the courtroom and shot him. I clearly remember the news of his death reverberating round the city like thunder that evening. He is still spoken of in Azerbaijan and indeed all over Iran and is regarded as an honest historian and social critic.

Izzat's neighbours, who were mostly either retired peasants or villagers who had come to Tabriz to work, talked of Pishavari and his land reform with admiration. They were disappointed when his government did not last and wondered why Pishavari had fallen from power. The question of Pishavari's fall has long preoccupied the people of Azerbaijan and Iran as a whole. My father and his friends believed that the central government's army was much stronger than Pishavari's forces (which were not meant to constitute an army and could not stand up against such an army). Furthermore, the Soviet Union failed to give practical support to the Democratic Government of Azerbaijan, which was resented by my father and his friends. Some argued that because the Pishavari government was put into power by the Russians, it did not have local and national support. (Mir Jafar Baqir, the president of Soviet Azerbaijan, had played an important role and had misled Pishavari.) More sophisticated and political commentators argued that Qavam (the Iranian prime minister at the time) had met Stalin and promised the Soviet Union an oil concession, and therefore Stalin had decided to withdraw his support for Pishavari. Among all these speculations, however, people knew that the conservative central government in Iran, backed by Britain and the United States politically (through the United Nations) and militarily, was chiefly responsible for the fall of Pishavari's government.

There were, however, some people in Britain who were critical of the British and American governments' stand against Azerbaijan and their support of the central government in Iran. Philip Price, MP, wrote in the *Manchester Guardian* on 20 December 1945:

> . . . a dangerous situation has now arisen in which Russia supports an autonomous regime of reforms in Persian Azerbaijan while we and the Americans are in fact supporting the most reactionary elements in the country . . .

Britain was particularly worried about the strong influence of Socialism and the democratic movements in the Middle East, and regarded the government of the Democratic Party of Azerbaijan as a threat against its interests in the area. According to John Kimche, writing in the British weekly, *Tribune*:

> Arab leaders have told me that they regard present-day British strategy as a defence against Russian penetration into the Middle East. They see a line of British military bases extending from southern Persia through Iraq, Syria, Lebanon, Palestine and Egypt to Greece to protect the Persian Gulf, the Middle East, the eastern Mediterranean and to back Turkey in her stand.
>
> (25 January 1946)

Whatever the causes, the fall of the Pishavari government, and the massacre of thousands of his supporters (especially in the cities of Zanjan, Miyaneh, Sarab, Ardabil and Tabriz), were devastating. William O. Douglas visited Azerbaijan and wrote in his book *Strange Lands and Friendly People*:

> When the Persian Army returned to Azerbaijan it came with a roar. Soldiers ran riot, looting and plundering, taking what they wanted. The Russian Army had been on its best behaviour. The Persian Army — the army of emancipation — was a savage army of occupation. It left a brutal mark on the people. The beards of peasants were burned, their wives and daughters raped. Houses were plundered; livestock was stolen. The Army was out of control. Its mission had been liberation; but it preyed on the civilians, leaving death and destruction behind.
>
> On the heels of the Army came the absentee landlords. They demanded not only the current rentals; they also laid claim to the rent which had not been paid while Pishavari was in power. These back payments were a severe drain on the food supply of the peasants.

One early morning my father sent me to buy fresh *sangak* bread. I bought the bread and came out of the bakery. A few metres away I saw a soldier running towards Izzat's district. Someone stopped him and asked what was happening. He said, "It is all over, our forces are defeated in Zanjan . . ." A woman standing next to me cried out, "Alas . . ."

Pishavari crossed over to Soviet Azerbaijan and at least lived to tell his tale. He died in exile. If he had not escaped he would have faced Khiyabani's fate. This is a child's memory of Pishavari, but there are still many people in Azerbaijan, outstanding historians among them, who could write or say more if they were allowed.

At the moment "spirit", both in the human body and in bottles, is forbidden in Iran. But one should not despair. Living in similar circumstances, Mu'jiz believed that the Muses have an inspiring and powerful influence in society:

> My poet, don't regret; this is a transient world.
> Only the spiritual world will last, believe my word.

Now go, in service to mankind seek your reward.
Only in truth can lasting joy be found, so let your word
By all the world, by all humanity be heard . . .

7

Mossadeq, Our National Father

I lived under Mossadeq. Dr Muhammad Mossadeq (1881-1967) was a European-educated aristocrat who had studied law in Switzerland. Since 1921 he had served as minister of justice, finance and foreign affairs, as well as governor of Fars and Azerbaijan. He was famous for his opposition to Reza Shah's dictatorship and for his liberal views, and was trusted by the public for his independent nationalism. I first heard of him in 1951 and was very much impressed by his nationalisation of Iranian oil and his idea (which I heard on the radio) that "the Shah must reign not rule".

After leaving Elmieh School I worked for six months, between July and December, in a chemist shop in Armanistan (the Armenian district of Tabriz). I was by then about 13 or 14 years old. I remember it was one of the coldest winters that I had ever experienced. Sometimes it was 10-20 degrees below zero and the roads were cracked and covered by ice and snow. Mr Saadati, the owner of the shop, used to send me to the drug wholesale bazaar or to other chemist shops to collect the drugs which were required for his customers. Inside my woollen gloves and socks my hands and feet would freeze and remain numb for several hours. But I did not complain to Mr Saadati or the young man who prepared the prescriptions because I did not want them to think of me as a child; I wished to be regarded as an adult or a serious person who wanted to learn.

My purpose in working in the chemist shop was to learn the names of the drugs and which drug was suitable for particular diseases. I thought that it would be a good idea to write the names of the drugs and diseases in a little notebook and after a while, when I had learned a sufficient number, then I could open my own clinic and serve the very poorest people.

The young man who worked in the chemist shop did not like to see me taking notes and sometimes seemed rather nervous and anxious in case I learned his job and took his place. He himself had learned this profession

Dr Muhammad Mossadeq, 1951.

through an apprenticeship, which he had begun at the age that I was at the time. In order to avoid upsetting him I started to take my notes during his absence. Most of the drugs had French names and so I decided to attend private evening classes and learn French.

Mr Asmai was my French teacher. He held his classes next to his house. There were few students in the class and Mr Asmai was a good teacher. He was a rather amusing old man who spent a good deal of time talking about his son, who was studying medicine at Tabriz University. He told us that his son was top in everything and how polite and obliging a son he was. This made my fellow students rather envious and they wished to be so popular with their parents. In later years I had a friend called Dr Chaichi who used to live in Amir Khiz (Izzat's district) and was a fellow student of my French teacher's son. Once, as a matter of interest, I asked him about Dr Asmai and how good a student he was. Dr Chaichi laughed and said nothing. Later on I insisted on knowing the reason for his laughter when I had mentioned Dr Asmai. He told me that he had been well known in the university as a fanatical supporter of the Shah and a close friend of Haji Abulqasim Javan, the owner of the largest carpet factory in Tabriz and again a sworn supporter of the Shah and enemy of Pishavari and Mossadeq.

I had met this man through my father. In fact he respected my father because he was the most skilled person in his profession and they had known each other since childhood. I once asked my father how Mr Javan had acquired such a big factory. My father answered, "I have known Mr

Javan and his older brother Ahmad since I was a child. When I had my small carpet factory Ahmad used to sell potatoes at Gajil Gapisi (the South Gate in Tabriz) and his brother Abulqasim was with him. Later on my friends and I helped Ahmad to start making carpets. Ahmad worked hard and started the factory but Abulqasim took over. Ahmad is a better person than his brother."

I sensed that my father disliked Abulqasim, not because he supported the Shah but because he was arrogant both towards the public and his workers. Once I heard that he had beaten a worker to death and evaded justice by bribing the police.

The owner of the chemist shop had a brother called Mr Karim, a pleasant-looking, tall man with sharp green eyes, who had a shop opposite my father's office. Mr Karim and his father melted down brass scraps which they then cast into objects such as water taps, bells, samovar bases and a myriad of little household articles. The furnace was at the corner of the shop. They used to place the brass scraps and pieces in special containers and stretch them into the furnace, which was kept burning brightly by leather bellows which were pushed backwards and forwards by a child. I found this fascinating and used to stand and watch them for hours. Mr Karim and his father were very kind to me. He once made me a toy gun out of brass, which I still have in Tabriz; it was a most valuable present for a child in those days.

After working for six months in the chemist shop I did not become a doctor as I had originally intended, but at least I had learned how to read the names of drugs in the Latin alphabet! This helped me to learn English in the following year after taking the examination of sixth-year elementary level.

Instead, I started my secondary education at Nizami School, which was situated between Amir Khiz and Davachi districts. I was excited at going to a new school: I was going to see new faces, new rooms, a new yard, new teachers — a whole new world. I was full of enthusiasm to discover what a state school would be like, as I was attending one for the first time.

I found it to be much better organised than my previous schools and the students more serious and disciplined. The teachers were all well qualified. We had excellent teachers in Persian, history, mathematics and English, but I did not like our Arabic teacher, who sat and read his university books and expected everybody to be quiet. In fact by good fortune I was already well versed in Arabic; I had learned it at Mirza Ibrahim's *maktab* and through private tuition. Another teacher who frightened us was the one who taught Persian. He was very well dressed and smart but rather strict and dry. In his class we were forbidden to speak Azerbaijani — our mother tongue.

The competition within our class was very intense. Although I managed to come third among 35-40 students, I nevertheless decided to leave the school and study at night-school so that I could try to pass two years' exams in one

Nizami Ganjavi, the poet.

year. This was not the only reason why I left a school and fellow students which I liked: what I did not like was the sense of suppression and suffocation of creative work and independent thought. Some teachers, particularly the Arabic and Persian ones, treated us like children. Of course we *were* children — but their attitude did not encourage the development of either the mind or the personality. I had already acquired a sense of independence and appreciated the opportunity for creative thinking — this perhaps others had not experienced. Consequently I preferred to study on my own, although there were more risks involved. If I passed the examination in the following June I would be one year ahead of my fellow students; if I failed then I would have fallen one year behind.

Nizami School was called after a great Persian poet — Nizami Ganjavi. Nizami Ganjavi (his real name was Ilyas ibn-Yusuf), a great poet and thinker from what is now Soviet Azerbaijan, was born in Ganja in 1141, where he lived all his life and where he died in 1209. His most famous works, which are a worthy contribution to world literature, are five long poems, of 30,000 couplets, known as the *Khamsa* (five books). "There is not a house in Iran," wrote Sa'id Nafisi (the famous Persian writer and critic of the present century) "where books of Sa'di and Hafiz can not be found and the *Khamsa* of Nizami would not be among them. Every old and young Persian-speaking person knows these books from elementary school."

Nizami was not a court poet and he criticised those who were in the service of the rich and powerful and extolled their masters' virtues for money. However, Nizami himself was obliged to dedicate his poems to rulers and eminent people, driven to this by poverty and the need to find patronage. One of his poems that I remember from childhood and read in school is "The Story of Sultan Sanjar" (who died in 1157) and "The Old Woman", which begins:

> A poor old woman was harassed,
> And came to Sultan Sanjar to complain:
> She said: "O Sultan, I have not seen any justice in you,
> All through the years I have seen oppression from you.
> A drunken officer came to my street,
> Kicked, knocked me down,
> He dragged me, innocent, out of my house,
> Pulling my hair as if he wanted to kill me.
> He yelled: 'You hunch-backed hag, tell me
> Who killed a person at your house?'
> He entered my house in search of the murderer.
> O Shah, what greater humiliation than this?
> The reason for murder was the officer's being drunk,
> Why, then, yell and treat an old woman like this?
> The officers of the Sultan ransack the land,
> But old women are accused as criminals!
> He who has committed this oppression
> Has harmed my reputation and your justice . . ."

In the rest of this poem Nizami draws the comparison between the sultan who lives upon his subjects by plunder and oppression and the sultan who protects his subjects by justice and even-handedness.

During the summer holiday I decided to find another job somewhere other than my father's factory. I thought that if I worked for my father I would not be able to study as much as I wanted. Besides, I wanted to support my own education, that is, pay my own fees and travelling expenses. My parents did not expect any money from me. The relationship between parents and children in Iran and the East in general is rather different from that in the West. Parents in Iran do not charge money for food and accommodation unless they are poor and unable to support themselves. In this case the children work and support their parents.

Through a friend I found a job in a material shop at Amir Bazaar, which was one of the best and most crowded bazaars in Tabriz. Many people shopped for their weddings in this bazaar, particularly for the dresses and jewellery. It was well arranged and brightly lit, with goldsmiths, jewellers, perfumeries and material shops of all kinds. There was another bazaar parallel to Amir Bazaar where there were herbs and haberdashery shops. I used to like passing this bazaar, which was full of the smell of fresh herbs.

I worked in Haji Ali-Asghar Turchiyan's shop from 9 a.m. to 4.45 p.m. and went to my evening classes at 5 p.m. I had to leave the shop almost three hours before closing time. There are no fixed hours for shops in Tabriz and in other cities of Iran. The bazaars usually close between six and seven in the evening but the shops in the streets are open, especially in summer, until midnight. This gives an air of liveliness to the evening streets, with people strolling up and down, shopping and window-shopping. Most shops close for two or three hours at midday for the afternoon siesta. This is an especially welcome break during the hot summer months.

My job in the shop was to help the customers, measure the materials, arrange and pack them. Mr Turchiyan handled the money. At noon Mr Turchiyan would go to the mass prayer at the nearby mosque and I used to sit, if there were no customers (the shop was usually very quiet in the afternoons), and revise my lessons. We ate our lunch together — fresh bread with butter and honey in winter and fresh bread, cheese and fruit in autumn and summer. Then twice a week I was sent to different places to collect money from Mr Turchiyan's debtors. These hours were most pleasant ones when I had a chance to read my books and go through my English vocabulary while waiting for the people from whom I had to collect the money.

On the whole, my employer was a kind and polite man who did not interfere with my studies while the shop was quiet. I was paid 25 tomans (about £3 at that time) per month, excluding my lunch. I paid 12 tomans for the evening class and spent 13 more on travelling and books. I managed to save some money from my wages and tips so that I would have something to spend during the three months (April to June) when I left work to concentrate on my studies and prepare for the final examination.

I stayed at home during these months to revise. I spent part of April in the library and May and June in our garden under the fruit trees. It was pleasant to be able to revise and think in the fresh air and spring sunshine, especially since I could help myself to the fruit which hung above my head as I sat and studied underneath the trees. At lunchtime my mother would call me in for a meal. I never wanted a big lunch in case I felt sleepy afterwards and could not study, but enjoyed sitting with my parents, brothers and sisters. I was always anxious not to miss the melon or water-melon after the meal.

After this effort I managed to pass all the subjects and had thus completed both the second and third years of secondary school. I had now moved one year ahead of my former classmates at Nizami School. This year (1950-1951) when I attended the Azar night-school, Bungah-i Azar, was a year of change for me. I was introduced to the outside world. I met many people from different levels both in the bazaar and at night-school. There were workers, army and air-force personnel, businessmen and young students like me in my class. We had well-known teachers in physics, chemistry, history, Persian and other subjects. Our physics teacher was called Murtaza Alasti. He was a good teacher but very strict and treated us like schoolchildren. Nobody was allowed to enter his class after he had started the lesson. I remember one day one of the workers, a Mr Dabbagh, who worked in a textile factory in Tabriz, arrived five minutes late and knocked at the classroom door. The teacher did not let him come in. I protested and said, "Sir, Mr Dabbagh is no schoolboy, but a worker who is returning from his work. It is not fair to keep him outside." My words fell like a bombshell in the classroom. Mr Alasti lost his temper and said sarcastically, "A new barber has arrived and cuts our hair differently." He meant that I had opposed tradition and his programme. Perhaps he was right, but I could not bear to see the innocent face of Mr Dabbagh outside the door and deprived of attending one of our most important subjects.

After speaking these words, Mr Alasti stalked out of the classroom. The reaction in the classroom was mixed: some believed that the teacher was right and some believed that I was right. A member of the air force who was sitting next to me (and in fact supported me) said, "You'd better go and apologise to Mr Alasti and ask him to return to his class." Worried about the loss of the physics lesson, I took his advice and went to the principal's room, where I found Mr Alasti. The principal, without hesitation, advised me to stay out of class for two weeks while Mr Alasti decided whether to accept me back or not.

For a fortnight I stayed away from the physics classes. One evening I went to Mr Alasti's house and knocked on the door. A woman answered and I asked for him. She said, "Wait, while I go and call him." Shortly afterwards Mr Alasti appeared at the door. I greeted him and apologised for disturbing him in his class. He said, "I appreciate your feelings but you put me on the spot in the classroom and made me feel guilty. You know, there are many individual rich students who want me to teach them privately but I prefer to teach the students at Bungah-i Azar. You may come back to my classes." In June when we received our examination results, Mr Dabbagh received the highest marks in the classroom. I was delighted.

During the following summer I worked in the shop next to the one owned by Haji Ali-Asghar Turchiyan. The name of the shop owner was Mr Qari-Zadeh. My work was rather dull and less stimulating in this shop, nor did I have the same freedom that I had in my previous employment. Mr Qari-

Zadeh neither showed any interest in my studies, nor did he talk to me about bazaar matters.

Before the summer ended I decided to work with Hassan, Haji Turchiyan's nephew. We both had a small amount of savings with which we bought some material. His father, who also owned a large material shop opposite his brother's, let us use the outside corner of his shop to sell our goods. This suited me very well, because I was my own boss and could sit and read or prepare my lessons and meanwhile serve any customer who wanted to buy some material.

I had enrolled at Bungah-i Azar to study the fourth and fifth years of secondary level. These years were equivalent to 'O' level or Scottish 'O' grade. As in the previous year, I worked in the bazaar until 5 p.m. and then attended my evening classes. This year I had much to do. Mathematics, physics and chemistry were much harder. In addition we had Arabic, English and Persian examinations. In April I stopped working in the bazaar and started to revise for the final examination. My father, who had seen that I was studying very seriously, did not bother asking me to do any odd jobs in the factory. But I still went there sometimes and talked to the workers.

I took my examinations in June and passed all of them. It seemed like a miracle. Some of the students who attended the classes with me had tried several times and failed. Their talk of failure had frightened me and made me anxious. A few weeks before the examinations I had talked to myself sternly: "Those who have attempted the examinations several times and have failed are those who attend the classes but do not do their homework and do not revise properly before the examinations. Look at those who frighten you. They spend most of their time in front of the girls' school and watch them or chat with them on their return home. If you study all the allocated books and answer all the questions in mathematics, physics and chemistry, and translate Arabic into Persian correctly, then there is no reason for worrying." This talk to myself had helped me.

By now I was two years ahead of my former fellow students at Nizami School. Most of my friends there knew what I was doing and in fact seemed proud of me. Their positive attitude had encouraged me and I was pleased that I had not disappointed them.

The following summer, 1952, I did not work in the bazaar but I helped my father at the factory and at home. I was also busy thinking about my future: whether to enrol in the military academy and become an officer after three or four years of study, or to enrol in a day-school and do the sixth and final year of secondary school, which is equivalent to 'A' level or Highers in Scotland. I finally decided on the latter and enrolled at Firdausi day-school.

Firdausi Secondary School was one of the largest and oldest schools in the city centre. It was a three-storey brick building surrounded by a large schoolyard. It had large laboratories for chemistry, physics and physiology. Dr Kishavarzi taught chemistry. Mr Alasti (who also taught at the night-school) taught physics and Dr Taymuri, the principal of the night-school, taught physiology a few days a week and also worked at the university hospital. He had a degree in physiology and a degree in medicine. Our teacher of Persian literature was Mr Batman-Qilinj, whom I liked very much; he had a sense of humour and stimulated and encouraged creative writing. I remember once we were asked to write about the meaning of "knowledge". I wrote a very short essay in Persian explaining that there are two kinds of knowledge: one is acquired through one's own daily experience and the other is taught by others. I trusted and preferred the former to the latter. Mr Batman-Qilinj called me to his office and told me how he liked my essay and encouraged me to write on the basis of my own experience rather than relying on the information of others.

The school had a huge hall where we could gather to watch plays and films or listen to speakers. I found some of the lectures very boring, especially those of the principal, Mr Mirfakhrai, who taught French. He was a cultured, upper-class man who tried to translate French novels into Tabriz life! Our English teacher, Mr Lazar, on the other hand, was an Assyrian who told us dirty jokes and often talked about his Chevrolet car, which was well known in the city. He taught *Essential English*; and *A Tale of Two Cities* by Charles Dickens. Mr Lazar was one of the best English teachers in Tabriz. He had learned the language while working for the British in southern Iran during the Second World War.

The students at Firdausi School came mostly from middle-class families. In our class there were about 60 students, who were aiming to study either engineering or medicine. I intended to study dentistry. My close friend Mr Tisheh-Zan, who hoped to study medicine, combined his studies with helping his father in their carpenter's shop. We often studied together at each other's houses. At the end of the year we both passed the sixth-year examinations. He could enrol at Tehran University to study medicine but I could not. I decided to study in the Faculty of Arts — English and Persian language and literature.

After the final examinations I decided to travel to other parts of Iran. I went to Tehran with my brother Ismail, where he went to a lung specialist for treatment of his tuberculosis. While attending the hospital he stayed with my cousin in Tehran. I, meantime, visited Esfahan and Shiraz. I found these ancient cities very beautiful and cultured. In Esfahan I visited blue-tiled mosques, which had the most beautiful mosaics on their domes; there were also huge squares with fountains and wide streets with tall trees and the bridge over the river, whose unusual architecture attracts many visitors from all over the world. The bazaars in Esfahan were also full of interesting handicrafts. However, I was anxious to visit Shiraz before returning to

A mosque in Esfahan.

Tehran to rejoin Ismail, so I did not stay there more than a few days.

Shiraz did not seem to me to have as many historical buildings as Esfahan, but its being the home town of Sa'di and Hafiz Shirazi, the great Persian poets, was more than enough for me. I had longed to visit Shiraz and roam through the narrow alleys and bazaars that Hafiz and Sa'di perhaps had once frequented. I wished to see the rose gardens of Sa'di's poetry and the meadows and cypress trees I knew from Hafiz, or the beautiful Shirazi and Turke-Shirazi girls whose beauty made Hafiz ever drunk and filled his imagination and poetry with energy and inspiration.

Creative imagination or poetic genius in man can be used as a weapon against dogmatism and social injustice. Hafiz attacked those hypocrites who condemn their progressive and creative opponents as being irreligious or unbelievers. He was not against Islam, in fact he knew the Quran by heart; he opposed the mullahs who used religion (in this case, Islam) as a means of negation, domination and exploitation of the people. Those who did not fast during Ramadan and did not go to the mosque were regarded by such people as unbelievers. Hafiz, satirising such religious leaders, wrote:

> Ramadan has passed. The day of Festivity (Id) has arrived and hearts rise. We
>   must call for wine.
> The turn of the leaden-hearted hypocrite is over.
> The time for freedom and enjoyment for freedom-lovers has arrived.
>
>   . . .
>
> Drinking, which has no hypocrisy or cunning in it,
> Is better than piety based on hypocrisy or cunning.
> What does it matter if you and I drink a few cups of wine?
> Wine is the blood of grapes, not of you [the people].
>
>   (From the *Divan* by Hafiz.)

Hafiz is the most loved and popular classical Persian poet in Iran. His *Divan* is put side by side with the Quran; the people read or refer to Hafiz even more than the Quran. They find that Hafiz talks their language and reflects their feelings and aspirations. Both literate and illiterate find something to think about or cling to in the poems of Hafiz. Even the Western élite and great writers and poets such as Goethe found their idol and a long sought meaning and definition of imagination or poetry in Hafiz Shirazi.

Hafiz spurns the dogmatic believers' concept of a remote, all powerful God in the sky, believing rather the power of creative genius or divine power in man. Here is a translation of part of one of his poems:

> For many years my soul was searching for a mirror in which it could see the
>   world,
> And was begging from strangers the very thing it had itself.
> The elusive pearl which cannot be found in the shell of time and place,
> My soul was requesting it from those who were lost on the sea-shore.
> Last night I took my problem to the old man
> Who solved problems with the help of visions.
> I saw him full of joy and laughing,
> Holding his bowl of wine which gave back the sight of hundreds of different
>   visions.
> I asked of the wise old man: "When was this bowl given to you?"
> And he replied: "When this blue dome was unfurl'd".
>
>   (From the *Divan* by Hafiz.)

Before I started at Firdausi School I had met two final-year medical students, Mr Chaichi and Mr Madani. I met Mr Chaichi in the bus which ran

Handicrafts on sale at a bazaar in Esfahan.

between Amir Khiz and the city centre, and I met Mr Madani through Mr Chaichi. Both had been among the first group of students who entered the medical school during the period of Pishavari's government, when the University of Tabriz was founded. They were interested in politics; most students from Tabriz University were politically minded, supporting either Mossadeq or the Tudeh Party. Mr Chaichi was pro-Mossadeq and defended him passionately and I learnt from him a lot about this man. Mr Madani also thought well of Mossadeq, but supported the Tudeh Party. They both talked to me about politics and also visited my sister Sakineh and my brother Ismail when they were ill. Indeed, they used to help and treat poor people and friends without charge.

In later years Mr Chaichi (now Dr Chaichi) opened a private clinic serving the people in the Amir-Khiz district, and charged them very low fees. I once visited his clinic. After seeing a patient, he turned to me: "Mr Sabri, most of my patients are not really ill, but need proper food. They are poor and often instead of prescribing medicine I give them some money to buy food." Dr Chaichi became well known in Tabriz for his good treatment of the people. Mr Madani (now Dr Madani) worked in the military hospital until 2 p.m. and held his private clinic in the evening. He also treated the poor without charge.

My friendship with Dr Chaichi was much closer. We visited each other's houses, dined together and discussed politics. Indeed, meeting him before going to Firdausi School helped me to find my way in the intense political atmosphere there. Among the students there were different groups, some supporting Mossadeq, some of the Tudeh Party, some Ayatollah Kashani, some the neo-fascist party, SOMKA, and some Dr Baqai.

Mossadeq, by this time, was premier and leader of the National Movement (*Jibhe-ye Milli*), which stood against British imperialism. The Tudeh party was Marxist-Leninist, supported Mossadeq and was pro-Soviet. Ayatollah Kashani was the leader of the religious zealots who were supported by the bazaar. He had initially been a supporter of Mossadeq, but later turned against him. Baqai, who was the leader of the workers' party, had also initially been a supporter of Mossadeq. Later, when I was at Firdausi School, his supporters attacked the Mossadeq government and were fanatically against the Tudeh party. The fascist groups were active under the name of SOMKA (I did not know the meaning of the word), who wore the Nazi swastika and clashed with other groups, especially the Tudeh Party and the National Movement. I remember on one occasion that the SOMKA supporters threw their opponents from the second-floor balcony on to the school yard. They were armed with knives and sticks. The supporters of Ayatollah Kashani, Dr Baqai and SOMKA frequently united to attack the supporters of Mossadeq and the Tudeh Party. I remember the students from the latter group being badly wounded.

The SOMKA members were mainly from land-owning and military backgrounds, whereas the supporters of Kashani and Baqai were sons of landlords and some sections of the bazaar, religious organisations and the rich intellectuals. When there was a conflict between the supporters and opponents of the Mossadeq government the SOMKA and Baqai groups would bring or hire supporters from outside the school. These were often hooligans or well-known delinquents from the city. We were really terrified to face them in front of the school. As soon as we knew they were congregating in front of the school we would try to escape through doors at the back or over walls. I never saw the supporters of Mossadeq and the Tudeh party using knives, sticks or bricks against their opponents, whereas the supporters of Baqai, SOMKA and Kashani even carried knives and sticks in the classrooms.

These days were a time of joy and grief, days of certainty and uncertainty — the days of gaining social consciousness. We were proud and full of joy to see and feel that — for the first time — a democratically elected government under Mossadeq's premiership had been established. There was a deep sense of pride and unity among the ordinary people of Iran. When the Mossadeq government faced an economic blockade (Britain stopped the export of Iranian oil) the people offered Mossadeq their own savings and precious possessions. This was one side of the coin but there was an ugly side as well: the opposition, who were supported by internal and external enemies of Mossadeq's government, did their best to destroy what had been achieved during the past 50 years of struggle since the Constitutional Revolution of 1905. Mossadeq was a manifestation of a long national struggle against internal despotism and external imperialism. Mossadeq was the embodiment of a suppressed nation. But his enemies were many, and the strongest of all was Great Britain.

I remember that the first open move by the Shah against Mossadeq was in the summer of 1952. He enlisted as his ally an old experienced politician, Qavam (also the butcher of the Pishavari government), and asked him to form the government. This move against the Mossadeq government and his subsequent dismissal as premier brought a flood of protests from the public. I was in Tabriz at the time. I went to Mr Hussein Hariri's house in our neighbourhood. He and his family (father, brothers and sisters) were all Constitutionalists and pro-Mossadeq. We went together to the post office in the city centre, where a big crowd had gathered, to send a telegram of support for Mossadeq and opposition to the Shah's support of Qavam. Many speeches were delivered. Mr Hariri spoke and several poets recited their revolutionary poems in support of freedom and the nationalisation of Iranian oil. I remember this poem in particular:

> London has developed by our oil
> But our city Abadan remains in ruins.
> The English live in brightness by our black oil,
> While we Iranians have no lights.
> In England the welfare state expands,
> While the people of Iran live in poverty.
> Under our feet is oil,
> While we have no oil in our lamps.
>
> (From "Jouya" (Mohammad Ali Mahmid,
> contemporary Iranian poet, born 1920.)

After the speeches had been made and the telegrams supporting Mossadeq and condemning Qavam had been sent, the crowd started moving towards the Town Hall. There were workers, businessmen, bazaar people and intellectuals. The cart and *doroshka* drivers had brought along their carts and *doroshkas* (horse-driven carriages), which the children in the procession had clambered up and were riding on. It was a lively and humorous procession and the opposition did not (as far as I remember) dare to face the crowd in Tabriz. But in Tehran it was a different story: there was a bloody clash between the Shah's army and the supporters of Mossadeq. Many of Mossadeq's supporters were crushed to death by moving tanks or were killed by gun-fire.

However, the Shah was forced to back down and Qavam resigned. Mossadeq regained his premiership and succeeded in weakening the position of the Shah. I remember Dr Chaichi and his friends were very active during this period. They organised meetings and discussion groups in schools and private houses. I took part in some of these meetings.

Apart from Ayatollah Angaji (Muhammad Ali Angaji), to whom I was introduced by Dr Chaichi, Ayatollah Milani and some junior mullahs, the religious leaders did not support Mossadeq. Even if they seemed to do so it was often only because they did not want to alienate themselves from the people who were their life-line (financial support).

Religious leaders, under the leadership of Ayatollah Kashani, had previously allied themselves with Mossadeq when, at the beginning, he was supportive of the traditional bazaar guilds and observed their religious laws. But as soon as the Mossadeq government began to talk about land reform, nationalising industry and oil, suffrage for women (Kashani, opposing this, said that "the government should prevent women from voting so that they can stay at home and perform their true function — rearing children") and permitting breweries and distilleries to continue production, then Ayatollah Kashani and landed ayatollahs turned against him.

I remember Ayatollah Milani, who lived between Izzat's and my parents' house, was attacked by other ayatollahs and their followers because he had voted for the production and sale of alcohol. Milani was a comparatively poor man, who had been elected by the people of Tabriz as their representative during the 16th Majlis. I remember that when Mossadeq and Dr Hussein Fatimi (Minister of Foreign Affairs) talked about their reforms the mullahs made public speeches in the mosques warning that Islam itself was in danger. At the time I could not understand how Islam could be threatened by these social reforms. Later, however, I realised that these ayatollahs and mullahs interpreted Islam as a set of religious laws, traditions and internalised superstitions which kept their social and economic positions intact and prolonged the status quo. Any social change which endangered the interests of the ruling class and the position of the ayatollahs was regarded as a threat to Islam. But for Ayatollah Milani and other progressive men like Ayatollah Taliqani, whom I knew through Dr Chaichi and Ayatollah Angaji, these social reforms and the application of social justice constituted the basic principles of Islam.

I attended the various meetings and listened to Dr Chaichi and his friends. Dr Chaichi was himself a devout Muslim and firmly believed in the principles of Islam. It was then that I began to realise that Islam was being used as a cloak and weapon by both conservative and progressive parties and groups to promote their social and economic positions. I well remember one occasion when I was sent from Tabriz by Dr Chaichi and his friends to take part in a meeting of the National Movement in Tehran. Ayatollah

Taliqani, Mr Bazargan, Mr Ghani-Zadeh, Allahyar Saleh (Mossadeq's ambassador in the United States) and many others were at this meeting. A discussion arose on how to organise committees and accept members to promote the ideas of the National Movement. Explaining what was required in selecting committee members, Mr Bazargan said, "We must even observe every individual to see if he prays five times a day and fasts in Ramadan . . ."

Taliqani reacted to Bazargan's views by commenting, "Prayers and fasting is an individual and private issue and should not be regarded as criteria for social and political awareness . . ." Through these kinds of meeting I came to understand the difference between a reactionary and progressive Muslim. One, for example, regarded the *chador* worn by women as their virtue, while the other regarded it as a matter of personal choice and of no relevance to virtue.

Just as the year 1951-52 was the year of change, so 1952-53 was the year of enlightenment for me, and others. Iranian oil was nationalised and British Petroleum expelled from the country. Iran was the first state in the Middle East and the Indian subcontinent to effectively challenge the British Empire. Mossadeq was now regarded as the leader and father of the nation. Both old and young felt proud.

My father also supported Mossadeq, mainly because his government encouraged native handicrafts, national products and exports. My father's carpets were exported and sold for higher prices than ever before. In order to promote the Iranian textile industry, Mossadeq himself wore clothes made of Iranian wool and material. Thus he encouraged others to use Iranian materials rather than imported ones. During Mossadeq's premiership exports increased tenfold and imports decreased.

Despite sanctions by Britain and her allies, the country's economy gained in strength. Many schools and hospitals were built and the social position of working women and men improved. Women were allowed to vote, but the religious leaders, and Ayatollah Kashani and pro-British Sheikh Hassan Lankarani in particular, attacked the government's liberal policies and continued to say that the woman's place was in the home bringing up children.

The opposition of Kashani, Baqai and other anti-Mossadeq forces — land-owners, top army personnel and above all the Shah — was not restricted to political debates. They used all sorts of violence: in the schools, streets, bazaars and among the military and police force. Afshar-Tus, the Chief of Police, was murdered in Tehran and many social and political figures who supported Mossadeq suffered at the hands of well-organised groups of terrorists. Religious fanaticism played an important role in carrying out terrorist actions. They accused their enemies of being anti-Islamic, atheist or Communist. This was a terrifying weapon and proved very effective on those people who believed passionately in Islam and Allah.

Communism did not have any objective meaning, but was seen as a bogeyman, a threat to their culture, religion and identity. Naturally, the conservative and reactionary forces used this weapon of "Communism" as often and as effectively as possible.

It was later revealed in a BBC film on Mossadeq (in 1985) that Britain was instrumental in magnifying the supposed threat of Communism in Iran, which was used as a scarecrow to frighten the United States into agreeing to get rid of Mossadeq. Eventually the CIA and MI6 acted together to overthrow Mossadeq in August 1953.

In July 1953 I went to Tehran to spend the summer preparing for the entrance examination to Tehran University. I stayed at the house of my father's friend (Mr Rajabi). I used to go to the city parks and sit under the trees next to running water and revise my physics, chemistry, biology and English. In the heat of a Tehran summer this was the coolest and quietest place for studying. There were many other students from different parts of Iran who, like myself, intended to take part in the entrance examination. I also used to study under the shade of the huge trees beside running water at Kakh Avenue (Palace Avenue), which was next to the Shah's winter palace. In the past I had always felt anxious sitting or walking in the streets next to the palace, in case I might be attacked by the guards. But now I felt secure, as if I was in a place which belonged to the public not to a despotic Shah. Mossadeq had created this sense of peace and security within me and perhaps within millions of others.

I used to walk up and down Kakh Avenue and read my schoolbooks. Once I dared to speak to one of the guards who, to my surprise and delight, was from Azerbaijan and spoke my language. We chatted for a while. He told me that he was very homesick and missed his family. He was a peasant's son and doing his military service. The lifestyle and atmosphere in Tehran was alien to him; moreover, he could not speak Persian. He told me that he had three sisters and four brothers who had never been out of their village except for the time when he and his elder brother had taken their mother to a hospital in Tabriz: "We took our mother on a donkey and travelled on foot for eight or ten hours. By the time we arrived in Tabriz it was night-time and the doctor's clinic was closed and the hospital did not allow our mother in. My brother, mother and I had to sleep all night in front of the hospital. My mother had an illness related to women and was bleeding. The night was cold and my brother and I tried to cover her as well as we could. We both put our coats over her. But before dawn she died and we had to return with her body on the donkey to our village. It was the longest and worst journey that I had ever done. My brother and I wished that we had been attacked by wolves and killed on the way rather than have to face my elderly father, my sisters and other brothers."

It was 19 August 1953, a few days before the entrance examination, I went to Tehran University to enrol for the examination and collect my card and seat number. Having done so, I came out of the university campus and sat in front of its big gate. I suddenly noticed a busload of women, who looked like prostitutes, followed by two buses full of gangs of thugs holding sticks and shouting "Long live the Shah! Down with Mossadeq!" There were a number of people on foot around the slow-moving buses inviting the people in the street to join in. Those who refused (in fact all the people I saw refused to repeat what the men wielding sticks demanded) were punished. I was shocked to witness this scene. I jumped up and rushed towards my friend's home.

On the way I saw crowds of people outside Mossadeq's house. They were supporting him. After a while some soldiers arrived, accompanied by a group of men and women, again shouting "Down with Mossadeq! Long live the Shah!" They were followed by tanks and yet more troops. In front of the defenceless people, who were supporting their democratically elected Premier, the soldiers attacked Mossadeq's house, using their tanks. At that moment I felt as if my father had died and I had become an orphan. For Mossadeq was regarded as our father — the personality and hero of a nation which was struggling to free itself from internal despotism and external imperialism.

Mossadeq gave himself up a few days later. Hussein Fatimi, who had been hidden by the Tudeh Party, was arrested after a three-month search. As Mossadeq's foreign minister, he was hated by the Shah and his sister. Fatemi was executed while he was ill and suffering from wounds inflicted by the Shah's thugs (their leader was known as "Sha'ban", the brainless). Lutfi, Mossadeq's minister of justice, was murdered. The treatment of the Tudeh Party members, however, was much harsher. As the Tudeh underground was gradually discovered, the security forces executed 40 party officials, tortured to death another 14, sentenced 200 to life imprisonment and arrested over 3,000 rank-and-file members. Hundreds of intellectuals, with varying political views, were also imprisoned or killed. Karimpur Shirazi, a well-known journalist under Mossadeq (his newspaper was called *Shuresh*), was burned alive by the Shah's police in front of the Shah's sister, Ashraf, who particularly despised this journalist. Muhammad Reza Shah, like his father, Reza Shah, could now rule without any organised opposition. Another cycle of despotism in Iran had been started by the coup of 1953. The Shah returned to Iran from Rome and General Zahedi, who led the coup d'état, became Prime Minister. Britain, America and other Western monopolies also returned to Iran. The country's oil was denationalised and put under a consortium.

The success of the ayatollahs in Iran after the Revolution in 1979 has its roots, I believe, in the past — particularly in the fall of Mossadeq. In order to understand the current situation in Iran and probably give an answer to these questions: "Where did the ayatollahs come from? What happened to Iran's deep-rooted culture and literary heritage? Why could the National Movement, the Tudeh Party, the Mujahedin, the Fida'is and other radical groups not succeed?" — we have to show why and how Mossadeq became the victim of a Western plot.

Mossadeq's fall disturbed me deeply and I was unable to think and study as before. I did not do well in the entrance examination. On the night of 19 August when I returned to my friend's house I found his family and the people in that area all very sad. In the following days the arrests and murders of Mossadeq's supporters continued. Ayatollah Kashani, Ayatollah Bihbahani and a number of powerful businessmen in the bazaar supported the coup. I heard that millions of dollars were distributed among prostitutes, gangs of brigands, religious leaders, army officers and many other hired thugs (some even wearing police uniforms). It became known later that the money was supplied by the CIA and the operation was jointly supervised between London and the US State Department. When I came to Britain in 1960 I found that my American and British fellow students and teachers were shocked and disbelieving when I said that Mossadeq was toppled by the CIA (I had not even mentioned the involvement of MI6 or the British Intelligence service). They clearly did not believe me and politely said nothing. But when, 25 years later, the BBC film on Mossadeq confirmed this, a few old acquaintances remembered what I had told them a long time before. This was a fact that many people in Iran had always known, but in the West people were told that Mossadeq was brought down by a popular uprising.

Iranians' deep resentment of the United States in particular is mainly rooted in bitterness at her involvement with the coup of 1953 and the reinstallation of the Shah. Most Iranians believed that a major crime was committed against the people of Iran and now I believe that 25 years of the Shah's dictatorship, followed by the ayatollahs' rise to power, are the results of Mossadeq's fall and the violation of the democratic movement in Iran. For Mossadeq's government was an evolution and materialisation of the constitutional and democratic movements which had started in 1905 and were manifested through Sattar-Khan, Khiyabani and Pishavari. But the internal reactionary and external imperial forces nipped this democratic movement in the bud. In their place religious fanaticism and reactionary forces were encouraged and given freedom (under the Shah's rule) to operate through mosques, schools, universities. Civil servants and religious organisations such as Hujjatiyeh (which apparently opposed the Bahai religion but secretly had many mysterious links even with SAVAK, the Shah's secret police), played an important role after the Revolution of 1979 in giving direction to support for the Islamic Republic of Iran, encouraging terrorism and suppressing democratic forces (such as the Mujahidin, the Tudeh Party,

Fida'is and other radical forces). Hujjatiyeh still has a strong influence among the ruling ayatollahs, Parliament and the Council of Guardians, whose members (five chosen by Ayatollah Khomeini) are the watchdogs over the parliament, and most of the social reforms, in particular land reform, have been blocked by this council.

After the coup d'état and my examination I returned to Tabriz. My parents, Izzat and Humai were all anxious to know if I was keen to go to Tehran if I had passed the university entrance examination. My reply was negative. I did not feel that I could go to Tehran and see the streets where the coup had taken place and many people had been killed. I felt nervous and agitated. I did not want to talk about the coup; I was still deeply shocked and affected. But I could not stop thinking about Mossadeq and his supporters who had been arrested and imprisoned.

During the days immediately after the coup pro-Shah newspapers and the radio started repeating and manufacturing all sorts of accusations and lies against Mossadeq, his government and supporters. Mr Karrubi, the local lawyer who helped me change my birth certificate, had to flee from Tabriz because his newspaper *Akhtar-i Shomal* had supported Mossadeq's government. His house was searched by the police, terrifying his family. Mr Karrubi was respected by the people in our district; I especially respected and loved him because of the help he had given me, which had enabled me to continue my education. The state of terror continued and grew in momentum. The people could not even mention Mossadeq's name: being associated with Mossadeq and his National Movement was regarded the same as being a Communist or sympathetic to Communism, which in either case meant imprisonment or death.

Dr Chaichi and his friends went underground. Tudeh Party members also went into hiding. I used to visit Dr Chaichi in his house or he would come to my parents' house. He was well respected and loved by my parents because he treated them whenever they were ill. He was especially kind to our womanservant, Zahra, who was deaf and dumb and would bring vitamins and a tonic for her whenever he visited. Dr Chaichi kept cursing Ayatollah Kashani, Dr Baqai and others who had turned against Mossadeq and helped the foreign powers (the United States in particular) to bring him down. However, he apportioned most of the blame to the internal reactionary and opportunist elements in the National Movement: "If the body is healthy it does not accept germs from outside. The National Movement was made sick by germs like Kashani, Qanatabadi, Baqai and other conservative and traditional elements. So it became susceptible to outside attack . . ."

By the end of September 1953 I felt better and decided to enter Tabriz University and study Persian and English language and literature. We were not allowed to study the language and literature of Azerbaijan. It is ironic that study of my own mother tongue was forbidden and was regarded as treason against Iran's independence, while studying English language and literature was encouraged, even regarded as essential. (A desire to study the Azerbaijani language was interpreted as an intention to separate Azerbaijan from the rest of Iran and to join North Azerbaijan in the USSR!) Therefore I chose English as my main subject.

There were about 40 students on my course, only four of whom were women. One was a teacher in the primary school; she could only attend the afternoon classes and used to borrow notes from me and others. The three other female students did not work and came from rich families. Miss Igtisad-Khah, the primary teacher, supported her mother and brother as her father had died. Miss Kashani was the daughter of a merchant and her friend Miss Lazar was the sister of a dentist at the city centre. Miss Atai was the daughter of the headmaster of the famous Sa'di School in Tabriz. My male fellow students came from a variety of backgrounds. Among them were Muslims (the majority), Armenians, Assyrians, Jews and Bahais. There was also an army captain (Mr Razmju) who attended the classes to learn English. He was a young man and did not take sides in our controversial discussions. On the whole we avoided talking about politics, though everybody knew who was who.

It did not take more than a few months before we managed to organise a protest against the new regime. The Shah had already returned home and knew that he owed his throne to the CIA. Now he had the full backing of America and Western Europe to rid himself of his opponents. He dismantled the National Movement as well as the Tudeh Party.

In our classrooms and other gatherings any mention of the names of Mossadeq, the National Movement and the Tudeh Party was dangerous, and could probably cost a man's life. Nevertheless, the opposition against the regime of the Shah took different and sophisticated forms. The language of politics began to change. The people in the street and the students in universities used symbolic words or wrapped their opposition in religious terms. Dr Chaichi, for example, used to call the Shah "Buzmachcha", an invented derogatory name. Whenever he used the name among his friends, they knew what he meant. In the streets and bazaars the name Yazid (the man who killed Imam Hussein, who was the grandson of Muhammad and son of Ali and who has become the symbol of political martyrdom for Shi'ites in Iran and other parts of the Muslim world) was used to refer to the Shah.

Again, when I came to Britain in 1960 I was surprised to see how the newspapers highlighted and praised the Shah's regime and belittled or denigrated Mossadeq. Even one prominent professor of Iranian Studies described Mossadeq as "a puzzling figure of fun" — but admired Reza Shah. On my first Sunday in London I saw a big photograph of the Shah and his wife Farah on the front of the *Sunday Times*. The accompanying article was full of praise, which purported to represent the feelings of the

Iranian people towards the Shah. I became interested to know what the papers had written about Mossadeq in 1953 and set myself the task of finding out.

Quoting Ayatollah Kashani, the *Times* correspondent wrote from Tehran on 30 July 1953 (a few weeks before the 28th Mordad coup on 19 August 1953):

Referendum "Step to Dictatorship": A statement issued by Mullah Kashani, former president of the Majlis, today condemns Dr. Mossadeq's proposed referendum under the protection of the armed forces as a stepping stone to dictatorship.

"Twenty-eight months of empty promises characterize Dr. Mossadeq's government" says the statement . . . "Our constitutional regime does not admit a referendum, and those resorting to a referendum are punishable for treason . . . It may be utilized by traitors for separatist purposes.

"After 28 months Mossadeq has seized on the oil question to prolong his hold on office, repeatedly promising an immediate solution . . . Mossadeq's action has hitherto been advantageous to foreigners."

In conclusion, the statement appeals to the people to defend their freedom, which, it says, is endangered by Dr. Mossadeq, pointing out that foreigners can extract concessions from one man more easily than from the whole nation.

I myself had heard Mossadeq complaining against certain members of the Majlis who put the interests of foreigners before the interests of Iran. As he believed in democracy, Mossadeq consulted the people in the only possible way, through a referendum. I, along with millions of others, took part in this referendum and, from my point of view, it was not conducted under "the protection of the armed forces" as suggested by the *Times* correspondent. I believe that this referendum was the most free and democratic one ever held in Iran.

Kashani may have regarded this as a "stepping stone to dictatorship" and Mossadeq to be "punishable for treason" but he, together with a number of other ayatollahs, welcomed the 28th Mordad coup and so embraced the coup d'état government of General Zahedi and the Shah, which served the aims and interests of the foreigners. Thus it was the action of men like Kashani (not Mossadeq) which was "advantageous for foreigners". Mossadeq did not want to give away the oil in exchange for conditions that Britain and the United States tried to impose upon Iran, but the coup d'état government accepted their conditions. So Mossadeq has "seized on the oil question" not "to prolong his hold on office", as Ayatollah Kashani had stated but to protect the interest of the whole nation. The whole nation trusted Mossadeq, but mistrusted foreigners.

An editorial in *The Times* ("Persian Oil", 26 August 1953) written a week after the coup d'état and imbrued with a sense of satisfaction at what had happened, still could not hide the fact that the new government was too frightened of the Iranian people to accept the conditions that the United States and the British government were imposing on the exploitation of Iranian oil:

> Since the overthrow of Dr. Mossadeq there has been a natural diffidence about discussing the question of Persian Oil, but General Zahedi and his colleagues are bound soon to come face to face with this problem and that of regulating Persia's relations with the outside world. General Zahedi's reported decision not to go on with the attempt to sell oil at half price is possibly a cautious beginning . . . Persian pride is as touchy under one government as under another, and no set of Persian leaders is likely to wish to show itself less nationally conscious than Dr. Mossadeq was. As the awkward subject of oil is approached, this fact will make difficulties.

Although Ayatollah Kashani, the United States and the British government did not speak the same language, they seemed to have a common aim: the overthrow of Mossadeq's government. Mossadeq's fall had been mooted to the British government by the oil company ever since 1951. Their offer of an oil settlement can be seen as purely tactical. One can appreciate this more by reading Farhad Diba's *Mohammad Mossadegh, a political biography.* I will quote only the following passage from this valuable book:

> When Churchill met Truman in January 1952 in Washington, a top secret paper was prepared to indicate points for discussion as how best "to assure access of the Western world to Iran's petroleum, and as a corollary to deny access to the Soviet bloc". This paper started with the premise that the Shah was the only source of continuity of leadership and, therefore, all assistance to Iran had to be through him. Also, since the oil dispute was recognised as "the principal factor affecting the security of Iran", its settlement would have to be negotiated with the Shah. However, "While a settlement might be easier with Mossadegh replaced, neither is this certain nor is there any present indication that he will fall. The talks which both of our representatives have had with the Shah concerning the possible replacement of Mossadegh have had no effect." The failure to obtain any positive action from the Shah, despite the insistence of the Anglo-American representatives, was because the Shah did not consider himself sufficiently strong to attempt such action. By early 1952, the British and US governments were both agreed that Mossadegh had to be removed.

Mossadeq, as we have seen, was removed from power on 19 August 1953. Eden, expressing his feeling and reaction to Mossadeq's fall, wrote in his memoirs, *Full Circle*:

> The news of Mussaddiq's fall from power reached me during my convalescence, when my wife and I, with my son, were cruising the Mediterranean between Greek islands. I slept happily that night.

Eden spent a restful night after Mossadeq's fall, but Iranians have had sleepless nights for over 35 years and are still suffering from the consequences of this coup. Thus an international crime against democracy and human rights was committed; the West is therefore answerable to what is happening in Iran under the ayatollahs and its effect on the Middle East as a whole.

For a student who journeys from his home country, as I did, it is strange to listen to the comments made by British teachers and the media concerning the affairs of Asia or Africa, and his own country in particular. There is a gulf between what the native people believe about their leaders and what the newspapers write about them abroad. When my professor innocently approached me in the corridors of King's College in London and congratulated me on the birth of the Shah's long-awaited son, I was taken aback and rather annoyed. I said nothing, however, but began to think about the two different worlds in which my professor and I lived.

Most of the people that I met in London thought that all Iranians were as rich as the Shah. Even my fellow students at college assumed that everyone in Iran had an oil well in their backyard. This impression was probably created by those few very rich Iranian students who drove expensive sports cars and lived in luxury flats. In fact, the lifestyle of these students often aroused the jealousy of their fellow students, who could not even afford to buy a bicycle or take their girlfriends to a decent restaurant or to the theatre. Nevertheless, there were some people who understood that Iran was formed of two nations: a very rich minority of about one thousand families and a vast majority of poor people. There were a few students like me in London who came from middle- or lower-middle-class families. Most of us did not receive grants, either from Iran or Britain. In order to cope with the expense of living in London we had to work unofficially some evenings in restaurants or similar places.

In 1962 I was fortunate to be offered part-time work in the Persian section of the BBC, through a friend who was working there while studying for a postgraduate degree. My job in the BBC, however, did not last very long. I remember one evening we were broadcasting a round-table discussion in which I and my friend participated. The theme of the discussion was "Different temperaments among different nations". The discussion led to the question of why the people of Asia and Africa are quick-tempered while the British people are calm and cool-tempered. Some argued that this stemmed from the difference in climate while others argued that it was the result of different education. Disagreeing with both these views, I said that if a child is sure of its mother's milk and care it will not cry unnecessarily. It is the insecurity of life in Asia and Africa which is the main cause of violent reactions among the people. Why, only the previous week in Britain, farmers protesting at the government's agricultural policy had poured into the

Houses of Parliament and were so angry that they almost pulled down the roof on the members of parliament. It was surely living conditions rather than climate or cultural differences which determined people's behaviour, I suggested. After this programme (the following day) the Director of the section called me to his office and informed me: "We no longer need your services — you are a Marxist and your views will not suit our listeners." In Iran, however, my mother and friends had been delighted to hear me in Tabriz on the BBC World Service, and had taken my comments to be facts of life. In those days my friends and I had not even read Marx or really knew what he stood for — and my mother who could not even pronounce his name! So it was that I lost my weekly income of eight guineas, but I was left wondering how I was Marxist in my views and outlook. Perhaps every thinking person who has a modicum of imagination becomes what is termed a "Marxist" when he experiences for himself the deprivation and injustice of poverty.

This reaction to my views did not come as any surprise to me. When Mossadeq had defended the poor people of Iran against the ruling classes and their Western supporters and nationalised the oil industry in 1952, all conservative and reactionary forces and their mass media accused him of being a Communist. But Mossadeq's speeches in the Majlis, in the street, and in the International Court of Justice in the Hague were understood and well received by millions of Iranians as conveying the true facts of their life and an expression of their very deepest thoughts. He spoke for them.

I remember when Mossadeq made the following speech at the 17th Majlis in March 1952:

We know that among press owners and members of both Parliament and Senate there are people who are in the service of and supported by foreigners. They are so prejudiced in this matter that they do not hesitate to accuse and abuse their fellow-countrymen . . . It is obvious that those who are damaged by my words and deeds are trying hard to defeat me by words and are even prepared to go to the extent of killing me.

If I turn against my national dignity and honour, abandon my country's freedom and independence and ignore all the historical achievements of our nation, then I accept the chain of slavery and dependence; and have to accept all conditions that the international banks are imposing on us. This is the way which will lead us to Hell. The oppressed nations, who are caught under greedy and cruel claws of colonialists, must sacrifice so that they achieve their freedom and independence and free their God-given resources from the hands of others and benefit from them themselves.

To achieve this holy aim we have to accept self-sacrifices and disappointments: no pain, no gain. History has shown that a nation cannot achieve her freedom and independence without facing difficulties.

Under the screen and scream of "reds under the bed" and rumours that Mossadeq would hand over power to the Communists, there was one issue and one interest: Persian oil. The United States made speeches about freedom from colonialism and Communism and criticised Britain for her treatment of Iran (Britain's main aim and activities in Iran — supporting, changing, bribing — were to force the Iranian government and parliament to ratify the 1933 Oil Agreement under Reza Shah, which meant that Britain had almost total authority over Iranian oil production and its selling price, with Iran only receiving a small share). Many intellectuals, politicians and a number of eminent members of the National Movement believed that the United States wished only to free Iran from British imperialism and protect her against Soviet expansion. I remember, for example, that two of my friends in Tabriz, a lawyer and a teacher, supported Khalil Maliki, who was a political thinker from Tabriz who broke away from the Tudeh Party in 1946 to form his own party called "The Third Force". They believed strongly that the United States was the representative of the free world and that the policy of the State Department in Washington was to help all developing countries; the United States was regarded as a friend of Iran. I once acted as a translator between my lawyer friend and an American Consulate official in Tabriz. My friend argued that the Shah was not strong enough to fight Communism. If the United States supported "The Third Force" and similar anti-Communist groups in Iran it could both achieve its aim and also please the people who did not want the Shah.

Only after the coup d'état of 1953 and the fall of Mossadeq did many of my friends in the National Movement realise that the motive behind the United States' opposition to Britain was essentially to share with the British its exploitation of Iranian oil and to achieve political superiority. After Mossadeq, the Iranian oil was given to a consortium of British (40%), American (40%) and other West European (20%) interests.

The United States hoped to win Mossadeq over to its side and then rule Iran through his popular and democratically elected government and thus take over the position held by Britain in Iran and the Middle East in general (for Iran has the longest border with the Soviet Union in the Middle East). But Mossadeq was too honest and too independent a premier to give in to the wishes of the United States or other foreign powers. Britain had learnt this lesson before the United States. When, in 1950 Mossadeq, at the suggestion of Hussein Fatimi, first decided to nationalise Iranian oil and subsequently passed the necessary legislation through the Majlis with great support from the Iranian masses (on 1 May 1951, the Nationalisation Act became law), then the United States joined Britain in an attempt to save their interests — namely the oil. Mossadeq was brought down essentially because of oil, because of his opposition towards imperial powers and their punitive economic policy. Mossadeq's speech in his final defence in front of the Shah's military court (December 1953) is very revealing:

> Some people wanted my government to fall and believed this would happen for two reasons: firstly the government could not survive long without oil revenue; secondly Iran had to appear before an international court and answer British claims. As soon as she would be defeated in this court, public opinion would turn against her and as a result the government would fall. The hearing took place but the result was the opposite of what was expected. In the UN Security Council Iran won and also defeated its opposer [Britain] in the International Court of Justice. Some people appreciated that if the government was given a further chance she would be able to manage the economic state of Iran in such a way that the country would continue to survive, as she had done for centuries, without oil revenue . . . I must say that the oil revenue is useful so long as it does not destroy our freedom and independence.
>
> Some people thought that if Iran gained independence through her oil revenue then other oil-producing countries would follow suit so that they could achieve freedom and independence. As a result they would lose their income from oil and influence over these governments. With regard to Iran three things were considered:
>
> 1. If the National Movement was able to continue economically then other oil-producing countries would follow our example . . . so interested countries had to solve the problem with us.
> 2. Strategic position of Iran: I believed that we were practically in the Western bloc, but would be better if we were not formally part of the Western alliance. Geographically, it is in Iran's interest to preserve her neutrality because in the face of a probable world war, the Western bloc cannot help Iran militarily at all. If war broke out and Iran's neutrality was not observed then the West could help us. In these circumstances the outcome would be the same whether Iran was part of the Western bloc before the war or not. If Iran is not attacked it is in her interest to be neutral and also it is in the interest of both East and West . . .
> 3. The renewal of relations with Britain should take place after an agreement through which the rights and duties of the two countries are observed . . . otherwise the British Government will gradually bring back the conditions of the past through the governments that she herself puts in power in Iran . . .
>
> Now as my final defence I relate the following. According to Constitutional Law and history no prime minister can be dismissed without a debate and vote of confidence by the Majlis. At one o'clock in the morning on August 16, 1953, the handwriting of His Majesty the Shah was brought to me [in his letter the Shah had dismissed Mossadeq]. The Majlis existed and according to law or the country's interests I did not want to give up my duty and wanted to solve the problem of oil honourably . . .
>
> Certainly my only sin, my very great sin, is this: that I have nationalised Iranian oil and have removed from this country the colonial base and the political and

economical influence of the world's greatest empire and challenged the dreadful organisations of international intelligence and colonialism at the cost of my own and my family's life and property. I am glad that God gave me this chance to challenge this terrifying system through the support and determination of the freedom-loving people of this country. Throughout all these pressures and difficulties, all these threats and dangers, I have not forgotten the essential reasons behind these troubles. I know well that my destiny must be an example for men throughout the Middle East who in the future might wish to break the chains of slavery and bondage of colonialism . . .

I had lost my job at the BBC by being a supposed Marxist, but Iran lost many lives, especially that of its beloved national father, and its independence through the same scarecrow — Communism. The Shah was brought back in August 1953 to give away Iranian oil and, in return, to receive mainly sophisticated American weapons which were used against the people in Iran and the liberation movements in the Persian Gulf. Britain and the United States continued to cooperate and share their power in Iran throughout the Shah's rule.

8

The End of the Persian Empire

The fall of Mossadeq had a deep, negative and tragic effect on Iranian society in general and on the supporters of Mossadeq in particular. A number of my friends totally withdrew from politics and became fanatically religious. Others who were already religious and had not previously drunk alcohol, became heavy drinkers. In fact one friend in particular died a few years later from a heart attack directly related to his alcohol consumption. The Iranian people, both the ordinary man in the street and intellectuals, seemed shocked and submerged themselves within their own home and country. They were trying to escape from reality — from what had happened — or perhaps they were looking for some kind of identity or amusement, and often for a selfish, limited, materialistic and individualistic end. Fear, insecurity, mistrust, punitive attitudes and hostility to each other, and lack of responsibility all became more common. I remember how people who had once offered their valuables and money to the Mossadeq cause lost their communal and human feelings and became self-centred and indifferent towards social matters. They were building psychological, social and material walls around themselves. The nation had lost its pride, personality and identity. It seemed bewildered by the invading and aggressive forces of the Shah and his Western backers. American military, political and economic influence was the most obvious social phenomenon after Mossadeq's fall.

After finishing my second year at university, I became translator-interpreter for the American military advisers who had offices and headquarters all over Azerbaijan and Iran. I was employed by Tabriz headquarters and would accompany officers and sergeants to the cities of Ardabil, Rasht, Maragheh, Miyandoab, Mahabad, Urmiyeh and sometimes to the borders between the Soviet Union and Iran. The purpose of the United States' presence in the Third World countries in general and Iran in particular was essentially to monitor or possibly eliminate any seriously democratic movement. This, however, was camouflaged by its provision of aid in military, educational and health spheres. American officers told me over and over again that they had come to Iran to save Iranians from Communism!

I used to get up very early in the morning in order to arrive at the American Army headquarters by 7 a.m. Sometimes I walked there, which took half an hour. The headquarters were situated in the city centre, next to Pahlavi Street, the main street in Tabriz. In winter, when the streets of Tabriz were usually covered by deep snow, travelling on foot was difficult and I had to take a shared taxi which at that time would cost only the equivalent of 20 pence.

All Americans, regardless of their rank, travelled from their lodgings to their headquarters in specially heated jeeps and trucks. Most of them drove their own vehicles, except when they went from one city to another; then Iranian military drivers would be engaged. I remember one particular occasion when we were going from Tabriz to Maragheh. The American officer was called Captain Fur and the driver was an Iranian army sergeant called Mr Akbari. We had not travelled more than a few miles beyond Tabriz when Captain Fur started swearing and wanted me to tell Mr Akbari that his feet were smelling. I refused to translate Captain Fur's remark. Captain Fur then lost his temper and became insistent that I tell Mr Akbari that his feet were smelly. Still I could not. I felt embarrassed to say this to Mr Akbari, who was very polite and a kind person. The captain still insisted and we eventually began to quarrel. Finally, Mr Akbari realised what was happening. He stopped the car in the middle of a valley surrounded by mountains, got out, walked round to Captain Fur's side of the vehicle and opened the door, saying, "Tush Ashaya! (Get down!)". As soon as Captain Fur got out of the car Mr Akbari grabbed him by his collar and pushed him against the car. He was gripping the captain so tightly that the captain's face turned red. Mr Akbari looked into his eyes and said, "This is my motherland. You have come from thousands of miles dictating, insulting and swearing at me. I receive 180 tomans a month and you receive 16,000 tomans a month. You live in the best houses and eat the best foods, but I live with my wife and four children in poor conditions. You can take a bath or shower every day, but I can only afford to go to the public bath-house once a fortnight. You can change your clothes and uniform every day, but I have only one uniform which I have to wear throughout the year. We treat you kindly because we regard you as guests, but you treat us like dirt — in our own motherland." Then Mr Akbari became emotional and pushed Captain Fur onto the road.

The captain, understanding a few Azerbaijani words and guessing from Mr Akbari's reaction what he meant, swore and, insultingly, replied, "We have come here to look after you and save you from Communism." But here I had to interfere and translate. Mr Akbari was furious. Grabbing the captain again, he said, "Who asked you to come and save me from Communism? You have not come to save me. You have come to save your own interests and the Shah's. I do not want you to save me. I can look after myself well enough. You are ignorant of our feelings and behave so arrogantly. My feet may smell (in fact I wash them every day) but your mind stinks and whenever you open your mouth you utter 'shit' and many swear words and insults."

Captain Fur was shaken and had turned pale. I intervened and tried to stop Mr Akbari from going too far. I took them both to a tea-house across the road, where we had tea. Both men sat there and said nothing. Mr Akbari was still upset and I did not think he was fit to drive. We sat for two hours and had lunch before we left. Mr Akbari insisted that he should pay for the lunch! The captain seemed pleased.

We set off again and arrived in Maragheh before sunset. During the rest of the journey we all remained silent, but I was worried about the consequences of the quarrel. Captain Fur could do anything against Mr Akbari, and could even have him sentenced to imprisonment or death through the Iranian generals, who usually treated these American officers as their masters and followed their instructions. Furthermore, the American army advisers had a say in the promotion of these Iranian officers; they also selected officers to go to the United States to attend military courses.

When we arrived at Maragheh Captain Fur and I stayed overnight at the Officers' Club. The following day he asked for Mr Akbari and I told him that he had been sent back to Tabriz and that we would have another driver for our return journey to Tabriz. I also advised the captain not to mention the event to General Mir Jahangiri, or if he did that he ought to tell the whole story. We returned to Tabriz after a week, but I never saw Mr Akbari again in the army!

Captain Fur became increasingly ill-tempered and I did not really like working in his office. However, I liked working with him in the Quartermaster's section (which dealt with the army's food, supplies and kitchens). We used to visit the soldiers' kitchens and dining-rooms to examine their food and also checked whether they had the proper clothing for winter and summer. I remember once we called very early in the morning at an army barracks in Tabriz and saw the soldiers getting up and preparing for their daily exercise. I asked one of the soldiers what he had eaten for his breakfast. He answered, "I had my breakfast last night." I asked him what he had had the previous night for his breakfast, to which he answered, "I had walnuts and dates and I have sent my tea and sugar to my mother in the village."

Captain Fur was very critical of the kitchen utensils and food in the army. Once, I remember, we were visiting Mahabad (the capital of Kurdistan, Iran), which is a day's journey from Tabriz. We arrived at night and stayed at the Officers' Club. The following morning we toured the army kitchens and finished by midday. Captain Fur wanted to see General Varahram, who was from Azerbaijan and the son of a famous landlord. General Varahram refused to see the captain that day and his secretary arranged a meeting for the following day, which annoyed the captain, who was accustomed to walking into the offices of other generals without a prior appointment.

Captain Fur and I went to see General Varahram on the following day, as arranged. His office was a large, well-furnished room and General Varahram sat behind a huge desk and held a baton in his hand. He received the captain very coldly, but asked me, in Azerbaijani, to sit next to him. He told Captain Fur to sit by the door and then asked me what he had come for. Captain Fur started to explain how the food and the kitchen facilities were of a poor standard and how the army needed good facilities. With regard to the soldiers' breakfast, Captain Fur believed that bread and cheese were not enough and that the soldiers needed a cooked breakfast. The general had been listening patiently, but at this point, moving forward in his chair, he turned to me and asked, "What do you usually have for breakfast?" "Bread, cheese and tea; sometimes butter and honey," I answered. "So do I," the general added. "What does America want us to give our soldiers for breakfast?" he asked. Captain Fur began to tell him: "Some kind of cooked food and . . ." The general, however, did not seem to have the patience to listen to Captain Fur's lecture on how his soldiers should be fed. Moving his army baton in his hands, he told Captain Fur, "Go and tell your President and generals what I tell you. If you want me to fight against our common enemy — Russia — then we must have the same facilities that the US army has. Do not assume that I, as General Varahram, regard my blood to be any cheaper than yours. You expect a lot from us without providing means and material. Imagine if a war starts tomorrow between us and Russia. Then I will have to beg Khrushchev to hold back his army and not attack until I have distributed stew to our soldiers from a huge pot which is carried from the barracks to the top of a mountain. After the soldiers have had their stew in this fashion, then allow Khrushchev to start the battle! I believe that either you are kidding us or kidding yourself. Do you think you are going to face Russia with these medieval methods and facilities? Oh, America wants to use us as a meat barrier against Russian guns — I for one do not want to give my blood [life] so cheaply. Go and tell your President and generals that we do not want to be used for an American war against Russia."

Captain Fur's face had turned very pale and all he could say was "Yes, sir." Before we left, General Varahram invited me to his house for the evening meal, which I accepted.

At about six o'clock I went to General Varahram's house, which was modern and apparently newly built. It was autumn and the night air was cold. I knocked on the door. An old lady opened the door and the general soon appeared and welcomed me into a small, dimly lit sitting-room. The light was so weak that you could hardly see. General Varahram, pointing to the light on the ceiling, said, "Look, this is the light in an army general's house. You have to light matches in order to find the bulb. Imagine what the rest of the people have." The general kept talking about the way the Iranian army was treated by the United States, which tried to crush its personality and identity. As I found the general to be rather patriotic and friendly, I said to him, "Is it not the Shah and the Iranian government who put water-melon under American arms (encourage them and make them feel important)? Why don't you tell the Shah, to whom, I understand, you are very close?" General Varahram said, "I have told the Shah and complained about American policy in Iran. The Shah perhaps does not want to hurt them." He seemed to be deeply troubled by the American presence in Iran, especially in his own Azerbaijan.

Our conversation was interrupted by the entrance of a young officer who brought the dinner which was, to my delight, *bozbash* (a special meat stew of Azerbaijan). The young officer joined us at the table for dinner.

After dinner our conversation turned to more general topics for the rest of the evening. I was fascinated to see the lifestyle of an Iranian general, and how he preferred to speak in Azerbaijani — his mother tongue (usually high government and army officials speak in Persian even though they might be from Azerbaijan). However, one cannot and should not judge the sincerity and patriotism of a person only by his speaking the language of the people; a number of generals from Azerbaijan of Iran played an active role in the suppression of the Democratic Movement in their own motherland.

My work with Captain Fur continued. Another time, I remember, I had a rather different experience when he and I were returning to Tabriz after a visit to Ardabil. It was winter and snow had blocked the roads. At one point we had to stop until it had been cleared and while we were waiting Captain Fur went to use the toilet which was beside the tea-house. After some time he had still not returned so I went to find out what had happened to him. To my surprise I found him covered with dirt and trying to clean his soiled uniform and boots. He was swearing furiously but I could not help laughing. I asked the owner of the tea-house to help and he did so by providing some hot water and a cloth.

When we had returned to the car, I asked the captain what had happened. "Damn," he said, "I bent my head down to look at the hole and my cap fell off into the hole. I tried to get it out and I got covered with dirt." Again I could not help laughing. The smell was still with us when we arrived in Tabriz, much later than expected.

Perhaps this is a good point to give a brief mention of Iranian lavatories. If one had a strong stomach and a weak sense of smell, one could make a fortune from Persian toilets. Many people drop and lose their gold and jewellery down the toilets. My sisters and mother, for example, lost their gold rings and bracelets. Sometimes, too, people fall into the cesspits. Once, in our neighbourhood, a cloth merchant fell into a cesspit while returning from the bazaar and someone was duly sent for to bring him out. The merchant (while he was half submerged in dirt) asked the man, "How much do you want to get me out?" "Ten tomans, sir." "No thank you. I don't want to come out for ten tomans!" shouted the merchant.

There was deep corruption in the Iranian army, especially among the higher ranks. Blankets, shoes, oil, wheat flour, meat and many other items were sold on the black market and the officers and some sergeants obtained a regular income from this source. Without this their salary, at least in 1958, was not enough for comfortable living. I remember a visit in the autumn of 1959 to Rasht garrison on the Caspian Sea. By this time Captain Fur had been replaced by another officer called Major Gray, who was a much more practical, enthusiastic and friendly person.

When we arrived at the garrison we discovered that the soldiers had not yet been issued with winter clothes. The commander-in-chief was Colonel Pahlavan, a relative of the Shah. We were not able to meet the colonel, but we informed his assistant that the soldiers should have already received these.

I was staying at the Officers' Club and Major Gray with other Americans in the city. During the course of the evening a young officer, who spoke Azerbaijani, was sent by Colonel Pahlavan to meet me. The officer, who was a captain, asked me not to report the division's shortcomings to Tehran. I said, "If you promise to distribute all the winter allowances to the soldiers at once, then I shall ask Major Gray not to report the matter." The following day we left the city for another destination, and never found out if they had kept their promise.

Major Gray was a farmer's son and had worked hard to reach his present rank in the army. Once he told me that other officers looked down on him because he did not attend the same schools, nor did he have a similar social background. But Major Gray was a very fine person who knew how to relate to people. I frequently discussed politics with him: he was a liberal-minded person, but regarded my support of Mossadeq as having a Communist ideology — which surprised me. However, since he was honest and frank in his conversation, I deeply respected him and accepted the difference in our views. He also encouraged me to continue my studies. When I said I could not afford to go to the United States he argued that I could combine working with studying as he had done.

My work with American military advisers brought me into contact with many army officers, government officials and American Consulate personnel in Tabriz.

I came to know an American family, Mr and Mrs Walsh. Mr Walsh worked as American Advisor in the Department of Education in Tabriz and also taught English at the university. There was also a Mr Fonset, who worked at the American Consulate. The American Consulate used to hold parties at Christmas and New Year and at other national festivals. Sometimes they invited students to their homes for discussion of different matters, including politics. Once or twice a year the Consulate offered some students a study trip to the United States. The students were selected by means of an English test and an interview. I once took part in the test and was then sent to the capital, Tehran, to have an interview with a person called Mr Miller. I arrived in Tehran and, after some difficulty, found the address. To my surprise it was a church and Mr Miller was a priest, who made me sit in the church while he was attending to other people. When he had finished he came over and sat in front of me and started to question me about my ideas, beliefs and how I should represent Iran in the United States. Then he started talking about the importance of the Christian faith, saying that all doors would be open to me if I accepted his advice and worked with them. I was taken aback to hear this, and could not understand what the Church had to do with my studies in America. I got up, left for Tabriz and never contemplated taking part in any such scheme again. In the summer of 1959 I left the American army headquarters and decided instead to go to Turkey to study.

While working with the American military advisers as an interpreter-translator I had also taught English to final-year students at Taqi-Zadeh secondary school in Tabriz. The school was newly built and named after an intellectual and diplomat who had played an active role during the Constitutional Revolution and both the Pahlavi shahs' reigns. He had signed the 1933 Petroleum Agreement between Reza Shah's government and Great Britain.

I taught two classes and there were about 40 students in each. Most of the students were between 17 and 18 years of age, although some were the same age or even older than me. This did not trouble me; in fact I felt proud to be able to help them. I was fond of all the students and found that I enjoyed teaching. Dr Kishavarzi, who had taught me chemistry at Firdausi School, was the headmaster. A Mr Ahmadi was the assistant head; he tended to bully these older students, so whenever he called them out of my classes and wanted to talk to them I refused and made the excuse that my class would be disrupted. Consequently I was popular with these students and not so popular with Mr Ahmadi, whom the students did not take seriously.

The students I taught came from different social backgrounds and places. Two or three were sons of big landowners, some were from middle-class families and the rest were from poor or working-class families. Some of the poorer students used to work outside school hours. They were predominantly building workers. One of the students, called Mr Husn-i Khulq, was a hard-working but poor man. His mother, too, worked to support the family. One day I called him to the blackboard and asked him to translate some sentences from Persian into English. He was very reluctant to come forward and I assumed that this was because he had not prepared his homework. However, when he eventually came to the blackboard I noticed that his trousers were torn and his shoes had holes in them. He appeared to be self-conscious and embarrassed and after he had translated one sentence I asked him to sit down. After class, he came and talked to me about his personal life and I found it rather distressing.

Most of the students did not have proper winter coats. A Mr Dirakhshani, also in my class, would come to school during the cold winter wearing only a shirt and a thin jacket. His face would turn blue and his intelligent eyes were sunken behind his glasses. I could not bear to look at him in the street; I felt ashamed and sad. Once I talked to him and asked if his parents were alive. He told me, "My parents live in Maragheh city. I live with my brother in Tabriz." I then asked what his brother did. He said: "My brother is in prison on political charges." When I asked Mr Dirakhshani how he and his brother's family managed, he said, "My parents send bread and other things or money from Maragheh." I did not see Mr Dirakhshani again, but I later heard that after he had left school he studied medicine and worked outside Tabriz.

In our discussion group at Tabriz University many students had spoken in favour of Mossadeq and criticised the CIA for its role in bringing down Mossadeq. By 1959, when I was preparing to leave Iran for Istanbul, Mossadeq was seen as the living symbol of the nationalist movement in Iran. He remained so for many people despite being imprisoned and held in solitary confinement for three years and thereafter remaining a prisoner at his residence in Ahmad-Abad, a village near Tehran, until the last days of his life. He died on 5 March 1967. The governments after the 28th Mordad coup were very unpopular. The United States became anxious to bring a Mossadeqist government back into power and approached Mr Allah-yar Saleh, who had been Mossadeq's Ambassador in Washington.

A month or so (about September 1959) before I left for Istanbul I paid a visit to Mr Allah-yar Saleh in his house near the University of Tehran. We sat together in his front room and talked about political life in Iran and American policy towards the recent developments. Allah-yar Saleh said, "The Americans invited me and suggested that I form a government. They were prepared to support me to gain the premiership, but with some conditions. The first one was that Iran should build up her army and buy the arms that American advisers recommended. Since I did not accept this and said that Iran, as an independent nation, must decide for itself what it needs for defence, the Americans ceased their negotiations with me."

I left Iran for Turkey by land. Travelling by bus from Tabriz I passed the cities of Marand, Khoy and Maku and arrived at Bazargan, a customs post at the north-west of Iran and south-east of Turkey.

Leaving Tabriz and my family (mother, father, sisters and brothers) and stepping into an unknown land made me dizzy — and I could not think of anything but watching aimlessly the people in the streets, villages and fields. I had not wanted to say goodbye to my people and homeland. The magnificent sight of the Ararat mountain (where, it is said, Noah's Ark once rested) with white snow on its summit reminded me of Sabalan and Talish mountains near Ardabil — the land of Babak. I felt at peace with myself. I stayed at Bazargan overnight: if buses arrived in the late afternoon or evening at Bazargan they had to wait until the following morning as the custom and passport offices are closed. When the offices did eventually open, passing through customs was a tiring process and, if you happened to have interests in politics, much heartache and anxiety was involved. This sort of worry makes travelling unpleasant. It is a well-known saying that one becomes happy twice in Iran: once after leaving Iran and again on re-entering the country. (In either case you do not know whether or not you will be arrested by the police.)

After two days and one night I arrived in Istanbul. There was a good atmosphere on the bus. The passengers were friendly and we shared our joys and griefs. When we arrived in Istanbul some people left for Europe and the rest stayed put.

My first two nights, spent in a hotel seemed endless to me. Afterwards, my Azerbaijani friends found me a room with a family. My landlady was a Jewish lady, aged about 40 with a daughter of ten or twelve years old. Madam Rose had lost her husband a year or so before; he had died after a gas explosion while working in a factory. She lived in a working-class area called Dolap-Dara. Once I was late returning to the house, and arrived to find her sitting in the hall waiting anxiously. I apologised and promised never to be late again. In fact I liked her being concerned about my life and my whereabouts.

A few weeks passed. One night I heard someone crying in the next room to mine. I could not sleep and got up and went to find out what had happened. I saw Madam Rose sitting at the window and her daughter asleep. I asked the reason for her crying but she did not want to tell me. The following day I insisted that she tell me the reason for her crying. She said that at the end of every month she became anxious and worried about how to pay the rent. "This worry has been with me day and night since my husband died. I work part-time and my wage is enough only for bread and butter and sometimes I buy meat and cheese." I asked her how much she paid as rent. "Three hundred Turkish lira," she said. "You give me 150 for your room and I am still 150 lira short." I wrote to my father, telling him the whole story. To my delight, he advised me to pay 300 lira for my rent and also suggested that I ought to buy food and have a meal with them instead of eating out. This created a happy family atmosphere.

My parents and sisters could not write letters to me. They had to ask my brothers or their children to write for them. Ibrahim usually wrote for my parents. In their first letter to Istanbul my parents had stressed two points: that I should pray five times a day and mix with the "right kind" of people. The rest of the letter was about how they would send me money and how much they missed me at meal times. My mother said, "Gholam-Reza, I wish I could write and express my feelings myself. When I cook nice meals I wish you were here. I cannot bear going to your study because I miss you. Sometimes I wonder whether it was necessary for you to go abroad. Then I tell myself: 'I should be patient. Perhaps my child's success and future depends on this trip.' The only thing I wish is that God may protect you from troubles in a strange land. That is all I can wish . . ."

Most of the letters written by Ibrahim referred briefly to my parents and the rest would be about business: the price of carpets; the state of the market; how they had managed the money that I had left with them; what they had done about the small area of land that I had bought at Taza-Kand (a village near Khusraw-Shah, about 100 kilometres from Tabriz) and what was happening at the old factory . . . I found it rather disturbing both to study and have to think about the financial news from Iran!

I stayed in Istanbul for nine months. Then, just before the summer of 1960 (on 27 May) General Gürsel engineered a coup d'état and all the universities in Turkey were closed. Accordingly, I left Istanbul for Tabriz.

My family were delighted to see me, especially my mother and Humai. But my father began to worry more about the ideas that I now expressed openly. Until the military coup, Turkey had been a much more open society than Iran. There were many books in Istanbul University which I had not seen before. Although I found the people and students in Turkey less politically conscious than in Iran, this access to political literature was something special for Iranian students.

I asked my father if I could go to Britain to collect material for my studies. He reluctantly agreed, and gave me money both for travelling and my living expenses in London. I went to the British Council in Tabriz and asked the director, a Mr Popplestone, for some guidance and help in finding libraries and colleges in London. During our conversation he remarked that my pronounciation of English was not correct. In answer to this I asked him, "How long have you been in Tabriz, sir?" "Two and a half years," he answered. "Why don't you speak with me in Azerbaijani, sir?" He seemed surprised by my question and quickly changed the subject. However, Mr Popplestone was helpful. He gave me a letter of introduction for the British Council in London.

When I arrived at London's Victoria Station it was evening. A gentleman from the British Council met me and took me by taxi to a hotel in South Kensington. I did not have any cash on me and asked the driver if he could cash a traveller's cheque for me. The gentleman from the British Council said that I should change it in a bank, so he lent me some cash. Meanwhile, I asked the taxi driver if he knew Hamlet (assuming that everybody in Britain must have read Hamlet). "I don't know that chap," he answered.

The bedroom at my hotel was so beautiful and the bed was so comfortable that I could not sleep. Instead I had a bath and then sat and looked out of the window, which faced Hyde Park. At breakfast a lady brought a bowl full of cereal, which to me looked like crumbled *lavash*. I said to myself that the women in London must be extremely clever and hard-working, getting up so early in the morning to cook *lavash* and prepare all this breakfast. Later, I discovered that the "crumbled *lavash*" was called cornflakes and came in packets!

I was accepted at King's College, London, to attend a postgraduate course and also work on William Blake. I found a room at Lancaster Gate and was eager to learn how to cook. One Saturday I decided to do some shopping and went to the greengrocer's near my house. I asked a lady in the shop for sparrows (I meant sprouts, which we do not have in Tabriz). The lady did not know what I wanted. She asked me kindly if I could show her what it was I wanted. When I pointed to the sprouts she could not help laughing.

I regularly received letters from my parents, but none from Izzat and Humai. Neither they nor their children could write. My mother sent me home-made *halva* and parcels of dried fruit. She could express her feelings and affection better in this way than by telling Ibrahim to put them into words in a letter. Whenever my mother was able, she would sit with Farideh and Shafiqeh (my sister Batul's daughters) and ask them to write a letter for her. I enjoyed these letters immensely: they told of what my sisters were doing and who had recently had a child; how she enjoyed the arrival of a new baby and the visits from the older grandchildren. In spring she would describe the flowers and blossoms in our garden, and in summer she would write and tell me about how much the fruit trees had produced and promise to keep some of the pears, grapes, apples and pistachio nuts for me. At the end of the letter Farideh and Shafiqeh often added — without my mother knowing — "Uncle, please write to our parents and tell them to keep us in secondary school. We want to continue our studies . . ."

My father often wanted me to send him special medicine and ointment to rub on his rheumatic arms and legs. He did not understand when I wrote and explained that chemists would not give the medicine without a doctor's prescription. To keep him happy I used to send some vitamin tablets and ointment which I could buy across the counter without a doctor's prescription.

By 1961 opposition to the Shah was growing stronger in Iran. The elections were rigged and political parties and trade unions were not recognised. Suppression and the imprisonment of intellectuals still continued. The National Movement and democratic movements, on the other hand, opposed and criticised all these social and political conditions.

The United States, under President Kennedy, was pressing the Shah to make some reforms. The Shah's "White Revolution" referendum of 1963, Dr Ali Amini's premiership (in 1962), and the half-hearted freedom for Mossadeqists to hold a political rally all came about because of this American pressure. The British government, traditional supporters of the big landowners in Iran, did not seem to support the pro-American government of Dr Amini, which intended to carry out land and other reforms.

When, in 1962, Dr Amini stopped over in London on his way to the United States a protest demonstration was organised by Iranian students in front of the Iranian Embassy, in which I participated. I found the police unusually cooperative and sympathetic with the demonstrators. But I did not understand the reason at the time.

The Iranian students knew what was going on in Iran through a number of different channels. The Shah's regime also knew all details of the students' activities, through SAVAK informers.

In 1962, the teachers in Iran came out on strike. At a rally in Tehran one of the leading teachers, Dr Khan Ali, was shot dead by the Shah's army in front of the Majlis. In London we held meetings and protests against Khan Ali's death. Being former teachers, Mr Salim from the University of Tabriz and I were among a group invited to speak about the position of teachers in Iran. I talked about my experiences in Tabriz schools. The following day we went to the Iranian Consulate in Kensington High Street and presented our protest resolution to Mr Ardashir Zahedi, the Iranian Ambassador and also the Shah's son-in-law and son of General Zahedi, who had led the coup in 1953. As we were leaving the Consulate, reporters from the BBC were waiting. I was the first person that the reporters accosted and was showered with questions: "Why do you protest? Which part of Iran do you come from?" When I said that I came from Azerbaijan, the reporter immediately asked, "Are you a Communist then?" "Nonsense. My being Azerbaijani does not mean I am a Communist," I answered. Nevertheless, this interview and the protest rally were enough evidence for the SAVAK to arrest me and others when we next returned to Iran.

My father died in the summer of 1963 and I could neither afford to nor dared to go home for my father's funeral. By this time I was running short of money. The Iranian government did not help me, nor did I want to ask my family to send me more money. Those who were pro-Shah or worked for the government received money. I had to work during the Christmas and summer holidays at Sainsbury's supermarket, and at a restaurant. At Sainsbury's I worked as a porter in the stockroom. All kinds of goods were brought by lorry and delivered through a trap door opening to the side street. Some of the cartons, especially those containing raisins, dates and other dried fruits which came in tin boxes, were very heavy. You had to catch them quickly and then pass them on to other workers. An Englishman called Fred and an Irishman called John worked with me. I remember one day I had a bad cold and my arms were not strong enough to catch the heavy boxes and I fell back. Fred lifted me up and said, "Son you seem unwell. You go upstairs and rest in the tea-room. I shall do your job." I did not want to bother him, but he insisted that I should rest. I went upstairs and rested until 3 p.m., and then came back to resume my work; but Fred still would not let me. He told me I should rest all that day. I felt that Fred was the nearest person to me in London and in fact he taught me a valuable lesson. This incident reminded me of my father's factory in Tabriz and of his friendship with Jabbar.

In October 1963 I moved to Edinburgh, to do a PhD on William Blake in the Department of English. Two things seemed to surprise my friends and my teachers at King's College. One was my deep interest in William Blake; the other was why I chose Scotland in which to study for a PhD. They gave me the impression that Scotland was at the North Pole and that it would take me several days and nights to reach there.

Nevertheless, when I boarded the Edinburgh coach the warmth of the company soon made me feel at home. A lady who was returning home to Edinburgh with her grandchildren offered me coffee and sandwiches; I had never experienced such hospitality in England. The driver was full of jokes. Feeling the weight of my suitcase, he commented that there must be a dead body in it — or gold! But it was full of all my books. To my surprise, we arrived in Edinburgh the following morning.

Edinburgh was bathed in bright autumn sunshine. It struck me as being the most beautiful city in Europe. The grandmother in the coach did not let me go: "Today is Sunday and everywhere is closed. Come with us and have a meal and then go to your lodgings." I accepted her kind invitation and accompanied her to her house. Her daughters were bus conductresses and I did not see her husband; perhaps he was dead and I did not ask. I enjoyed my stay and having lunch with her family. I really felt at home. Afterwards I went to my lodgings and met Mrs White, my landlady. I was met with a fierce list of rules. When I saw my room in the attic with a window facing the sky my heart sank and I wished I had stayed with the Scottish grandmother. I preferred her small kitchen to my isolated room at the top of the building.

Until the university had arranged a postgraduate grant for me I had to work at Christmas and other holidays. I got a job that first Christmas at Edinburgh's Waverley Station. I remember that it was a cold Christmas. The other students and I had to unload the mail bags from one train and distribute them among other trains. We worked during the night and early morning. One night in particular was exceptionally cold and the wind was cutting our faces and hands like a sword. One of the railwaymen came over to us and invited us downstairs to have tea and sandwiches. "Don't worry," he told us, "when the train arrives we'll all come out and finish the job together." We went downstairs and had plenty of hot tea and sandwiches. We chatted, told jokes and laughed. This was repeated on the following nights. I felt as though I was among the workers in my father's factory. This affection from a Scottish railwayman, who came from Glasgow, built a bridge in my heart between the people of Tabriz and Scotland. Scotland did not seem like the North Pole any longer, but next to my motherland — Azerbaijan. In fact the people of Scotland and Azerbaijan have much in common: most important of all are their kind hearts, poetry, music, highlands and spring waters.

When I visited Baku in Soviet Azerbaijan in 1987 I presented a gift from Scotland to the museum of Uzeir Hajibeiov (1885-1948), the celebrated composer and the founder of the Azerbaijani operatic art. His opera *Leili and Majnun* was first staged in 1908 and was based on a poem of the same name written in Azerbaijani by the great 16th-century Azerbaijani poet Muhammad Fuzuli, who was born in Karbala (Iraq) in 1498. He wrote in three languages — Azerbaijani, Arabic and Persian — and used all the genres and artistic forms known in the Islamic literature of his time. Fuzuli lived in constant need, as we know from his numerous complaints against the times he lived in, which brought nothing but ruin, chaos and destitution. He died of cholera in Karbala in 1556. The following lines are the translation of some lines taken from his *Leili and Majnun*. Leili is speaking to a lamp, but hesitates to impart to it all of her sad history:

> O thou whose eyes are closed and heart is worn
> Whose feet are bound, whose spirit is forlorn,
> Let us together sigh, together weep;
> Disclose to me the secret that so deep
> Within thy heart thou keepest hid from all.
> Why moanest thou, why dost thou softly call
> As if thou wert a wounded nightingale?
> Why is thy flame screened by a smoky veil?
> Why burnest thou with such intensity?
> What spark hath set thee blazing? — Answer me! . . .
> But, O, forever loyal 'twill remain
> To him I love . . . O lamp, they'll never wrest

My secret from me. Always in my breast
I'll keep it locked . . . until the day I die
Their threats and their abuse will I defy!
And e'en to thee my tale I'll not impart
Lest that it break thy simple, aching heart . . .

The political atmosphere in Iran was a little better in 1964 than 1963, so I went to Iran and my wife stayed with her parents in London. (I had met my wife at King's College, London in 1960 and we became friends. We married in Edinburgh in 1964.) After having been away from home for four years, during which time I had little communication with my mother, Humai and my sisters, my return to Iran had special meaning for me. I wanted to rediscover Iran and especially Azerbaijan. I wanted to rediscover the Tabriz streets, the bazaars and the places and people that I had known in my childhood — the *cheshmas, karvan-sarais* and *chai-khaneh* (tea-house), the beetroot and ice-cream seller (to find out if he was still alive), my schools, my father's factory and his workers.

The day after I arrived in Tabriz I visited Humai and Izzat. I found them both well and that their sons had married. Majid and his wife lived two streets away, but Hamid and his wife lived with Humai and Izzat. They had built a room on top of the roof where we used to sleep in summer. Humai was very happy to see me. She kept smiling and looking at me. She asked only one question: "Have you become a doctor in order to open a clinic and treat the people?" "Not yet," I answered. "But I am not studying to be a medical doctor," I added. She did not say anything but each time I visited Iran in later years she encouraged me to return to Tabriz and treat her painful feet. "Other doctors cannot treat me. You should come back and treat me yourself," she said to me when I last returned to Iran, in 1982.

Visiting people and places I knew well and, in particular, talking to people in my mother tongue was relaxing, delightful and made me feel free inside. I called to see some of my father's former workers who now worked for themselves. Some had one loom and others two looms in their homes and worked with their families. Since I left Tabriz they had married and had children. Most of them lived on the outskirts of Tabriz. At one time Humai and Izzat's house had been situated on the very edge of the district, but now their house seemed to be in the middle of the city as many people had moved to Tabriz from the surrounding villages.

Many people I met did not know that I had been living abroad for the past four years. They thought I worked in Tehran. Those who did know asked me many questions: "How do the British live and how do they get married?" "Is it expensive to get married and who pays for the wedding?" "How much does a worker earn per day?" "Are the hospitals and schools free?" "Do they speak our language and know about Azerbaijan?" "What is the difference between the English and the Scots?" "Where do you live?" and "What kind of food do they eat?" Their questions seemed endless, yet they were not merely inquisitive but sincerely interested in other people. I answered as many as I could and sometimes I found myself encircled by people in the tea-houses, like the story-teller dervish. In the tea-houses they served me endless cups of tea and in people's homes I was constantly offered generous quantities of cakes, fruit and other delicious food.

My mother and sisters cooked all the kinds of food that I might have missed while I was in Britain. My mother, who was grieving over my father's death, needed to talk to me. She wanted to sit with me for hours, but she never showed any weakness. She still seemed to be the centre of power and affection for her children and the entire family. In the mornings we would all sit round the samovar and my mother served tea with fresh *sangak* or *lavash* bread with white cheese. Our house and garden, with its abundance of flowers and fruit trees and the pool in the middle were unchanged. At this time the garden had not yet been divided and my brothers had not built their new houses. It seemed like a garden in paradise.

Soon after my arrival, we had a constant stream of visitors to the house, paying the customary courtesy visit to the newly returned traveller. Again, following custom, I had to repay each visit.

Apart from rediscovering Tabriz, I also wished to rediscover its writers, poets and thinkers, both past and present. I spent many days with my former fellow students, writers and my books at home. Among my books I found the works of Khaqani Shirvani, a famous twelfth-century poet from Azerbaijan, and for the first time I found out that he was buried not far from my parent's house and near Muhammad Khiyabani's memorial tomb. I visited the place, which was called "Sayyid Hamzeh", and to my great surprise I saw that this great poet's grave was deserted and in ruin. However, during a later visit to Soviet Azerbaijan, in November 1987, I was able to see, to my delight, his valuable works in the Nizami Museum in Baku. His poems were written on walls, carpets and stones.

Khaqani, like other great poets from Azerbaijan such as Nizami Ganjavi, wrote in Persian and Arabic. Professor Mobariz Alizadeh of Baku University has translated Khaqani's Persian poetry into Azerbaijani. Here, in English, is an extract from Khaqani's famous Persian poem "The Ruins of Madain":

My soul, come, draw lessons from life, look around
A mirror to help you in old Madain can be found.

Beside the Tigris lie the ruins of great Madain
The river's long banks with bitterest groaning resound.

More blood flows than water from Tigris' suffering eyes
No tears touch its cheek, dried by flames that from smouldering ruins arise.

See — the Tigris is foaming — foam curls on the lips of each wave . . .
How mournful those ruins burying hearts and their sighs!

The heart of the Tigris is burnt by sorrow and fear.
Can flames be so intense that the water itself they rear?

. . .

This place speaks of chambers of justice once ruined by hate.
The throne fell to tyrants who rose unaware of their fate.

Yes, once long ago Madain was a work of great art.
The palace had gateways that blazed with mosaics and gold . . .

Imagine this place that once held a whole land in its sway,
The fort as it was, not the ruins that lie here today.

The walls would say, "Weep! For you, too, have good reason for sorrow,
To dust all must crumble and you, man, are just living clay!"

. . .

You ask where such rulers have gone, since today there are none —
The earth has embraced all these kings, every shah and khagan . . .

The great Madain is still witnessing the horrors of an undesirable war between Iraq and Iran!

Seeing the derelict state of Khaqani's grave in Tabriz made me conscious of the fact that there were other great poets who had been born in Azerbaijan and had died there but are not celebrated. In Iran, Azerbaijani poets and writers have suffered discrimination while they lived and after their death. Humam Tabrizi was equally as great as Sa'di Shirazi, if not greater; Khaqani was as great a poet as Firdausi. Unfortunately, neither Humam nor Khaqani are introduced to the people of Iran, at least to the people of Iranian Azerbaijan, as are Sa'di and Firdausi. Contemporary Azerbaijani poets still live and die unrecognised. Habib Sahir, for example, whom I met in 1977, wrote beautiful poetry in Azerbaijani. He died, unnoticed, in 1982 in Tehran. Here are some lines from his poem, "My Ancient Beauty":

I know my own ancient beauty,
    She is in Egypt a statue made of gold!

Once she was like a mortal human being,
    But today she is an immortal beauty . . .

In her dreamy, large black eyes
    There is the everlasting sunshine of the desert.

She is a bewitching and a rare beautiful blossom;
    This flower only blossoms by the Nile.

Shahriyar, a famous Azerbaijani poet who is still alive today, is reduced to poverty and writes his poetry under political and psychological pressure. His son was arrested and accused of having Marxist-Leninist sympathies and Shahriyar was informed that his son would not be released unless he composed poetry in praise of the Islamic Republic of Iran. I was introduced to Shahriyar by Dr Chaichi and met him several times before I went to Istanbul in 1959. During my time in Istanbul he would send me poetry written in his own handwriting. I later donated two of these poems to the Istanbul Museum of Manuscripts.

Shahriyar's poem "Haydar-baba Salam" has become very well known and is often considered as his masterpiece. Here I translate some lines from this poem ("Haydar-baba" is the name of a mountain in Azerbaijan):

> Haydar-baba when it thunders,
> Floods, waters, roaming down,
> Girls standing in line and watching.

> I hail your glory and your people,
> May you remember our name too.

> When your partridges take flight,
> When your rabbits rise and run out of bushes,
> When your gardens have burst into blossoms,

> May you remember our name too.
> Make our depressed hearts happy.

> Haydar-baba may the sun warm up your back,
> Make your face laugh and make your springs run,
> Your children collect bunches of flowers.

> When the wind blows send it to us.
> Perhaps this may awaken my sleeping fortune . . .

I did not stay in Iran more than two months before returning to Britain, but I met many people and learnt a lot. Between 1953 and 1964 the Shah had appointed several governments and many plans had been implemented, the most important of which was his so-called "White Revolution". There was a noticeable improvement in the living conditions of people. Nevertheless, all these socio-economic changes were uneven, and the political atmosphere in Iran was stifling. All political parties, except those approved by the Shah, were banned. Only the "National Party", under the leadership of Manuchihr Iqbal, and the "People's Party", under Asadullah Alam, were free to operate openly. Both these leaders were very close to the Shah and both came from big land-owning families. Iqbal served as prime minister in 1957 and was later in charge of Iranian oil. His National Party was later replaced by the New Iran Party and Hassan Ali Mansur became its chairman.

While he was prime minister, Mansur was assassinated in January 1965 and the Shah gave the premiership to Amir Abbas Hovida, who served until 1977. Hovida was executed after the Revolution of 1979.

Alam was an influential court minister and quite close to most leading ayatollahs. After he had rigged the election for the 21st Majlis, he served as prime minister in 1963. It was he and Pakravan (the chief of SAVAK) who arranged Ayatollah Khomeini's exile to Turkey after the bloody riots which occurred in many Iranian cities in June 1963. A retired colonel who had worked for the SAVAK told me (after the Revolution of 1979) that Alam and Pakravan had used Ayatollah Shariatmadari to save Ayatollah Khomeini from execution. According to the colonel, the Shah had ordered Pakravan to get rid of Khomeini, even by execution if necessary. Pakravan went to Alam to discuss the situation. Since a leading ayatollah cannot be executed, they decided to go to Ayatollah Shariatmadari, explain the situation and ask him to issue a decree saying that Khomeini was a leading mujtehid (the highest rank of religious leader). Ayatollah Shariatmadari complied with their request. Alam took the decree to the Shah and, as prime minister, prevented the execution of Ayatollah Khomeini. Although the Shah lost his temper, he eventually agreed to the exile of Khomeini to Turkey. Ayatollah Khomeini was later removed from Turkey to Iraq and stayed there until 1978.

Ayatollah Khomeini kept in contact with the leaders of religious students and bazaar merchants in Iran. In the absence of political parties and democratic freedom, religious leaders, such as Ayatollah Khomeini worked steadily and continuously, using hundreds of mosques and playing thousands of tapes which contained their sermons. Even the government encouraged religion. The Shah and the royal family, in order to impress the religious population, visited Mashhad regularly and also paid visits to Karbala and even Mecca. Influential persons such as Alam and even the Shah regularly met with religious leaders. As part of their programme to combat democratic movements and Marxist ideology in Iran, they believed that the Islamic religion was the most effective deterrent for the illiterate people. In this way the Shah, while suppressing all intellectual and political activities, succeeded in replacing the political mechanism with religion — and thus undermined his own regime.

While the Shah accepted the traditional, orthodox religion and its leaders, he nevertheless was the enemy of radical religious groups like the Mujahidin. I visited Iran again in the summers of 1965, 1971 and 1978 with my family. When I visited in 1971 I realised that among the students and intellectuals there were two political movements: Islamic and Marxist. The Mujahidin, which did not adopt its name until 1971, was formed from the religious wing of Mossadeq's followers and especially from the Liberation Movement. Over 90 per cent of its members were intellectuals and were mostly from bazaar merchant families; thus they also received financial support from this source. They believed that the Pahlavi regime had little support beyond that of the big businessmen and landowners and that the Shah ruled mainly through terror and propaganda. The only way to destroy this terror, they felt, was through heroic acts of violence. The Shah's regime labelled the Mujahidin "Islamic Marxists", thereby showing its fear, not of Islam, but of Muslims who combined Islam with Marxism. In fact, the Mujahidin later developed in two groups, in 1970: Islamic and Marxist.

The other political group, the Fida'i organisation, which had basically branched out from the Marxist-Leninist Tudeh Party and the Marxist wing of Mossadeq's National Movement, like the Mujahidin, had emerged in the early 1960s. This organisation adopted its name in March 1971 and, again like the Mujahidin, was composed of two subgroups.

Although the guerilla movement represented by these organisations failed to bring down the Shah's regime, it was to play a crucial role in late 1977, during the revolutionary upsurge. Of all these guerrilla organisations, the Mossadeq group from the Fida'i played a decisive role in combating the Shah's forces during the Revolution of 1979. But they did not manage to maintain and develop their unity after the Revolution. This internal disintegrity made it easier for Khomeini's government to establish itself and suppress other political groups.

The Shah's regime acted decisively against these political organisations and killed many of their members. In order to discredit the Mujahidin and Fida'i, a number of mullahs were recruited into the SAVAK, who organised numerous religious meetings in mosques and other public places. At these meetings the mullahs condemned these radical organisations, thus discrediting them in the eyes of the illiterate and the working people. At the same time they were also putting the political and social initiative into the hands of the mosque.

Moharram ceremonies were encouraged. Generally the SAVAK ignored the distribution of religious tapes, including those of Ayatollah Khomeini, but possessing the works of a progressive writer such as Samad Behranghi, would cost a man several years in prison. A certain colonel once told me that a branch of SAVAK, under the direction of Alam, was distributing these tapes and collecting money in support of Ayatollah Khomeini after 1964. The Shah's regime, and even the West, preferred to use the traditional religion and the mullahs in order to attack and weaken the radical Muslims and Marxists in Iran.

In the summer of 1965 I met for the first time many of my writer friends. Samad Behranghi, Behruz Dihqani, Kazim Sa'adati and, some time later, Dr Ghulam-Hussein Sa'idi (Sa'idi lived in Tehran and was visiting his home town of Tabriz). At first they would come to my parents' house. Samad Behranghi was writing short stories for children taken from Azerbaijani folklore and a book about the problem of education in Azerbaijan. I once asked him what he was writing and why he had aroused such opposition among the older teachers and the Department of Education. He answered, "I do not write anything extraordinary. I write what I see."

Later we used to meet at Intisharate Shams (Shams Publications). My friendship with Samad Behranghi, Behruz Dihqani and Ghulam-Hussein Sa'idi became deeper when I learned that they were honestly and passionately devoted to serving the masses by their pen and voicing their silent griefs and shortcomings. At a time and in a society where all political parties are banned, freedom of speech is outlawed and historians do not dare to write the truth, the works of such writers and their socio-political literature becomes very valuable. In order to understand the history, the society and the political and economic conditions of the people in Iran (especially since the coup of 1953) we must read and understand the works of writers like these.

Although the Shah's "White Revolution", with its modernisation and social reforms, offered the peasants, workers and civil servants relative prosperity or advancement, this prosperity or advancement remained uneven and was often short-lived. The peasants, for example, who had benefited from the land reforms implemented in the 1960s could not make their living from the land which they had bought. There were many reasons for this. First, the piece of land allocated to each peasant was too small to produce enough crops to provide both food for his family and a surplus to sell. Second, he could not afford to pay for water, seeds and the repayments for his land. Third, even if he produced more crops than he needed for his own consumption, the price of grain in the market was so low (because of subsidised imported grain from the United States and other countries) that he could not make a profit. Most peasants eventually had to abandon their land and move to the cities, where they became construction labourers or were swallowed up by the factories as cheap labour. Those who could not move to the cities sold back their land to the landowners or others, in order to repay their debts. They then became labourers or casual workers for the big landowners.

At this time, Samad Behranghi had completed teacher training college in Tabriz and was teaching in the villages in Azerbaijan. He had noticed the uneven distribution of wealth in the villages and in the cities of Azerbaijan, which is a comparatively prosperous province of Iran. In his stories he effectively highlighted the gulf between the rich few, who enjoyed the financial and moral support of the Shah and his government, and the poor majority. He also stressed the gulf between the theory and practice, the moral teachings and deeds, of the government.

In his story *Oolduz and the Crows* (Oolduz is a popular name for girls in Azerbaijan) Samad criticised social injustice and abstract moral laws. The crow tells Oolduz how it steals soup from courtyards or catches fish from pools. "Why steal?" asks Oolduz. "It is a sin," she adds. "Do not be childish, my dear," replies the crow. "What is sin? It is a sin not to steal when my children and I die of hunger. That is a sin, my dear. It is a sin not to be able to satisfy my hunger. It is a sin to see so much soup everywhere and be hungry . . . you ought to know that it is impossible to prevent stealing by such abstract and empty advice. For as long as everyone seeks only his own interest, there will be stealing."

By 1965 Samad Behranghi had reached the conclusion that the Shah's regime suffered from two main weaknesses: one was lack of a proper educational and political mechanism and freedom; the other was social injustice, especially towards the honest and good-hearted peasant villagers. In his book *Twenty Four Hours Day Dreaming*, he showed the difficult life of a man who has gone to Tehran to seek a better life. (Most of the peasants from Azerbaijan went to Tehran and were employed in the construction industry. The people from Sistan and Baluchistan emigrated to Gorgan and became labourers in the large cotton fields there.)

Perhaps it was these two weaknesses in the Shah's regime which caused his downfall. Samad Behranghi had projected this idea in his book *Kachale Kaftar Baz* (*The Bald Pigeon Flier*), which tells the story of Kachal, who was a poor boy who had an old mother, a goat and some pigeons. He and his mother lived in a smoke-blackened hut. Kachal collected dry thorny bushes in order to feed his goat, and to fuel the stove in the middle of their room. His mother had a spinning-wheel on which she spun wool. Thus they managed to make a living.

In front of Kachal's hut was the magnificent palace belonging to the king. The princess used to sit on her balcony and watch Kachal's pigeons fly. She fell in love with Kachal and wanted to convey her feelings to him through gestures and her servants. Kachal also loved the princess, but could not show his feelings because he knew that the king would never allow him to marry his daughter.

After a while the princess became ill because of her love for Kachal. The king summoned all the learned men and asked them to cure his daughter. They could not cure her. But the princess told the king her secret. He became angry and threatened the princess. She would be banished from the country if she loved "this dirt".

The king decided to get rid of Kachal and his pigeons. He ordered his prime minister to send the army to punish Kachal, kill his pigeons and forbid him to fly pigeons again. The princess sent her trusted servant to warn Kachal and his mother of the king's order. Kachal was feeding his pigeons when the king's soldiers suddenly stormed into his hut. They killed his pigeons, beat Kachal and broke the leg of his mother's spinning-wheel.

A few days later, Kachal had recovered a little. He came out of the hut and was sitting under the mulberry tree in their yard, where his goat used to eat and sleep. He suddenly noticed that two pigeons on top of the tree were whispering to each other and one was saying to the other: "Sister, if Kachal feeds his goat on the leaves of the mulberry tree — which will fall after we fly away — and then milks his goat and rubs the milk on the necks of his dead pigeons, then the pigeons will wake up from their death-sleep and do things that ordinary pigeons cannot do." (This refers to those who were arrested or tortured by the SAVAK. After their release they knew things about the SAVAK that other people did not. They knew the SAVAK from the inside.)

Kachal did what the pigeons on the tree suggested. All of his pigeons awoke and flew away. After a while they returned to Kachal bringing with them a special hat for him. The hat was magic and anyone who put it on became invisible. When Kachal's mother heard of the magic hat she begged her son not to steal. Kachal promised not to take things which did not belong to him.

He put on the hat and went to the district where the rich factory owners such as Haji Quli Parchabaf lived. "How has Haji Quli gained his wealth and money?" Kachal wondered. "From his factory," he thought. "Who works in his factory?" he asked himself. "The workers work and make money for Haji Quli and Haji Quli does not dirty his hands," he exclaimed out loud. Then he argued, "If the workers do not work, then the factory will close and Haji Quli will lose his money. So the money and wealth of Haji Quli comes from the work of the workers and this should belong to the workers."

Therefore, Kachal, believing that Haji Quli's wealth was not rightly his own, walked into Haji Quli's house and saw him sitting with his wives having afternoon tea in the garden. Kachal saw honey, cream, toast and tea in front of Haji Quli. Because he was hungry, Kachal tried some of them. He lifted Haji Quli's glass of tea and drank from it. Haji Quli started praying fervently and his terrified wives screamed and ran away. Kachal entered Haji's house, collected many valuable items, opened the safe and took all Haji Quli's money. He came out and distributed all the money and items among the workers. He told them, "This belongs to you. Spend it on your family." When he had finished a little money was left over. Kachal bought some food with it for his mother and himself. Kachal also used the hat to visit the princess in her palace.

Haji Quli and the other rich manufacturers and landowners went to the king and persuaded him to act against Kachal. They said to the king, "What sort of king are you? Can't you protect our property?" The king set his entire army against Kachal. A battle began, between Kachal and his pigeons on one side and the king's army on the other. While the commander-in-chief tried to catch Kachal, his pigeons flew over the army and showered the soldiers with goat droppings. The soldiers were alarmed and the commander-in-chief was wounded. Finally, the army were forced to withdraw. (Ironically, the Shah's army was defeated by the poor in the shanty town of southern Tehran. In the story Kachal symbolises a social outcast, and a poor but a wise character.)

The princess was united with Kachal and she was taught how to spin wool by Kachal's mother. Kachal and the princess lived happily ever after.

Samad Behranghi's story might seem rather simple and childish, but his vision is sharp and the prediction is apt. In the story the king, while giving support to Haji Quli and the other rich factory-owners, suppresses social relationships and love. He was prepared to kill the pigeons, who symbolise freedom, and Kachal, who represents reason or wisdom. Society lacks justice and political freedom. Although the book was written for children, it was also meant to be read and understood by adults. It was written in this style in order to avoid the attention of the SAVAK, who would have prohibited its publication. Nevertheless, the SAVAK came to fully understand the meaning of Samad's works soon after his death, because of the influence he left behind among the people.

Ghulam-Hussein Sa'idi, a well-known Iranian psychiatrist and leading playwright, who died in 1985, realised the power of superstition and influence of the mullahs in the villages and even in the cities of Iran. In his *Tars va Larz* (*Fear and Trembling*) he takes us to the fishing villages of Southern Iran, where life is dominated by the sea and its changes. If the sea is calm and fish plentiful, the villagers are cheerful and the village itself bustles with activity. But when the sea is rough and the fishermen are unable to work, the shadow of fear and superstition covers the village and everything becomes lifeless.

The villagers live in fear of want, and tremble at the threat of death. It is not only the sea or natural elements which cause this fear in the village, but the existence of certain parasitic beings, such as the mullah and a man called Isaac, who calls himself a doctor. The mullah is after women and good food; the doctor is after money. Originally, the village did not have a mullah. One day, however, a man with a briefcase arrives at the village. The villagers are naturally curious about the stranger. One says, "He has come to round up conscript soldiers"; another says, "The gendarmerie always collects conscript soldiers; he has perhaps come to issue birth certificates."

The stranger meets the headman of the village and asks if there is a mullah in the village. The headman replies, "What do we want a mullah for? We neither need to write letters nor do we need prayer, thank Heaven." The stranger says, "Just as well you have not got a mullah, because I am a mullah and know how to write. If anyone wants to send a letter or needs a prayer note, he or she could come to me — I want to stay here for some time."

After some conversation, the headman, as a matter of custom, invites the stranger to stay at his house. The mullah eats a large meal and then goes to bed. The following morning the mullah gets up early and walks through the village, returning in time for breakfast. He recounts the different kinds of palm tree he had seen in the village. "You know, Kadkhuda," says the mullah. "I like to eat these dates very much . . . all of them are blessings from God, and each has a special benefit. One kind of date cures a pain in the waist, another cures headache and another is suitable for a married man." "That is obvious," answers Kadkhuda. "If somebody can find all these and eat them, he will certainly feel better. But, mullah, there is not so much here that you can eat them every day. Haji Mostafa is the only one who is fairly well off, but his orchard is not very large. He has a big family and also helps the needy. He is a man of God." "That is true," replies the mullah "but I have read in a book that all these dates that grow in orchards bear a secret . . . You know, Kadkhuda," continues the mullah, "every village that does not have good women, good dates and good water should be deserted. How old do you think I am? I am much older than you. Look, I have not got even one grey hair on my head. But can you show me even a single black hair on yours? Do you know why? I have always taken life easy and enjoyed myself. Wherever I travel I find a good woman. I also eat well. By the way, Kadkhuda, who is the owner of that large door at the top of the alley?" "Which door?" asks Kadkhuda. "There are two horns mounted on the top of the door, which has large decorative nails." "Oh, I know," says Kadkhuda, "it is Zakariyya's house. Why?" "I was passing by," answers the mullah, "and saw a pretty woman who was carrying water and who went to that house. By the way, Kadkhuda, has that lady got a husband?" "Oh, she is Zakariyya's sister, and has not got a husband. She was married, but her husband divorced her and went to the island." "I knew," said the mullah, laughing, "that she did not have a husband. It was obvious from the way she walked. Now you see, Kadkhuda, what a nice place I have come to. After an hour, go to Zakariyya's house and propose that I marry his sister. See if he agrees to let me marry her. Tell him that I am a servant of God — a mullah. I can write, I also have money. If he agrees, congratulate him, and sort out the problems on my behalf."

A few days after his arrival in the village, the mullah marries the woman. After a while he deserts her and she dies giving birth to a child. The mullah, it turns out, has been following the same pattern in the surrounding villages.

Again, in his *Chub bi-dastha-yi Varazil* (*The Stick-Wielders of Varazil*), Sa'idi shows how non-political the masses are and how the only place they know of to escape to is the mosque. The Shah had closed all political doors, but he kept the doors of mosques open.

Varazil is an imaginary village which is attacked by wild boars. Many peasants lose their crops and finally all get together to debate the matter.

One suggests that without a gun and gunpowder they cannot kill the boars. Thus they decide to employ some hunters who can do the job for them. After a lengthy investigation they are told about a man, called Monsieur, who lives in the city. One of the villagers is appointed to go and ask for Monsieur's help. Monsieur is interested in the story because of the boars, and decides to send two of his hunters to the village on condition that they are provided with good food and accommodation.

When the hunters arrive at the village 'they are given the use of a large house, and the villagers agree to take turns to provide them with food. The hunters eat an enormous amount. They hunt at night and eat and sleep during the day. This continues even after all the boars have been killed. Finally, they exhaust all the food supplies in the village. When the villagers protest and, armed with sticks, ask them to leave, the hunters threaten to turn their guns on them. In despair, the villagers return to Monsieur, who advises them to employ two more hunters to dislodge the first two.

The same pattern of food and accommodation is repeated. After eating and sleeping well, the new hunters challenge the original hunters who are lodged in the building opposite. The two groups confront each other with their guns. The villagers gather in the square to watch. The hunters take aim at each other, and prepare to fire. Then suddenly, they turn their guns towards the villagers. The crowd panics and tries to flee to the mosque. (The two sets of hunters clearly represent the British and the Americans.)

By the end of 1970, crop production in many villages had reached such a low level that the villagers were forced to buy grain from the cities. Then there was an oil boom between 1970 and 1975 and agriculture was further abandoned by the government. Hovida, who was prime minister at the time, boasted that Iran could afford to import anything it wished. So wheat and rice came from America, eggs and chickens from Israel and fruit from Spain and other countries.

The Shah offered loans and grants to European, African and Asian countries. At the same time he neglected the villages, the hospitals and the homeless people in Tehran and other big cities. If the Shah had spent the money given to the Western countries on the people of Iran, and had given political freedom to the political parties (at least to the liberal parties such as the Mossadeqists), a real political foundation would have been built which would have established a relationship between the government and society. Then he might have survived external pressure. But the Shah did not have or establish a social and political foundation, whereas the mullahs already had one. He was not close to the people, but the religious leaders were. For this reason, when the Revolution took place and all the underground groups participated, the mullahs were the only organised group who could fill the vacuum. Europe, realising that the mullahs were the best bid to combat the radical and democratic forces in Iran, backed Ayatollah Khomeini and his Islamic Republic.

In February of 1979 when I wanted to fly from Tabriz to Tehran, the weather was bad and all flights were cancelled. There were many Iranians and foreign correspondents from *The Guardian, Washington Post, New York Times* and other newspapers — waiting in the airport departure lounge. We decided to travel by train and went by taxi to Tabriz railway station, a few kilometres away. When we arrived at the station there was a long queue at the ticket office. We stood in the queue and started chatting. I learned that these foreign correspondents were returning from a province in Kurdistan, where they had interviewed Izziddin Husseini and other Kurdish leaders. The correspondent from the *Washington Post* was standing next to me. "How do you see the situation in Iran?" I asked him. "The situation is frightening," he said. "We do not want the guerrilla organisations to take over the Revolution."

In the train they were preoccupied with Kurdistan and Azerbaijan and kept asking me questions. One asked me if I thought Kurdistan and Azerbaijan wished to be autonomous. I replied that I did not know. When, in turn, I asked him for his opinion, he said, "It would be disastrous if the Marxists take over the government in Iran." "Do you mean Russians?" I asked. "Oh no, there are enough Iranian Marxists to take over the government if they get a chance." But I did not hear a single word against Ayatollah Khomeini and his prime minister Bazargan.

9

The Hi-jacked Revolution

When my family and I went to Iran in the summer of 1978 the wind of change was blowing across the country. In Tabriz the people talked about the upheaval of February 1978 and explained, with a sense of pride, how the police and SAVAK systems had been paralysed and the city was out of their control. Although the city had fallen into the hands of the people they rarely indulged in physical attacks on individuals or private property.

The upheaval continued for three days during which time police stations, Resurgence Party offices, banks, and cinemas specialising in foreign "X"-rated films were attacked. The people set upon police stations and Resurgence Party offices because they represented the Pahlavi state, and on banks because they were owned by the royal family, the state and foreign investors who helped the rich and discriminated against the poor and small businessmen. Many eye-witnesses told me that no one attempted to steal anything. They set fire to the banks but did not touch the money. They attacked cinemas because of foreign "pornographic" films. The banks symbolised the physical exploitation and the cinemas symbolised the cultural exploitation and negative influence of the West. Neither in Tabriz nor in other cities were the people opposed to Western technology and modernisation as such; they were against the exploitation and negative aspects of the West. Later on, the ayatollahs exploited this anti-foreign and particularly anti-Western feeling of the people. Thus they managed to rally the people behind them. In this way they began to hi-jack the revolution of 1979: using anti-West and anti-American propaganda as camouflage, the ayatollahs developed relations with the Common Market countries and maintained secret links with the United States (Irangate can be seen as an example of this).

When I met some members of the Iranian Writers' Association in Tehran, I learned more about the influence of writers and poets on the political atmosphere in the country. Poets and writers played an extremely important role during 1977 through their popular gatherings in Tehran, in which over 10,000 intellectuals and students participated. During the Shah's rule this sort of gathering was rare and was paid for with people's lives. In the face of SAVAK's intimidation by threats, physical attacks and even death, this action by the Iranian Writers' Association was a daring move against the Pahlavi regime. Lawyers, teachers, doctors, especially women students and teachers, were secretly and wholeheartedly supporting the opposition. Almost all female students I met during my stay in Iran, from whichever walk of life, expressed views and revolutionary vision which I found encouraging. I became very optimistic about the prospects for change because I believed that without the participation of the women of Iran the Revolution would not be successful.

I could clearly feel the wind of change and the current of revolution underneath the "island of stability" (a phrase used by President Carter to describe Iran when welcoming the Shah at the White House about a year before the Revolution of 1979). I thus decided to stay a few months in Iran and witness the outcome. I was, fortunately, on sabbatical leave for the following two terms (October 1978-April 1979). I took my family back to Britain and returned to Tehran on 7 September 1978 (one day before "Black Friday").

My brother Mohsen had come from Tabriz to meet me at Tehran airport. (Following my arrest by the SAVAK at Tehran airport in the summer of 1977, Mohsen always anxiously travelled from Tabriz to meet me.) When I arrived the SAVAK did not ask their usual questions: What do you teach in Britain? What are your political activities? Do you support anti-Iran groups and organisations? and so on.

The SAVAK had arrested me in March 1977 partly because I had read three papers — one was on "The concept of 'Devil' in Persian mythology" (Ann Arbor, Michigan 1967) at an international conference on the Middle East, at which I had also voiced my criticisms of the Shah and Israel's occupation of Arab lands; the second was on the works of Jalal-Al-e Ahmad and Samad Behranghi, in Brussels in September 1970, and the third on the works of Dr Ghulam-Hussein Sa'idi, in Paris in August 1973. The SAVAK informed me that both Samad Behranghi and Ghulam-Hussein Sa'idi were threats to the security of the state.

I remember one amusing incident that happened while I was under arrest. I had been locked in a very hot room and the heat soon melted the chocolates that I was carrying in my pockets to give to my sister's children when I arrived at her house in Tehran. I realised this when I wanted to find a tissue to wipe the perspiration from my forehead, which was starting to trickle onto my glasses. I inadvertently dipped my right hand in the melted chocolate. I then, without thinking, tried to find a tissue in another pocket to clean my dirty hand. My left hand then became sticky with the melted chocolate in my

Tabriz, November 1978.

other pocket. I did not know what to do, lost my temper and banged on the door. A policeman opened the door. He told me off, in an Azerbaijani accent, and ordered me to stop making a noise. When he saw the brown-stained stuff on my hands and on my jacket, he asked me what was the matter. Realising that he was from Azerbaijan, I spoke to him in my own language and asked him to keep the door open so that I could have some fresh air. (The temperature in Tehran at the time was over 100°F. Inside the room it must have been much higher!) He told me he would be reprimanded but, however, kept the door slightly ajar to allow some fresh air to filter through. Thus I sat, still covered in chocolate, until a police officer came to question me.

On the evening of 7 September 1978 the Shah had forced the Cabinet to declare martial law in Tehran and eleven other cities. Mohsen told me what had happened during the past few days in the streets of Tabriz and Tehran. He had witnessed the events first-hand. The following morning (Friday 8 September) my friend Mahmud, who had completed his studies in architecture in London and returned to Iran to work, called at my sister's house and asked me to accompany him to a street demonstration. By the time we arrived near Jaleh Square in eastern Tehran it was about 8.30 a.m. Thousands of people were converging on the square from all directions, while helicopters were hovering over the area. Just as Mahmud and I were approaching the square itself (about 8.45 a.m.) we heard shooting. Mahmud became very excited when he heard this; he wanted to rush into the square but I stopped him. "There is no point in going with empty hands to face armed soldiers. You see they are shooting at people. It is pointless to waste our lives without doing anything useful."

Mahmud agreed and we sheltered behind huge trees near Jaleh Hospital. We could still hear the shooting and hundreds of wounded people were being rushed into the hospital, into houses, or bundled into cars and taken away. There were many people trying to help the wounded, when tanks and armoured cars appeared from behind the old Majlis building with mounted machine-guns firing at the people in the street. The soldiers did not look like Iranian soldiers to us. They had long fair hair or were very dark. Mahmud and I squatted with many other people, sheltering behind huge trees or in the narrow alley next to Jaleh Hospital.

In Jaleh Square that day hundreds of people were shot dead by the soldiers firing from the ground and helicopters. (Houses were also attacked by the helicopters. There were bullet marks on the walls and the people were hit through their heads and shoulders.) It was not safe to walk on the streets of Tehran. Mahmud and I returned home in the late afternoon. I heard an eye-witness saying that he had seen in all 3,672 dead men, women and children in Bihisht-i Zahra (a burial ground in Tehran) by 4 p.m. on Friday 8 September. This day became known as "Black Friday". Significantly, I did not see a single mullah either at Jaleh Square area or among the wounded or killed.

Most of the wounded in the streets of Tehran were saved from being taken away by the army. I heard another eye-witness saying that the army buried the dead and wounded together. Some of the doctors in Tehran had made their clinics available free of charge for the treatment of the wounded people. Dr Akbar Sa'idi (the brother of Ghulam-Hussein Sa'idi), who is a surgeon, had organised 24-hour portable surgical units which carried out operations in Tehran. I visited one of his units in the city centre (near the city park) where Dr Sa'idi had full surgical equipment and a standby nurse. Ordinary people were also helping. I was impressed by his courage, enthusiasm and love for the people in saving their lives.

"Black Friday" neither intimidated the people nor deterred them from taking part in further street demonstrations. It was clear that the Shah had lost any chance of a peaceful reform. There seemed only two ways forward: either a revolution or a military counter-revolution. The atmosphere reminded me of a poem, "Birds of Storm" by Shafi'i Kadkani (a well-known contemporary poet from Mashhad):

O birds of storm! May you fly high.
How did you so lovingly accept
In your own blood
The impact of lead bullets,
So kindly!
. . .

I want to question the breeze,
How will the sea move today
Without the tide of your heartbeat?
O birds of storm! May you fly high.

The 40th day after Black Friday fell on 16 October. A national strike was declared by political and religious leaders. The strike was very successful. All shops and bazaars were closed in Tehran and other Iranian cities. Thousands of people gathered at Bihisht-i Zahra to honour their martyred relatives. They made speeches opposing the Shah and prime minister Sharif Imami and his Cabinet. The place was surrounded by army commandos and armoured cars mounted with machine-guns. The University of Tehran was also surrounded by Scorpion tanks and commandos. This was the most successful strike of the past eight months and all schools, universities, factories and civil servants participated. In Dizful and Andimeshk and other Iranian cities the army opened fire on demonstrators and killed dozens of students and workers.

On 11 October 1978, in order to censor and silence the press, soldiers were sent to the *Keyhan* and *Ittilla'at* newspaper offices. They wanted to censor every article and all news. This had been common practice since the coup d'état of 1953 and the press employees were forced to accede to the suppressive regulations. However, on this occasion, the press employees, being aware of the political atmosphere in Iran and the need for a free press, refused to co-operate with the censorship and rules imposed under martial law — and went on strike. The strike was a complete success, and lasted for over two months. The government tried to persuade the writers and reporters to return to their work, making numerous promises, including freedom of the press without interference, but they did not succeed. The writers told the military government, "You can kill people by arms, you can censor by force, but you can never write by bayonets. Writers belong to the people." This political stand by writers and reporters brought them closer to the people.

I knew one of the writers (a Dr Mojabi) who worked for *Ittilla'at* newspaper who told me, "During these years of dictatorship we writers and reporters suffered a lot. We appeared to be working for the newspapers who supported the Shah and did not write about the shortcomings in the country and what was happening to the people. But we writers were, at heart, with the people and wanted to defend their interests, rights and independence. It is very frustrating for writers or reporters who love their country and people but cannot help them by using their pen in freedom. Censorship negates the development of constructive ideas in society and all dictators are afraid of these ideas. We have still a long way to freedom . . . but it will be gained by our people. Our writers have an important responsibility in this process . . ."

The strike of workers in the oil industry, in copper and other mines, and factories began in October 1978 and lasted until the Revolution of February 1979. The Iranian oil industry workers were to play an important role in the Revolution itself.

I could not stay in Tehran indefinitely and I was anxious about what was happening in Tabriz, so I travelled to my home town by coach. The passengers talked about their recent experiences and current affairs more openly than ever before. A lady sitting in the next seat told me that she made this journey to Tehran every fortnight to see her son in Evin prison. "How long has he been in prison, and why?" asked a gentleman next to me. "He has been in prison for more than seven years. My daughter was also imprisoned, but she was set free after two years. Both my son and daughter were at Tabriz University. My son was in the third year of an engineering course and my daughter the first year studying Persian literature. One night the police — two civilians and two commandos — stormed into our house and began to search everywhere. They pulled out all the books, newspapers, papers and whatever we had in our cupboards. They were looking for books and weapons. They did not find any weapon; in fact my children did not have any. But they found books of stories by Samad Behranghi, two books of Azerbaijani tales by Behruz Dihqani (who was tortured to death in prison in 1973), the *Defences* of Khusraw Ruzbih (a professor at the Officers' College who was executed along with other Tudeh Party officers after the coup of 1953), the collected poems of Hakimeh Billuri and Marzieh Usku'i (two well-known Azerbaijani female poets. Marzieh, a teacher, was killed by the Shah's forces in 1974). They took the books and my two children. I begged them to take from the house whatever they wanted but to leave my daughter and son. They refused and said that after they had been questioned they would be sent back home. When I heard nothing after searching for a year and a half and spending all my savings on travelling and police bribes, I finally discovered my daughter and son in Evin Prison!"

Here I translate from Azerbaijani a poem by Hakimeh and a poem by Marzieh:

> I love my people much, very much,
> Not because I am related to them;
> They appreciate one's service —
> > Because of this I love them.

They love guests —
      Because of this I love them.
They are not interested in lining their pockets,
But in filling their hearts,
Thinking about others' pain.
My people understand minute particulars,
My people support truth,
They carry pride in their heart and dignity in their hand,
They are down to earth,
Dignified, patient and content.
I have observed all this.
Their patience is like a mountain,
Their natural ability like a spring.
They have a patience like that of Canaan.
I love their youth very much,
Because they are loyal.
I love their old very much,
Because their words are meaningful.
The mothers' words are influential,
Their vision is long-sighted.
My people have good habits.
They have open and bright hearts.
From childhood it is a habit among us:
To respect the old.
Affection cannot be bought and sold,
Love and service cannot be hindered,
Work is regarded Holy.
For these reasons my people make me live —
      the people's affection.
And this longing to see my motherland
      Can also kill me.

                    (A poem by Hakimeh Billuri)

I was a small and slow-moving river
Running through forests, mountains
And valleys.

I knew that stagnant waters
Die within themselves.
I knew that in seas,
In the bosom of the waves,
New life is born
For small rivers.

Neither the length of the road
Nor dark fissures,
Nor the fear of being stopped from running,
Held me back from movement.

Now I have joined
To the eternal waves.
Our existence is in effort;
Our death is in idleness.

("The Wave" by Marzieh Usku'i)

On 25 October 1978, 1,126 political prisoners (men and women) were set free. Among these were some well-known names, for example Vida Hajibi (a university lecturer, the campaign for whose freedom I had been involved in), Muhsin Yalfani (a theatrical actor and stage manager) and Abu Turab-i Baqirzadeh (a writer and translator).

In the midst of the freed political prisoners stood an old, dignified man called Safar Qahramani from Azerbaijan, who was regarded as the world's longest-serving political prisoner. He had been in prison for 30 years, 15 of which he had spent in the terrifying Burazjan prison. When he was freed in Tehran he did not know even one street. He had asked his fellow prisoners, "What does an 'apartment' look like?" He was interviewed by a newspaper reporter in his sister's house in Tabriz. Replying to questions, he said, "After 30 years of imprisonment, this freedom was unexpected. I owe my freedom to the people. If it were not for the right struggle of the people I would have stayed in prison until the end of my life. I regard this freedom dearly, because many faced bullets and lost their lives.

"Thirty years ago, after being active in the Democratic Party of Azerbaijan for five years, which had successes and failures, I was arrested and imprisoned. My activities were against the rule of the feudals but, knowing this, they still sentenced me to life imprisonment. Two years ago they took me and 60 other political prisoners to Evin prison and wanted me to write to the Shah and ask to be pardoned. I refused. For this reason they kept me in the worst conditions of Evin prison. The prison warden told me, 'You'll stay here until you disintegrate.' I laughed and said, 'I am unperishable. The people are behind the prison's walls'.

"Because of my continual protests against the prison authorities I was sent to the 'green cell' in Evin. This is a place where one cannot tell night from day. Air is pumped into the cell. Besides this more recent experience, the terrifying Burazjan prison has swallowed 15 years of my life. I had been without a visitor for years. Don't be surprised if I do not know the city and any street. Still, every second, I think with my whole being about those who remain political prisoners. All of my life is hidden in my past. I still live in prison because the rest of the children are in prison. I have seen young people, who had not yet grown hair on their faces, imprisoned for merely reading a book. All of my being is full of memories. I have left some prisoners behind with whom I have spent 25 years. What can I say about my own freedom?

"I cannot appreciate the beautiful word of freedom at the moment . . . I beg you to tell this to the people of Iran: We have been freed by the struggle of the people. Using the word 'amnesty' for our freedom is not fair. The people freed us and will free the rest of the political prisoners. We believed in this and still believe. Even when our friends were taken for torture and we could only hear their protesting agony, still we did not lose our hope of the people. My chest is a book, written in blood, 30 years of my memories. You ask me what do I desire? I explicitly answer, 'My desire is the freedom of political parties and freedom of all political prisoners . . .'

"You ask me about recent government policy. I am very pessimistic. I believe that the government of Iran is more afraid of people's unity than anything else. Hearing of the arrest of Bihazin, during the final minutes of my 30 years of imprisonment, is the reason why I am pessimistic." (Mahmud I'timadzadeh, known as Bihazin, was a prominent writer and translator, who had translated Shakespeare's *Othello* and had written novels and short stories including a collection entitled *Besu-yi Mardom* (*Toward the People*). He was the chairman of the Iranian Writers' Association and founder of the "Democratic Unity of Iranian People". He is still in one of the prisons of the Islamic Republic of Iran, one among hundreds of other political prisoners.)

Many political prisoners had met Safar Qahramani and were inspired by his strong personality and dignity. He was a symbol of resistance against the Shah's dictatorship. The Shah's regime could not break him. He had created the legend of "No" against the regime.

When I was in Tabriz he was being received by thousands of people. My brother Mohsen and I went to "see him in". The Tabriz streets were full of flowers. One of his fellow prisoners was a lorry driver who had spent a few years with him and had put his feelings about Safar Khan in a poem called "The Man", which was published in the first issue of *Iran-Shahr*, a Persian weekly newspaper edited by Ahmad Shamlu, in September 1978. I include a translation of this poem below.

> I am writing about the man,
> The man who has stayed thirty
> Springs of his life in a city
> Without even seeing that city, even for a day.
>
> He is a village man.
> In the city of restless people
> He is the bearer of troubles and patience.
> This man with broad shoulders,
> With strong stature and broad chest,
> With the strong arms of dignity,
> He is an everlasting man.

In patience he is a very Job of the time,
His broad forehead is a mirror to all
The sufferings of the prison.
In frozen and hard days
Safar Khan is warm and resilient.

This man from Azerbaijan
With olive-coloured face,
And eyes like black-velveted angels,
He is a man without a mask.
He is equal to the sun
In this permanent winter.

Thirty springs have passed,
But he is still upright and content
Like a tall cypress standing in winter.
In the summer of love,
Safar Khan has the secret of understanding.

This sun which can move at night,
Without showing dismay on his face,
Stood on firm for thirty years of deprivation
Still hoping to see the rebirth of spring.

He has roots in the heart of earth,
He has opened his arms to the universe,
He has sheltered many imprisoned tigers.
A world of dignity resides in his heart,
In this dark house he is in love with light.
In front of Ahriman [Satanic power]
He is like fresh verses of Ahura [divine power].
Without fear from the horror of storm
Safar Khan is a man of eternity.

This is indeed the literature of resistance and Persian modern literature
has many examples of this. Ahmad Shamlu himself, writing under the name
of "Bamdad", is a well-known Iranian contemporary poet. He, too, suffered
under the Shah's regime. Here I translate from Persian one of his poems,
"On the Pavement" (published in November 1978):

My unknown friends
Like burnt out stars,
So many of you have fallen cold on the dark earth,
That you might say
The earth
Will ever continue
Having night without stars.

Hey!
Look at streets from behind the window
See the blood on the pavements! . . .
This is the blood of dawn, as if on the pavement
Such beats the heart of sun
In its drops . . .

Faridun Tonikabuni (another contemporary writer) wrote in his *Notes on Prison Memories*, "Even Paradise without freedom is hell. But prison is twofold hell." (*Keyhan*, 23 October 1978.)

While in Tabriz I joined the National Solidarity of University Teachers at Tabriz University. I was invited to give a talk on the nature of "Cultural Exploitation" on 1 November 1978, which was published in *Keyhan* newspaper. Explaining in this talk how cultural exploitation was linked with economic exploitation, I referred to the experiences of Samad Behranghi, as related in his *Study of Educational Problems in Iran*.

On completion of his course at the teacher training college in Tabriz in 1957, which was based on modern and American theories on education, Samad became a teacher in a village school. The school consisted of one room and a toilet. The windows needed repairing and the roof leaked on rainy days and during winter. The school was located outside the village itself and the pupils walked to school. In winter those who did not have proper shoes were forced either to stay at home or work in a neighbouring carpet factory. American or Western educational theories could not be put into practice under these conditions. Thus Behranghi in the book wrote, "Until we see an environment or society closely, until we live in it, mix with the people and hear their griefs and learn about their wants, it is vain and useless to show ourselves sympathetic to that society and people, and even to write stories for them . . ." A person who is living comfortably in Europe or Tehran and writes books about the education of poor villagers cannot be objective and aware of the difficulties resulting from living conditions.

When the Iranian students and others denounced the Shah and the West they were, in fact, opposing social injustice and the culture of an unjust society where the ruling classes controlled books, schools, the mass media and the entire educational system. The people were thus being exploited both economically and culturally, bodily and spiritually.

While the Shah was busy buying hundreds of Phantom bombers, Chieftain tanks and many other sophisticated weapons from the West, the villages in Iran needed schools, teachers, doctors, roads and other basic necessities of life. The Iranian people had seen and experienced social injustice and had identified the West with the Shah through their close cooperation and common interest. So the students, teachers and the people as a whole did not believe in the fine words — "democracy", "human rights" and "love" —

which were taught by the Shah and his Western backers. In his article, "Literature for Children" (published in June 1968), Samad Behranghi criticised the passive and conventional moral and social laws, saying, "The time of limiting children's literature to passive propaganda and rigid instructions has passed away. Instructions such as cleanliness of the hands, face and body, obedience to parents, listening to grown-ups, laugh and the world laughs with you, helping the poor in the style of Charity Clubs, and many other examples like these, whose total and final result is to keep children ignorant of the important and urgent problems of life and their living environment. Why should we suffocate a child in the cocoon of vain luck, happiness and hope, while his elder brother is desperate for free breath and freedom. Does not a child need other things than learning about cleanliness and obedience to grown-ups, and listening to his teacher (which teacher?), and ethics (which ethics?) that men of power, comfortable and of dominant class, support and propagate? Should we not tell the child that there are children in this country who have not seen the colour of meat or even cheese for months or years? Because there are a few people who always desire to have 'goose cooked in wine' on their table! . . . Should we not tell our children that more than half of the world's population is hungry; why they are kept hungry; and what ways there are to cast off their hunger? Should we not teach a child a scientific and correct concept of the history, development and evolution of human societies?" Behranghi concluded his article by commenting, "Fine words about obedience and human love from those who have the largest slice of the cake are certainly to be expected, but for those who have only crumbs, these words are valueless . . ."

In October 1978 the teachers in Tabriz and other cities were on strike, and held a gathering in the hall at Firdausi Secondary School. The National Solidarity of University Teachers in Tabriz also met and decided to support the teachers' strike. The teachers were mainly opposed to the dictatorship and wanted to elect their own headmasters and local educational authorities. The university teachers had written a letter of support, which was to be presented at the teachers' meeting. I offered to take the letter there. When I arrived, the school was surrounded by police, commandos and many civilian SAVAK members. However, I went into the hall, gave the message and sat and listened to the speakers. The teachers eventually succeeded in many of their demands.

Meantime, I taught in the department of English and helped a number of postgraduate students who were working on the social importance of Persian literature. Some of my colleagues at the university were American. One was an ex-serviceman who had served in Vietnam and South-East Asia. There was also a married couple (Mr and Mrs Peach), who seemed to be more than simple teachers; most of the university believed that they worked for the CIA. These American teachers received a much higher salary than their

Iranian counterparts. There were also hundreds of American advisers in different governmental departments and industries, most of them former army officers or servicemen from Vietnam. They did not seem to know much about the job for which they were being paid. One American lady admitted that she had been employed without knowing what she was going to do in Iran. Only after her arrival was she placed in charge of a computer, about which she knew very little; but she had managed to save her face through the kind help of Iranian engineers! One can imagine how these well-qualified Iranian engineers, who received barely half her salary, felt about the situation; especially since many of these same Iranians had once been students in the United States, where they could find only the lowest-paid jobs in restaurants and other places where white Americans did not want to work.

As the street demonstrations and public meetings continued in Tabriz and other cities, political actions became more frequent on the basis of belonging to the main Muslim communities, for example the Shi'ite community, which accounts for approximately 90% of the population of Iran and 10% of all the total world population who profess Islam. Belonging to one or other community did not in itself determine the political character of such actions. While the Shi'ite clergy in Iran made a positive contribution to the development of the initial stage of the Revolution, at the same time the counter-revolutionary activity (the Shi'ite community) in Afghanistan had a different political character. While in Iran the Islamic factor initially helped to highlight the anti-Shah and anti-Imperialist (the United States in particular) content of the Revolution, in Afghanistan the banner of Islam was used to launch a counter-revolutionary drive backed by the United States through Pakistan. I noticed that both in the university meetings and the street demonstrations Islam was used by the religious-bourgeoisie in order to take the Revolution out of the class struggle.

Mahmud Dawlatabadi, a well-known contemporary writer, made a series of speeches during what was known as the Week of National Solidarity of the Universities in Iran (the first week of November 1978). He warned his audiences against volcano-like eruptions of emotions:

> The truth is that, contrary to many people who think they are living at an exciting point in history, I feel that we are experiencing a very dangerous process in the nation's social and political history. I do not think I am the only one to realize this. Without doubt many of our learned political scholars have reached this understanding before I have. But the practical atmosphere in society is ahead of their views, and this has created fear among intellectual observers. This fear of the general and actual atmosphere of society has forced many of our learned men to take an indecisive stance, they accept and even praise the current phenomena of society without having the courage and frankness to warn of possible dangers, of a future avalanche.
>
> This very fear and lack of frankness in principles have also given a chance to a

group of notorious people who are more Catholic than the Pope in demanding freedom. It is generally noticed that these people who only yesterday were openly and deeply involved in corruption and a parasitic lifestyle, are today still involved although not so openly as before. They pretend to be more sympathetic nurses to our children than their mothers. They have stepped in this market and are trying to take the bridle of this bolting horse . . .

This revolt is in itself acceptable because it is genuine. On the other hand it is dangerous because it is out of control. It is so much out of control that it drags men of thought and ideas behind like helpless people. The revolt is likeable because it has roots in the heart of the masses. It is fearful because it has no place in the mind of the masses . . .

The protests are based in blind instinct and excitement. They are not equipped with wisdom. The masses are hoodwinked and allowed to say whatever they want. One who has not got anything wants everything. Taking an extreme stance is either side of the same coin. It is putting imagination before reality and entrusting the heart to one's own deceit. The unhindered marching pleases the heart and open space removes petty conflict, if there is one, from the mind. But awareness and limitations are lost. Yardsticks are dropped. Excitement is increased in vain. The movement is becoming monopolized and dragged to extremes and will finally lose its way in extremity and chaos. Since they lack a united ideology and political organization and are not equipped with necessary political techniques at this social, historical point in time, these rapid emotions do not seek a vehicle for their aims and ideals . . . It has not even got a chance to select its mottoes. Naturally, in these circumstances, the movement becomes monopolistic and dogmatic. The leading men of thought and ideas have not been allowed during the past quarter of a century to walk along with the people, alive, at the same pace, slowly and creatively, together and on a reciprocal basis, they have been dragged behind the people. And — alas — actions run before thoughts . . .

The Revolution does not belong to one group. It belongs to all people of Iran, to all ideological and religious groups. Thus the most comic and at the same time the most dangerous political phenomenon of today is the replacement of one dictator by another dictator . . .

The workers in the factories, on a wide scale, are still demanding their historical and justified rights. They are suffering and are in need of the most elementary living conditions. Miners and factory workers, who have been kept in the conditions of the medieval ages, are protesting against these conditions. The idle peasants, who are more than three millions, are still scattered all over the country like homeless refugees.

(*Keyhan*, 4 November 1978.)

By the end of November 1978 it became clear that Ayatollah Khomeini had gained control of the Revolution. Ayatollah Shariatmadari was being undermined, even in his homeland of Azerbaijan. Just talking about Ayatollah Shariatmadari in the university was frowned upon by those who later gained important positions in the Islamic Republic government. There were even conflicts of opinion about the two ayatollahs within individual families in Tabriz. However, Ayatollah Khomeini's resolution and firm position against the Shah were winning the people in Azerbaijan over to his side.

In December 1978 the Shah appointed Bakhtiyar as prime minister. Bakhtiyar was a follower of Mossadeq and a liberal-minded man; he appeared on national television with a picture of Mossadeq in the background. By offering a series of reforms, he tried to win over the opposition. One of my Tabriz University colleagues commented, "I wish the opposition would accept his offers and cooperate with him and save us from an unforeseeable future." I said, "I doubt the people would accept Bakhtiyar because he was appointed by the Shah. But I admit that Bakhtiyar's announcement of the Shah's leaving Iran (apparently for a vacation), cancelling $7 billion worth of arms contracts, stopping the sale of oil to Israel and South Africa, withdrawing from CENTO, releasing political prisoners, dismantling SAVAK, freezing the assets of the Pahlavi Foundation, etc., seems the most radical move ever announced since Mossadeq's government."

Many political personalities expressed their views about Bakhtiyar's government and in general they had a negative opinion of his Cabinet. But Dr Sadiqi, a prominent professor of sociology at Tehran University and ex-member of Mossadeq's Cabinet, supported Bakhtiyar. In one interview, he said:

"Dr Bakhtiyar, as I know him, has two distinct qualities. First, he has a strong personality which makes him outstanding among many national leaders. He has the courage to step forward in these circumstances, when all are thinking about how to become a hero or achieve a position. Second, he loves and is interested in his own homeland. His interest in the independence of his country is a theme that he has stood by unwaveringly for many years; and I think, at this time in history, it is a victory for our nation to see someone like Dr Bakhtiyar in charge of forming a Cabinet and highlighting the everlasting name of Dr Muhammad Mossadeq . . . a man whose name the mass media could not even dare mention.

"Bakhtiyar had the courage to step in and it is our duty and that of all national leaders to help him and save the country. Now it is not a question of Dr Bakhtiyar in person, the National Movement, or you and I and even His Majesty the Shah, but it is a question of a country which we have to save . . ."

Although Bakhtiyar described Ayatollah Khomeini as the "Ghandi of Iran" and allowed him to return to Iran, his own government was rejected by Khomeini, who called for further strikes and demonstrations and declared that any government appointed by the Shah was illegal. But Ayatollah Shariatmadari declared that he (among other moderate religious leaders) would support the new premier and expressed his anxiety about the country's future. Meantime, Bakhtiyar warned that if the opposition rejected his plans on the basis of constitutional laws, the army would follow the example of

Chile and establish a military dictatorship. But Bakhtiyar knew that the
American General Hoyzier had been specially sent to Iran to supervise the
transfer of power and neutralise any possibility of a coup by Iranian
generals.

Many demonstrations were staged in Tabriz and the masses came out in
large numbers not only to oppose the Shah but also to denounce Bakhtiyar's
government. On 13 January, over one million people marched in the streets
of Tabriz (many travelled to be there from other cities of Azerbaijan),
demanding the resignation of Bakhtiyar and the return of Khomeini from
France.

On 16 January, I heard at two o'clock in the afternoon that the Shah had
left Iran. I rushed out with my brother Mohsen, taking my camera as I wanted
to go to the city centre to record what was happening. I saw that our street
was already packed with people. Some were dancing; some were mounted on
crowded lorries. All cars, taxis and other vehicles had their headlights on.
Men and women, including mothers with their children, lined the pavements
or were sitting on their rooftops watching the crowds and the celebration.
The soldiers had confined themselves to the inside of lorries and were
holding up pictures of Ayatollah Khomeini to save themselves from possible
attack.

By the time my brother and I reached Danishsara Square, which was
dominated by a large statue of the Shah, the crowd were just preparing to
climb up and pull down the statue. I filmed the fall of the Shah's statue, and
its replacement with pictures of Khomeini and Shariatmadari. Before filming,
however, I noticed that a quarrel had broken out between the two soldiers
who were guarding the statue. When the crowd approached the statue, one
soldier wanted to fire into the crowd but his comrade stopped him by hitting
him on the nose, which began to bleed violently. The crowd encircled them,
saying that it was not time to quarrel but to be united against the common
enemies — the Shah and America. People offered flowers and sweets to the
soldiers by the statue and in army vehicles. Women were giving away
sweets and encouraging their brothers and husbands by standing on the
pavements and raising their fists.

In the past, during bloody street battles, the women had played an
important part by turning their homes into first-aid centres to treat the
wounded. In this way they prevented the arrest and interrogation of hundreds
of combatants or demonstrators. When the crucial days of the Revolution
were approaching and the conflict between the Shah's army and the masses
was becoming more and more violent and bloody, women in Iran were very
active and played a decisive part in the Revolution. In Tabriz I saw women
piling up sandbags, wearing jeans or army uniform, and sitting behind
machine-guns. In Tabriz women showed such courage and resoluteness that
it became a saying among the Shah's commandos "You can move rocks but

you cannot move women". As so often happens, these women have been betrayed by the Revolution they helped to bring about.

After the crowd had toppled the Shah's statue in Danishsara Square, Mohsen and I moved toward Saat Qabaghi (City Council Square). By the time we arrived the people were pulling the body of the Shah's statue along the street, while a tall person carried the head of the statue above his head — mimicking the Shah. All the streets were still packed and buses and cars were unable to move. I could hear this poem being relayed through a loudspeaker:

> It is night and the face of motherland is dark.
> We have lost many brothers,
> They have been drowned in blood.
> For the sake of freedom,
> Take your daggers, your weapons
> Fight to bring the revolution to fruition . . .
> Let us unite and free ourselves from slavery and despotism,
> Workers and peasants unite . . .
> Rise up and bring down the palace of tyrant.

I met some university students, who told me that they were on their way towards Tabriz Prison, which was situated on the outskirts of Tabriz on the road leading to Tehran. They intended to free the political prisoners. I decided to join them.

When we arrived, one group had already attacked the prison and was trying to open the gates. Another group was approaching the prison. They were mainly workers, students and poor peasants who had moved to Tabriz and made their homes in the valleys of the Own-Ali mountain, where they lived in mud huts without electricity or proper heating. The students and I lost each other among the crowd. As the crowd approached the prison building, commandos suddenly appeared on the roof and started to fire at the crowd. People took shelter behind concrete structures and stone walls. I hid behind a concrete structure while I was filming the shooting. The hail of bullets was so fierce that I abandoned filming and lay down on the ground. Red-hot bullets were whizzing over our heads so closely that I could feel their heat. Someone pulled me back saying, "Doctor, don't go so close to the edge. You might be shot. We need you . . ."

After the shooting stopped and the crowd began to disperse, I talked to the young man who had pulled me back. He was a worker and lived at Own-Ali mountain, which is not very far from my parents' house. We started walking towards the city centre. I asked him about his life and about his reasons for opposing the Shah's regime. He said, "I work here and there. Sometimes I work at the carpet factory and in summer I prefer to do construction work. I work to support my mother and little sister. My father became ill and died last year. They said he had rheumatism and bronchitis. Our house is damp. A high electricity pylon passes over our valley but underneath we live without electricity and heating. It is very hard to live like this."

"What has the Shah got to do with this?" I asked. He answered, "After all he is the head of our country. We expect him to think about our living conditions. We suffer from cold in winter and from heat in summer. While we do not have drinking water and electricity, the rich people on the other side of the city have plenty of electricity and water. They even have swimming pools. Two kilometres away from our area you can see blocks of luxury flats built for the families of army and air force personnel. We do not expect to have those kinds of flats, but we want at least to have water, electricity and work. I tell you we live worse than animals. We are not regarded as human beings and members of this society. I know your brother Mohsen. Ask him about our living conditions and you are welcome to my home to see for yourself."

I asked Hassan, the young man, if he had taken part in other demonstrations. "A few days ago I took part in a protest demonstration in front of the American Consulate in Tabriz. My shoes were torn and when we were attacked by the police I could not run fast enough and fell in the gutter next to the pavement and broke my glasses. Now I can neither see properly and work nor can I afford to buy a new pair of shoes. I wished I was dead then . . ."

I met Hassan a week later and he took me to his house. His mother seemed embarrassed by her son's showing me their home. They lived and slept in one room. There was neither a kitchen, nor a bathroom. At the corner of a small yard was a toilet and in another corner of the yard was a pot next to an old paraffin oil stove. The place looked more like a dumping ground than a home. Hassan showed me the entire area, where hundreds of desperately poor people lived. I was allowed to film the area and talk to some of the men and women who lived there. I had previously filmed this area, and the high-voltage pylon which crossed above the lower parts of the Own-Ali mountain, in December 1978, about two or three months before the Shah left. At that time many people did not dare to come out and talk in front of the camera. I had only managed to interview one man who was building his home while it was snowing and one woman who lived further down towards the bottom of the valley. The man told me that they had been to the electricity board and asked for electricity, but the electricity board asked for money and the man did not have the two thousand tomans (equivalent to £60) to pay for it. The woman said, "We live in this room and do not have heating in this cold weather. There is no water either. I have to leave my young children alone in the room and travel to the other side of the valley to collect water. We went and asked for electricity and they wanted two thousand tomans for each pole. We do not have that money to give. The Shah promised us water and electricity many years ago, but we did not get it . . ." While I was interviewing this woman I could see on the other side of the hill many Phantom bombers on the ground of a military base next to Tabriz airport. There were still over 50,000 American military advisers living in Iran at the time, receiving huge salaries from the government.

This area, called Dabbakhana Usti (upper part of the skin factory), did not have a single doctor or a clinic. Many children suffered from dysentery, especially in summer. For treatment they had to travel to the children's hospital in the centre of Tabriz. I also filmed in this hospital soon after the Revolution of February 1979 and interviewed Dr Baradaran, who was in charge.

There were queues of children waiting for urgent treatment. Dr Baradaran told me, "You can see for yourself. We have to put two or three children in one cot because there is a shortage of beds and facilities. In this situation one baby passes infection to another, or when one child cries and moves it disturbs the next child. It often happens that one baby causes the death of another by disturbing and disconnecting the tube which supplies water to the sick child's body! We have not got enough nurses to watch them constantly. We simply cannot cope with so many sick children. This is the largest children's hospital in Tabriz. It is a pity to see so many children die. It is really a waste. The government could have spent much more on hospitals and child care . . ."

After the Revolution Dr Baradaran and I organised a clinic at Dabbakhana with the generous help of medical students in Tabriz. This clinic was open for 20 hours a day and treatment was free, with only a nominal charge for medication, and was able to drastically reduce the number of sick children, especially in summer, by attacking the causes of dysentery. Later on I heard that the clinic was shut down by the Komiteh, a committee which was formed after the Revolution in every district, mainly composed of militia men, who were very diverse in their social outlook, and claimed to protect the Revolution and the Islamic Republic, on the charges that the medical students belonged to left-wing political groups.

On 1 February 1979 Ayatollah Khomeini returned to Iran and millions of people in Tehran welcomed him as the leader of the Revolution. The state disintegrated and Bakhtiyar could no longer govern. Power passed into the hands of the Komitehs and city councils. In Tabriz and other parts of Azerbaijan many of the Komitehs were taken over by clerics. In Tabriz there were large-scale demonstrations in support of Ayatollah Khomeini and his provisional government headed by Mahdi Bazargan, a mechanical engineer and leading member of the Liberation Movement, which was a religious branch of Mossadeqists. On 9 February, in Tehran, the Imperial Guard withdrew after intense fighting with the people, in which the Left (Fida'is,

Mujahidin and Tudeh members) played a crucial role. Large quantities of arms were distributed to the people. On 11 February at 6 p.m. Tehran radio announced the end of the 2,500-year monarchy and the success of the Revolution.

The same course of events took place in Tabriz the following day, 12 February, where General Bidabadi attempted to crush the Revolution. First he distributed arms to all SAVAK members, but withdrew his commandos from the streets. In fact he neither ordered the police to withdraw nor to refrain from shooting. When a big crowd of people converged on the police station near the city park, Gulistan Baghi, to take it over they faced the policemen who, in desperation, fired at them, killing many and wounding hundreds. I was with my friend and saw people collecting white sheets in which to wrap the dead. When the city hospital announced shortages of blood, ice and medicine, within an hour hundreds of people queued to donate blood and had taken with them so much ice and medicine (bought from chemists) that Tabriz radio had to broadcast announcements asking them to stop bringing more. A food shortage had also been declared and foodstuffs such as eggs had been requested. An eye-witness said that a heap of eggs and ice was piled up in front of the hospital. The hospital refused to accept more contributions.

Two things above all remain distinct in my memory about the Revolution. First, people offered whatever they could afford, even their own lives, especially those members of the poorer sections of society. Second, people were not frightened of anything — even death. "It is rather death which is frightened of these brave people," I commented to my friends at the time.

On 13 February a Tabriz City Council, formed of local dignitaries, teachers, workers, clerics and merchants met and decided to appoint people to organise their local Komitehs. With two other people from Davachi (Shams-Tabrizi Street) I was appointed to organise Komiteh No. 3 and to supervise local security and cooperate with air force cadets and officers. When we went to the local police station (the place assigned to be Komiteh 3) we found it in ruins and decided to go instead to the next building, which belonged to the City Council's Cleansing Department.

We organised some tables and arranged the rooms. Several young militia men came with us. One of them, a short and unintelligent-looking person about 30 years of age, came along and wanted to be my bodyguard. Although I refused to have a bodyguard, he still insisted on staying with me. Later on, Captain Bayburdi, an air force officer and commander of the cadets in our Komiteh, discovered that my bodyguard was a weapons smuggler and an agent for Mullah Binabi, who supported Khomeini and opposed Shariatmadari.

Within three days we had organised the Komiteh and arrested and disarmed a number of SAVAK members, who had fired into the air to create panic among the local people. Then the mullahs took over the Komiteh and the man who was supposed to be my bodyguard stopped me entering the Komiteh building and threatened to kill me. I returned home.

That evening, Captain Bayburdi came to see me at home and announced his resignation and the withdrawal of his cadets and personnel from the Komiteh. We parted on good terms. Later on, in 1983, I heard that Captain Bayburdi had committed suicide in mysterious circumstances.

I recall three events from those days when I was working with Captain Bayburdi. The other two people, both merchants, who were supposed to be working with me as local representatives, did not turn up either through fear or expediency. Thus I had to rely totally on Captain Bayburdi and take his opinion into consideration. The first night of the Revolution the captain, a few young dedicated militia men and I were sitting and having a cup of tea after a long, tiring day. It was midnight. One of the militia brought in an old man who was very drunk but could still talk and joke. He had four bottles of wine in his pocket. I asked him why he was so drunk and where he had bought the bottles. He replied, "Sir, all my life I used to pass the wine shops and look at the bottles from outside the window. Today these shops were open and everything was free. I drank more than four bottles and took some more bottles away with me. It is the happiest day of my life." I asked the young man who had brought him if he knew where his house was. He said, "He lives at Dabbakhana." Captain Bayburdi and I decided to ask our driver to take the man and deliver him to his family, as we were afraid that something might happen to him on his way.

The second event happened on the second night. Two policemen were brought by some Gurichai people (from a mainly working-class area) who demanded that these policemen should be executed. They had allegedly taken part in shooting the demonstrators opposing the Shah's regime. The policemen were shivering with fear and could not talk. Captain Bayburdi and I said that we could not decide about their case; there should be a trial and if they were found guilty then the court should decide what to do. Besides we could not be sure whether they had fired on the people or not. The men insisted that these policemen *had* fired on demonstrators. Finding ourselves in this awkward situation, we promised to make an investigation and collect evidence from eye-witnesses and then we would send the case to the House of Justice. Fortunately, the crowd left, but the two policemen refused to go, being frightened to leave the building in case of attack. We let them sleep in one of the back rooms.

Before we decided to keep these policemen in the Komiteh building, we asked them to tell us the truth about whether they had killed any person during the recent demonstrations. We even promised to help them because they each had a family and children. Both of them admitted that they had fired in the air, not to shoot anyone but to protect themselves from attack.

Our investigations proved this to be true. When we told them that they could leave the Komiteh, they said that they were drug addicts and asked our help. The only thing the captain and I could do was to send them to a hospital and ask for them to be treated. They agreed with this decision and were pleased to be safe. Their families were informed.

The third event occurred on 15 February 1979. Captain Bayburdi and I visited Amir-Khiz, Davachi and Dabbakhana, which were all covered by the Komiteh 3 area. Some air force personnel accompanied us. We wanted to find out what was happening in these areas. The sound of machine-guns could be heard here and there. Were people being shot or was it merely to create chaos? I heard the BBC World Service saying on the radio that hundreds of people were killed in Tabriz on that night. Actually only a few people were shot dead that night; those who used machine-guns were SAVAK members and were disarmed within 24 hours by air force members.

Captain Bayburdi and I were surprised to see two or three young men brandishing sticks and guarding the Gurichai district at 2 a.m. They were so proud and determined, believing that they could face any enemy. We asked them what had happened to the member of the militia who had been sent by Komiteh 3 to guard the area. They said, "He is sleeping in the mosque. He had not slept for the past two nights so we wanted him to rest while we guard the area for him!" We were truly impressed by the sincerity and courage of these people. Captain Bayburdi said, "You people deserve freedom and I kiss the feet that support your body . . ."

Soon after the Revolution, the government forces attacked the Kurdish and Turkman people. Many were killed. I learned about the situation in Kurdistan through Dr Khaliqi, my colleague at Tabriz University. Dr Khaliqi was himself a Kurd and knew the area inside-out. He described how the people had been bombed and killed by government forces. Upset and angry at this news, I telephoned Mr Bazargan's house in Tehran that night. He was not available so I left a message expressing my anxiety about Kurdistan. His wife kindly promised to convey my message. After three days I heard that Mr Bazargan had sent Ayatollah Talqani to Kurdistan on a fact-finding mission. I later heard that Ayatollah Talqani's report stated that the innocent people in Kurdistan needed food and housing not bullets. Kurdistan needed urgent attention. Despite this report the bombing and shelling continued. Thousands of people died or lost their homes and fled to other cities as refugees. We were told by the government-controlled media that those who died in Kurdistan were "anti-revolutionaries".

A few days after I heard the news about Kurdistan, I talked again to Dr Khaliqi and suggested that he ought to return to Kurdistan and try to bring peace to his motherland. At the same time I also suggested that we both travel to Tehran and meet Mr Furuhar, who was minister of labour in Bazargan's Cabinet. Mr Furuhar had known me since Mossadeq's time. I had met him with Mr Ghani-Zadeh on several occasions. Both men were sincere supporters of Mossadeq.

Dr Khaliqi and I accordingly travelled to Tehran the same day. We met Mr Furuhar and discussed the matter. He was pleased to put forward Dr Khaliqi's name to the Home Secretary as a possible secretary of state for Kurdistan. While in his office, Mr Furuhar expressed anxiety about unemployment in the country. He asked me if I could be helpful in allocating proper jobs to those students who had returned home from abroad. I showed my willingness to help and also wished to work in Azerbaijan. He agreed and suggested that I should immediately contact Mr Muqaddam Maraghei (the newly appointed governor-general of Azerbaijan) and tell him about our conversation. Mr Furuhar added, "An official letter, appointing you as director of labour in Azerbaijan, will be issued shortly." Before I left we decided to meet on Friday 2 March at his home to discuss the matter further. I had written down some suggestions about the situation in Azerbaijan, which I gave to Mr Furuhar and asked him to pass on to Mr Bazargan.

I returned to Tabriz, contacted Mr Muqaddam Maraghei and told him about Mr Furuhar's suggestion. After a few meetings we decided that I should work on a plan for opening the closed factories, providing jobs for both skilled and unskilled workers, and particularly deal with unemployed carpet-makers who had lost their jobs during the Revolution when the carpet market was bad. At the same time Mr Murtazavi, the vice-governor-general, suggested that I organise the Social Democrat Party in Tabriz. Mr Muqaddam Maraghei himself was the leader of this party and Mr Murtazavi hoped that he would be prime minister in the near future. I did not show any interest in this and said that I preferred to be helpful in solving the unemployment and labour problems in Azerbaijan.

I sat and worked for a whole week and prepared a plan with the help of an economist friend who had recently completed his PhD studies at the London School of Economics. We both took the plan to Mr Maraghei and gave it to him to study and make any necessary suggestions. We agreed to meet again and discuss the matter, and hoped that by then an official letter confirming my new appointment would have reached Tabriz.

I met Mr Maraghei after a few days. Without being specific, he said, "Dr Sabri, your labour programme is similar to that of Pishavari." I was surprised to learn that Mr Maraghei did not approve of my suggestion that the closed factories should be opened and put under the management of a committee democratically elected by the workers of the same factory; or that instead of depending on loans or temporary unemployment benefits, the workers should be employed in construction works to build schools, hospitals, roads and houses. Neither I nor my economist friend could understand how we could solve the problem of unemployment without carrying out some practical and essential work in the area. In the end both Dr Khaliqi and I failed to receive any letter from Tehran. Many, like us, who had been prepared to carry out all sorts of service without expecting big salaries, remained idle. Bazargan's government seemed indecisive and more afraid of revolutionary forces than the anti-revolutionary ones such as big landowners, major businessmen and traditional religious leaders. I became even more convinced that this was so when Bazargan and his Cabinet visited Tabriz a month later.

When Bazargan visited Tabriz with his entire Cabinet, on 25 March 1979, I was one of three representatives from Tabriz University (the other two were Professor Manuchihr Murtazavi, ex-principal of Tabriz University and Professor Rawshan-Zamir) who met him and attended a lunch party held in the governor-general's official building. Mr Bazargan talked about the workers and said that they should return to their factories and the peasants to their villages. Afterwards the workers' representative rose and read out a list of their needs and made several suggestions. Mr Bazargan seemed annoyed. A long silence followed. I then stood up and commented both on what Mr Bazargan had said and on the suggestions made by the workers' representative. I said, "Mr Bazargan, you suggest that workers must go back to the factories. Now most of the factories are closed and their owners have either fled the country or are sitting in their country villas waiting to see what will happen next. Your government ought to invite these factory owners to reopen their factories in two weeks' time. If they fail to open them within two weeks then your government itself should open these factories and let a workers' committee run them. The products of these factories could be sold in co-operative shops and the profits used to both pay the workers and plough back into the factories.

"About the peasants whom you have suggested should be sent back to their villages: this suggestion seems to me like someone throwing a big stone at Mount Own-Ali (we could all see the mountain from where we were sitting) and then order the stone to stay on the mountain. There must be energy to hold the stone on the mountain otherwise it will fall down. Similarly, if there is nothing in the villages to attract the peasants — no land, no water, no seeds, no proper houses, no doctors or many other essentials of life — then how can we expect these desperate peasants to go back to their villages and stay there? Land, water, seeds, proper houses and other essentials of life must be provided, then they will return without persuasion or force."

When I had finished, Mr Bazargan said, "Why do you expect everything from my government?" He sarcastically concluded by adding, "I am glad that a university teacher has risen in defence of workers." Someone reacted to these statements and said, "If we do not ask your government to provide for our needs then should we ask our neighbours to help us? You have accepted the responsibility of being the government of Iran after the Revolution. We have made the Revolution to promote the needs of workers and peasants; otherwise why would we have gone through all those terrible days?"

After lunch I spoke with General Madani, Minister of Defence. In the middle of a conversation about the political situation in Tabriz University and the position of university teachers, we were joined by Amir Intizam, the government spokesman. I asked Amir Intizam when the government would introduce land reform and the other radical reforms which the country badly needed. He replied, "It is too early to think about land reform. The Revolution is still in danger." He did not, however, specify who it was that threatened the Revolution. Later, I learned how the Bazargan government had attacked and brutally suppressed patriotic and national forces in Kurdistan, Turkmanistan and in various political groups. Only then did I understand what Amir Intizam meant by "anti-revolutionary" elements. In fact, right from the first days of Bazargan's government ex-SAVAK members and people who had been influential civil servants during the Shah's rule, grew beards and filled very sensitive governmental jobs and positions. To my surprise, there were quite a number of these kinds of people in Tabriz and they pretended to be more revolutionary than the true revolutionaries. I remember a certain person called Muhammadi, a well-known SAVAK member at the machine and ball-bearing factory. He disappeared during the Revolution, but returned to Tabriz and the factory after February 1979 with a long beard saying that he had been pardoned by Imam Khomeini. He had said to the workers in the factory, "I told Imam Khomeini that I was in SAVAK, but my work had been to catch Communists, and the Imam told me to return to my job and continue catching Communists."

It seemed to me that the people were divided into three groups. First there were those who had suffered and been deprived for years, and in whom the pent-up energy and desires had now erupted like a volcano without mind and control. These people faced the Shah's army and death. Thousands of lives were lost. Second, there were those who had held influential positions under the Shah and were from comfortably-off traditional middle-class families. These people were aware of where their interests lay and the directions they should follow. They were using religion as a cover. They were to be found among the workers, teachers in schools and universities and among businessmen. These people often wrote slogans for and gave directions to the first group, which consisted of thousands and even millions of innocent men and women in the streets of Tabriz and other cities of Iran. If the second group wanted to label a person or political enemy as Godless and anti-revolutionary it did so through these honest ignorant masses. I remember in February 1979 when the Fida'is tried to organise a demonstration in front of the American Consulate in Tabriz. They were faced by a large group of men wielding sticks or sitting armed on motor bikes and shouting, "Fida'is are Godless" and "We do not want Communists". In the end they were forced to cancel their demonstration. One of my friends commented that "America must be delighted to see that she is not without support . . ."

The third group was a combination of political groups and parties: the Mujahidin, Tudeh Party, Fida'is, Mossadeqists and so on. These groups came under systematic attack, and in a concerted way. Their meetings were disrupted by ordinary people (often mere youngsters) who were directed by a mullah or members of the second group I have mentioned. I remember one night when the students occupied Tabriz University demanding the return of Ayatollah Khomeini from France to Iran. I stayed with the students. There were a few very fanatically religious students who barred the third group from taking part in this sit-in at the university.

Thus, soon after the Revolution had occurred those who were truly revolutionary and had played a crucial role during the uprising against the Shah were now denounced as being anti-revolutionary, anti-God, Communists, Western-oriented, spies and Bahais. The reactionary forces, important businessmen in the bazaars and major landowners raised the flag of Islam and Revolution shouting, "There is no party but the party of Allah", "There is no leader, but Ruhullah". By "Ruhullah' they meant Ruhullah Khomeini. I heard this slogan for the first time in December 1978 in Tabriz, when a group of young people came from the city to Tabriz University led by a young mullah.

Ayatollah Khomeini, in fact, in a message to school and university students on 8 October 1978, clearly accused the Left and Communists of being dependent on foreigners and deceived by them. This created a wave of criticism among non-religious groups in Europe and Iran. Afterwards, whenever other political groups or parties held a meeting, a group of "Hizb Allah" or "Party of God" members appeared, shouting out the same slogan over and over again until the meeting was disrupted and forced to disperse. There was, I believe, an underground organisation for such disruption and other serious crimes. The anti-revolutionaries began to shout louder than the revolutionaries.

On 4 March 1979 I paid a visit to Dr Karim Sanjabi, the minister of foreign affairs after the Revolution and an important member of Mossadeq's Cabinet in 1953. He received me warmly in his office at the Ministry of Foreign Affairs in Tehran. Leaving his huge desk he came and sat next to me. He was dignified and courteous, but his eyes seemed tired and his smile was mixed with sadness. I congratulated him on his important job and said, "You must be glad to see this freedom after years of imprisonment and suppression under the Shah. Iranians, Azerbaijanis and Kurds in particular need a strong and well-organised united democratic front to fight against injustice, unemployment and illiteracy, and to carry out radical and revolutionary programmes." Dr Sanjabi agreed with me but then stated, "There is much to be done. One does not know (or is not allowed to know) where to begin. I feel old. My friends and I have spent our youth and energy either under a suppressive atmosphere or in prison. Now that the time of working and fulfilling the essential needs of the Revolution has arrived we feel too old to carry out such duties. In addition, certain social and political relationships have also tied my hands. I blame the Shah for all this. He committed a big crime by the 28th Mordad coup d'état."

When I questioned him in general about the minority peoples of Azerbaijan, Kurdistan and Baluchistan, and in particular about the Kurdish troubles, Dr Sanjabi did not seem to have such clear ideas as had Mr Furuhar. I suggested, for example, that priority must be given to the mother tongue in Kurdistan, Azerbaijan and other parts of Iran. In schools a Kurdish and an Azerbaijani child should first learn to read and write in his or her mother tongue and only afterwards learn Persian as an official language of the country. Dr Sanjabi commented, "The Kurdish language differs in Mahabad from Kirmanshah. In other words, the Kurdish language is not the same all over the area." I responded by pointing out that "the difference is rather in the dialect than in the language. We see similar differences in Azerbaijani, Arabic and even Persian. Once children start learning Kurdish from text books then this will gradually create a common literary language, understandable all over Kurdistan. This is also true about other minority languages in Iran." This was perhaps of little importance for a minister of foreign affairs, but he listened kindly and showed interest.

Before returning to Tabriz, I called on Mr Dariyush Furuhar in his office. He regretted to hear that neither Dr Khaliqi nor I had received any communication from the minister of the interior.

The University of Tabriz was reopened after the Revolution. Special classes were organised in the afternoons and evenings to prepare the students for their finals. I started teaching night-classes and enjoyed the work. My subject was the art of essay writing. I discussed the concept and origin of "imagination" in a literary and social context: whether art and literature have class roots and how "imagination" works in a class-based society.

I also taught English language and literature to the first-year students. There was a mixture of men and women students: most of them worked during the day as teachers, army personnel, farmers, joiners — all manner of jobs. I found them extremely enthusiastic, eager to learn and appreciative of any help. They did not like to be regarded as students, or at least to be treated like children. Creating a sense of personality and self-respect among them worked wonders. Many students passed, although I did not think their standard was as high as it should have been and much was based on rote learning. This perhaps stemmed from the social and educational restrictions that all the universities had suffered during the previous years.

Many students talked to me about their work and private life. One of the women explained how she had attended classes in the university without telling her father. "He disapproves of girls studying at university. I attended the classes secretly until my mother told him about my attendance. He was upset about it but realised that it was too late to change my mind." By 1979, 133,000 students were studying in colleges and universities in Iran. One third of these were girls. The fees were so high that low-income citizens had little chance of entering the colleges. A few years before the Revolution, the government had announced a scheme whereby any student wishing to study could do so on condition that for each year of study they should work for the government for two years after finishing their studies. Many students preferred to both work and study at the same time.

The situation of women in Iran worsened after the Revolution of 1979. In his speech, Ayatollah Khomeini had rightly said, "We owe our revolution to women." Unfortunately, the Islamic Republic of Iran has repaid its debt to women by denying them the most essential human rights. There are still many Iranian girls and mothers who are tortured in prison for political reasons. They want freedom, independence, social justice and peace. Iranian women have long suffered on two fronts, by socio-economic exploitation and sex discrimination, yet they have struggled alongside freedom-fighting men throughout history, particularly during the Revolutions of 1905 and 1979. Iranian women are closer to the bitter experiences of life under the regime of *Vilayat-i Faqih* (the rule of a religious leader). They have endured all manner of sacrifices and have suffered most through the loss of their sons and husbands during the past eight years of the Iran-Iraq war.

In a society where women are mostly barred from employment, the poverty and hardship that results from these deaths pushes women into yet more dependent and humiliating positions. The government's solution was to encourage men to marry more than one wife! But these women and their daughters will appear again in the streets of Iran with more determination and unity. The Shah's army could not move them and "You can move rocks but you cannot move women" had become the proverb of the Revolution of 1979 in Tabriz. The regime of clerical dictatorship cannot be an exception, although it is more devastating to women than the Shah's regime because it has the weapon of religion.

Here are two poems I wrote at the time:

Poem from Tabriz:

You may see me under veil,
You may see me in prison,
You may see me in the fields,
You may see me at work.

Don't look on me as helpless!
Under my veil I have a loving heart,
Inside prison walls a strong heart,
In the fields I have waiting eyes,
At work I have strong arms.

I shall heal our wounds by love,
I will break the prison walls,
I shall meet the waiting eyes,
And embrace all in my loving arms.

Palestinian mother

I have waited for years,
I have waited for days,
I have waited for hours,
I have waited for minutes,

To see my freedom at my door,
To see my children at home,
To have a land for my own,
To have the freedom for all.

The sun is rising behind the barbed wires,
The wind of change blowing through the prison walls,
The birds began returning home,
And want to be free in their home.

At the beginning of the Revolution I supported it and felt that Khomeini was a radical religious leader who could pave the way in a religious society for social justice and eventually for Socialism. I saw Khomeini as similar to the philosopher-poets like Rumi and Attar, who opposed the ruling dogmatic system and rigid religion of their time. They opposed social injustice. Khomeini, furthermore, seemed the only leader since Mossadeq who was able to unite the people against the Shah's regime, and millions supported him. Khomeini made many moralistic and revolutionary speeches highlighting the position of workers, peasants and the oppressed masses. He said that "The Prophet of Islam kissed the hand of a worker saying that a worker's hands are holy". He presented the Revolution as one of the oppressed rising against their oppressors.

Within two years I realised that a gulf existed between the words of Ayatollah Khomeini or the Islamic Republic of Iran and their actions. The workers and peasants were abandoned or left at the mercy of factory owners and landowners. Labour laws passed were anti-working-class; political and opposing religious groups were persecuted. Many intellectuals, doctors, engineers and teachers were sentenced to death for holding contrary political and religious views.

The first election after the Revolution, in which I myself participated, was rigged and the votes of other political parties ignored. I noticed in one polling station that the votes given to Mujahidin-i Khalq and the Marxists were more than those for the supporters of the Hizb-Allah. Musa Khiyabani (for Mujahidin-i Khalq), for example, polled 478 votes and Hujjat al-Islam's Sayyid Hussein Musavi 305. Sayyid Hussein Musavi, however, was the one elected. I interviewed several people who were in charge of polling booths. They confirmed that the votes for groups other than the Hizb-Allah were suppressed. I argued with some of those who attended at the polling stations. Armed men, however, were everywhere and I thought it dangerous to protest too strongly.

There is a long dark story attached to Mullah Hussein Musavi mentioned above. He later ordered the execution of hundreds of young political prisoners and those from minority religious groups such as the Bahais. One Bahai was a prominent ear, nose and throat specialist, Dr Faramarz Samandari. He was arrested and executed the same night. The following day all medical doctors went on strike, but their action was stopped by military force.

In the summers of 1981 and 1982 when I revisited Iran, I remember that Sayyid Hussein Musavi used to fly once or twice a week from Tehran to Tabriz to sit as a judge in the city prison. People were accused of being "anti-revolutionary" or "corrupted on earth". In summary trials he used to sentence to death many young men and women.

> . . . I have not fulfilled my youthful desires
> And have remained with the young eternally young,
> I have given my unperformed song to the river
> So it can sing it with the young.
>
> The spring which gushes out of a mountain: is me
> It is the one that springs from the heart of rock!
> The fire is made bright by the fire in my chest
> The thunder is my voice.
>
> Anywhere fists are raised they are my fists!
> Any wound caused by slashes is on my back!
> Anywhere you hear the voice of freedom: It is me!
> I breathe through all these protests . . .
>   (Extract from "Spring in the Sun", by H. Sayeh.)

In the evening of the days that he was in Tabriz the spectre of death used to cover the sky. The dreadful sound of execution by firing squad could be heard in the streets by the mothers and families of those who were imprisoned. Every mother and every family used to sit in agony and wait for news of their loved ones, not knowing whether they had been spared or not. They only heard definite news of the execution the following day, when a prison guard would call at their house to demand payment for the bullets that had been used. If an unmarried girl had been executed the guard would hand over a token "bride price" to the family: to protect themselves from the possible wrath of God for executing a virgin the guards would hurriedly "marry" a condemned girl to one of their number. This practice does not, of course, exist in Islam and, indeed, the execution of women is a controversial issue in religious dogma.

I cannot say more than this about that hellish time and atmosphere. I know only that two of my friends' mothers had heart attacks and died on the evenings that they waited for news of their child's fate. I have recently heard that Ayatollah Khomeini has dismissed Mullah Musavi from all his posts because of his corruption and for committing adultery with female prisoners and prisoners' wives. Various members of his family, who had risen with him, were also dismissed. Such a mullah is the real enemy of the Revolution, not the unfortunate "anti-revolutionaries" he had put to death. The irony is that Ayatollah Khomeini himself had appointed this mullah to such a position.

I monitored all the government elections. The number of votes cast in every poll steadily dropped after the first referendum. About 20 million people took part in the first referendum; 15.7 million in the constitutional referendum; 14.1 million in the presidential elections; figures for the parliamentary elections showed a steep drop in the number of voters. The most important reason for the decline was political. The vagueness and ambivalence surrounding the aims and objectives of the Revolution and the constant efforts by certain powerful circles to attract the attention of the masses through empty promises and high-sounding slogans were instrumental in dampening a great many people's enthusiasm.

I talked to Izzat on 28 March 1980. He complained bitterly about price rises and the shortage of paraffin. "Mr Khomeini has made everything upside-down," he declared. "It is not Khomeini's fault; the mullahs and big businessmen have done this," I commented.

Izzat reacted angrily: "It is Mr Khomeini who has let these dogs out against the people. We have lost everything. Even one kilo of potatoes costs 80 rials. What has happened to paraffin? What has the Revolution got to do with paraffin? During the Russian Revolution paraffin and other goods were brought from North Azerbaijan and the price did not change. So long as the system is the same, so long as these people who possess everything rule the country, nothing will change. Now those who have money and are strong get whatever they need and the poor and weak are left helpless. I have no knowledge and education; my experiences have taught me that mullahs and these religious leaders do not care for the working class and the poor. Their words never match their deeds. They are good actors and they know how to deceive people." "It is partly the fault of the people who support the mullahs and vote for them," I replied. "In the parliamentary election I did not receive many votes." (I had stood as an independent candidate for the Majlis in March 1980.)

"Many people voted for you," Izzat answered. "I myself saw that many of my friends and neighbours voted for you. I was standing at the mosque in front of our house and someone said you had 950 votes just in one box. I heard people at the voting box saying that if you write your votes inside the mosque you must only vote for the mullahs. I tell you, this whole election seems suspicious and I have my doubts about it. What happened to so many educated people — doctors, teachers, lawyers, writers — and the workers who we know in our district? They were really popular, honest and kind men. None of them are elected! Only mullahs come out of the boxes . . ."

I chatted further with Izzat and recorded him speaking in his vegetable shop. He had recently converted part of his vestibule into a small shop selling fresh vegetables. I then went into the house to see Humai. I had to pay Humai a visit because it was Nawruz and I had brought her a present. We sat down and talked for an hour or so. My brother Mohsen joined us later. Humai told me how clever her sons, daughters and grandchildren were: "I don't really want for anything in the world. My daughters and grandchildren visit me often. Two of Marzieh's daughters and three of Fatima's daughters are newly married. My sons, Majeed and Hamid, are also married and have their own homes, thank Heaven. My only problem is the pain in my legs. I cannot walk far. I used to walk to your parents' house — carrying two children. I never felt tired."

I offered to take her to a doctor for treatment. She asked me again as before: "Cannot you treat me yourself? Come back to Tabriz and open a clinic and treat me properly." This time I did not repeat that I was not a medical doctor.

Izzat died in 1984 but Humai is still alive and living with her son Hamid. I can contact her by telephone: although she cannot hear half my conversation, I still feel delighted to hear her affectionate words in Azerbaijani, "*Sagh ol oghlum ke mani Yada salmisan*" ("Be healthy, my son, for remembering me").

On the same day that I visited Izzat and Humai, I also called on some carpet-makers in their district. I interviewed one of the master carpet-makers called Mr Sarkhush Dildari. I asked his opinions about the Revolution and about his living conditions. He said: "At the beginning of the Revolution we got together (160 families), collected money and built gutters in the middle of our alleys. We covered them with iron sheets. These gutters could take rain-water and all dirty effluent out of our alleys and houses. The city council provided some unemployed workers and we kept them well supplied with food to encourage them to do the job properly. We all worked together. In the end we were in debt (14,000 tomans). Mr Maraghei, the governor-general after the Revolution, did not pay attention to any requests for help. We therefore decided against asking the governor for money to pay our debt. One of our neighbours, Haj Aziz, contributed 8,000 tomans and the rest was paid by the rest of the neighbours. The problem has not been solved yet. We need urgent attention from the government. There is the problem of the sewage system. The cesspits in our houses are full. If we want to have them emptied, a special machine is needed. This machine cannot enter our narrow alleys. A hose of between 600-700 metres in length is needed to stretch from our houses to the main street. This problem has not so far been solved.

"After the Revolution the government decided not to charge for water. We do not want free water; we would rather the government charge us money and instead do something about the sewage system. We are even prepared to help. Neither the city council nor the city governor have paid any attention to our conditions. Our head men are frightened to approach the government and ask for help. Several times the leading men in our district have been taken away by government forces and either beaten up or harassed in different ways. Now they are frightened to approach the governor's office for help. They only want to protect themselves. And so the district committee which was organised at the beginning of the Revolution is now defunct. No one wants to take part in local meetings.

"We are told by Ayatollah Khomeini and his Government that the Revolution of 1979 was the revolution of the 'Mostazafin' (the deprived). We are 'Mostazafin'. This does not mean that I do not have clothes and a home. I have these. But I need other things — a hospital for example. If a samovar overturns on my child there is no emergency hospital in this part of town. I have to carry my child to the main road, find a taxi (if I am lucky to get one quickly) and take my child to Imam Khomeini Hospital, right on the other side of the city. All this would take at least an hour. That is, if I can find a taxi, the traffic is not busy and all goes well, my child will reach hospital in an hour. Heaven knows what could happen to the child in an hour. It depends on how serious the accident is.

"If there were a clinic in our district to deal with the sick and emergency patients one of our problems would be solved. During the Shah's rule they set up a clinic which still exists, but it does not have proper doctors or medicine. It merely dispenses some patent medicine for the relief of stomach-ache, for example. They hand this out for both children and adults. Our children often become ill with gastro-enteritis, for example, and pass germs on to other children in school. If a child is treated in time he will not pass on infection to another 60 pupils or so in a classroom. If the Islamic Republic wishes to help us, we need a health service. We need work. We expected the Revolution to give us what we needed. A revolution has taken place and we are told that the factories are nationalised, that is to say, they have become the property of the people. I am prepared to do anything: I can make carpets,

I can work as an electrician. I can drive. When I go to the office of the governor-general in Tabriz and ask for work, they either label me as 'anti-revolutionary' and beat me up or send me to the Department of Unemployment where they put me on a waiting list. My number is 10320. This means after 10319 people have found a job then it will be my turn. The other day I decided to go and see either the governor or his assistant. I managed to see his assistant and expressed my desire to work and help the Revolution. Instead of giving me a job or something to do he offered me a loan. I refused and said that if I accepted the loan what should I do after I had spent it? I added that this is a bad and anti-revolutionary act to give a loan to a worker who is able and willing to work. If we have made a revolution and the factories are nationalised, then we workers have the right to work in these factories. I still support the Revolution. We don't demand much from the Islamic Republic. I have two children, support my wife and mother and need work and a hospital. My children need an education and I want them to have a good future."

I recorded this interview about a year after the Revolution, in March 1980. The workers, peasants and the poor people in general, who had gathered under the umbrella of Islam in the hope of realising their social and economic needs had already begun to doubt. They questioned whether this umbrella of the ayatollahs would offer them secure shelter. Many people (including myself) had begun to realise that there were two umbrellas and two Islams in the country: those of the rich and those of the poor. Each had their own interpretation of Islam in terms of land reform, property ownership, labour laws and many other social and political matters.

Those political groups or individuals who defended land reform and demanded social justice and political freedom were labelled and accused of being "anti-revolutionary", non-Muslim, Godless, Communist and Monafiq (trouble-makers). All institutions were taken over by seemingly fanatical and dogmatic Muslims. Many teachers were accused of being left-wing or Marxist and were sacked. To even mention a poet like Gulsurkhi and utter the word *khalg* (the people) brought the charge of being a Communist, which usually cost a man his life. This also became a common occurrence in the universities and classrooms. I was accused of being a Communist because I discussed Samad Behranghi and interpreted the works of great Muslim writers such as Allama Muhammad Iqbal, the "poet of the East" (1877-1938).

After the Revolution various ideological discussions and serious disputes started in the University of Tabriz and other seats of learning. They ranged from the philosophy of Marxism to the role of "*Vilayat-i Faqih*" (supreme Islamic judge: Ayatollah Khomeini is regarded as the "*Vilayat-i Faqih*"). I remember that I was once invited to read a paper on Allama Muhammad Iqbal. I had originally written this paper in 1977 for an international seminar on the Iqbal Centenary held in New Delhi and Lahore. My paper, a summary of which I shall give here, caused great controversy among the students and teaching staff. I said:

"Informed Muslim scholars who have rejected the Islam of princes and kings have returned for inspiration to what they see as the original, pure spirit of Islam. The late scholar Ali Shariati argued in Iran that Islam was originally in revolt against the oppressive rulers of the time, but was soon taken over by these same rulers to be used as another 'instrument of oppression'. Like Christianity, Islam was taken over as a state religion by leaders who advocated acceptance and humility while they themselves lived in splendour. Muhammad Iqbal, one of the great Muslim poets of the 20th century, wrote when India was still under colonial rule and condemned this kind of exploitation:

> What shall I say about the poor, suffering Muslim,
> valuable only as a human being?
> He has neither energy nor excitement in his blood.
> His hands are as empty as his pockets.
> Do not tell me that God has done this.
> You can wash away dust by this excuse.
> Turn upside down this world — where
> the unjust steals from the just.
>
> (From *Armaghan-e Hejaz.*)

"Iqbal was against the mullahs who supported the rich and kept people ignorant of social justice and human understanding. Like other religions, Islam has both progressive and conservative followers, according to their socio-political outlook. There are parallels with Christianity. In the days when the official Church worked hand-in-glove with the ruling class, there arose revolutionary Christian writers who returned for inspiration to the original concept of Christ, the saviour of the poor and wretched. When socio-political needs arise, people use the nearest intellectual weapon against their social enemies. William Blake, for example, the revolutionary Christian poet, defended his vision against that of the official Church and social system:

> The Vision of Christ that thou does see,
> Is my Vision's Greatest Enemy . . .
> Thine loves the same world that mine hates,
> Thy Heaven doors are my Hell gates . . .
> Both read the Bible day and night,
> But thou read'st black where I read white.
>
> (From *The Everlasting Gospel.*)

"This vision is still active in present-day Latin America and Iqbal's vision is alive in Iran, Pakistan and throughout the Middle East, where the working classes and the poor use religion as a weapon against the ruling classes and American imperialism."

This weapon, which was wielded in the 1979 Revolution against the Shah and the ruling classes, was now steadily turning against those who had made the Revolution, who had made sacrifices and suffered the most. Major commercial interests, landowners and other reactionary forces persuaded the influential ayatollahs (especially those in the Council of Guardians) to use their religious weapon under the name of "*Vilayat-i Faqih*". They turned it on the workers, land and social reformers, democratic forces and political parties and organisations who demanded these reforms. To divert the people's attention from the main aims of the Revolution and essential social reforms, the leaders of the Islamic Republic first exploited the American hostages episode.

The seizure of the American Embassy and 66 of its American occupants by militant students on 4 November 1979 had become a major issue. Conservative and ruling interests in both Iran and the United States fully exploited the episode for their own advantages. Ronald Reagan owed much of his success in the 1980 presidential election to the hostage issue. It is little wonder that he had wished the hostage case to be continued and not to be resolved before the election. I later heard rumours that he had promised Khomeini's regime more arms than President Carter had offered in exchange for American hostages.

When I visited Iran in the summer of 1980 and closely followed events in Tehran around the American Embassy, I became convinced that it was much more than a simple hostage affair. A counter-revolution was taking place against democratic and revolutionary forces. By these means the Western world and Israel achieved their political initiative and regained the ground lost during the Revolution. Day and night anti-American slogans continued to appear in the streets and the media and Ayatollah Khomeini called America "the Great Satan". Meanwhile, the import of goods from America, Western Europe and Japan continued unabated. I saw sacks of rice imported from America with "Death to America" stamped on the outside. One of the mottoes of the Islamic Republic was "self-sufficiency", yet agricultural imports for the first eight months of 1987 alone cost $2.5 billion; this in addition to the purchase of arms which amounted to billions.

The West was worried about the left-wing element in Iran, especially the Tudeh Party. In February 1980 I discussed the situation with a long-serving British expert on Iran. He told me that the Revolution in Iran had taken the West by surprise; the West was anxious to keep Bazargan in power because the clergy were incapable of governing and sooner or later the Tudeh Party would take over. I disagreed with him, pointing out that

Ayatollah Khomeini had millions of supporters and the Tudeh Party was not strong enough to take over the government in Iran. The British expert commented, "It is true that Ayatollah Khomeini is supported by millions, but millions cannot govern the country. A number of technocrats, like Bazargan, are needed to govern and also keep in check the activities of the left." Later on, the West, realising that the ayatollahs were accommodating their purposes (namely the suppression of the democratic forces and the continuation of trade with the West), decided to support, discreetly, the regime.

The following summer I met Sayyid Musavi. He was then minister of foreign affairs and is at present the prime minister of the Islamic Republic of Iran. We met in his office and discussed the political situation in Iran and the country's foreign policy. After complaining that there were too many decision-making centres in the country, he revealed his anxiety about the influence of "left-wing" literature in the universities and schools. He said, "We need some dedicated Muslim writers to counteract this trend among the young, who are easily influenced by the left." He suggested that I should apply for a government position and send my publications to him. When I returned to Britain I sent him a copy of my book on William Blake and my articles on Allama Muhammad Iqbal. I never received a reply. I still kept wondering how the anxiety of the British expert about the left was repeated by Mr Musavi.

During 1980 attacks on the left and on democratic forces in general continued on a wider scale in the universities under the slogan of the "Cultural Revolution". In April 1980 a speech was given by Mr Hashimi Rafsanjani (the present Speaker of the Majlis) at Tabriz University, in which he referred to the activities of the "anti-revolutionaries" and the need to purge and purify the educational institutions of undesirable elements. Immediately afterwards, a huge well-organised mob wielding clubs attacked the university, beating and ejecting all the left-wing student organisations. They called themselves "Muslim Revolutionaries" and aimed to rout those "anti-God" elements who were left-wing or Communist and thus "anti-revolutionaries"! Many of my friends witnessed this event in Tabriz. I later witnessed similar scenes myself.

At the same time as the Tabriz demonstrations parallel events occurred in the universities of Tehran and other cities. All offices of the left-wing organisations were forced to close; they were burnt and looted and their members savagely attacked, wounded and killed. Meetings addressed by the President, Mr Bani-Sadr, were also disrupted. In all these events, too, the attackers used the slogan of "Muslim Revolutionary" against the "anti-revolutionary" Communists! They were similarly organised, armed and all used the same savage tactics. Behind all these events there was an organised corps of former SAVAK agents, reactionaries in the government circle who wanted to suppress intellectual freedom in the universities and establish a "pure Islamic State with its own Islamic Education System". The universities were closed for over two years and hundreds of students, mostly female, were disqualified for being left-wing or "anti-revolutionary". Many university teachers and top scientists were forced to leave the country and become "God-sent" brains for Western institutions. Canada and the United States managed to attract thousands of them. Thus the so-called "Cultural Revolution" turned out to be against the culture and valuable human achievements of the country.

I Live Under War

Saddam Hussein of Iraq declared war on Iran on 11 September 1980. This further strengthened the position of the traditional clergy and pleased the West, especially the United States, for a number of reasons. Iraq counted on a swift military victory over the Shi'ite theocratic government in Iran because it was seen as a revolutionary and a regional power centre. Hussein thus hoped to deprive the Shi'ite separatists in Iraq of outside support. The Revolution of 1979 in Iran roused hope and gave moral support to the Shi'ite population of Iraq who had been governed by the Sunni minority. While Ayatollah Khomeini counted on Iraqi Shi'ites, Saddam Hussein relied on the nationalist sentiments of the Arabs in Iran's province of Khuzistan.

Scenes from the war.

Saddam Hussein wished to kill two birds with one stone. A victory over the theocratic government in Iran would strengthen his position at home on the one hand, and make him a regional power centre on the other. American encouragement and Saudi Arabia's promise of support tempted Saddam into a senseless war which is almost eight years old. (It is said that Henry Kissinger, President Saddam and Fahd met in Riyadh a day or so before 11 September.) The *Times* editorial wrote on 24 September 1980: "The trip which the Iraqi President, Saddam Hussein, made to Saudi Arabia this summer took the world by surprise . . . The Saudi royal family would seem to have little in common with the Baath socialist regime in Baghdad." I heard Ayatollah Khomeini announce in a radio broadcast: "This war is a God-given gift."

In the summers of 1981 and 1982 I experienced the hell of war in Tabriz and Tehran. Both Tabriz and Tehran were bombed and hundreds of civilians were killed or wounded. There was a mixture of revolutionary patriotism and mourning. Thousands of men, young and old, from Azerbaijan and indeed from other parts of Iran rushed to the front hoping to push back the Iraqi army, which had penetrated 60 kilometres into Iranian territory on 22 September 1980. This was regarded by Iran as "the start of the Iraqi aggression". Meanwhile, black flags hung mournfully on the doors, roofs and mosques, in memory of fathers, brothers and sons killed in action. Those who had lost their sons or husbands were celebrated with flowers and greetings. Being killed in action was regarded as martyrdom and a sign of true devotion to Islam and the Revolution. The parents of the martyred offered sweets, cakes and tea to their visitors; their families were favoured and helped by the government of Iran.

The war stimulated patriotism and fanaticism among the general public, although for the children and mothers it was a terrifying experience. When Iraqi bombers appeared over the city, many faces grew pale. The children were told that as soon as they heard the warning sound they should rush and hide under the stairs (they used under the stairs as a shelter — as if bombs would not affect the stairs!). Mothers carried their babies and hid them in the basement or under stairs. Once the Iraqi aeroplanes came at midnight while everyone was asleep and my sisters and their families were in my mother's house. They rushed into the basement carrying the sleeping children and babies. The aeroplanes bombed the Tabriz oil refinery. The sound was so loud that it seemed as if a bomb had fallen next door. The entire building shook. One blast followed the other and all of us felt that we were in danger of being hit. Suddenly my youngest sister, Aghdas, realised that Yusif, her youngest son, had been forgotten in the panic and was left upstairs. She began to cry. I ran up to bring him downstairs. I saw that he had just been woken up by the noise and was looking for his mother. I took him to his mother and he complained, "Mum, I hate these planes. They make too much noise."

> Look at our homeland!
> It is a cage of mourning birds
> Which have bleeding beaks.
> Look at its earth!
> The torn remnants of red tulips rise up from it.
> Look at its roads
> A caravan of poverty and refugees are waving.
> Look at its sky
> Where the angry clouds are rolling . . .
>
> (Extract from a poem by Siyavush Kasrai.)

I asked people about their opinion on the causes of the Iran-Iraq war. The majority believed that Saddam Hussein had started the aggression, backed by America and Israel. This is what the Islamic Republic of Iran had stated through the government-controlled media. The war was, therefore, between the just (the Islamic Republic) and the unjust (Saddam Hussein and his backers). I rarely heard people say that the dispute was between the Shi'ite and Sunnites, as the Western press often asserts.

More sophisticated Iranians believed that the imperialist powers showed a significantly great interest in the dispute between Iraq and Iran. Shortly before hostilities began, the media in the United States and western Europe started to discuss both the threat to the Islamic Revolution from Iraq and the threat to Iraq from Iran. Ahmad, my friend who had graduated from Edinburgh and taught English in Tabriz, argued that the Iran-Iraq war was essentially planned and encouraged by the United States. He said, "America had three aims. First, they wanted to distract revolutionary Iran from essential social reforms inside the country. They also wanted to strengthen the position of important businessmen in the bazaar and landowners who would benefit from the war by price rises and hoarding of essential goods. This would create false shortages and mean they could sell their goods for vastly inflated prices." (This indeed has happened during the past eight years.) "Second," my friend continued, "America wanted to turn conservative Arab states (such as Saudi Arabia) against revolutionary Iran and sell them more arms. Above all, they wanted to have a military base and presence in the Persian Gulf and Arab countries who, in the past, were reluctant to admit America. Even countries like Kuwait, who used to take a somewhat neutral stance, were forced to take shelter under the American wing." (Kuwait's tankers, in 1988 for example, sail under the protection of the American flag. Now the United States has the largest fleet in the Persian Gulf and military bases in the Indian Ocean, Middle East and North Africa, i.e. Egypt.) "Thirdly, America intended to destroy two strong armies, namely those of Iran and Iraq, and thus save Israel from possible danger at the hands of these power centres." (America not only managed to bring about the destruction of most sophisticated weapons in Iran and Iraq by letting them turn against each other, but also sold billions of dollars worth of weapons to Iran. London was also used as a centre for financial and weapons transaction (as was reported in the *Observer*, 28 February 1988). Iraq bought a great deal of weapons from France after the start of war in September 1980.)

In the summer of 1982, Samad (my nephew, who was 18 years old) returned to Tehran from the war. I had a long talk with him. He described the situation at the front. "It is a selfless atmosphere. We were six in one trench. We were fighting day and night. Although we were hungry and tired, everybody put his fellow soldiers' interest before his own. When we had little food left, everyone said he was not hungry in case the others were more in need of food . . ." Samad had an ideal, heroic and spiritual vision of the war. Knowing he was potentially a good student I tried to persuade him to stay behind, finish his education and thus serve his country better. We returned to Tabriz together. On the way we had a long discussion about the nature of the Iran-Iraq war and its negative effect on the peoples of Iran and Iraq.

While in Tabriz Samad told me that he had lost his cousin Ali in the war and had brought his "testament" with him. "Ali wrote this statement before attacking the enemy positions," Samad said. He handed it for me to read. The paper stated, ". . . My dear parents, don't cry or be sad after my death. This is the way that I have chosen, the way that leads to the bosom of Allah, to eternity . . . My ultimate desire is to be martyred as Imam Hussein was in Karbala . . ." Samad seemed to be feeling guilty. "Ali is martyred but I am sitting, eating and living in comfort." Samad could not overcome his sense of guilt. His friends called on his house every day and urged him to rejoin them at the front. My sister Aghdas was disturbed and worried about Samad's state of mind. She told me one day: "I cannot sleep. I have nightmares. The other night I dreamed Samad had returned to the war front and was killed like his cousin — I cannot bear to see him leaving Tabriz." Although Samad had promised to stay in Tabriz and finish his education, after I returned to Scotland I heard that he had been killed in the war.

Aghdas later went alone to visit her son's grave in Tabriz in the middle of winter. She fainted on the grave. She lay in the snow for a long time until someone found her and informed her family. This experience and her grief made her so ill that she had to stay in bed for months and she still suffers from a sore back and neck. My mother's death was hastened by her grief for Samad. Countless numbers of young men have been killed in the years of fighting, from both the Iranian and Iraqi sides. According to UN estimates, more than a million people, including women and children, have been killed. Over a million Iranians and three hundred thousand Iraqis have been crippled. The material damage has reached over 500 billion dollars.

All those killed were once children like Samad, whom we see in the photograph holding his cousin's hand.

People in Iran and Iraq are all sick and tired of the war; mothers in particular hate the fighting:

> I wish war had never been created,
> I wish the seed of war had never been sown.
> War has swallowed so many children,
> War has destroyed so many blossoms.
> Our earth has experienced so many wars,
> Our earth is left in ruins by wars.

Samad with his cousin, winter 1965.

My children are murdered by war,
My heart has shed blood by war.
I wish war had never been created,
I wish the seed of war had never been sown.

I have received many letters from Iran since 1982. One mother wrote:

. . . my husband earns 1000 rials a day [on the black market £1 is worth about 1600 rials]. There are nine in the family. My children are hungry and have become ill. In the past cheese and bread were cheap and we could afford to eat these with vegetables. Now cheese is 1200 rials per kilo, and we cannot afford to buy it. War has caused nothing but hardship for us. I wish it would stop soon. Ayatollahs do not want to stop the war. The Speaker of the Iranian Parliament, Hashemi Rafsanjani, said the other day "If we accepted a truce we would accept the downfall of our regime".

Another letter says:

. . . I am writing this letter by paraffin light. Saddam's planes are coming to Tehran and the power is cut. My mother is shivering in the corner of the room. My little daughter Mona [five years old] has told me to wake her up when the planes come . . . The other day, Mona said "Mum, I don't want to die. I am too young to die".

Here I end my story, but Iranian mothers have a lot to say — in the future.

O mother, O mother, I hate bombs
They frighten me to death when they drop
For it shakes our house and city
It shakes my heart, I tremble inside.

I dream every night of war planes
Appearing above my head in the sky
I scream and cry in my dreams
I am disturbed all through my sleep.

O mother, how long will this war last?
How many of my brothers will be lost?
I have already lost two, O mother
I cannot afford to lose another!

Bibliography

Literature

Where not otherwise indicated, the translations are my own; the story of the rise of Mazdak from Firdausi was cast into geraldines by Owen Dudley Edwards; unidentified poems are my own.

Amini (Maftun), Yadollah, *Divan-e Koolak* (a collection of poems), Shams Publications, Tabriz, 1965

Arberry, A. J., *Kings and Beggars* (translation of the first two chapters of Sa'di's *Gulistan*), Luzac & Co., London, 1945

Ashrafi, M. M., *Persian — Tajik Poetry* (14th & 15th century miniatures), Tajikistan, 1974

Attar, Farid ud-Din, *The Conference of Birds*, translated by Afkham Darbandi and Dick Davis, Penguin Classics, 1984

Musibat-nameh (Book of Laments), Zawwar, Tehran, 1959

Bargoshad, Jalal, *Babak*, translated by Reza Anzabi and Rahim Ra'sniya, Negah Publications, Tehran, 1987

Behrangi, Samad, *Kandokav Dar Masail-e Tarbiyati-ye Iran* (Study of Educational Problems in Iran), Tabriz, 1965

Mahi-ye Siya-he Kuchulu (Little Black Fish), Tehran, 1968

Majmu'e-ye Maqaleha (The Collected Articles), Shams Publications, Tabriz, 1969

Para Para (collection of Azerbaijani poems), Sina Bookshop, Tabriz, 1965

Qesseha-ye Behrang (Stories of Behrangi), Shams Publications, Tabriz, 1967

Billuri, Hakimeh, *Shirlar* (a collection of poems), Baku, 1980

Blake, William, *The Complete Writings of William Blake*, edited by Geoffrey Keynes, The Nonesuch Press, 1957

Browne, E. G., *Literary History of Persia*, Vol. III, Cambridge, 1951

Curzon, George N., *Persia and the Persian Question*, Longmans, London, 1892

Dihqani, Behruz, *Afsanaha-ye Azerbaijan* (Tales of Azerbaijan), Vol. 1, Tabriz (1965), Vol. 2, Tehran (1968)

Majmu'e-ye Maqalat (The Collected Articles), Tabriz, 1967

Firdausi, Hakim Abulqasim, *Shah-nameh (The Book of Kings)*, Javidan Publications, Tehran, 1985

Fuzuli, Muhammad, *Divan* (Persian poems), compiled and edited by Hasibe Mazioghlu, University of Ankara, 1962

Gink, K. and Turanszky, I., *Azerbaijan, Mosques, Turrets, Palaces*, Budapest, 1977

Gulsurkhi, Khusraw, *Barguzide-ye Ash'ar-e Khusraw Gulsurkhi* (Selected Poems of Khusraw Gulsurkhi), Murvarid Publications, Tehran, 1979

Hafiz Shirazi, *Divan*, compiled and edited by Muhammad Qazvini and Dr Qasim Ghani, Gulshan Press, Tehran, 1982

Iqbal, Muhammad, *The Complete Writings of Iqbal* (in Persian), Lahore, 1975

Ishqi, Mirzadeh, *Kulliyat-e Mosavvar-e Ishqi* (Illustrated Poetical Works of Ishqi), Amir Kabir Publications, Tehran, 1950

Javanshir, M. F., *Hamasi-ye Dad* (socio-political analysis of Firdausi's *Shah-nameh*), Tudeh Publications, Tehran, 1980

Kashani, Jamal, *Iran's Men of Destiny*, Vantage Press, New York, 1985

Khalkhali, Muhammad Baqir, *Rubah-nameh* (The Book of Foxes, known as *Sa'labiyyeh*), Tabriz, 1900

Khayyam, Omar, *The Rubaiyat of Omar Khayyam*, The Richards Press, London, 1947

The Rubaiyat of Omar Khayyam (in Persian), Amir Kabir Publications, Tehran, 1965

Mahmid ("Jouya"), M. A., *The Mirrors: Eyes, Hearts and the Universe*, Doran Publishers, London, 1986

Mu'jiz Shabistari, Mirza Ali, *Kulliyyat-e Mu'jiz Shabistari* (The Complete Works of Mu'jiz Shabistari), two vols., Tabriz, 1977

Nizami, Ganjavi, *Ghazaliyat*, edited by Saeed Nafisi, Tehran, 1958, Baku, 1981

Makhzan al-Asrar, Vol. 1, Ibn-e Sina Publications, Tehran, 1955

Nizami Aphorisms, Baku, 1982

Quli-Zadeh, Jalil Muhammad, (Mullah Nassradin), *A Few Stories*, translated by M. Farzaneh, Ashna Press, Tehran, 1951

Rumi, Mawlana Jalalu'ddin, *The Mathnawi of Jalalu'ddin Rumi*, translated by Reynold A. Nicholson, Vols. 6, 7, 8, London, 1937

Rypka, Jan, *History of Iranian Literature*, edited by Karl Jahn, D. Reidel Publications, Holland, 1968

Sabir (Tahir-Zadeh, Mirza Ali-Akbar), *Hup Hup Nama*, Azar Publications, Baku, 1922

Sabri-Tabrizi, G. R., *The 'Heaven' and 'Hell' of William Blake*, Lawrence & Wishart Ltd., London, 1973

"The 41st International P.E.N. Congress" in *Bulletin of the British Association of Orientalists*, Vol. 9, 1977

"Iqbal's Relevance to the Present Day World: Persian Writings of Iqbal" in *Iqbal Commemorative Volume*, edited by Ali Sardar Jafri, New Delhi, 1978

Sa'di Shirazi, *Gulistan* (Rose Garden), translated by Edward Rehatsek, edited by M. H. Tasbihi, Furughi Books, Tehran, 1957

Sadiq, H., *Haft Maqala* (Seven Articles) (about Azerbaijani folklore and literature), Dunya-ye Danish Publications, Tehran, 1968

Sa'idi, Ghulam-Hussein, *Tars va Larz*, Tehran, 1969

Gav, Tehran, 1971

(see also Sabri-Tabrizi, "Social Values in Modern Persian Literature" in *Bulletin of the British Association of Orientalists*, Vol. 8, 1976)

Shafi'i Kadkani, Reza, (M. Sirishk), *Dar Ķuche Baghha-ye Nishabur* (a collection of poems), Raz Publications, Tehran, 1971

Shahriyar, Muhammad Hussein, *Barguzide-ye Ash'ar-e Turki* (Selected Azerbaijani Poems), compiled by Ismail Tajbakhsh, Yaran Publications, Tabriz, 1984

Sarybelli, Osman (Ed.), *Azerbaijan Poetry* (an anthology), Moscow, 1969

Usku'i, Marzieh, *Khatirat* (Memoires), Fida'i Organisation, Tabriz, 1974(?)

History

Abrahamian, Ervand, *Iran between Two Revolutions*, Princeton University Press, UK, 1982

Battuta, Ibn, *Travels in Asia and Africa 1325-1354*, translated and selected by H. A. R. Gibb, London, 1929

Diba, Farhad, *Mohammad Mossadegh: A political biography*, Croom Helm, 1986

Kumaramangalam, Mohan, *Iran at the Crossroads*, Bombay, 1946

Mahmid, M., *Tarikh-e Diplomasi-ye Iran* (Diplomatic History of Iran), Mitra Press, Tehran, 1983

Mussadeq, Muhammad, *Difa'iyyate Mussadeq* (The Final Defence of Mussadeq), edited by Col. Jalil Buzorg-Mehr, Iran-History Publications, Tehran, 1984

Nutqha-ye Dr Mussadeq (Mussadeq's speeches during the 16th Majlis), Vol. 1, 1968, Vol. 2, 1970, Mussadeq Publications, The Association of Iranian Students Outside Iran

Pishavari, Sayyid Jafar, *21 Azar: Nutqlar va Maqalalar*, Tehran, 1980

Polo, Marco, *The Travels*, translated by Ronald Latham, Penguin, Great Britain, 1958

Ra'isniya, Rahim, *Heydar Amu-Oghli Dar Guzar-e Tufanha*, Dunya Publications, Tehran, 1981

Koroghlu (In Myth and in History), Nima Publications, Tabriz, 1983

Ra'isniya, Rahim and Nahid, Abdul-Hussein, *Du Mubariz* (The Constitutional Movement), Shafaq Press, Tabriz, 1972

Tabari, Ehsan, *Jahan-biniha va Jonbishha-ye Ijtimai Dar Iran* (The World Outlook and Social Movements in Iran), Tudeh Publications, 1970

Index

This index only includes names and places of some historical significance.

ملّا دیسر 'حرامیدی' سیندیرقفاسینی

سیندیرقفاسینی

میرزا علی معجز شبستری

انسان اولان بلینه خنجر تاخماز

آما حیف کور تو تد وعون بیراخماز!

محمد حسین شهریار

"He is not a mullah but a
'thief' Better break his neck!"

Mu'jiz Shabustari

"The one who is a human
being,
Does not wear a dagger in his
belt,
But alas the blind man
Does not give up what he
holds."

Muhammad Hussein Shahryar

حقیقت را باید گفت

شیخ محمد خیابانی

"The truth must be told"

Muhammad Khiyabani

از پاسخ های دکتر محمد مصدق به شاه :

رجال خیرخواه و مبارزک هستند که با سیاست خارجی ارتباطی ندارند

و در راه آزادی و استقلال وطن حاضرند که از همه چیز بگذرند ...

عکس هر دم از آزادی و استقلال می زد چون مخالف با مصالح استعمار

بود و مال بیگانه ، او را افراطی قلمداد و متهم می کردند به کمونیستی ...

دکتر محمد مصدق

"Men of good will and
freedom fighters are people
who have no connection with
foreign policy makers, and are
prepared to sacrifice
everything for the sake of the
freedom and independence of
their country. . . .

Any one who talked about
the freedom and
independence, since he was
against the interests of
colonialism and foreign

capital, he was regarded as an
extremist and was accused of
having communist
ideology. . . ."

Dr Muhammad Mossadeq

زنده باد ایران

ستارخان سردار ملی

"Long live Iran"

Sattar Kham, The National Leader